I0754346

THE PAST, THE PRESENT,

AND

THE FUTURE.

BY

H. C. CAREY,

AUTHOR OF "PRINCIPLES OF POLITICAL ECONOMY," &c.

IF ANY MAN WILL DO HIS WILL, HE SHALL KNOW OF THE DOCTRINE, WHETHER IT BE OF GOD, OR WHETHER I SPEAK OF MYSELF.
JOHN VII. 17.

PHILADELPHIA:
HENRY CAREY BAIRD,
INDUSTRIAL PUBLISHER,
No. 406 WALNUT STREET.
1872.

STEREOTYPED BY L. JOHNSON AND CO.
PHILADELPHIA.
PRINTED BY COLLINS.

THE PAST, THE PRESENT,

AND

THE FUTURE.

BY

H. C. CAREY,

AUTHOR OF "PRINCIPLES OF POLITICAL ECONOMY," &c.

IF ANY MAN WILL DO HIS WILL, HE SHALL KNOW OF THE DOCTRINE,
WHETHER IT BE OF GOD, OR WHETHER I SPEAK OF MYSELF.

JOHN VII. 17.

PHILADELPHIA:
HENRY CAREY BAIRD,
INDUSTRIAL PUBLISHER,
No. 406 WALNUT STREET.
1872.

STEREOTYPED BY L. JOHNSON AND CO.
PHILADELPHIA.
PRINTED BY COLLINS.

PREFACE.

THE volume now offered to the public is designed to demonstrate the existence of a simple and beautiful law of nature, governing man in all his efforts for the maintenance and improvement of his condition, a law so powerful and universal that escape from it is impossible, but which, nevertheless, has heretofore remained unnoticed. The further object of these pages is, by aid of this law, to examine and to solve various questions of great interest. In doing this, it has been necessary to refer to the history of various nations, in order to show that certain causes have invariably produced certain effects; and thus to account for the differences observable in their present condition, and in their modes of thought and action. If in so doing the author be found to have expressed himself strongly in regard to some of the nations of Europe, he begs the reader to believe that he has done so not because he is not of them, but because *they* are not of those who have maintained peace and permitted the laws of nature to take effect: and if, on the contrary, he has spoken highly of the course pursued by the United States, and has placed in a strong point of view the results here realised, he begs the reader also to believe that he has done so, not merely because he is of them, but because they have, to an extent hitherto unprecedented, followed "the things that make for peace;" and because they, less than any other people, have interfered with the great natural laws under which man lives, and moves, and has his being. "God," says the wise man, "hath made man upright, but he has sought out many inventions." We find fewer of these "inventions" in the history of the United States than in that of any other nation, and it is due to the great cause of Truth and Human Happiness to exhibit as strongly as possible the contrast between the unrestricted operation of the laws of God on the one hand, and the results of the "inventions" of man, on the other.

TABLE OF CONTENTS.

THE LESSON OF THE PAST

TO

THE PRESENT.

CHAPTER I.

MAN AND LAND.

THE first cultivator, the Robinson Crusoe of his day, provided however with a wife, has neither axe nor spade. He works alone. Population being small, land is, of course, abundant. He may select for himself, without fear of his title being disputed. He is surrounded by soils possessed, in the highest possible degree, of the qualities that fit them for yielding large returns to labour. They are, however, covered with immense trees that he cannot fell, or they are swamps that he cannot drain. To pass through them even is attended with no small difficulty. The first is a mass of roots, stumps, decaying logs, and shrubs, while into the other he sinks half leg deep at every step. The atmosphere, too, is impure. Fogs settle upon the low lands, and the dense foliage of the wood prevents the circulation of the air. He has no axe, but if he had, he would not venture there, for to do so, would be attended with certain loss of health and great risk of life. Vegetation, too, is so luxuriant, that before he could, with the imperfect machinery at his command, clear a single acre, a portion of it would be again so overgrown that he would have to recommence his labour, which would be almost, if not quite, that of Sisyphus. The higher lands, comparatively bare of timber, are ill calculated to yield a return to his labour. Nevertheless there are spots on the hill where the thin soil has prevented the growth of trees and shrubs, or there are spaces among the trees, that can be cultivated while they still remain standing, and when he pulls up by the roots the few shrubs scattered over the surface, he feels no apprehension of their being speedily replaced. With his hands he may even succeed in barking the trees, or, by the aid of fire, he may so far destroy them that time alone is needed to give him a few cleared acres, upon which he may plant his grain, with little fear of weeds. To attempt these things upon the richer lands would be loss of labour. In some places the ground is always wet. In others, the trees are too large to be seriously injured by fire, and its only effect would be to stimulate the growth of weeds and brush. He, therefore, commences the work of cultivation far up the hill, where, making with his stick holes in the light soil that drains itself, he drops the grain an inch or two below the surface, and in due season obtains a return of double the amount of his seed. He pounds this between stones, and obtains bread. His condition is improved. He has succeeded in making the earth labour for him, while himself engaged in trapping rabbits or squirrels, and in gathering fruits. In process of time, he succeeds in sharpening a stone, and thus obtains a hatchet by aid of which he is enabled to proceed more rapidly in girdling the trees, and in removing the sprouts and their roots, which is nevertheless a very slow and laborious operation. At the next step, we find him bringing into activity a new soil, whose food-producing powers were less obvious to sight than those of that first attempted. He finds an ore of copper, and by the aid of some of his fallen and decayed timber, succeeds in burning it, and thus obtains a better axe, with far less labour than was required for the first. He has also something like a spade.

He can now make holes four inches deep with less labour than with his stick he could make those of two. He penetrates to a lower soil, and being enabled to stir the earth and loosen it, the rain is now absorbed instead of running off from the hard ground, and he finds his new one far better and more easily worked than that upon which he has heretofore wasted his labour. His seed, better protected, is less liable to be frozen out in winter, or parched in summer, the consequence of which is that he gathers thrice the quantity sown. His new soil gives him larger returns with less labour. At the next step, we find him bringing into action another new soil. He has found that which, on burning, yields him zinc, and by combining this with his copper he has brass. His machinery improves, and he proceeds more rapidly. He sinks deeper into the land first occupied, and is enabled to clear other lands upon which vegetation grows more luxuriantly, because he can now exterminate the shrubs with some hope of occupying the land before they are replaced with others equally valueless for the supply of his wants. His children, too, have grown, and they can weed the ground and assist him in removing the obstacles by which his progress is impeded. At another step, we find him burning a piece of the iron soil which surrounds him in all directions, and now he is enabled to obtain a real axe and spade, inferior in quality, but still much superior to those by which his labour has been thus far aided. He next, with the aid of his sons, grown to man's estate, removes the light pine of the hill-side, leaving still untouched, however, the heavy oak of the river bottom. His cultivable ground is increased in extent, while he is enabled with his spade to penetrate still deeper than before, thus bringing into action the powers of the several soils lying within half a dozen inches of the surface. He finds, with great pleasure, that the light soil is underlaid with clay, and that by combining the two he obtains a new one far more productive than that first brought into activity. He finds, too, that by turning the top soil down, the process of decomposition is facilitated, and that thus, with each new operation, he receives an increasing reward for his labour. His family has increased, and he has obtained the important advantage of combination of exertion. Things that were needed to be done to render his land more rapidly productive, but which were to one man impracticable, become simple and easy when now attempted by himself and his half dozen sons, each of whom obtains far more food than he alone could at first command, and in return for far less severe exertion. He next extends his operations downwards, towards the low grounds of the stream, girdling the large trees, and burning the brush, and thus facilitating the passage of air so as to render the land by degrees fitted for occupation. He now finds that his sons can perform all the labours of the field, and that by devoting his own attention to the cultivation of the iron soil, he can render more aid, and with less severe labour, than in any other manner. He invents a hoe, by means of which his grandchildren are enabled to keep the ground free from weeds, and to tear up some of the roots by which his best lands —those last brought into cultivation—are yet infested. He has succeeded in taming the ox, but as yet has had no use for his services. He now invents the plough, and by means of a piece of twisted hide is enabled to attach the ox, and to turn up a deeper soil, while extending his cultivation over land more distant from the place of his first little cabin, on the spot first occupied. His family grows, and with it grows his wealth. He has better machinery, and he has reduced to cultivation more and better lands. Food and clothing are more abundant, and the air on the lower lands is improved by the clearing of the trees. His house, too, is better. In the outset, it was a hole in the ground. Afterwards it was composed of such decayed logs as his unaided efforts could succeed in rolling and placing one upon the other. A chimney was an unhoped-for luxury, and he must live in perpetual smoke, or almost perish of cold. A window was a luxury unthought of. If the severity of the weather required him to close his doors, he was stifled with smoke, and he passed his days in darkness. His time, therefore, during a large portion of the year, was totally unproductive, while his life was liable to be shortened by disease produced by foul air within, or severe cold without, his miserable hut. With increase of population he has acquired wealth, derived from the cultivation of new and better soils; and he has acquired also the power of combining his labour with that of others, thus rendering that of all more productive. They now fell the heavy oak and the enormous pine, and avail themselves thereof for the construction of additional houses, each in regular succession better than the first. Health improves, and population increases more rapidly. Some of the sons are now employed in the field, while others prepare the skins and render them more fit for clothing: and a third set make axes, spades, hoes, ploughs, and other implements calculated to aid the labours of the field, and those of construction. The supply of food increases rapidly, and with it the power of accumulation. In the first years, there was perpetual danger of famine. Now, there is a surplus, and a part is stored to provide against the danger of short crops. Cultivation extends itself along the hill-side, where deeper soils now laid open by the plough, afford a better return, while down the slope of the hill each successive year is marked by the disappearance of the great trees by which the richer lands have heretofore been occupied, the intermediate spaces becoming meanwhile enriched by the decomposition of the enormous roots, and more readily ploughed because of the gradual decay of the stumps. A single ox to the plough can now turn up a greater space than in the outset could be done by two. A single ploughman can now do more than on the ground first cultivated could have been done by a hundred men armed with pointed sticks. The family are next enabled to drain some of the lower lands, and copious harvests of grain are obtained from the new soil now first cultivated. The oxen have heretofore roamed the woods, gathering what they could. The meadow is now granted to their use, the axe and the saw enabling the family to enclose them, and thus to lessen the labour attendant upon obtaining supplies of meat, milk, butter and hides. Heretofore their chief domestic animal has been the hog, which could live on mast. Now, they add beef, and perhaps mutton, the lands first cultivated being abandoned to the sheep. They obtain far more meat and grain, and with less labour than at any former period, although their numbers have so greatly increased. The father and grandfather have passed away, and the younger generations are now profiting by the wealth they had accumulated, while applying their own labour with daily increasing advantage: and obtaining a constantly increasing return, with increasing power of accumulation, and decreasing severity of application. They now bring new powers to their aid, and the water no longer is allowed to run to waste: the air itself is made to work. Windmills grind the grain, and sawmills cut the timber, which disappears more rapidly, while the work of drainage is in course of being improved by more efficient spades and ploughs. The little furnace makes its appearance and charcoal is now applied to the reduction of the soil yielding iron, when it is found that the labour of a single day becomes more productive than was before that of half a dozen.

Population spreads itself along the faces of the hills and down into the lower lands, becoming more and more dense at the seat of the original settlement, and with every step we find increasing tendency to combination of action for the production of food, the manufacture of clothing and household utensils, the construction of houses, and the preparation of machinery for aiding in all these operations. The heaviest timber: that growing on the most fertile land: now disappears, and the deepest marshes are now drained. Roads are next made to facilitate the intercourse between the old settlement and the newer ones that have been formed around it, and to enable the grower of corn to exchange his product for improved spades and ploughs, and for clothing and furniture. Population again increases, and wealth still further increases, and therewith man acquires more leisure for reflection on the results furnished by the experience of himself and his predecessors. His mind becomes more and more stimulated into action. The sand in the neighbourhood is found to be underlaid with marl, and by the aid of the improved machinery now in use, the two are brought into combination, thereby producing a soil of power far exceeding that of those heretofore cultivated. The return to labour increases, and all are better fed, and clothed, and housed, and all are incited to new exertions, while improved health and the power of working in-doors and out-of-doors, according to the season, enable them to apply their labour more steadily and regularly. Thus far, however, they have found it difficult to gather their crops in season. The harvest time is short, and the whole strength of the community has been found insufficient to prevent much of the grain remaining on the ground until, over ripe, it was shaken out by the wind, or in the attempt to gather it: and not unfrequently it has been totally ruined by changes of weather after it was fit to be harvested. The progress of cultivation has thereby been arrested, and labour has been superabundant during the year, while harvest produced a demand for it that could not be supplied. The reaping-hook takes the place of the hand, and the scythe enables the farmer to cut his hay. The cradle and the horse-rake follow, and all tend to increase the facility of accumulation, and thus to increase the power of applying labour to new soils, deeper or more distant, more heavily burdened with timber, or more liable to be flooded, and thus requiring embankment as well as drainage. New combinations, too, are formed. The clay is found to be underlaid with the soil called lime, which latter, like the iron soil, requires preparation to fit it for the task of combination. The road, the wagon, and the horse facilitate the work, by enabling the farmer readily to obtain supplies of the carbon-yielding soil, called coal, and he now obtains, by burning the lime and combining it with the clay, a better soil than at any former period: one that will yield more corn, and that requires far less severe labour from himself, his oxen, or his horses. Population and wealth again increase, and the steam-engine facilitates the work of drainage, while the railroad and the engine facilitate the transportation to market of his products. His cattle are now fattened at home, and a large portion of the produce of his rich meadow-land is left at home, in the form of manure, to be applied to other soils, yet found incapable of yielding a return to labour. Instead of sending food to fatten them *at* market, he now obtains *from* market their refuse in the form of bones, and the productiveness of labour is greatly increased. Passing thus, at every step, from the poor to the better soils, the supply of food, and of all other of the necessaries of life increases daily, and men consume more, while accumulating wealth with constantly increasing rapidity.

The danger of famine and disease passes away. Increased returns to labour and daily improving condition render labour pleasant, and man applies himself more steadily as his work becomes less severe. Population increases, and the rapidity of its increase is seen to be greater with each successive generation; and with each is seen an increase of the power of living in connection with each other, by reason of the power of obtaining constantly increasing supplies from the same surface: with each is seen an increase in the tendency to combination of action, by which their labours are rendered more productive—their wants increased—the desire and the facilities of commerce augmented: tending to produce harmony and peace, and security of person and property among themselves, and with the world: accompanied by constant increase of numbers, wealth, prosperity and happiness.

Nearly forty years have elapsed since Mr. Ricardo communicated to the world his discovery of the nature and causes of rent, and of the law of its progress. The work by means of which it was first made known has since been the text-book of that portion of the English community, who style themselves, *par excellence*, political economists, and any thing short of absolute faith in its contents is regarded as heresy, worthy of excommunication, or as evidence of an incapacity to comprehend them, worthy only of contempt. Nevertheless, imitating in this the action of the followers of Mahomet, in regard to the Koran, the professors, one and all, who have undertaken to teach this doctrine, insist upon construing it after their own fashion, and modifying it to suit their own views and the apparent necessities of the case ; the consequence of which is, that the inquirer is at a loss to determine what it is that he is required to believe. Having studied carefully the works of the most eminent of the recent writers on the subject, and having found no two of them to agree, he turns, in despair, to Mr. Ricardo himself, and there he finds, in the celebrated chapter on rent, contradictions that cannot be reconciled, and a series of complications such as never before, as we believe, was found in the same number of lines. The more he studies, the more he is puzzled, and the less difficulty does he find in accounting for the variety of doctrines taught by men who profess to belong to the same school, and who all agree, if in little else, in regarding the new theory of rent as the great discovery of the age.

In looking round, he sees that all the recognised laws of nature are characterized by the most perfect simplicity, and the greatest breadth. He sees that they are of universal application, and that those by whom they are taught are freed from any necessity for resorting to narrow exceptions to account for particular facts. The simplicity of Kepler's law of 'equal areas in equal times' is perfect. Its truth is universal, and all to whom it is explained feel assured not only that it *is* true, but that it must continue to be so in relation to all the planets that may be discovered, numerous though they may be, and however distant from the sun and from us. A child may comprehend it, and the merest novice may make himself so fully master of it as to enable him to teach it to others. It needs no commentary, no modification. Such is not the case with the law to which we now desire to call the attention of our readers. Whatever else may be its merits, it cannot be charged with either simplicity or universality.

At first sight, it looks, however, to be exceedingly simple. Rent is said to be paid for land of the first quality, yielding one hundred quarters in return to a given quantity of labour, when it becomes necessary, with the increase of population, to cultivate land of the second quality, capable of yielding but ninety quarters in return to the same quantity of labour: and the amount of rent then paid for No. 1 is equal to the difference between their respective products. No proposition could be calculated to command more universal assent. Every man who hears it sees around him land that pays rent. He sees that that which yields forty bushels to the acre pays more rent than that which yields but thirty, and that the difference is nearly equal to the difference of product. He becomes at once a disciple of Mr. Ricardo, admitting that the reason why prices are paid for the use of land is that soils are different in their qualities, when he would, at the same moment, regard it as in the highest degree absurd if any one were to undertake to prove that prices are paid for oxen because one ox is heavier than another: that rents are paid for houses because some will accommodate twenty persons and others only ten: or that all ships command freights because some ships differ from others in their capacity.

A certain portion of the world now thinks that it sees in this difference in the qualities of soils the reason why rent is paid for any soils. It is not a very large portion, for the theory has made but little way out of England. It is taught by a few in France, and by some in America, but elsewhere, it has, we believe, made no progress whatsoever, which would certainly not have been the case had it been, like other of the laws of nature, characterized by that simplicity which is essential to universality of application.

In former times it was obvious to the whole world that the earth remained unmoved, and that the sun performed a daily revolution around it. It was not to be doubted that such was the case, but if any one so far ventured, he was referred to the Scriptures for unquestionable evidence of the fact. Careful observers, however, detected numerous other facts whose existence was incompatible with that of the one great and universally admitted fact. Further observation confirmed them in the doubts thus raised, and it was found, at length, that, patch the Ptolemaic theory as its professors might, it could not be made to cover facts whose existence was undeniable. It was too long for some, and too short for others. To disbelieve it, however, was rank heresy, worthy not only of excommunication, but of punishment by fire. Copernicus nevertheless dared to declare his disbelief, and to proclaim to the world that the sun stood still, and that the earth it was that moved. Persecution embittered the remaining years of his life, and his disciple Galileo was compelled, on his knees, to recant his declaration of belief in the monstrous doctrine, yet the whole civilized world now unites with him in the assertion that "still it moves."

The doctrine of Mr. Ricardo has, in like manner, been found quite too long for some facts, and as much too short for many others, and hence the numerous modifications it has undergone.* Every new teacher tries to stretch it

* Among the earliest and most distinguished of the advocates of Mr. Ricardo's doctrine was the author of the Templar's Dialogues. In a recent work by the same author we find the following passage :—

"The *tendencies* of a natural law like that of rent it is always right to expose, and Ricardo first *did* expose them. Others had discovered the law; he first applied his sagacious sense to its consequences upon profits, wages, price; and through them upon universal economy. That was right; for that we are irredeemably his debtors. But it was *not* right to keep studiously out of sight that eternal counter-movement which tends, by an equivalent agency, to redress the disturbed balance. This concealment has had the effect of introducing marvels into a severe science; since else, what other than a miracle is it that rent has not long since absorbed the whole landed produce—a result to which it so manifestly tends. * * * Our own social system seems to harbour within itself the germ of ruin. Either we must destroy rent, *i. e.* that which causes rent, or rent will destroy us," &c.—*Logic of Political Economy*, p. 190.

in the direction necessary to cover some well-observed fact, the consequence of which is, that others are left uncovered. In the effort to conceal the head and arms, the feet are exposed, and when the cloak is stretched so as to cover the feet and head, the arms present themselves to view. Such precisely was the case with the system of Ptolemy. It was neither broad nor simple. It was based on a few facts, omitting all reference to a thousand others, and hence its downfall, the necessary consequence of its untruth.

Proposing, as we do, to submit some views in opposition to this doctrine of the cause of rent, we would beg leave respectfully to suggest to the disciples of Mr. Ricardo, into whose hands this volume may chance to fall, that their confidence in its truth is not greater than was that of the followers of Ptolemy: that the evidence of the great fact upon which it rests is not as obvious as was that of the revolution of the sun; nor the belief therein quite as universal: that as Ptolemy was ultimately proved to be in error, so may Mr. Ricardo, at some time, be: and that it is, therefore, within the bounds of possibility that it may not be an entire waste of time to read the brief examination of their favourite system that we shall now offer for their consideration.

That theory, in its simplest form, is contained in the following propositions:—

First: That in the commencement of cultivation, when population is small and land consequently abundant,

---

Mr. Ricardo taught that as population increased, the return to labour diminished, and the power of accumulation became less. Mr. De Quincey would have had him teach that as population increased, the power of accumulation also increased, and that by aid of the capital accumulated, the return to labour increased. Mr. Ricardo did not conceal this. He did not see it. Mr. De Quincey does see it, and a very little reflection will satisfy him that the facts and the theory are totally inconsistent with each other.

the best soils: those capable of yielding the largest return, say one hundred quarters, to a given quantity of labour: alone are cultivated.

Second: That with the progress of population, land becomes less abundant, and there arises a necessity for cultivating that yielding a smaller return; and that resort is then had to a second, and afterwards to a third and a fourth class of soils, yielding respectively ninety, eighty and seventy quarters to the same quantity of labour.

Third: That with the necessity for applying labour less productively, which thus accompanies the growth of population, rent arises: the owner of land No. 1 being enabled to demand and to obtain, in return for its use, ten quarters, when resort is had to that of second quality: twenty when No. 3 is brought into use, and thirty when it becomes necessary to cultivate No. 4.

Fourth: That the *proportion* of the landlord tends thus steadily to increase as the productiveness of labour decreases, the division being as follows, to wit:—

	Total.	Labour.	Rent.
At the first period, when No. 1 alone is cultivated	100	100	00
" second period " No. 1 and 2 are cultivated	190	180	10
" third period " No. 1, 2 and 3 "	270	240	30
" fourth period " No. 1, 2, 3 and 4 "	340	280	60
" fifth period " No. 1, 2, 3, 4, and 5 "	400	300	100
" sixth period " No. 1, 2, 3, 4, 5 and 6 "	450	300	150
" seventh period " No. 1, 2, 3, 4, 5, 6 and 7 "	490	280	210

and that there is thus a tendency to the ultimate absorption of the whole produce by the owner of the land, and to a steadily increasing inequality of condition: the power of the labourer to consume the commodities which he produces steadily diminishing, while that of the landowner to claim them, as rent, is steadily increasing.

Fifth: That this tendency towards a diminution in the return of labour, and towards an increase of the landlord's proportion, always exists where population increases: and most exists where population increases most rapidly: but is in a certain degree counteracted by increase of wealth, producing improvement of cultivation.

Sixth: That every such improvement tends to retard the growth of rents, while every obstacle to improvement tends to increase that growth: and that, therefore, the interests of the landowner and labourer are always opposed to each other, rents rising as labour falls, and *vice versa.*

We hope that this statement of the theory will be deemed by its advocates unexceptionable. We desire to state it with perfect fairness, but we know of few things more difficult, because of the numerous exceptions and modifications that have been required to make it fit the facts. So difficult, notwithstanding, has the operation of fitting been found, that some of its most distinguished advocates have seemed much disposed to think the fault is in the facts themselves.*

It will be perceived that the whole system is based upon the assertion of the existence of a single fact, viz., that in the commencement of cultivation, when population is small, and land consequently abundant, the soils capable of yielding the largest return to any given quantity of labour alone are cultivated. That fact exists, or it does not. If it has no existence, the system falls to the ground. That it does not exist; that it never has existed in any country whatsoever; and that it is contrary to the nature of things that it should have existed, or can exist, we propose now to show.

---

* "The one [the practical man] draws his notion of the universe from the few objects which compose the furniture of his counting-house; the other [the philosopher] having got demonstration on his side, and forgetting that it is only a demonstration *nisi*—a proof at all times liable to be set aside by the addition of a single new fact to the hypothesis—*denies* instead of examining and sifting the allegations which are opposed to him."—*J. S. Mill.*

The picture presented by the theory differs materially from that which we have offered to the consideration of the reader. Mr. Ricardo places his settler on the best lands, and the children of that settler on those which are inferior. He makes man the victim of a sad *necessity*, increasing with his numbers, whereas, we have shown him exercising constantly increasing *power*, derived from combined exertion by those numbers. He had never witnessed, as at this moment we do from the window at which we write, the progress of a new settlement. Had he done so, we doubt not his strong mind would have enabled him to study out the true cause of rent, and the law of its progress and decline. We propose now to show that in every part of the world, and in every age, the order of events has been such as we have stated it to be, and if this can be done to the satisfaction of our readers, it will be obvious that the theory of Mr. Ricardo has no foundation. It rests on the assumption of a single and simple fact, and if that fact can be shown to have no existence, the system must be abandoned, and we must seek elsewhere for the cause of rent: and it may prove that we shall find the law of its progress to be directly the reverse of what it is, by many, supposed to be. We shall commence our examination with the United States. Their first settlement is recent, and the work being still in progress, we can readily trace the settler, and mark his course of operation. If we find him invariably occupying the high and thin lands requring little clearing and no drainage: those which can yield but a small return to labour: and as invariably travelling down the hills and clearing and draining the lower and richer lands, as population and wealth increase: then will the theory we have offered be confirmed by practice: American practice at least. If, however, we can thence follow him into Mexico, and through South America; into

Britain, and through France, Germany, Italy, Greece and Egypt, into Asia and Australia, and show that such has been his invariable course of action, then may it be believed that when population is small, and land consequently abundant, the work of cultivation is, and always must be, commenced upon the poorer soils: that with the growth of population and wealth, other soils, yielding a larger return to labour, are always brought into activity, with a constantly increasing return to the labour expended upon them: and that with this change there is a steady diminution in the proportion of the population required for producing the means of subsistence, and as steady an increase in the proportion that may apply themselves to producing the other comforts, conveniences and luxuries of life.

The first settlers of the English race are found establishing themselves on the barren soil of Massachusetts, and founding the colony of Plymouth. The whole continent was before them, but, like all other colonists, they had to take what, with their means, they could obtain. Other settlements are formed at Newport and New Haven, and thence they may be traced, following the courses of the rivers but occupying in all cases the higher lands, leaving the clearing of timber and the draining of swamps to their more wealthy successors. Were the reader desired to designate the soils of the Union least calculated for the production of food, his choice would, we think, fall upon the rocky lands first occupied by the hardy Puritans, and thus we find that here at least the most fertile lands are not first taken into cultivation. If we look to New York the process is the same. The unproductive soil of the island of New York, and the opposite shore of New Jersey, and the higher lands on Long Island, claimed early attention, while the more productive soils came later into cultivation. Here, again, we find population spreading and following the course of the Hudson towards the Mohawk, but in all cases it will be found keeping the higher and drier lands, away from the river bank. The settlers desire food, and if they undertake to cleaı the forests and drain the meadows, they must starve. In New Jersey we find them occupying the higher lands towards the heads of the rivers, while neglecting the lower grounds that require drainage.* That state still abounds in fine timber that covers rich lands, which need only to be cleared to yield larger returns to labour than any of those cultivated a hundred years since, when land was far more abundant than now. On the shores of the Delaware, we find the Quakers selecting the light lands that produce the pine: and that, even now, with the aid of manure, will scarcely produce wheat: while forests of oak still cover the opposite shore of Pennsylvania. Every settler selects, too, the higher and drier parts of his farm, leaving the meadows, many of which have remained until now in a state of nature, while others have been drained within the last five years. The best portions of every farm are, invariably, those which have been most recently brought into cultivation, while the poorest lands of the various neighbourhoods are always those on which are seen the oldest farm-houses. If we pass further through the sandy lands of New Jersey, we shall find hundreds of little clearings more than half a century old, long since abandoned by their owners, who have left behind their little orchards and other evidences of their existence, to attest the character of the soil that men cultivate when population is small, and fertile land most abundant. Having cleared the lands that produce the oak, or drained those which yield the white-cedar,

* The reader may see this by reference to the map of East Jersey in 1682, recently republished.

they abandon those which produce the pine of that state, the poorest of all pines. The Swedes settle Lewistown and Christiana, on the sandy soil of Delaware. Crossing that state towards the head of Chesapeake Bay, we find in the little and decaying towns of Elkton and Charlestown, once the centres of a somewhat active population, further evidence of the poverty of the soils first occupied, when fine meadow-land, on which are now the richest farms in that state, was abundant, but held as worthless. Penn follows the Swedes, and profits by their expenditure and experience. He first selects the high lands on the Delaware, about twelve miles north of the site which he afterwards chooses for his city, near the confluence of the Delaware and Schuylkill. Starting from this latter point, and tracing the course of settlement, we find it not at first extending downwards towards the rich meadow-lands, but upwards along the ridge between the two rivers, where the village of Germantown, which half a century since exceeded three miles in length, and was for a village very closely built, remains to mark the tendencies of early colonists. If, now, we pass, right or left, to the river banks, we shall see, in the character of the buildings, evidences of later occupation and cultivation. If further evidence be desired, and we look to the maps of that early day, we find the fertile lands in the vicinity of the Delaware, from New Castle almost to the head of tide-water, a distance of more than sixty miles, marked as held in large tracts, and dotted over with trees, to show that they are still uncleared, while all the upper lands are divided into small farms.* Passing northward and westward, and keeping near the Schuylkill, we see the oldest habitations always most distant from the river; but later times, and increase of population and wealth, have carried cultivation to the water's edge. With every additional mile, we find stronger evidence of the recent cultivation of the best soils. The original

* See Holmes's Map, published in 1681, and recently republished.

timber still stands on beautiful meadow-land. The trees and shrubs in and near the fence rows on the lower lands become more abundant. The valleys in the rolls of the hills, a little distant from the river, become studded with trees. The lowest ground in the meadow-field, from time immemorial a ditch in which leaves have rotted, remains in a state of nature, from want of drainage. The banks of the little tributaries of the river become more and more wild. Long strips of meadow land are met waiting for embankment. Cows are seen pasturing in fields the character of whose vegetation shows that the operations of the owner have been limited to clearing and enclosing them, and that a proper system of drainage is, as yet, unthought of. Little islands appear, capable of yielding a large return to labour, but as yet covered with weeds and shrubs. Everywhere around we see the higher lands in a high state of cultivation, and affording proof of the length of time that has elapsed since they were cleared. Arriving in the vicinity of Reading, we see in lands abandoned, evidence of the want of fertility in the soils first cultivated, and other evidence of the superiority of the new soils now coming into activity, in the fine fields that have been restored by combining the inferior lime with the superior clay. In our further progress up the river we meet, at every step, farms on the hillsides, while the lower lands become more and more wild and rough. Patches of wood standing thereon are now of frequent occurrence, while the stumps in others attest the recent date of their subjugation to the plough: and finer crops standing among the stumps equally attest the superiority of this soil to that of the long-cleared dry land of the hills, first cultivated. The rough and undrained land nearest the river will, with increased population and wealth, furnish fine meadows, but in its present state is of small value. Further on, cultivation almost leaves the river bank, and if we would seek it we must pass outward, where, at the distance of half a mile or more, we may find farms half a century old. If we travel up the little stream that leads to Orwigsburg, the seat of justice for Schuylkill county, we shall find a beautiful valley with the hill-sides cleared to the top, while below, the rivulet meanders through patches of wood-land, and the flat is interspersed with remnants of the timber that originally covered the whole: the intermediate spaces being frequently occupied by fields the date of whose clearing may readily be determined by the greater or less decay of the stumps with which they are in part covered. If now we follow the old road, winding about, apparently in search of hills to cross, and in quire the cause of thus lengthening the distance, we find that it was made to suit the early settlers: but if we follow the new roads, we find them keeping near the stream, on the low and rich lands last cultivated. Returning to the river and passing on our course, the trees become more and more numerous, and the meadow-land less and less drained or occupied; and at length, as we pass up the little branches of the river, cultivation disappears, and the original woods remain untouched, except so far as the wants of the recently established coal trade have tended to their extermination. If we desire to see the land chosen by the early settlers, we have but to ascend the hill-side, and on the flat above will be found houses and farms, some of them half a century old, many of which are now abandoned. If, passing northward from the river, we trace its little tributary, Mill Creek, to its source, we see miles of fine meadow-land, still covered with the original timber, with but here and there a patch of cleared land: while on the hill-sides may be seen occasional little farms, the houses on which bear every mark of considerable age. Arriving at the little town of St. Clair, the site of which three years since was covered with timber growing on land fitted to make the finest meadows, but much of it then a mere marsh, we see, far up the hill, the residence of the first owner of this large body of fertile land, and may judge for ourselves the original character of the soil selected focultivation from the small pines and hemlocks on that immediately adjacent; and yet the style of the house proves him to have been of the better class of the settlers of half a century past, when population was thin, and good land abundant, but wealth scarce. Crossing Broad and Locust mountains, we see near their tops the habitations of early settlers, who selected the land of the pine, easily cleared, and whose pine-knots afforded at one time tar, and at another, substitutes for candles that they were too poor to buy. Immediately afterwards we find ourselves in the valley of the Susquehanna, on meadow-lands whose character is proved by the great size of the timber by which they are covered: but upon which neither the spade nor the plough has yet made its mark. Passing onward, we meet a row of small farms occupying a ridge between the mountains, while below them, distant two or three hundred yards, the little stream runs through fine white-oak timber lands, upon which the axe has scarcely yet been heard. Good land thus abounds, but the settler prefers that which will yield the largest return to labour, which the richer lands would not, as the cost of clearing them would be more than they were worth when cleared. Descending the little stream, we reach the Susquehanna, and with every step of our progress, we find cultivation descending the hills. The valleys become more cleared of timber, and meadows and cattle appear, the most certain signs of increasing population and wealth.

Passing up the west branch of the Susquehanna, the order is again inverted. Population diminishes, and cultivation tends to leave the river bottom, and to ascend the hill-sides. Arriving in the vicinity of Muncy, if, leaving the river and ascending the bank, we pass to the foot of the Muncy hills, our road will cross fine limestone land whose food-producing qualities being less obvious to the early settlers, whole tracts of it, containing hundreds of acres, passed from hand to hand in exchange for a dollar, or even a jug of whiskey. They preferred the oak-producing soils, whose trees they could girdle, and afterwards destroy by fire. With increasing population and wealth, we find them returning to the lands at first despised, combining the inferior and superior soils, and obtaining greatly increased returns to labour. If now we could take a bird's-eye view of the country, we might trace with perfect accuracy the course of every little stream, by the timber still standing on its banks, conspicuous among the higher and cleared lands of the neighbourhood. Passing again up the river, we find the timber in the low lands increasing in quantity, and if we desire to see cultivation we must seek it at the head-waters of the Bald Eagle, in the county of Centre: or we may pass up the Sinnemahoning, amid tens of thousands of acres of timber, much of which would yield, as we are assured, a hundred thousand feet of lumber to the acre, which yet have felt no implement but the axe of the lumberman. So nearly valueless are the fertile soils which produce these fine trees, that we have just now heard of the sale of two thousand acres, estimated to average thirty thousand feet to the acre: the whole for the sum of $1250—or £260. Attaining the head of the stream, we find ourselves again in the midst of cultivation, and see that the settlers here, as everywhere else, have selected the high and dry lands upon which they might commence with the plough, in preference to the more fertile soils that required the axe. If, instead of turning southward towards Clearfield, we advance northward to the newly settled counties of Potter, McKean and Tioga, we find the centre of population of each occupying the highest lands, near the head of the several little streams which there take their rise. If, passing westward, we cross the ridge of the Alleghany to the head-waters of the Ohio, we find again the order of things inverted. Population at first is scattered, and occupies the higher lands, and the best timber is still standing: but as we descend the river, population and wealth gradually increase, the lower lands become more and more cleared, and at length we find ourselves at Pittsburgh, in the midst of a dense population, actively employed in bringing into connection the several soils containing carbon, lime, and iron, with a view to the preparation of machinery to enable the farmer of the west to sink deeply into the land of which heretofore he has but scratched the superficial soil, and to clear and drain the fertile soils of the river bottoms, instead of the higher and drier lands from which he has heretofore derived his supplies of food.

The early settlers of Ohio, Indiana, and Illinois, uniformly selected the higher grounds, leaving the richer lands for their successors. The immediate valleys of streams, fertile as were the soils, were and still are avoided on account of danger to be apprehended from the fevers which even now sweep off so many of the emigrants to the new states. The facility of getting some small crop always prompted, as it still prompts, to the selection of the land which was most readily brought into cultivation: and none so well answered the purpose as that which was slightly clothed with timber, and clear of undergrowth. The constant fall of leaves had by their decay kept the ground covered with a light mould, and prevented the growth of grass: and by deadening the trees to let in the sun, they could obtain a small return to labour. The first great object was to have a dry place for the dwelling. Land which is entirely covered with timber has very imperfect drainage, and therefore the settler was found always selecting dry ridges of land on which to begin the work of cultivation; for the same reason which prevented him from commencing the work of artificial drainage to secure a place for his dwelling equally prevented him from so doing for any other purpose.

In the prairies, the richest land is found in the centre of the prairie, and there can water be most readily obtained; while on the outer edges, as the surface descends towards the timbered land, it is less healthful, and water is obtained only by boring to a considerable depth, while the soil is far less rich: yet here invariably does the settler commence, as the centre requires drainage, and three or four yoke of oxen to break up the tough sod. With each step in the progress of wealth and population, the new settlers are seen approaching nearer to the centre and obtaining better soils at less cost of labour. While thus passing inward towards richer portions of the prairie, others gradually make their way down to the lower lands near the margins of the streams, but for want of drainage these are frequently overflowed, and then the labour is in a great measure lost.

Descending the river from Pittsburgh, we reach the confluence of the Ohio and Mississippi, where we lose sight of all signs of population, except that of the poor wood-cutter, who risks his health while engaged in providing wood for the numerous steamboats. Here, for hundreds of miles, we pass through the most fertile land, covered with timber of gigantic size. With all its powers of production, it is valueless for all purposes of cultivation. Unembanked, it is liable to occasional overflow from the river, and its neighbourhood is destructive to life and health: for which reason hundreds of thousands of acres that, when population and wealth shall have further increased, will yield the largest return to labour, remain uncleared and undrained: while the higher lands, whose "original and indestructible powers" are less, are in a state of cultivation. Descending further, we meet population and wealth in the act of ascending the Mississippi, from the shores of the Gulf of Mexico. Embankments, or *levées*, keep out the river, and the finest plantations are seen on land corresponding in every respect with the wild and uncultivated region through which we have just passed. If, now, we desire to seek the habitations of the early settlers, we must leave the river bank and ascend the hills, and with every step we shall find new proof that cultivation invariably commences on the poorer soils. If we interrogate the pioneer settlers why they waste their labour on the poor soil of the hill-tops, while fertile soils abound, their answer will invariably be found to be, that the one they *can* cultivate as it stands, while the other they *cannot*. The pine of the hills is small, and easily cleared. It gives them good fuel, and its knots furnish artificial light. To attempt to clear the land that bears the oak would ruin them. If, instead of descending the Mississippi, we ascend the Missouri, the Kentucky, the Tennessee, or the Red River, we find invariably that the more dense the population and the greater the mass of wealth, the more are the good soils cultivated: and that as population diminishes with our approach to their head-waters, and as land becomes more abundant, cultivation recedes from the river banks, the timber and the undrained meadow-lands increase in quantity, and the scattered inhabitants are seen obtaining from the superficial soils a diminishing return to their labour, accompanied with diminishing power to command the necessaries, conveniences, and comforts of life. If we cross the Mississippi into Texas, and mark the site of the town of Austin, the centre of the first American settlement, we find it to have been placed high up on the Colorado, while millions of acres of the finest timber and meadow lands in the world, totally unoccupied, were passed over, as incapable of paying the cost of simple appropriation. If we look to the Spanish colony of Bexar, we find further illustration of the same universal fact. The whole tendency of colonization is towards the head-waters of the rivers.

We know of no exception to the rule, and we feel assured that none exists, or can exist. That it should do so, would be contrary to the laws of nature. The same reason that prompts the settler to build himself a log-house, to provide shelter while waiting until he can have one of stone, equally prompts him to begin cultivation where he can use his plough, and not to risk the starvation of his family by endeavouring to do so where he cannot: and where fevers, perhaps to be followed by death, would be the inevitable result of the attempt. In every case on record, in which settlements have been attempted on rich lands, they have either failed totally, or their progress has been slow, and it has been only after repeated efforts that they have thriven. The reader who desires evidence of this fact, and of the absolute necessity for commencing with the poorer soils, will obtain it if he study the history of the French colonies in Louisiana and Cayenne, and compare their repeated failures with the steady growth of those formed in the region of the St. Lawrence, where numerous and somewhat prosperous settlements were formed at places where the land is now held to be almost utterly valueless, because better soils can be obtained elsewhere, by sinking deeper into the earth, or removing to a little distance. He may obtain additional evidence, if he will compare the gentle, but steady, growth of the colonies planted on the sterile soils of New England, with the repeated failures of colonization upon the richer lands of Virginia and Carolina, which latter could not be reduced to cultivation by men working for themselves; and hence we find the richer colonists purchasing negroes, and compelling them to perform the work, while the free labourer seeks the light sandy lands of North Carolina. Slavery would never have existed there could free labourers have been obtained, but no man, left to himself, will commence the work of cultivation on the rich soils: because it is from those soils that the return is then least, and it is upon them, throughout all the new countries of the world, that the condition of the labourer is the worst, where the work is undertaken in advance of the wealth and combination that come, or ought to come, with time. The settler who sought the high light lands obtained food, although the return to his labour was small. Had he undertaken to drain the rich soils of the Dismal Swamp, he would have starved, as did those who settled the fertile island of Roanoke.

If the reader will now cross with us the Rio Grande, into Mexico, he may find further illustration of the universality of this law. At his left, near the mouth of the river, but at some distance from its bank, he will see the city of Matamoras, of recent date. Starting from that point, he may follow the river through vast bodies of fine lands in a state of nature, with here and there a scattered settlement occupying the higher ones, to the mouth of the San Juan, following which to its source, he will find himself in a somewhat populous country, of which Monterey is the centre. If, standing here, he cast his eyes to the north, he sees cultivation advancing among the high lands of Chihuahua, and keeping, invariably, away from the river banks. The city of that name is distant twenty miles even from the little tributary of the great river, and more than a hundred miles from the mouth of that tributary. If he pass west from Monterey, through Saltillo and thence south, his road will lie over sandy plains whose existence is evidence of the general character of the region. Arriving in Potosi, he finds himself in a country without rivers, and almost without the possibility of irrigation, and where any failure of the periodical rains is followed by famine and death, yet if he cast his eyes downwards towards the coast, he sees a magnificent country, watered by numerous rivers, and in which the cotton and the indigo plant grow spontaneously: a country in which the maize grows with a luxuriance elsewhere unknown: one that might supply the world with sugar, and in which the only danger to be apprehended from the character of the soil is, that the crops might be smothered by reason of the rapid growth of plants that spring up in the rich earth, without aid, or even permission from the man who might undertake to cultivate it: yet there he sees no population. The land is uncleared and undrained, and likely so to remain, because those who should undertake to work, with the present means of the country, would starve, if they did not perish by the fevers that there, as everywhere, prevail among the richest soils until subjected to cultivation: and often long afterwards.

Passing on, he sees Zacatecas, high and dry like Potosi, yet cultivated. Keeping the ridge, he sees on his left Tlascala, once the seat of a great and wealthy people, far removed from any stream whatsoever, and occupying the high land from which descend little streams seeking the waters of both the Atlantic and the Pacific. On his right he sees the valley of Mexico, a land capable of yielding the largest returns to labour, that by slow degrees, with the growth of population and wealth, was once drained and rendered fit for cultivation. In the time of Cortes, the people were numerous and rich, and the fertile soils they had brought into activity produced food in abundance for forty cities. Population and wealth have declined, and the remaining people have retired to the high lands bordering the valley, to cultivate the poorer soils; and the single city that still remains draws its supplies of food from a distance of fifty miles, in a country where roads scarcely exist, the consequence of which is that corn is higher in price than in London or Paris while wages are very low. Fertile land is here superabundant, over which roam half-starved cattle, seeking to obtain from the top soil: the only one used in this second childhood of agriculture: that nourishment which would be afforded in endless abundance, did the people possess the means and the industry to penetrate to those lower soils which were cultivated when population abounded. Not an acre in the hundred is cultivated at all, yet even with their imperfect machinery each one would yield twenty bushels. The people fly from it, whereas, according to Mr. Ricardo, it is that which would be first appropriated.

Passing southward, we see Tabasco almost unoccupied, yet possessing highly fertile lands. Next we reach Yucatan, a land in which water is a luxury: yet here we meet a large and prosperous population, near neighbours to the better soils of Honduras that are covered with trees of the most enormous size, and that, when population and wealth shall have sufficiently increased, will yield returns to labour as large, if not larger, than any hitherto known: yet now they are a wilderness, affording subsistence but to a few miserable logwood and mahogany cutters.

If, now, the reader look northward, towards the Caribbean sea, he will see the little dry and rocky islands of Montserrat, Nevis, St. Kitts, St. Lucia, St. Vincent, and others, cultivated throughout, while at his right stands Trinidad, with the richest of soils, remaining almost in a state of nature. If he will cast his eyes on the map and mark the position of Santa Fe de Bogota, and the city of Quito, the centres of population, where men cluster together on the high and dry lands while the valley of Oroonoko remains unoccupied, he will see exhibited on a great scale the same fact which, on a small one, we have shown to exist on the banks of the Schuylkill and the Susquehanna. If, next, he will take his station on the peaks of Chimborazo and look around, he will see the same great fact in relation to all southern America. He will see the only civilized people of the days of Pizarro occupying high and dry Peru, drained by little streams whose rapid course forbids the possibility that marshes should be formed in which vegetable matter may decay, to give richness to the soil for the production of timber before the period of cultivation, or of food afterwards. It was poor and easily cleared. It wanted no artificial drainage. It was therefore occupied.

If, now, he turn his face to the east, he will see before him the rich valley of the Amazon, affording soils inferior to none on earth, yet to this day a wilderness. Let him next trace the numerous tributaries of that great river to their sources, and he will there meet the various Portuguese towns and cities, occupying the high lands, and waiting the further growth of population and wealth for the clearing and draining of the rich soil lying between them and the ocean: soils whose crops, transported on steamboats, will at some future day yield to the labour employed a return ten times greater than can now be obtained by cultivating the poor ones, and transporting the produce across hills and mountains on the backs of mules. The laws of nature require that if man would improve his condition he must work, and he must let others work in peace. He must let wealth and population grow, and if he will not do this: if he will commit wholesale robbery and murder under the pretence of making wars for "the public good," or the hollow one of maintaining "the liberties of Europe:" she punishes him by shutting him out from those lands that would yield the largest return to his labour, and compelling him to travel on foot across barren mountains, when he might have a railroad car that would transport him rapidly through fertile valleys, where at every step he would see evidences of prosperity and happiness.

Let the reader now cast his eyes south, and compare the steep declivity occupied by the people of Chili, advancing rapidly in population and wealth; with the great valley of the La Plata, and its tribes of barbarians encamped upon lands capable of yielding the largest return to labour: and that will do so when man shall relinquish the trade of war, and permit the earth to enrich himself and his neighbour. Here, as everywhere, he has evidence that cultivation invariably commences on the poorer soils.

Crossing now the ocean, let him next take up a map of Roman Britain, and after a little study determine for himself where agriculture should first take root. Throughout the southern portion of the island, Britannia Prima, he will see the small streams passing almost directly to the ocean, and thus affording evidence of a tolerably rapid fall, and of the absence of marsh and heavily-timbered land: and here, accordingly, we find the commencement of cultivation. As he approaches the valley of the Thames, he may see the marks of population on the high lands bordering it, but in the valley itself he sees little except in the existence of a single town. Passing northward, population is everywhere seen on the flanks of the central ridge, occupying the high grounds at the heads of the streams, but we look in vain for signs of life in the lower lands: on the banks of the Humber or its tributaries, or on those of the several streams emptying into the Wash. If, now, he inquire for the seats of early cultivation, he will be referred to the sites of the rotten boroughs: to those parts of the kingdom in which men who can neither read nor write, still live in mud-built cottages, and receive nine shillings per week for their labour: and those commons upon which, to so great an extent, cultivation has recommenced.* If he seek the palace of the Norman Kings, he will find it at Winchester, and not in the valley of the Thames. If he ask for the forests and swamps of the days of Richard and of Ivanhoe, he will everywhere be shown cultivated lands of the highest fertility. If he seek the land whose morasses had nearly swallowed up the army of the conquering Norman, on his return from the devastation of the north: that which daunted the antiquary Camden, even so late as the age of James I.: he will be shown South Lancashire, with its rich corn-fields covered with waving grain, and meadows on which pasture the finest cattle. If he ask for the land most recently taken into cultivation—the newest soils—he will be taken to the fens of Lincoln; to the late sandy wastes of Norfolk; where his companion will exhibit to him the marl, yielding the largest and best crops of England: and then perhaps will accompany him on an excursion to Northumberland or Cumberland, counties occupied two centuries since by a population who found plunder more profitable than labour. Southern England possessed the land best fitted for early cultivation and for that reason least fitted for a more advanced state of population and wealth. Peru and Chili stood first on the list, but Brazil will win the race. Cultivation commenced in upper Brazil, but the banks of the Amazon will give food to a population ten times, and perhaps fifty times, greater. Lower Canada took precedence of Louisiana, but the latter has left her competitor far behind. New England preceded Pennsylvania, but

* Such are the lands described by Eden, about fifty years since, as "the sorry pastures of geese, hogs, asses, half-grown horses and half-starved cattle," and existing by thousands of acres, but which wanted only "to be enclosed and taken care of, to be as rich and as valuable as any lands now in tillage."

the soil of the latter will, at some future time, enable her to produce food for ten times the number of inhabitants per acre that can be supported from that of Massachusetts or Rhode Island. The highest cultivation will ultimately be found where there exists the greatest variety of soils, and where man is enabled to pass in succession from the poor to the better, and thence to the best: the last resulting from the compounding of new soils by aid of the machinery which constitutes wealth, and which increases most rapidly where there exists the greatest tendency to an increase of population. The variety of soils in the north of England is far greater than in the south, and hence the superiority of the former over the latter: a superiority that will continue to be maintained.

If we pass north, into Scotland, and inquire for the ancient seats of cultivation, and the residences of the great chiefs by whom the peace of the country was so frequently disturbed, we shall find them in the higher regions of the country. If we desire to see what has been styled "the granary of Scotland," we shall be referred to the light and easily cleared and cultivated soils of the Moray Frith. If we ask for the newest soils, we shall be taken to the Lothians, or to the banks of the Tweed, inhabited but a short time since by barbarians, whose greatest pleasure was found in expeditions, for the purpose of plunder, into the adjacent English counties. If we seek the forests and swamps of the days of Mary and Elizabeth, we shall find the finest farms in Scotland. If we ask for the poorest people, we shall be taken to the isles of the west: Mull or Skye: which were occupied when meadow-lands were undrained: or to the Orkneys, deemed in former times so valuable as to be received by the King of Norway in pledge for the payment of a sum of money, far greater, we doubt not, than the poor islands would but recently have commanded had the sale included the land itself as well as the right of sovereignty. If we stand on the hills of Sutherland, we see around land that has been, from time immemorial, cultivated by starving Highlanders; but if we cast our eyes on the flats below, we see rich crops of turnips growing on soil that was, but a few years since, a waste. Stand where we may: on Arthur's Seat, or Stirling's towers; or on the hills which border the great valley of Scotland: our eyes rest on fertile soils, almost, even when not wholly, undrained and unoccupied, while around may be seen high and dry lands that have been in cultivation for centuries.

In the days of Cæsar, the most powerful nations of Gaul are seen clustering round the Alps, and occupying the lands that now yield the smallest return to labour. If we seek on the map for the cities with whose names we are most familiar, as connected with the history of France in the days of the founder of the Capetian race, of St. Louis, and of Philip Augustus: Chalons, St. Quentin, Soissons, Rheims, Troyes, Nancy, Orleans, Bourges, Dijon, Vienne, Nismes, Toulouse, or Cahors, once the great centre of the banking operations of France: we shall find them far towards the heads of the rivers on which they stand, or occupying the high grounds between the rivers. If we seek the centres of power at a later period, we may find them in wild and savage Brittany, yet inhabited by a people but little removed from barbarism: at Dijon, at the foot of the Alps: in Auvergne, even yet a "secret and safe asylum of crime, amidst inaccessible rocks and wilds, which nature seems to have designed rather for beasts than men:"* in the Limousin, which gave to the church so many popes that the Limousin cardinals at length were almost enabled to dictate the proceedings of the Conclave, yet is now the poorest part of France: or on the side of the Pyrenees, in Gascony, the country of the Armagnacs, and of crimes almost unparalleled. If we look, at any of these periods, towards the lands further down the slope, we find the tend-

* Flechier.

ency to their occupation very small indeed, in regard to any of those forming a part of the kingdom of France: but greatly increasing as we reach Guienne and Normandy, the two provinces in which population and wealth increased most rapidly, by reason of their connection with England, under whose sway their rights were respected to a degree entirely unknown to the other provinces. In these grew up the love of labour and the habit of trade. In the others, the love of plunder and the contempt for all honest industry, common to all men who cultivate the poorest soils.

If we look to the state of France at present, we shall see that the poor soils alone are almost universally cultivated. Immense forests: the same in which roamed the hogs raised by the Gauls for the market of Rome: still cover many of the best lands, while from those which are cultivated the return is frequently but thrice the seed, because of the extreme imperfection of the machinery used in the work of ploughing and drainage: the poor farmer doing little more than scratch the surface to bring the top-soil into use. France is buying bad land in Algeria, at the cost of hundreds of thousands of lives and hundreds of millions of treasure, which, if applied to bringing into activity the best soils of her old lands, now dormant because of the poverty of the people, would perhaps enable her to maintain the position in the world she appears to be so rapidly losing. In that country population increases very slowly, and wealth but little faster, as must be the case always with those who cannot clear and drain the better soils, invariably last in being cultivated. The mountains and moors of Limburg and Luxemburg were occupied far in advance of the rich meadows of Holland, and while the fertile soils of Flanders and of Zealand presented to view only salt marshes and sandy wastes.

In the early history of Holland, we see a miserable people, surrounded by forests and marshes covering the most fertile lands, but living on islands of sand, and forced to content themselves with eggs, fish, and very small supplies of vegetable food of any kind. Their extreme poverty exempted them from the grinding taxation of Rome, and the unceasing vexations of Roman proconsuls, and by slow degrees they grew in numbers and wealth. Unable by means of agriculture to obtain food, they sought it from commerce. With further growth, we see them then extending themselves over the land that could be cultivated, and gradually clearing the woods and draining the marshes, until at length we find a nation the wealthiest in Europe. In this case population and wealth appear to have spread rather upwards than downwards, because they had their origin in commerce and not in agriculture. Here, however, we have further illustration of the fact that men always commence with the poorest soils. Commerce sought a shelter from Roman tyranny in the marshes of Holland, as we find it afterwards to have done among the lagunes of Venice, and behind the rocks of Amalfi, and the mountains of Liguria. These were the worst commercial soils, but they were those that could alone be cultivated, for they were those in which alone could security of person and property, so necessary to success in commerce, be obtained.

In Germany, we see the mass of the early population on the higher part of the eastern slope of the Alps, and as we pass towards the mouths of the rivers it becomes less and less dense, and the low lands are seen to exist more and more in a state of nature.

Passing into Italy, we see a numerous population in the high lands of Cisalpine Gaul, at a period when the rich soils of Venetia were unoccupied. As we advance southwards, along the flanks of the Apennines, we find a gradually increasing population, with an increasing tendency to the cultivation of the better soils, and towns whose age may almost be inferred from their situation. Thus Veii and Alba were built when the banks of the Tiber were unoccupied, and Aquileia filled a place in Roman history which was denied to the little place that then occupied the site of modern Pisa.

In Greece, we mark the same great and universal fact. The meagre soil of Attica, every foot of which drains itself, was among the earliest fitted for cultivation, and there population and wealth grew rapidly; while the fat Bœotia, requiring to be cleared and drained, followed slowly in the rear. Passing south, along the Isthmus, we have full in view on the left the short and steep eastern slope of Argolis, long since abandoned as incapable of yielding a return to labour; yet there stand the ruins of Mycenæ, of Tirynth and Trœzene, witnesses to the fact that the least fertile soils of Peloponnesus: those which were too dry to require drainage, and too poor to require to be cleared: were first selected for cultivation. On the opposite side of the ridge, the slope is much longer, and the movement of the waters more sluggish. Vegetation was far more rapid, and the land would have yielded a larger return to labour had it been accessible; but here we find precisely the same state of things that was observed in South America, where Peru was so early cultivated, while the great valley remains to this day an impracticable wilderness. On the short, steep, slope of Achaia we find another witness in the State of Sicyon, whose territory was cultivated when the richer lands of Arcadia and Elis, watered by the Alphæus, were still unoccupied.

If, now, we cross the Mediterranean and ascend the Nile, we find cultivation becoming more and more ancient as we rise, until at length far towards its head we reach Thebes, the first capital of Egypt. With the growth of population and of wealth, we find the city of Memphis becoming the capital of the kingdom: but still later, the Delta is occupied, and towns and cities rise in places that to the earlier kings were inaccessible, and with every step in this progress, there was increased return to labour.

Passing by the Red Sea, and entering the Pacific, we may see innumerable rich islands, whose lower lands are un occupied, because of their superior richness rendering them dangerous to life, while population clusters round the hills. Farther south, are rich valleys in Australia, uninhabited, or, if inhabited at all, by a people standing lowest in the catalogue of the human race; while on the little high-pointed islands of the coast, distant but a few miles, are found a superior race, with houses, cultivation, and manufactures. Here we find precisely the facts offered by South America and Argolis. Turning our steps northward, towards India, we meet Ceylon, in the centre of which are found the dominions of the king of Candy, whose subjects have the same aversion to the low and rich lands, unhealthy in their present state, that is felt by the people of Mexico and of Java. Entering India by Cape Comorin, and following the great range of high lands, the back-bone of the peninsula, we find the cities of Seringapatam, Poonah, and Ahmednugger, while below, near the coast, are seen the European cities of Madras, Calcutta and Bombay, the creation of a very recent day. Intermediate between the two, are seen numerous cities, whose positions, sometimes far away from the banks of the rivers, and at other times near their sources, show that the most fertile lands have not been those first cultivated. Standing on the high lands between Calcutta and Bombay, we have on the one hand the delta of the Indus, and on the other that of the Ganges. The former remains yet entirely unoccupied. Through hundreds of miles that river rolls its course, almost without a settlement on its banks, while on the higher country, right and left, exists a numerous population. On the Ganges, the first city that we meet, Patna, is distant from its mouth almost five hundred miles. Then follow Benares, Agra, and, at length, far up towards its head, we meet Delhi, the capital of all India while yet the government remained in the hands of its native sovereigns. Here, as everywhere else, man avoids the low rich soils that need clearing and drainage, and seeks in the high lands that drain themselves the means of employing his labour in the search for food:

and here, as everywhere else where the top-soil of the dry land alone is cultivated, the return to labour is small; and hence it is that we find the Hindoo working for a rupee, or perhaps two, per month: sufficient only to give him a handful of rice per day, and to purchase a rag of cotton cloth with which to cover his loins. The most fertile soils exist in unlimited quantity on land that is untouched, and close to that which the labourer scratches with a stick for want of a spade, making his harvest with his hands for want of a reaping hook, and carrying home upon his shoulders the miserable crop, for want of a horse and a cart. We have here precisely the state of things that, were Mr. Ricardo's doctrine true, should give the highest prosperity, yet famine and pestilence are frequent, and men rob and murder on the highway, to an extent and with a coolness unknown in any other country; because of the impossibility of obtaining subsistence by honest industry where land abounds and man is scarce.

Passing northward, by Caubul and Affghanistan, and leaving on our left the barren Persia whose weak dry soils have been cultivated through a long series of ages, we attain the Himalaya range, the highest point of the earth's surface. Looking down, we see immediately around the cradle of the human race, where head the streams that empty into the Frozen Ocean and the Bay of Bengal, the Mediterranean and the Pacific. *It is the land, of all others, suited to the purpose: that which will most readily afford to the man who works without a spade or an axe, a small supply of food.* Here we are surrounded by man in a state of barbarism: and standing here, we may trace the course of successive tribes and nations passing towards the lower and more productive lands, yet compelled in all cases to seek the route that is least disturbed with water courses, and therefore keeping the ridge that divides the waters of the Black Sea and the Mediterranean from those of the Baltic: standing here we may mark them, as they descend the slope, sometimes stopping for the purpose of cultivating the poor land that can, with their indifferent machinery, be made to yield a small supply of food; and at other times marching on and reaching the neighbourhood of the sea, there to place themselves, not on the rich lands, but on the poor soils of the steep hillside—those on which water cannot stand to give nourishment to trees, or to afford annoyance to settlers whose means are inadequate to the draining of swamps and marshes: or on little peaked islands, from which the water passes rapidly, as in the case of those of the Ægean, cultivated from so early a period. We mark some of these tribes gradually reaching the Mediterranean, where civilization is first found, and soonest lost under the weight of successive waves of emigration, while others are seen passing farther west, and entering Italy, and France, and Spain. Others, more adventurous, reach the British isles. Again, after a rest of a few centuries, we see them crossing the broad Atlantic, and commencing the ascent of the slope of the Allegheny, preparatory to the ascent and passage of the great range that divides the waters of the Pacific from those of the Atlantic; and in all cases we mark the pioneers gladly seizing on the clear dry land of the hillsides, in preference to the rich and highly wooded land of the river bottoms. Everywhere we see them, as population gradually increases, descending, equally gradually, the sides of the hills and mountains towards the rich lands at their feet: and everywhere, with the growth of numbers, penetrating the earth to reach the lower soils, to enable them to combine the upper clay, or sand, with the lower marl, or lime, and thus compounding for themselves, out of the various materials with which they have been provided by the Deity, a soil capable of yielding a larger return than that upon which they were at first compelled to expend their labours. Everywhere, with increased power of union, we see them exercising increased power over land. Everywhere, as the new soils are brought into activity, and as they are enabled to obtain larger returns, we find more rapid increase of population, producing increased tendency to combination of exertion, by which the powers of the individual labourer are trebled, quadrupled, and quintupled, and sometimes fifty-fold increased; enabling him better to provide for his immediate wants, while accumulating more rapidly the machinery by means of which he hopes further to increase his power of production, and to bring to light the vast treasures of nature. Everywhere, we find that with increasing population the supply of food becomes more abundant and regular, and clothing and shelter are obtained with greater ease; famine and pestilence tend to pass away; health becomes more universal; life becomes more and more prolonged, and man becomes more happy and more free.

In regard to all the wants of man, except the single and important one of food, such is admitted to be the case. It is seen that with the growth of population and of wealth men obtain water, and iron, and coal, and clothing, and the use of houses, and ships, and roads, in return for less labour than was at first required. It is not doubted that the great work produced at a cost of ten millions, by means of which the Croton river is carried through the city of New York, enables men to obtain water at less cost than was required when each man took a bucket and helped himself on the Hudson's bank. It is seen that the shaft which has required years to sink, and to discharge the water from which the most powerful engines are required, supplies fuel more cheaply than at first, when the settlers carried home the scraps of half-decomposed timber for want of an axe with which to cut the already fallen log: that the grist-mill converts the grain into flour at less cost of labour than was needed when it was pounded between two stones: and that the gigantic factory supplies cloth more cheaply than the little loom: but it is denied that such is the case with food. In regard to every thing else, man commences with the worst machinery and proceeds upward towards the best: but in regard to food, and that alone, he commences, according to Mr. Ricardo, with the best and proceeds downward towards the worst: and with every stage of the progress finds a decreasing return to his labour, threatening starvation and admonishing him against raising children to aid him in his age, lest they should imitate the conduct of the people of India and of the islands of the Pacific, (where land however is abundant and food *should* be cheap,) and bury him alive, or expose him on the river shore, that they may divide among themselves his modicum of food.

How far all this is true, we must leave to the reader to judge. All others of the laws of nature are broad and universally true, and we are disposed to hope that he may now agree with us in believing that there is one law, and one alone, for food, light, air, clothing, and fuel: and that man, in all and every case, commences with the worst machinery and proceeds onward to the best; thus enabled, with the growth of wealth, population, and the habit of union, to obtain with constantly diminishing labour an increased supply of all the necessaries, conveniences, comforts, and luxuries of life.

The second proposition is, that with the increase of population it becomes necessary to resort to soils of inferior fertility, yielding a smaller return to labour.

If man begins always with the best soils, then is this proposition true, and with every step in the progress of population, he loses more and more the control over his own actions—becoming the victim of *an overruling necessity*. If, on the contrary, he begins with the poor soils, and passes gradually towards the best, every step should be accompanied by increasing *power* to select such soils as are best suited to his purpose, taking sometimes the light sand, and at others the heavy marl: at one time the clay, and at another the lime: at one time the iron and at another the coal: the hill-top or the river bottom: the near or the distant: the superficial or the profound: as he deems them best calculated to minister to his wants and those of his family, and to enable him to accumulate the machinery required for exercising still greater power over the materials provided by the Creator for his use, and awaiting his draft. If increasing population produce necessity, the standard of man, physical, moral, intellectual, and political, must fall. If it give him power, the standard must rise, and he must feed better, clothe himself better, lodge better, act better, think better, and exercise in relation to all the actions of his life a volition increasing with every step in the growth of his power over the material world. Which of those two classes of phenomena it is that has been seen to appear, we propose now to examine.

In 1760, the population of England and Wales was 6,479,000. It is now about 16,000,000. The total quantity of grain produced in the former period was estimated at 15,349,000 quarters, and the exports exceeded the imports by 400,000 quarters. The whole quantity of land is about 37,000,000 of acres. Of this, a very large portion was unenclosed and uncultivated, so recently as the closing years of the last century. Eden, writing in 1797, speaks of Great Britain as a country "disfigured and burdened everywhere" with "immeasurable wastes, commons, and heaths," and resembling "one of those huge unwieldy cloaks worn in Italy and Spain, of which a very small part is serviceable to the wearer, while the rest is not only useless, but cumbersome and oppressive." He regarded it as containing, "in proportion to its size, more acres of waste land than any civilized kingdom in the world, Russia itself not excepted."

How great must have been the extension of cultivation since the period first named, may be judged from the fact that, independently of all private land that has since been cleared and drained, and manured, and limed, and marled, and thus rendered fit for the production of food, about eight millions of acres of commons and wastes: almost one-fourth of the whole surface: have been enclosed under acts of Parliament. We suppose it fair to infer that the quantity now in cultivation is, at the lowest calculation, twice as great as at the accession of George III., in 1760. With this extension over the surface, there has been a corresponding descent into the bowels of the land, and the lower soils have been to a wonderful extent combined with the superficial ones. The underlying marl of Norfolk and Lincoln has been combined with the sand, and throughout the kingdom lime has been, to an extent not to be estimated, combined with the clay, the power to accomplish which has resulted from the cultivation of the iron and coal soils, always among the last to be brought into full activity. The effect of this may be judged from the fact that the same land which in the former period yielded, in addition to the grain, but about forty tons of straw, now yields the same grain and more than five hundred tons of straw, hay, and turnips, as food for the cattle required to meet the demands of the meat markets of the kingdom: demands thrice exceeding those of the former period. The weight of food, per acre, is considerably more than twice as great as was then obtained, and the number of acres being doubled, we have five times the quantity of food to be distributed, while the population has increased but one hundred and fifty per cent.

To this must, however, be added the vast quantity of animal and vegetable food obtained from Ireland and Scotland, the imports from America and the continent of Europe: the sugar and coffee of the West Indies and Brazil: and the tea from China: the commerce in all of which existed to a very small extent in 1760. The weight of these three articles now consumed exceeds 300,000 tons, or 1,200,000 quarters, being nearly one-twelfth part as much as all the grain produced in 1760, when the export exceeded the import. The amount of food now imported is almost equal to the whole quantity consumed at that period, and this, added to the product of agriculture at home, would give six times the quantity of food, with only two and a half times the population making the average about two and a half times as much per head for the whole community.

The number of families in England and Wales, in 1831, was 2,900,000, and of these but 835,000 were engaged in agriculture. The average size of families is about five persons, and this would give about 4,200,000 as the amount of that class of the people. In 1760, the mass of the population was of that description, and we are disposed to believe that an allowance of one-half is far below the truth. If so, the result would be, that while the number of persons employed in agriculture had increased by only one-third, the product had increased five times, and that the return to the labour employed was, per head, almost four times greater than at that period. Such being the case, the new soils must be far better than the old, and the great increase of population, which, according to Mr. Ricardo's doctrine, should have brought with it increased *necessity*, has been accompanied by a steadily increasing *power* to consume the produce of rich meadow-lands that now yield fat beef, where, before, forests and swamps gave but the meat of the half-starved ox, or half-fed hog, upon which landlords banqueted when land was abundant: and thereto to add the produce of the soils of China and India, Mexico and Brazil, Cuba and Carolina. Wealth has grown faster than population, and the man of England has become lord of all the soils of the world, selecting at his pleasure the commodities that he prefers: whereas, when the poor soils alone were cultivated, he took what he could get, and as necessity had no law, the worst bread was then welcome, and a herring at harvest time was a luxury.

Nearly three millions of families are to be fed, where in 1760 there were but little over 1,200,000, and with the exception of the quantity of food imported, the whole is produced by the labour of a number of persons but little greater than was then employed in agriculture, which could not be the case did not the labour employed on the soils since brought into cultivation yield a greatly increased return. That they do yield such increase is evident from the fact that in 1760 the great mass of labour of the country was required for the production of vegetable food, whereas much of it is now employed in the cultivation of animals that yield hides that are almost equally with food essential to the comfort of man: much in producing the fuel required to keep him warm and preserve his health: and a vast portion of it in the fabrication of clothing, of which such vast quantities are consumed at home: other portions being exchanged for sugar, tea, coffee, rice, cheese, butter, &c., which millions have learned to regard as absolute necessaries, though but recently luxuries unattainable even by some who were ranked among the rich. At every step there is an increased consciousness in man of the existence of power to improve his condition, producing increased desire of improvement. Desire produces determination, and determination creates power.

At the close of the fourteenth century, the population was probably about two and a half millions. Fertile land abounded, but men cultivated the poor soils, because unable to clear and drain the rich ones. Of this we have evidence in various statements that have come down to us of the actual contents of farms and messuages, some of which are given by Eden. Six of these, of various dates from 1359 to 1400, contained one thousand one hundred and forty-two acres of arable, and but one hundred and fifty-one of meadow and pasture land. The return to the husbandman averaged less than a quarter to the acre, and if from this be deducted two bushels for the seed, we have six bushels as the product of labour. The population is now about six and a half times greater, but the number of persons who live by the labours of the field is not three times greater, while the land in cultivation is probably ten times as great; and the average yield per acre, estimating green crops as beef and mutton, and looking to the vast yield of potatoes and various other articles of vegetable food, is at least six times as great: probably even far more. If this be so, the return to labour employed on the soils brought into use since the days of the Edwards, is more than twenty times as great as when good land abounded, and when, according to Mr. Ricardo, none were required for cultivation but those which would yield the largest return. Hence it is that so large a population can be fed, while applying themselves to the production of fuel, clothing, and machinery of every description fitted to promote the comfort and happiness of man.

In "the good old times" of Ivanhoe and Richard, when fertile land was abundant and people rare, the Saxon hogs roamed the woods, living upon acorns produced from oaks that Cedric lacked the means to fell. Later, half-starved sheep fed upon lands incapable of yielding grain, but cows and oxen were few, because the fine rich meadow was covered with wood and so saturated with moisture as to be inaccessible. Maids of honour then luxuriated on bacon, and labourers banqueted upon "the strength of water-gruel," as did sixty years since many of the people of those northern counties,* which now present to view the finest farms in England, the rich soils composing which were then awaiting the growth of population and of wealth. A piece of fat pork was, in those days, an article of luxury rarely to be obtained by the labourer. Even within a century, the bread consumed by a large portion of the people was made of barley, rye, and oats, the consumption of wheat being limited to the rich; the quantity produced being small. It is now in universal use, although so recently as 1727 an eight acre field of it, near Edinburgh, was deemed a curiosity. As late as 1763, there was no such person as a public butcher known in Glasgow. It was the custom of families to buy a half-fed ox in the autumn and salt down the meat as the year's supply of animal food. The state of things there is an index to that which existed in the Lothians, and in Northumberland and other counties of the north of England, where

* Eden.

may now be seen the most prosperous agriculture of Britain. At that time men cultivated, not the best soils, but those which they *could* cultivate, leaving the rich ones for their successors: and in this they did what is done now every day by the settlers of Illinois and Wisconsin.

While wheaten bread has thus succeeded the compound of barley, rye, and acorns, once denominated bread, and which was supposed to afford more nourishment, because it remained longer in the stomach, and was less easily digested: an idea repeated in the present day by the poor Irish peasant, who prefers the miserable potato called *the lumper*, because it has, as he says, a bone in it: fat mutton and beef have succeeded the salt herring on the table of the artisan and labourer, and the mast-fed bacon on that of the landlord. Within a century the average weight of cattle has risen from three hundred and seventy to eight hundred pounds, and that of sheep from twenty-eight to eighty pounds, and the number consumed has increased more rapidly than the weight. The quantity of wool, of hides, and of other materials for manufactures of various kinds, is immense, and yet the agricultural population is certainly not three times as great as in the days of the Black Prince. The return to labour has therefore largely increased as, with increased numbers, man has acquired power over the various soils, then too deep or distant to be cultivated with the means at his command, but now required for the supply of the greatly increased and thriving population.

Mr. Ricardo's proposition is diametrically opposed to all the facts presented by the history of the United States: of England: and of the World: whereas the following is in strict accordance therewith:

With the increase of population there arises a habit of union, tending to promote the growth of wealth and to facilitate the acquisition of machinery to be used in aid of labour; and with each step in this progress, man acquires increased power over the materials of which the earth is composed, and increased power to determine for himself which to select for cultivation, as being most likely to promote the object of maintaining and improving his condition; and with every increase of this power he is enabled to obtain a larger return to his labour, and to consume more, while accumulating with still increased rapidity the machinery required for further improvement.

The third proposition is, that with the necessity for applying labour less productively which thus accompanies the growth of population, rent arises: the owner of land No. 1, yielding one hundred quarters, being enabled to demand and to obtain in return for its use, ten quarters when resort is had to those of second quality, yielding ninety quarters: and twenty when No. 3 is brought into use, yielding only eighty quarters.

Were all land of precisely equal productive power, this necessity could not be supposed to arise; yet compensation would still be paid for the use of a farm provided with buildings and enclosures, that would be denied to the owner of one which remained in a state of nature. *That* compensation is regarded by Mr. Ricardo as being only interest upon capital, and to be distinguished from what is paid for the use of the powers of the soil. When lands of different capabilities are in use, and all equally provided with fences, houses, barns, &c., he supposes the owner of No. 1 to receive the interest upon his capital, *plus* the difference between the one hundred quarters that it is capable of yielding, and the ninety, eighty, or seventy quarters that may be yielded by the soil of lowest power that the necessities of man have compelled him to cultivate. This *difference* he holds to be *the true rent.*

If, however, cultivation always commence on the poorer soils, and proceed from them to the better ones, the reverse course should be pursued; and the owner of the land first cultivated should receive interest, *minus* the difference between its powers and those of other lands that may, with the increase of population and wealth, be brought into activity with the same quantity of labour that had been expended upon it. The first little clearing on the hill side, with its miserable cabin, has cost a thousand days of labour, whereas a meadow of greater extent may now be cleared, and a good log-house erected, with half that quantity. If the first settler desire to let his land to his new neighbour, the latter will give him—not profits *plus* difference, but—profits *minus* difference. Daily observation shows that such is the course of proceeding, and that land obeys the same laws as all other commodities and things. The old ship cost a vast amount of labour, but she can carry only five thousand barrels; whereas a new ship, capable of carrying ten thousand barrels, can be built with half the labour. The owner of the first receives, as freight, profits *minus* the difference. The old house cost the labour of ten thousand days, but it will accommodate only ten persons. A new one, capable of affording better accommodation to twenty, can be produced with five thousand days of labour. The owner of the first will receive, as rent, profits *minus* the difference. And so is it with early steam-engines, railroads, mills, and all other machines.

The price of land is more or less in proportion to the rent that is paid. If the doctrine of Mr. Ricardo is true, the selling price should be the capital invested, *plus* the value of the true rent. If, on the contrary, man always commences with the poor soils, and proceeds onward towards the better ones, the price should be the capital, *minus* the difference between its power of paying rent and that of other land which could be brought into cultivation by aid of the same capital. If his doctrine is true, the power of the land and its representative over man, increases as population and the necessities of man increase: but if it is not true: if man commences always with the poor soils, and proceeds onwards to the richer ones: then must the power of man over land and its representative always increase; and then must he be enabled to obtain, at every step, land of equal powers with diminished labour; and then must those heretofore cultivated tend steadily towards diminution in their labour value. That such is the fact, we propose now to show. The whole land rental of England and Wales is about thirty millions, which, at twenty-five years' purchase, represents a capital of seven hundred and fifty millions. The wages of labourers and mechanics average about £50 per annum. The landed property of England and Wales thus represents the labour of fifteen millions of men for one year, or that of half a million of men for thirty years. Let us now suppose the island reduced to the state in which it was found by Cæsar; covered with impenetrable woods, (the timber of which is of no value because of its superabundance,) abounding in marshes and swamps, and heaths and sandy wastes; and then estimate the quantity of labour that would be required to place it in its present position, with its lands cleared, levelled, enclosed, and drained; with its turnpikes and railroads, its churches, school-houses, colleges, court-houses, and market-houses; its furnaces, forges, coal, iron, and copper mines; and the thousands and tens of thousands of other improvements required to bring into activity those powers for the use of which rent is paid, and it will be found that it would require the labour of treble the number of men for centuries, even although provided with all the machinery of modern times—the best axe and the best plough, the steam-engine, and the railroad car.*

The same thing may now be exhibited on a smaller scale. A part of South Lancashire, the forest and chase of Rossendale, embracing an area of twenty-four square miles, contained eighty souls at the beginning of the sixteenth century; and the rental, in the time of James I., little more than two cen-

* "Those who reflect for a moment on the many hundreds, or rather thousands of millions, that have been expended in fencing, draining, manuring, and otherwise improving, the land of Great Britain, and in the erection of farm buildings, must be satisfied that the return for this capital, though miserably inadequate, very greatly exceeds the other portion of the gross rental of the kingdom."—*McCulloch.* Such being the case, it might have been obvious that all rent was paid for the use of these improvements, and that there really was no other portion to be accounted for.

turies since, amounted to £122 13 8. It has now a population of eighty-one thousand; and the annual rental is £50,000, equivalent, at twenty-five years' purchase, to £1,250,000. We have never seen this land, but we have no hesitation in saying that if it were now given to Baron Rothschild, in the state in which it existed in the days of James, with a bounty equal to its value; on condition of doing with the timber the same that has been done with that which then stood there, he binding himself to give to the property the same advantages as those for which rent is now paid, his private fortune would be expended in addition to the bounty long before the work was completed. The amount received as rent is profit upon capital, and is interest upon the amount expended, *minus* the difference between the power of Rossendale to yield a return to labour, and that of the newer soils that can now be brought into activity by the application of the same labour that has been there employed. Such, likewise, is the case with the rents of London and Paris, New York and New Orleans. With all their advantages of situation, their selling prices represent but a small portion of what it would cost to reproduce them, were their sites again reduced to a state of nature. The power of man over mere brute wealth thus grows with every increase in the ratio of wealth to population.

There is not, throughout the United States, a county, township, town, or city, that would sell for cost; or one whose rents are equal to the interest upon the labour and capital expended.

Every one is familiar with the fact that farms sell for little more than the value of the improvements. When we come to inquire what "improvements" are included in this estimate, we find that the heaviest are omitted; that nothing is put down for clearing and draining the land, for the roads that have been made, the court-house and the prison that have been built, with the taxes that have been annually paid; for the church and the school-house that have been built by subscription; for the canal that passes through a piece of fine meadow-land, the contribution of the owner to the great work; or for a thousand other conveniences and advantages that give value to the property, and induce men to feel willing to pay rent for its use. Were all these things estimated, it would be found that the price is—cost, *minus* a large difference.

The great landholder of the world is the People of the United States, as represented by their Government. He obtains his land at a price that is apparently very low, yet he would be ruined were it not for his exemption from contributions. Population gradually approaches his limits. Canals and roads are made to or through them. By degrees a portion acquires the small value of $1·25, the minimum price, per acre. Settlers make new roads, and build churches and school-houses. He pays no taxes, but they do. Another section reaches the minimum price, and he sells it. Population increases more rapidly, and more roads are made, more churches and school-houses are built, but still he pays no taxes for these purposes. At length the whole is sold; and when he comes to foot up the account, he finds that by omitting many of the heaviest items of cost—those attendant upon affording protection to the settlers until they were able to protect themselves—a small profit is made to appear.

The price that is paid for land represents a portion, and often a very small portion, of its cost. Labour is frequently thrown away upon it, because it does not consist of the peculiar kind of soil that is needed *at the moment.* The settler that begins with clearing swamps, throws away his labour and dies of fever, unless he prevent that occurrence by running away. The land is rich, but its time is not come. The man who sinks into granite, searching for coal, throws away his labour. The land will be valuable when granite quarries come to be wanted, but its time is not come. The man who attempts to raise marl while surrounded by rich meadow land yet uncleared, throws away his time. The land is rich, but its time is not come. All soils have qualities tending to render them useful to man, and all are destined to come into activity; but it is the decree of nature that the best soils—those most fitted to yield a large return to labour—shall be obtained for his use only at the price of labour; and their attainment is the reward held out to him as the inducement to steady exertion, prudence, economy, and a constant observance of the great law of Christianity, which requires that every man shall respect in others those rights of person and property that he desires others to respect in himself. Where these exist, he is seen passing steadily and regularly from poor soils to those which are more productive; and with every step there is an increase of population, wealth, prosperity, and happiness. The last historian of the world, prior to its dissolution, will have, we doubt not, to say of the soils, as Byron said of the skies of Italy:

> "Parting day
> Dies like the dolphin, whom each pang imbues
> With a new colour as it gasps away,
> *The last still loveliest,* till—'tis gone—and all is gray."

Rent is paid for the use of the improvements which labour has accomplished for, or on, land, and which constitute items of wealth. Wealth tends to augment with population, and the power of accumulating further wealth increases with constantly accelerating pace as new soils are brought into cultivation, each yielding in succession a larger return to labour. Rent tends, therefore, to increase in amount with the growth of wealth and population. It is greatest in England, the wealthiest country of Europe. It diminishes as we pass thence to the poorer countries of France, Germany, Italy, and Spain, and at length disappears totally among the Rocky Mountains and the Islands of the Pacific.

The fourth proposition is, that as with the increase of population recourse is necessarily had to poorer soils, yielding a less return to labour, the *proportion* of the land-owner tends to increase.

If cultivation begins with the rich soils and proceeds to the poor ones, the power of the man who represents land, over its products, must always increase, and he must take a larger proportion, attended with increasing inequality of condition; but if, on the contrary, it always begins with the poor soils and proceeds to the rich ones, then must the power of man over land and its representative always increase, he being enabled to demand a constantly increasing proportion, leaving to the representative of land a constantly diminishing one; and thus with each step in the progress of cultivation there must be an increasing tendency to equality of condition.

It was observed, half a century since, that the proportion of the landlord was decreasing. Mr. Malthus admitted the fact, and regarded it as a proof that there was increased difficulty in obtaining food. The common impression, however, was, that men lived better than in olden times; that now they had meat and wheaten bread, and sugar, and tea and coffee; whereas, in times long past, they were obliged to be contented with barley, rye, and acorn bread. To prove that this was not the fact, Mr. Malthus asserted that whereas in the latter half of the fifteenth century the labourer could have one hundred and ninety-two pints of wheat as wages for a week, he then [1810] could have but eighty pints. Since then another writer has gone still further, and has asserted that in 1495 he could have one hundred and ninety-nine pints, or more than three bushels, for that amount of labour.

What were the precise annual wages of a labourer at that moment we have no means of ascertaining; but the change from century to century was very slow, and we shall not err very greatly in taking those of the last years of the previous one. In 1389, a plough driver had 7*s.*, and a carter 10*s.* *per annum*, without clothing, or any other perquisite; and it is esteemed doubtful if, in addition to this, he had *his own* wretched food. On an average of years these wages would command not more than a quarter of wheat, or eight bushels, and yet are we told that a labourer could earn three bushels *per week!* In the same year, four hundred and fifty days' labour were required for the harvesting of the produce of two hundred acres of land; and the average *net* yield was about six bushels per acre: in the whole, twelve hundred bushels, or two and two-third bushels harvested for each day's work. The week's return, at same rate, would be sixteen bushels, of which almost exactly one-fifth is allowed as the wages of every week in the year. Of the people who worked nearly all were employed in agriculture, and very few in manufactures or trade. Had all been so employed, with precisely similar returns and similar wages, it would follow that five weeks' wages would be equal to *the whole annual crop;* and such statements are put forth gravely by writers who know that at that very period the land and its representative took two-thirds, leaving but one-third for the labourer. The harvest labourer of the present day receives probably one-fortieth of the quantity harvested. He has work all the year, and harvest wages do not differ very greatly from those of other days; but in the fifteenth century employment during the year was rare, and those wages constituted an important portion of the year's revenue; as we see to be even now the case with the labourers of Ireland. Increased wealth facilitates the distribution of employment throughout all seasons of the year, and thus increases greatly the productiveness of labour.

The proportion of the landlord was supposed by Mr. Malthus, at the time he wrote, to be about one-fourth of the whole product. Recently Mr. McCulloch has reduced it to one-fifth; although, during the period that has elapsed, the quantity of labour and capital applied to the cultivation of new soils has been prodigiously great, and the proportion should have increased, there being more capital to draw interest, *plus* a greater difference.

If cultivation *does* always commence with the best soils, and man *is* compelled, as population increases, to descend to those yielding a less and less return to labour, the proportion of the landlord must increase. He must take profits, *plus* a constantly increasing difference; and he must ultimately absorb the whole product, except so far as he may find it to his interest to give something to his slave to keep him alive. If, however, cultivation always commences on the poor soils, and man proceeds, as population and wealth increase, always to the better soils, then the reverse must happen, and the landlord must have profits *minus* the difference, giving him a constantly decreasing proportion, and leaving to the labourer a constantly increasing one. In the one case the power of the land and its representative over the product must increase, and that of the labourer must diminish. In the other, the power of the labourer must rise, and that of the land must fall. That the latter does fall, is proved by the history of every nation of the world. The English landlord's proportion, formerly two-thirds, or more, was, in the days of Mr. Malthus, one-fourth; in those of Mr. McCulloch, one-fifth; and if population and wealth be permitted to increase, the day is not far distant when it will be one-tenth, or less, while the amount will be greater than now. If we look to other parts of the world, we shall see abundant evidence of this. In Prussia, forty years since, it was assumed that the peasant who retained one-third of the product had a decent subsistence. In France, where population and wealth grow very slowly, the proportion of the landlord is much greater than in England, and probably greater than in Prussia. In Spain and Sicily it is greater than in France. In Mexico it is greater than it is in Sicily. In India, greater than in Mexico. In all these countries the most fertile soils abound, uncultivated; and men scratch the surface, obtaining from the superior soil the most sorry return to their labour.

Whenever the time shall come when the rulers of their destinies shall permit population and wealth to increase—and they cannot be separated—the more fertile soils will be cultivated, the return to labour and the *amount* of rent will both be increased, and the landlord's *proportion* will be diminished.

In the time of the Plantagenets, the owner of land took the whole product, and gave what he pleased to his serf. From that day to the present, as population and wealth have increased, the labourer has obtained a constantly increasing control over the application of his labour, and over the distribution of the commodities that he produces; the result of which is that the labourer of England, where the various soils, superior and inferior, are cultivated to an extent elsewhere unknown, receives for his own use a larger proportion, and thus exercises more power over the product of his labour, than the labourer of any other portion of Europe. At no period has his proportion increased so rapidly as within the present century, when population has increased at a rate before unexampled; and in no part of England is his proportion so great as in that in which population has most rapidly increased; yet it is precisely there that the lower soils have been to the greatest extent brought into cultivation. How these facts are to be reconciled to the fashionable doctrine of rent, it is difficult to conceive. Seeing them, it is not extraordinary that one of the earliest and most enthusiastic admirers of Mr. Ricardo should have found occasion recently to reproach him with having furnished no explanation of these "miracles." The real "miracle," however, appears to us to be the fact that such a doctrine should have obtained so extensively, and should have so long continued to obtain.

Wealth tends to grow more rapidly than population, because better soils are brought into cultivation; and it does grow more rapidly, whenever people abandon swords and muskets and take to spades and ploughs. Every increase in the ratio of wealth to population is attended with an increase in the power of the labourer as compared with that of landed or other capital. We all see that when ships are more abundant than passengers, the price of passage is low—and *vice versa*. When ploughs and horses are more plenty than ploughmen, the latter fix the wages, but when ploughmen are more abundant than ploughs, the owners of the latter determine the distribution of the product of labour. When wealth increases rapidly, new soils are brought into cultivation, and more ploughmen are wanted. The demand for ploughs produces a demand for more men to mine coal and smelt iron ore, and the iron-master becomes a competitor for the employment of the labourer, who obtains a larger proportion of the constantly increasing return to labour. He wants clothes in greater abundance, and the manufacturer becomes a competitor with the iron-master and the farmer for his services. His proportion is again increased, and he wants sugar, and tea, and coffee, and now the ship-master competes with the manufacturer, the iron-master and the farmer: and thus with the growth of population and wealth there is produced a constantly increasing demand for labour; and its increased productiveness, and the consequently increased facility of accumulating wealth are followed necessarily and certainly by an increase of the labourer's proportion. His wages rise, and the *proportion* of the capitalist falls, yet now the latter accumulates fortune more rapidly than ever, and thus his interest and that of the labourer are in perfect harmony with each other. If we desire evidence of this, it is shown in the constantly increasing amount of the rental of England, derived from the appropriation of a constantly decreasing proportion of the product of the land: and in the enormous amount of railroad tolls compared with those of the turnpike: yet the railroad transports the farmer's wheat to market, and brings back sugar and coffee, taking not one-fourth as large a *proportion* for doing the business as was claimed by the owner of the wagon and horses, and him of the turnpike. The labourer's product is increased, and the proportion that goes to the capitalist is decreased. The power of the first over the product of his labour has grown, while that of the latter has diminished.

Nothing is more frequent than references to those "good old times," when the labourer obtained food more readily than at present, but no idea can be more erroneous. The whole quantity of food at this time consumed in England is at the lowest estimate sixty times as great as in the days of Edward III., while the population is but little more than six times greater. Divided among the whole people, the average per head would be ten times as great, in quantity, without taking into account the difference of quality. In those days of barbarous wassail, the waste among the nobles and their followers was prodigiously great. In our day economy prevails everywhere, and it prevails necessarily, for as the standard of living rises with the increase of production, the *proportion* that falls to the land, or to capital in any other form, tends to decrease. Increase of wealth tends therefore to beget economy, and economy begets wealth ; and the more fertile the soil cultivated the greater will be the power of the labourer, and the greater the necessity for economy on the part of those who represent landed or other capital, and who do not themselves work. The proportion now consumed by the wealthy and their attendants—by those who consume and do not produce—is very small compared with what it was in those "good old times," and therefore the proportion going to the labourer is very large, while the quantity to be divided is so greatly increased. The great mass of the present large product goes directly to the tables of those who work, while a very small proportion of it is prepared for the tables of those who do not work, and even of that a large portion is eaten at last by people whose position in society renders employment desirable. The Queen eats less in weight than the man who mines the coal that is used in her palace. Lord John Russell consumes less than any London porter, and Sir Robert Peel is, we doubt not, outdone by most of his servants.

Of the mass of food provided for the people of England, nine-tenths are eaten by the labouring class. If any be disposed to deny that this view is correct, let them endeavour to satisfy themselves what else becomes of it. That the whole is eaten is certain. That the class who do not labour is small, and that they cannot consume much more, per head, than others, are equally certain; and if so, it must be obvious that the proportion which their consumption bears to the quantity consumed must be very small indeed; and equally so that what they do not eat must be eaten by the great class who do labour.

Such is likewise the case with clothing. The quantity consumed is thousands of times greater than it was at the period to which we have referred, and it is chiefly consumed by the class who work. Ladies and gentlemen *buy* more than colliers and farm-labourers, but they do not *wear out* as much. They change frequently, but their cast-off clothes pass from hand to hand and are worn out by those who work. In no part of Europe is the mass of rent, or of profits of capital employed otherwise than on land, so great as there: yet in none do the people who pay that rent, or those profits—those who work—enjoy so large an amount of the conveniences, comforts, and enjoyments of life. In none is there so great a tendency to an increase of the labourer's proportion,—of his power over the product of his labour,—while in none is the quantity to be divided so great. In none, therefore, is there so great a tendency to elevation and equality of physical, moral, intellectual and political condition, because in none do wealth and population grow so rapidly, facilitating the cultivation of the lower and more productive soils. In no time past has there been so rapid an increase as now. Never has the tendency to cultivate those soils been so great, and yet never has the product of labour increased in so great a ratio: and never has the proportion of the landlord so rapidly diminished. Were the doctrine of Mr. Ricardo true, such "miracles" could not happen. The following table of the results of the two systems may be compared by the reader with what is now passing before his eyes, and he may then determine for himself which is most in accordance with the facts.

	RICARDO'S DOCTRINE.*			OBSERVATION.		
		Power of Land.	Power of Labour.		Power of Land.	Power of Labour.
First period	100	—	100	30	20	10
Second "	190	10	180	70	42	28
Third "	270	30	240	120	60	60
Fourth "	340	60	280	180	80	100
Fifth "	400	100	300	250	100	150
Sixth "	450	150	300	330	120	210
Seventh "	490	210	280	420	140	280
Eighth "	520	280	240	510	155	355
Ninth "	540	360	180	620	170	450
Tenth "	550	450	100	740	180	560
Eleventh "	550	550	00	870	190	680

The fifth proposition is, that wealth tends to counteract these laws, and to prevent the necessity for resorting to less productive soils, by producing improvements in cultivation. This proposition was interpolated by Mr. Ricardo into his system, because of the absolute necessity for leaving a place of escape for some of the thousand exceptions to his laws that presented themselves to his consideration, and its presence there is a direct admission of the unsoundness of his whole doctrine.

Wealth should grow, according to Mr. Ricardo, most rapidly when and where land is most abundant, and when and where the best soils only are cultivated. That his followers think so, is obvious from the fact that they, one and all, attribute the rapid growth of wealth in the United States to the abundance of land. Improvements of cultivation should, then, be most rapid where land is most abundant, but such

* See page 22.

has not been the case in England, nor is it now in any country of Europe. On the contrary, wealth grows more rapidly at this moment, when resort is daily had to the lower and more distant soils, than it has done in any time past, and the only manner in which it promotes improvements in cultivation is in facilitating the resort to those soils. The plough enables the farmer to go deep into the lower soil. The spade enables him to reach the marl. The wagon enables him to transport it. The railroad enables him to bring the coal to the lime, and thus facilitates the compounding of a new soil: and with each new one thus brought into activity the produce of labour and the growth of wealth should diminish, and therewith we ought to see a diminished power of effecting such improvements; yet with every extension of cultivation the power of man over the various soils is seen to increase. The new soils are better than the old ones, or they are worse. If the first, Mr. Ricardo's theory is false. If the second, then with every soil that is cultivated, the power of accumulation must diminish, and as population still goes on to increase, the necessity for applying labour with diminished return must go on, let man do what he may to prevent it. The law of nature in regard to the production of food can no more be arrested than that in relation to the gravitation of matter. All her laws are simple and universally true. That of Mr. Ricardo is complex and universally false. Had it been otherwise, he would have experienced no necessity for providing escape-valves for troublesome facts.

The sixth and last proposition is, that every such improvement tends to retard the increase of rent, while every obstacle to improvement tends to accelerate that increase; and that, therefore, the interests of the landlord and the labourer are always in opposition to each other.

If men commence with the cultivation of the most fertile

soils, and if with the progress of population there *does* arise a necessity for resorting to those of less fertility, yielding a constantly decreasing return to labour, such must be the case. The slower the increase in the supply of food, the more rapid will be the increase in the power of the owner of land in cultivation, and the greater will be the tendency to starvation and disease among those who work.* The landlord will take a constantly increasing proportion, and the labourer must eventually become his slave, thankful to be allowed to live and work, even although compelled to live on acorn-bread. Mr. Ricardo has, here, carried out his doctrine to its legitimate results, and those results must be reached at some future day, if his theory is correct. It signifies nothing to say that the downward progress may be arrested. Man must be always tending in that direction, and there must he arrive at last: even if it be a thousand years hence.† The experience of England and of Europe for thousands of years past, and that of America for the last three centuries, would lead us to opposite conclusions, but Mr. Ricardo says that such is the law. If so, when is it to begin to become operative? We know of no other of the natural laws thus hung up *in terrorem* over man: none, the action of which is thus suspended, in order that it may at some future time fall with a force increased immeasurably during the period of suspension. Population is growing daily, and with great rapidity, and the necessity for resorting to less productive soils must be increasing with every hour; yet man is permitted to go on to increase his species, in blind and blissful ignorance of the fact that his children, grandchildren, or great grandchildren

* "How slow soever the increase of population, provided that of capital be still slower, [believed by Mr. Mill to be the case,] wages will be reduced so low that a portion of the population will regularly die from the consequences of want."—*Mill.*

† "From the operation of fixed and permanent causes, the increasing sterility of the soil is sure, in the long run, to overmatch the improvements that occur in machinery and agriculture, prices experiencing a corresponding rise, and profits a corresponding fall."—*McCulloch.*

must inevitably see themselves deprived of the means of subsistence, while owners of land are to revel in abundance greater than ever before : the one class becoming masters and the other slaves.

If, on the contrary, cultivation commences invariably on the poorer soils and proceeds to the better, the reverse must be the case, and every improvement must tend to accelerate the growth of rent; and every obstacle to improvement, be it what it may, must tend to arrest that growth; and therefore must the interests of the landlord and those of the labourer be in perfect harmony with each other. Improvement of cultivation results from the increase of wealth. The more spades and ploughs, and the better their quality, the larger is the return to labour, and the greater is the rent. The more horses and cattle, the larger is the return to labour, and the greater is the rent. The more steam-engines, the easier is the work of drainage, the larger is the return to labour, and the greater is the rent. The more mills, the easier is the conversion of the grain into flour, the larger is the return to labour, and the greater is the rent. The more factories, the less is the labour required to procure a supply of clothing, the greater is the quantity that may be given to improving the land by making drains, roads, bridges and school-houses, the larger is the return to labour, and the greater is the rent. The interests of the landlord would seem therefore to be directly promoted by every measure that tends to augment the wealth of the nation and to aid in the improvement of cultivation.

How stands it with the labourer? He sees that with every increase in the number and quality of spades and ploughs: of engines and roads: of mills and factories: his labour becomes more productive. Again, he sees that with every increase in the ratio which spades and ploughs, engines and mills, bear to the men by whom they are to be employed, he takes a larger proportion; and that whereas, when the land in cultivation yielded a net product of six bushels to the acre, the owner took half, or more, leaving him three, or less;

now when it yields forty bushels, he takes but one-fifth, leaving him thirty-two. He *feels*, therefore, at every instant of his progress, that his interests are, like those of the landlord, directly advanced by every measure tending to the augmentation of wealth, and to the promotion of improvements in cultivation.

Here we have perfect harmony of interests, and it is only necessary that the two parties should fully understand that it exists, to have all unite in the removal of restrictions that tend to expel capital by rendering it unproductive; and to expel labour, to be employed elsewhere less productively than it might be employed at home, if aided by that capital. This understood, kindness and good feeling would take the place of jealousy and discord. The few would no longer believe that their interests were to be promoted by the waste of wealth on large fleets and armies; and the many would cease to feel that they were borne down by taxes. Wealth would increase more rapidly, as would the power of production and consumption. Neighbouring nations would be unwilling to lose rich customers, and equally unwilling to be deprived of their accustomed supplies of commodities needed for the gratification of their wants, and would carefully avoid all cause of hostility. The harmony of classes would thus beget the harmony of nations. The love of peace would diffuse itself throughout the earth. All would become satisfied that in the laws which govern the relations of man with his fellow man, there reigns the same beautiful simplicity and harmony everywhere else so abundantly evident: all by degrees would learn that their own interests would be best promoted by respecting in others those rights of person and property that they desired to have respected in themselves: and all become, at length, satisfied that the whole of the so-called Science of Political Economy is embraced in the brief words of the great founder of Christianity, "Do unto others as ye would that others should do unto you."

Mr. Ricardo's system is one of discords. Its parts do not

agree with each other, and its whole tends to the production of hostility among classes and nations. He professes free trade, while teaching that the monopoly of land is in accordance with the laws of nature. He professes a love for freedom of action, while teaching that if men and women *will* unite themselves together in marriage, thus doing that which tends most to stimulate them to exertion for the improvement of their condition, physical, moral, intellectual, and political, the consequence must be an increasing tendency to starvation: and thus he affords countenance to the thousand restrictions by which marriage is prevented and profligacy promoted. He is for free trade in corn, but he teaches the landlord that his interests will be injured by it. He is for promoting the growth of wealth, but he informs the landlord that all wealth appropriated to the improvement of cultivation must diminish the progress of rent. He would have the rights of property respected, while teaching the labourer that the interests of the land-owner are to be promoted by every measure tending to produce starvation and misery; and that rent is paid because of an exercise of power on the part of the few, who have appropriated to themselves that which a beneficent Deity intended for the common good of all. His book is the true manual of the demagogue, who seeks power by means of agrarianism, war, and plunder. The lessons which it teaches are inconsistent with those afforded by the study of all well observed facts, and inconsistent even with themselves; and the sooner they shall come to be discarded the better will it be for the interests of landlord and tenant, manufacturer and mechanic, and mankind at large.

The PAST says to the landlord of the PRESENT: "Study economy, private and public. Give your mind to the management of the treasure of materials placed in your hands. Permit wealth to grow, and your rents will rise, while you will be surrounded by happy and prosperous people. You will lose in power, but you will gain in happiness."

To the labourer it says: "Economize your time, your labour, and their proceeds. Improve your mind. Study to promote the growth of wealth, and your labour will become more productive, while your power over its product will increase, and you will experience a steady improvement in your physical, moral, intellectual, and political condition."

To all it says: "Respect the rights of your neighbour, as you would desire that he should respect your own." To all it says: "I have sinned. I have failed to respect the rights of others, and I have suffered heavily in consequence. Take warning by my example."

CHAPTER II.

MAN AND FOOD.

MAN commences by cultivating the poor soils. He works alone, and his labour is unproductive. As his numbers increase he is enabled to combine his exertions with those of his fellow-men, and to subdue to cultivation the better soils, obtaining a constantly increasing return to his labour; enabling him, while consuming more and better food, to accumulate more rapidly the machinery required to facilitate his further progress.

The prevailing doctrine of the time is that of Mr. Malthus, who teaches—

I. That population tends to increase with great rapidity.

II. That the tendency to increase in the supply of food is less than in the numbers of mankind.

III. That with every step in the progress of population there is a tendency to starvation.

IV. That improvements in cultivation may increase production, but that they are invariably followed by a still more rapid increase of population, neutralizing their effect by compelling a resort to less productive soils.

V. That the remedies provided by nature for preventing this excess of population over food, are war, pestilence, famine, vice, and misery, to be avoided only by the exercise of that moral restraint which shall tend to diminish the growth of the numbers of mankind.

The time *may* arrive when the world will be so fully occupied that there will not be even standing room, but we may safely leave that distant future to the benevolent care of the Deity. We know well that there is now, and always has been, an abundance of unoccupied land; and the question to be settled is: What are the phenomena which in time past have attended the increase of mankind up to the present point: with a view to determine what are those which may be expected to mark the further progress of our race towards the occupation of that almost infinite extent of soil capable of yielding food, which in both old and new countries yet remains unoccupied and unproductive. Mr. Malthus thought he saw that they were such as indicated "a constant effort in the population to increase beyond the means of subsistence," as constantly tending "to subject the lower classes of society to distress, and to prevent any great permanent melioration of their condition;" and this effort appeared to him quite as obviously to exist in countries in which the population was but one to the square mile, as in those in which it amounted to a hundred. Of course his theory refers, not to the state of things which may be supposed to arise when the whole earth shall come to be occupied, but to that which now exists and has existed for centuries past. In support of these views his book furnishes an infinite number of small facts, while the great and really important ones are totally overlooked. His work throughout wants breadth. His theory is, nevertheless, perfectly sound, if men commence the work of cultivation with the rich soils, and proceed downwards to the poor ones. If, however, they always commence with the thin, dry soils, and always proceed onward to the rich ones, then the reverse thereof must be true, and food must tend to increase faster than population, permitting wealth to increase, and combination of action to arise as men are enabled to live in closer connection with each other.

The first cultivator can neither roll nor raise a log, with which to build himself a house. He makes himself a hole in the ground, which serves in lieu of one. He cultivates the poor soil of the hills to obtain a little corn, with which to eke out the supply of food derived from snaring the game in his neighbourhood. His winter's supply is deposited in another hole, liable to injury from the water which filters through the light soil into which alone he can penetrate.* He is in hourly danger of starvation. At length, however, his sons grow up. They combine their exertions with his, and now obtain something like an axe and a spade. They can sink deeper into the soil; and can cut logs, and build something like a house. They obtain more corn and more game, and they can preserve it better. The danger of starvation is diminished. Being no longer forced to depend for fuel upon the decayed wood which alone their father could use, they are in less danger of perishing from cold in the elevated ground which, from necessity, they occupy. With the growth of the family new soils are cultivated, each in succession yielding a larger return to labour, and they obtain a constantly increasing supply of the necessaries of life from a surface diminishing in its ratio to the number to be fed; and thus with every increase in the return to their labour the power of combining their exertions is increased.

If we look now to the solitary settler of the west, even where provided with both axe and spade, we shall see him obtaining, with extreme difficulty, the commonest log hut. A neighbour arrives, and their combined efforts produce a new house with less than half the labour required for the first. That neighbour brings a horse, and he makes something like a cart. The product of their labour is now ten times greater than was that of the first man working by himself. More neighbours come, and new houses are wanted. A "bee" is made, and by the combined effort of the neighbourhood the third house is completed in a day; whereas the first cost months, and the second weeks, of far more severe exertion. These new neighbours have brought ploughs and horses, and now better soils are cultivated, and the product of labour is again increased, as is the power to preserve the surplus for winter's use. The path becomes a road. Ex-

* The *caches* of the savages of the Rocky Mountains, and the *silos* of the people of Castile, are instances of this course of proceeding.

changes begin. The store makes its appearance. Labour is rewarded by larger returns, because aided by better machinery applied to better soils. The town grows up. Each successive addition to the population brings a consumer and a producer. The shoemaker wants leather and corn in exchange for his shoes. The blacksmith requires fuel and food, and the farmer wants shoes for his horses; and with the increasing facility of exchange more labour is applied to production, and the reward of labour rises, producing new wants, and requiring more and larger exchanges. The road becomes a turnpike, and the wagon and horses are seen upon it. The town becomes a city, and better soils are cultivated for the supply of its markets, while the railroad facilitates exchanges with towns and cities more distant. The tendency to union and to combination of exertion thus grows with the growth of wealth. In a state of extreme poverty it cannot be developed. The insignificant tribe of savages that starves on the product of the upper soil of hundreds of thousands of acres of land, looks with jealous eyes on every intruder, knowing that each new mouth requiring to be fed tends to increase the difficulty of obtaining subsistence; whereas the farmer rejoices in the arrival of the blacksmith and the shoemaker, because they come to eat on the spot the corn which heretofore he has carried ten, twenty, or thirty miles to market, to exchange for shoes for himself and his horses. With each new consumer of his products that arrives he is enabled more and more to concentrate his action and his thoughts upon his home, while each new arrival tends to increase his *power* of consuming commodities brought from a distance, because it tends to diminish his *necessity* for seeking at a distance a market for the produce of his farm. Give to the poor tribe spades, and the knowledge how to use them, and the power of association will begin. The supply of food becoming more abundant, they hail the arrival of the stranger who brings them knives and clothing to be exchanged for skins and corn; wealth grows, and the habit of association—the first step towards civilization—arises.

The little tribe is, however, compelled to occupy the highland. The lowlands are occupied by dense forests and dreary swamps, while at the foot of the hill runs a river, fordable but for a certain period of the year. On the hill side, distant a few miles, is another tribe; but communication between them is difficult, because, the river bottom being yet uncleared, roads cannot be made, and bridges are as yet unthought of. Population and wealth, however, continue to increase, and the lowlands come gradually into cultivation, yielding a larger return to labour, and enabling the tribe to obtain larger supplies of food with less exertion, and to spare labour to be employed for other purposes. Roads are made in the direction of the river bank. Population increases more rapidly because of the increased supplies of food and the increased power of preserving it, and wealth grows still more rapidly. The river bank at length is reached, and some of the best lands are now cleared. Population grows again, and a new element of wealth is seen in the form of a bridge, and now the two little communities are enabled to communicate more freely with each other. One rejoices in the possession of a wheelwright, while the other has a windmill. One wants carts, and the other has corn to grind. One has hides to spare, while the other has more shoes than are required for their use. Exchanges increase, and the little towns grow because of the increased amount of trade. Wealth grows still more rapidly, because of new modes of combining labour, by which that of all is rendered more productive. Roads are now made in the direction of other communities; and the work is performed more rapidly, because the exertions of the two are now combined, and because the machinery used is more efficient. One after another disappear forests and swamps that have occupied the fertile lands, separating ten, twenty, fifty, or five hundred communities, which now are brought into connection with each other; and with each step labour becomes more and more productive, and is rewarded with better food, clothing, and shelter. Famine and disease disappear; life is prolonged; population is increased, and therewith the tendency to that combination of exertion among the individuals composing these communities, which is the distinguishing characteristic of civilization in all periods of the world, and in all nations. With further increase of population and wealth, the desires of man, and his ability to gratify them, both increase. The nation, thus formed, has more corn than it wants; but it has no cotton, and its supply of wool is insufficient. The neighbouring nation has cotton and wool, and wants corn. They are still divided, however, by broad forests, deep swamps, and rapid rivers. Population increases, and the great forests and swamps disappear, giving place to rich farms, through which broad roads are made, with immense bridges, which enable the merchant to transport his wool and his cotton to exchange with his now rich neighbours for their surplus corn or clothing. Nations now combine their exertions, and wealth grows with still increased rapidity, facilitating the drainage of marshes and thus bringing into activity the richest soils; while coal mines cheaply furnish the fuel for converting limestone into lime, and iron ore into axes and spades, and into rails for the new roads that are needed to transport to market the vast products of the fertile soils now in use, and to bring back the large supplies of clothing, sugar, tea, coffee, and the thousand other products of distant lands with which intercourse now exists. At each step population and wealth, and happiness and prosperity, take a new bound; and men realize with difficulty the fact that the country which now affords to tens of millions all the necessaries, comforts, conveniences, and luxuries of life, is the same that, when the superabundant land was occupied by tens of thousands only, gave to that limited number scanty supplies of the worst food . so scanty that famines were frequent and sometimes so severe that starvation was followed in its wake by pestilence, which, at brief intervals, swept from the earth the population of the little and scattered settlements, among which the people were forced to divide themselves when they cultivated only the poor soils of the hills.

Such is the course of events, when man is allowed to follow the bent of his inclinations, which, however, he rarely is. When men are poor, they are compelled to select such soils as they *can* cultivate, not such as they *would*. Although gathered around the sides of the same mountain range, they are far distant from each other. They have no roads, and they are unable to associate for self-defence. The thin soils yield small returns, and the little tribe embraces some who would prefer to live by the labour of others rather than by their own. The scattered people may be plundered with ease, and half a dozen men, combined for the purpose, may rob in succession all the members of the little community. The opportunity makes the robber. The boldest and most determined becomes the leader of the gang. One by one, the people who use spades are plundered by those who carry swords, and who pass their leisure in dissipation. The leader divides the spoil, taking the largest share himself, with which, as the community increases, he hires more followers. He levies black mail on those who work, taking such portion as suits his good pleasure. With the gradual increase of the little community, he commutes with them for a certain share of their produce, which he calls rent, or tax, or *taille*. Population and wealth grow very slowly, because of the large proportion which the non-labourers bear to the labourers. The good soils are very slowly improved, because the people are unable to obtain axes or spades with which to work, or to make roads into the dense forests. Few want leather, and there is no tanner on the spot to use their hides. Few can afford shoes, and there is no shoemaker to eat their corn while making the few that can be bought. Few have horses, and there is no blacksmith. Combination of effort has scarcely an existence. By very slow degrees, however, they are enabled to reduce to cultivation better lands, and to lessen the distance between themselves and the neighbouring settlement, where rules another little sovereign. Each chief, however, now covets the power of taxing, or collecting rents from the subjects of his neighbour. War ensues. Each seeks plunder, and calls it "glory." Each invades the domain of the other, and each endeavours to weaken his opponent by murdering his rent-payers, burning their houses, and wasting their little farms, while manifesting the utmost courtesy to the chief himself. The tenants fly to the hills for safety, being there more distant from the invaders. Rank weeds grow up in the rich lands thus abandoned, and the drains fill up. At the end of a year or two, peace is made, and the work of clearing is again to be commenced. Population and wealth have, however, diminished, and the means of recommencing the work have again to be created. Meanwhile the best lands are covered with shrubs, and the best meadows are under water. With continued peace, the work, however, advances, and after a few years, population and wealth, and cultivation, attain the same height as before. New wars ensue, for the determination of the question which of the two chiefs shall collect all the—so-called—rent. After great waste of life and property, one of them is killed, and the other falls his heir, having thus acquired both glory and plunder. He now wants a title, by which to be distinguished from those by whom he is surrounded. He is a little king. Similar operations are performed elsewhere, and kings become numerous. By degrees, population extends itself, and each little king covets the dominions of his neighbours. Wars ensue on a somewhat larger scale, and always with the same results. The people invariably fly to the hills for safety. As invariably, the best lands are abandoned. Food becomes scarce, and famine and pestilence sweep off those whose flight had saved them from the swords of the invader. Small kings become greater ones, surrounded by lesser chiefs who glorify themselves in the number of their murders, and in the amount of plunder they have acquired. Counts, viscounts, earls, marquises, and dukes, now make their appearance on the stage, heirs of the power and of the *rights* of the robber chiefs of early days. Population and wealth go backward, and the love of title grows with the growth of barbarism.* Wars are now made on a larger scale, and greater "glory" is acquired. In the midst of distant and highly fertile lands occupied by a numerous population, are rich cities and towns offering a copious harvest of plunder. The citizens, unused to arms, may be robbed with impunity, always an important consideration to those with whom the pursuit of "glory" is a trade. Provinces are laid waste, and the population is exterminated, or if a few escape, they fly to the hills and mountains, there to perish of famine. Peace follows, after years of destruction, but the rich lands are overgrown: the spades and axes, the cattle and the sheep are gone: the houses are destroyed: their owners have ceased to exist: and a long period of abstinence from the work of desolation is required to regain the point from which cultivation had been driven by men intent upon the gratification of their own selfish desires, at the cost of the welfare and happiness of the people over whose destinies they have unhappily ruled. Population grows slowly, and wealth but little more rapidly, for almost ceaseless wars have impaired the disposition and the respect for honest labour, while the neces-

* It is amusing to trace with each step in the progress of the decay of the Roman Empire, the gradual increase in the magnificence of titles: and so again with the decline of modern Italy. In France, titles became almost universal as the wars of religion barbarized the people. The high-sounding titles of the East are in keeping with the weakness of those by whom they are assumed, as are the endless names of the Spanish grandee with the poverty of the soil cultivated by his dependents. The time is fast approaching when men of real dignity will reject the whole system as an absurdity, and when small men alone will think themselves elevated by the title of Esquire, Honourable, Baron, Marquis, or Duke. Extremes always meet. The son of the duke rejoices in the possession of half a dozen Christian names, and the little retailer of tea and sugar calls his daughter Amanda Malvina Fitzallan—Smith, or Pratt: while the *gentleman* calls his son Robert, or John.

sity for beginning once more the work of cultivation on the poor soils, adds to the distaste for work, while it limits the power of employing labourers. Swords or muskets are held to be more honourable implements than spades and pickaxes. The habit of union for any honest purpose is almost extinct, while thousands are ready, at any moment, to join in expeditions in search of plunder. War thus feeds itself by producing poverty, depopulation, and the abandonment of the most fertile soils; while peace also feeds itself, by increasing the number of men and the habit of union, because of the constantly increasing power to draw supplies of food from the surface already occupied, as the almost boundless powers of the earth are developed in the progress of population and wealth.

These views are not in accordance with the doctrine of Mr. Malthus, yet look where we may, we shall find confirmation of their truth. If to India, we may see the rich soil relapsing into jungle, while its late occupant starves among the forts of the hills. If to other parts of Asia, we may see abandoned the rich countries on the banks of the Tigris, and of the Euphrates, while poor and barren Persia is still cultivated. If to Egypt, we may trace with its advance the gradual descent of population towards the Nile, bringing into activity the rich lands of the Delta: and with its decline, the abandonment of those lands, the filling up of the canals, and the concentration of the population on the higher and less productive lands. If to Italy, we see a growing people subduing to cultivation the rich lands of the Campagna and of Latium, to be again gradually abandoned, and now affording miserable subsistence to men, many of whom go clothed in skins of beasts, and whose number scarcely exceeds that of the cities that once there flourished. If we pass farther north, we may see the rich lands of the Siennese republic in cultivation until the sixteenth century, when the ferocious Marignan drove to the hills the small remnant of the population that escaped the sword, and gave to the world a pestilential desert, in lieu of the highly cultivated farms which before abounded. Still further north, may be seen the destruction of the canals of Pisa and the abandonment of its fertile soils, while its late inhabitants perish by pestilence within the city walls, or transfer themselves to the head of the Arno, to seek there the subsistence no longer afforded by the richer lands near its mouth. In France, we may see the perpetual ravage of the rich lands of the south by the ferocious tribes of the north, from the days of Clovis down to the period of the revocation of the Edict of Nantes, and at every fresh invasion, the people are seen flying to the hills and mountains for safety. In the days of the English wars, we may see the lower and richer countries ravaged by bands of fierce mountaineers: the wild Breton, the ferocious Gascon, and the mercenary Swiss: united for the plunder of the men who cultivated the more fertile soils, and driving them to seek refuge in the wild and savage Brittany itself. We may see the lands of the richer soils rendered utterly desolate: *la Beauce*, one of the most fertile parts of the kingdom, become again a forest: while from Picardy to the Rhine not a house, unprotected by city walls, is left standing, nor a farm that is not stripped. In later times we see Lorraine reduced to a desert: and fine forests but recently stood, if even now they have ceased to stand, where formerly the rich soil yielded liberal returns to labour. Throughout France are seen the effects of perpetual war, in the concentration of the whole agricultural population in filthy villages, at a distance from the lands they cultivate: there inhaling a foul atmosphere, and losing half their time in transferring themselves, their rough implements, and their products, to and from their little properties, whereas, the same labour bestowed upon the land itself would give to cultivation the richer soils.

If we trace the external history of that country, we see hosts of gentlemen followed by bands of savage Bretons, Gascons, and Swiss: all, noble and gentle, equally greedy and rapacious: engaged for successive centuries in the work of plundering and exterminating their neighbours, whose wealth enabled them to cultivate the fertile soils: the people of the Netherlands and Germany: of Italy and of Catalonia: and compelling them to abandon their rich fields and to seek refuge within the walls of cities, there to die of famine and pestilence. War is thus, everywhere, the trade of the barbarian who cultivates the poor soils and looks with greedy eyes upon the wealth of other men, whose honest industry and exertion have enabled them to bring into cultivation the better soils, with a constantly increasing return to labour.

If next, we desire to see the countries in which men cultivate the poorest soils, we must turn to those in which constant wars and oppression have most prevented the growth of wealth and population: to India and Sicily: and there we shall find the habit of combined exertion least existing. If we cross the Atlantic, and look to Mexico, we may see the fertile valley that surrounds the city, and that once afforded food for a vast population, now in a state of desolation; its canals choked up, and its cultivation abandoned; while from the poorer lands that border the valley, strings of mules bring from a distance of fifty miles loads of provisions to supply the wants of the city. For a specimen of the next class, we must turn to France, whose population requires for its duplication above a century; and whose labourer uses poor machinery that enables him to penetrate but little into the upper soil, leaving the more fertile soils beneath and around him for some future race that shall have learned that real glory and grandeur are not to be attained by endless wars.* If now we seek the countries in which the reward of the labourer most rapidly advances, we must turn first to Prussia, that has, since 1763, with the exception of the few years that followed the battle of *Jena*, enjoyed the blessings of peace: and there we shall find population

* "La Gloire est le Dieu de la France."—*M. de Beaumont.*

and the habit of union advancing with a rapidity unknown to the rest of continental Europe. Next, we must look to England, where we shall find vast wealth, the growth of internal peace, and a population increasing in numbers with a force constantly accelerated as the accumulation of that wealth has enabled them to bring into activity the better soils. In the days of the Edwards, it numbered two millions and a half. In 1700, it but little exceeded five millions. The increase was small, and the improvement of the condition of the people was slow. In the first seventy years of the past century, the increase was forty per cent. In the following thirty years, it exceeded twenty-five per cent. Population increased rapidly, and with it grew wealth and the power and habit of union, and cultivation was extended, with a rapid increase in the return to labour. It is now doubling itself in forty-six years, thus proceeding with accelerated force, and with its increase we see more fertile soils coming into cultivation, and affording larger returns: giving increased wages to the labourer and larger reward to the capitalist than is obtained in any other part of Europe. With every step in this progress, we see an increase in the habit of combined exertion: and an increased tendency towards union, personal, political, and economical: perpetually repressed, however, by the waste consequent upon frequent wars produced by an anxiety for "ships, commerce and colonies." The jealousy of the Scot and the Saxon has passed away. The Welshman and the Englishman, the Highlander and the man of the lowlands, have long since ceased to view each other with dislike: and the Cornishman and the Yorkshireman have learned at length to speak the same language. Lastly, we turn to the United States, which, during more than two centuries from the first landing of the Pilgrims, never were engaged in war but when forced thereto in self-defence, and whose history presents a course of peaceful action unparalleled in the world. From a few poor and scattered settlers, occupying the poor lands along the Atlantic coast, between whom communication was almost impossible, even if desired: and scarcely desired because of differences in their origin, and in their ideas of religious and political government: they have grown to a nation of more than twenty millions, in whom the habit of union exists to an extent elsewhere deemed inexplicable:* a consequence of the rapid growth of wealth, the fruit of peace and honest industry. Beginning necessarily with the poorest soils, they were widely separated from each other. Had they, like their neighbours of Canada, been perpetually engaged in war, they would have remained poor and scattered; but they worked while the others sought alliances with the Indians, and prosecuted the work of conquest. Few in number, and poor, they still cultivated poor soils, when England was already the wealthiest nation of the world, and had the power to bring into activity the best soils, if she would: but England preferred a war of twenty years attended with incalculable waste of life and treasure, the result of which is that she stands now but second in point of wealth.

Look where we may, we shall find similar results. If we desire to see men in a state of high prosperity, we must turn to those countries and to those periods in which their numbers grow. In Italy we shall find it in the days of Servius, before Rome undertook the mission of plundering the world and exterminating the free population, to be replaced by slaves. In Tuscany we shall meet it in the fourteenth century, before French princes and nobles had learned to interfere in their affairs, expelling the most useful of her citizens, and introducing a habit of war: to result in building up the colossal fortune of Cosmo de' Medici, derived chiefly from the profit of loans to the state for purposes of war, at enormous interest paid out of the proceeds of taxes on provisions, and collected at the gates of the city by his own

---

* "That tenacious spirit of unity which has hitherto so singularly characterized them."—*Edinburgh Review.*

clerks. In Athens it will be found in the days of Solon and the Pisistratidæ, before the depopulation and poverty produced by Persian armies gave power to men like Cimon and Pericles: men who saw in the expenditure of enormous taxes for the support of ruinous wars, the means of acquiring that distinction which otherwise they could never have obtained. In Egypt, in the days of the Ptolemies, before proconsuls drew from the impoverished inhabitants the means of maintaining their canals, to be applied to the support of the profligate and worthless people of Rome. In Spain, on the banks of the Guadalquiver, before the fortune of war had given power to Isabella and her successors to plunder and exterminate the industrious and prosperous Moors. In all these cases, increasing wealth gave man the power to cultivate the better soils. If, now, we desire to see man in poverty and distress, a prey to famine and pestilence, we must turn to those periods in which population decreases; and be they where they may, we shall be sure to find the object of our search. War diminishes population, but it destroys wealth. The farmer may live to return to his fields; but his house is burned, his crops are carried off, his cattle have been killed and eaten, and his plough and his harrow broken up; and he returns to the city a beggar, to die of famine: for his neighbours are like himself. Their property is gone, and they have no means of employing him, even as a labourer. Everywhere poverty goes in advance of depopulation, while everywhere increasing wealth goes far in advance of increasing numbers.

Such being the case, we may well doubt if war, which forces man to abandon the best soils and seek the poorer ones, be really the panacea furnished by the Deity for restraining population within the limits of food. It would rather seem to be one of the weak "inventions" of man, for counteracting the great law of nature which prescribes that if men will live well they must labour, and thus provide themselves with the machinery necessary for the development of the productive powers of the earth: powers so wonderfully great that it would be absurd, with our present limited knowledge, to attempt a definition of their extent. The use of those powers, with increased return to labour, is the reward offered to man for good conduct—for the full observance of the great law of Christ: and in every country he profits by their use in the precise ratio of his obedience.

Mr. Malthus recommends "moral restraint." Where shall it be found? Certainly not among the Esquimaux, where every woman is ready to prostitute herself for a nail, or a bead,—nor among the savages of the Rocky Mountains, or those of the islands of the Pacific,—*nor any where, where population does not grow*. It prevails to a certain extent in France, in whose great city, according to M. Dupin, it is only every third child that is a bastard; but it prevails more in Prussia, where labour is better rewarded, and men marry more freely; still more in England, where matrimony is still more common; and most in America, where everybody marries. In all countries population increases nearly in the ratio of morality; but where marriage is deemed a luxury,* bastards will abound, and foundling hospitals will be needed.† The remedy of Mr. Malthus would thus appear to produce the disease for the cure of which it was intended, and to stimulate instead of repressing, population.

Population asks only to be let alone, and it will take car of itself. Without its growth the power of union cannot arise, nor the love of harmony and of peace, essential to the

* "The temptation is great to show that the poor have no more right than the rich to indulge in luxuries which they cannot afford, and that it is decidedly immoral to bring children into the world to starve." — *Thornton on Over-Population.*

† In 1809, the number of foundlings in France was 69,000. Since the measure of 1811, (ordering a foundling hospital to be established in each arrondissement,) it has advanced to 84,500, in 1815; to 102,100, in 1820; to 119,900, in 1825; to 125,000, in 1830; and since then it has advanced with a still more remarkable acceleration. (In 1833, it had risen to 129,629.) At Paris, the proportion of foundlings to births was as one to ten; it is now little less than one to four. * * * The expense has advanced in a parallel proportion to the numbers. It amounts to 11,500,000 francs per annum, the Paris institution alone costing, some years since, 1,731,239 francs.

promotion of the growth of wealth and to the cultivation of the best soils, without which the return to labour cannot be large. With its growth production increases, and the labourer is enabled to take as his reward a larger proportion, thus producing a tendency to equality of condition. *The people* have everywhere loved peace, for such were its fruits. *Their masters* have everywhere loved war, because it tended to the maintenance of inequality; yet if they had been governed by the sense of an enlightened self-interest, they would have seen that the injury to themselves was as great as was that experienced by the labourers and mechanics by whom they were surrounded.

The PAST says to the sovereigns of the PRESENT: "Avoid war! It diminishes population and wealth, and union, and it tends to reduce nations into tribes. Its apparent grandeur is real littleness. It destroys the power of self-protection, in which consists real greatness."

To the representatives of land it says: "Avoid war! It destroys population and wealth, and the value of land is dependent upon the growth of both."

To the labourer it says: "Avoid war! It destroys wealth more rapidly than population. It diminishes your power over the product of your labour, and it tends to increase the existing inequality of condition."

CHAPTER III.

WEALTH.

The first cultivator commences his operations on the hill-side. Below him are lands upon which have been carried, by force of water, the richer portions of those above, as well as the leaves of trees, and the fallen trees themselves; all of which have there, from time immemorial, rotted and become incorporated with the earth, and thus have been produced soils fitted to yield the largest returns to labour: yet for this reason are they inaccessible. Their character exhibits itself in the enormous trees with which they are covered, and in their power of retaining the water necessary to aid the process of decomposition; but the poor settler wants the power either to clear them of their timber, or to drain them of the superfluous moisture. He begins on the hill-side, but at the next step we find him descending the hill, and obtaining larger returns to labour. He has more food for himself, and he has now the means of feeding a horse or an ox. Aided by the manure that is thus yielded to him by the better lands, we see him next retracing his steps, improving the hill-side, and compelling it to yield a return double that which he at first obtained. With each step down the hill, he obtains still larger reward for his labour, and at each he returns, with increased power, to the cultivation of the original poor soil. He has now horses and oxen, and while, by their aid, he extracts from the new soils the manure that had accumulated for ages, he has also carts and wagons to carry it up the hill: and at each step his reward is increased, while his labours are lessened. He goes back to the sand

and raises the marl, with which he covers the surface; or he returns to the clay and sinks into the limestone, by aid of which he doubles its product. He is all the time making a machine which feeds him while he makes it, and which increases in its powers the more he takes from it. At first it was worthless. It has fed and clothed him for years, and now it has a large value, and those who might desire to use it would pay him a large rent.

The earth is a great machine, given to man to be fashioned to his purpose. The more he fashions it, the better it feeds him, because each step is but preparatory to a new one more productive than the last; requiring less labour and yielding larger return. The labour of clearing is great, yet the return is small. The earth is covered with stumps, and filled with roots. With each year the roots decay, and the ground becomes enriched, while the labour of ploughing is diminished. At length, the stumps disappear, and the return is doubled, while the labour is less by one-half than at first. To forward this process the owner has done nothing but crop the ground: nature having done the rest. The aid he thus obtains from her yields him as much food as in the outset was obtained by the labour of felling and destroying the trees. This, however, is not all. The surplus thus yielded has given him means for improving the poorer lands, by furnishing manure with which to enrich them; and thus he has trebled his original return without further labour: for that which he saves in working the new soils suffices to carry the manure to the old ones. He is obtaining a daily increased power over the various treasures of the earth.

With every operation connected with the fashioning of the earth, the result is the same. The first step is, invariably, the most costly one, and the least productive. The first drain commences near the stream, where the labour is heaviest. It frees from water but a few acres. A little higher, the same quantity of labour, profiting by what has been already done, frees twice the number. Again the number is doubled, and now the most perfect system of thorough drainage may be established with less labour than was at first required for one of the most imperfect kind. To bring the lime into connection with the clay, upon fifty acres, is lighter labour than was the clearing of a single one, yet the process doubles the return for each acre of the fifty. The man who wants a little fuel for his own use, expends much labour in opening the neighbouring vein of coal. To enlarge this, so as to double the product, is a work of comparatively small labour; as is the next enlargement, by which he is enabled to use a drift-wagon, giving him a return fifty times greater than was obtained when he used only his arms, or a wheelbarrow. To sink a shaft to the first vein below the surface, and erect a steam-engine, are expensive operations; but these once accomplished, every future step becomes more productive, while less costly. To sink to the next vein below, and to tunnel to another, are trifles in comparison with the first, yet each furnishes a return equally large. The first line of railroad runs by houses and towns occupied by fifty or a hundred thousand persons. Half a dozen little branches, costing together far less labour than the first, bring into connection with it three hundred thousand, or perhaps half a million. The trade increases, and a second track, a third, or a fourth, may be required. The original one facilitates the passage of the materials and the removal of obstructions, and three new ones may now be made with less labour than was required for the first.

All labour thus expended in fashioning the great machine is but the prelude to the application of further labour, with still increased returns. With each such application, wages rise, and hence it is that portions of the machine, as it exists, invariably exchange, when brought to market, for far less labour than they have cost. The man who cultivated the thin soils was happy to obtain a hundred bushels for his year's work. With the progress of himself and his neighbour down the hill into the more fertile soils, wages have risen, and two hundred bushels are now required. His farm will yield a thousand bushels; but it requires the labour of four men, who must have two hundred bushels each, and the surplus is but two hundred bushels. At twenty years purchase this gives a capital of four thousand bushels, or the equivalent of twenty years' wages; whereas it has cost, in the labour of himself, his sons, and his assistants, the equivalent of a hundred years of labour, or perhaps far more. During all this time, however, it has fed and clothed them all, and the farm has been produced by the insensible contributions made from year to year, unthought of and unfelt.*

It is now worth twenty years' wages, because its owner has for years taken from it a thousand bushels annually; but when it had lain for centuries accumulating wealth, it was worth nothing. Such is the case with the earth everywhere. The more that is taken from it the more there is left. When the coal mines of England were untouched, they were valueless. Now their value is almost countless; yet the land contains abundant supplies for thousands of years. Iron ore, a century since, was a drug, and leases

* It will be observed that we consider the owner and farmer always as one and the same person, and it is when they are so that this operation is the most complete, and yet the most insensible. Such it is in the United States. All who write of land, in England, talk of the expenditure of capital on land. Land asks no such expenditure. It gives capital, when properly treated. In that country, the tenant starves it that he may gather up the rent, and if the landlord permits a small portion of its gifts to go back to the great producer, he considers himself as having given it something, for which it is his debtor. Had the tenant been the owner of the ill-treated machine, he would have given it twice as much, making no charge; but, on the contrary, crediting it with the portion that he retained for his own consumption. When English landlords talk of spending five and ten pounds per acre, it sounds very grand; but as in all other cases, the real grandeur is in the inverse ratio of that which is apparent. The man who cultivates his own land, puts on twice as much; but, he does it from year to year, insensibly, and the land is rendered twice as productive by the one operation as by the other. Nature performs all her operations slowly and gently, but steadily, and the nearer that man approaches her, the more nearly is he right. The man who improves his own land works with a long lever, and little power is required; whereas, the landlord works with a short lever, and greater power is needed to produce smaller effect.

were granted at almost nominal rents. Now, such leases are deemed equivalent to the possession of large fortunes, notwithstanding the great quantities that have been removed, although the amount of ore now known to exist is probably fifty times greater than it was then.

The earth is the sole producer. Man fashions and exchanges. A part of his labour is applied to the fashioning of the great machine, and this produces changes that are permanent. The drain, once cut, remains a drain; and the limestone, once reduced to lime, never again becomes limestone. It passes into the food of man and animals, and ever after takes its part in the same round with the clay with which it has been incorporated. The iron rusts, and gradually passes into soil, to take its part with the clay and the lime. That portion of his labour gives him wages while preparing the machine for greater future production. That other portion which he expends on fashioning and exchanging *the products* of the machine, produces temporary results, and gives him wages alone. Whatever tends, therefore, to diminish the quantity of labour necessary for the fashioning and exchanging of the products, tends to increase the quantity that may be given to increasing the amount of products, and to preparing the great machine; and thus, while increasing the present return to labour, preparing for a future further increase.

The first poor cultivator obtains a hundred bushels for his year's wages. To pound this between two stones requires twenty days of labour, and the work is not half done. Had he a mill in the neighbourhood he would have better flour, and he would have almost his whole twenty days to bestow upon his land. He pulls up his grain. Had he a scythe, he would have more time for the preparation of the machine of production. He loses his axe, and it requires days of himself and his horse on the road, to obtain another. His machine loses the time and the manure, both of which would ave been saved had the axe-maker been at hand. The real advantage derived from the mill and the scythe, and from the proximity of the axe-maker, consists simply in the power which they afford him to devote his labour more and more to the preparation of the great machine of production, and such is the case with all the machinery of preparation and exchange. The plough enables him to do as much in one day as with a spade he could do in five. He saves four days for drainage. The steam-engine drains as much as without it could be drained by thousands of days of labour. He has more leisure to marl and lime his land. The more he can extract from his machine the greater is its value, because every thing he takes is, by the very act of taking it, fashioned to aid further production. The machine, therefore, improves by use; whereas spades, and ploughs, and steam-engines, and all other of the machines used by man, are but the various forms into which he fashions parts of the great original machine, to disappear in the act of being used; as much so as food, though not so rapidly. The earth is the great labour savings' bank; and the value to man of all other machines is in the direct ratio of their tendency to aid him in increasing his deposits in the only bank whose dividends are perpetually increasing, while its capital is perpetually doubling. That it may continue for ever so to do, all that it asks is that it shall receive back the refuse of its produce: the manure: and that it may do so, the consumer and the producer must take their places by each other. That done, every change that is effected becomes permanent, and tends to facilitate other and greater changes. The whole business of the farmer consists in making and improving soils, and the earth rewards him for his kindness by giving him more and more food the more attention he bestows upon her.

The solitary settler has to occupy the spots that, with his rude machinery, he *can* cultivate. Having neither horse nor cart, he carries home his crop upon his shoulders, as is now done in many parts of India. He carries a hide to the place of exchange, distant, perhaps, fifty miles, to obtain for it leather, or shoes. Population increases, and roads are made. More fertile soils are cultivated. The store and the mill come nearer to him, and he obtains shoes and flour with the use of less machinery of exchange. He has more leisure for the preparation of his great machine, and the returns to labour increase. More people now obtain food from the same surface, and new places of exchange appear. The wool is, on the spot, converted into clőth, and he exchanges directly with the clothier. The saw-mill is at hand, and he exchanges with the sawyer. The tanner gives him leather for his hides, and the paper-maker gives him paper for his rags. With each of these changes he has more and more of both time and manure to devote to the preparation of the great food-making machine, and with each year the returns are larger. His *power to command* the use of the machinery of exchange increases, but his *necessity* therefor diminishes; for with each year there is an increasing tendency towards having the consumer placed side by side with the producer; and with each he can devote more and more of his time and mind to the business of fashioning the great instrument; and thus the increase of consuming population is essential to the progress of production.

The loss from the use of machinery of exchange is in the ratio of the bulk of the article to be exchanged. Food stands first; fuel, next; stone for building, third; iron, fourth; cotton, fifth; and so on; diminishing until we come to laces and nutmegs. The raw material is that in the production of which the earth has most co-operated, and by the production of which the land is most improved; and the nearer the place of exchange or conversion can be brought to the place of production, the less is the loss in the process, and the greater the power of accumulating wealth for the production of further wealth.

The man who raises food on his own land is building up the machine for doing so to more advantage in the following year. His neighbour, to whom it is *given*, on condition of sitting still, loses a year's work on his machine, and all he has gained is the pleasure of doing nothing. If he has employed himself and his horses and wagon in bringing it home, the same number of days that would have been required for raising it, he has misemployed his time, for his farm is unimproved. He has wasted labour and manure. As nobody, however, gives, it is obvious that the man who has a farm and obtains his food elsewhere, must pay for raising it, and pay also for transporting it; and that although he may have obtained as good wages in some other pursuit, his farm, instead of having been improved by a year's cultivation, is worse by a year's neglect; and that he is a poorer man than he would have been had he raised his own food.

The article of next greatest bulk is fuel. While warming his house, he is clearing his land. He would lose by sitting idle, if his neighbour brought his fuel to him, and still more if he had to spend the same time in hauling it, because he would be wearing out his wagon and losing the manure. Were he to hire himself and his wagon to another for the same quantity of fuel he could have cut on his own property, he would be a loser, for his farm would be uncleared.

If he take the stone from his own fields to build his house, he gains doubly. His house is built, and his land is cleared. If he sit still, and let his neighbour bring him stone, he loses, for his fields remain unfit for cultivation. If he work equally hard for a neighbour, and receive the same apparent wages, he is a loser by the fact that he has yet to remove the stones, and until they shall be removed he cannot cultivate his land.

With every improvement in the machinery of exchange, there is a diminution in the proportion which that machinery bears to the mass of production, because of the extraordinary increase of product consequent upon the increased power of applying labour to building up the great machine. It is a matter of daily observation that the demand for horses and men increases as railroads drive them from the turnpikes, and the reason is, that the farmer's means of improving his land increase more rapidly than men and horses for his work. The man who has, thus far, sent to market his half-fed cattle, accompanied by horses and men to drive them, and wagons and horses loaded with hay or turnips with which to feed them on the road, and to fatten them when at market; now fattens them on the ground, and sends them by railroad ready for the slaughter-house. His use of the machinery of exchange is diminished nine-tenths. He keeps his men, his horses, and his wagons, and the refuse of his hay or turnips, at home. The former are employed in ditching and draining, while the latter fertilizes the soil heretofore cultivated. His production doubles, and he accumulates rapidly, while the people around him have more to eat, more to spend in clothing, and accumulate more themselves. He wants labourers in the field, and they want clothes and houses. The shoemaker and the carpenter, finding that there exists a demand for their labour, now join the community, eating the food on the ground on which it is produced; and thus the machinery of exchange is improved, while the quantity required is diminished. The quantity of flour consumed on the spot induces the miller to come and eat his share, while preparing that of others. The labour of exchanging is diminished, and more is given to the land, and the lime is now turned up. *Tons* of turnips are obtained from the same surface that before gave *bushels* of rye. The quantity to be consumed increases faster than the population, and more mouths are needed on the spot, and next the woollen-mill comes. The wool no longer requires wagons and horses which now are turned to transporting coal, to enable the farmer to dispense with his woods, and to reduce to cultivation the fine soil that has, for centuries, produced nothing but timber. Production again increases, and the new wealth now takes the form of the cotton-mill; and, with every step in the progress, the farmer finds new demands on the great machine he has constructed, accompanied with increased power on his part to build it up higher and stronger, and to sink its foundations deeper. He now supplies beef and mutton, wheat, butter, eggs, poultry, cheese, and every other of the comforts and luxuries of life, for which the climate is suited; and from the same land which afforded, when his father or grandfather first commenced cultivation on the light soil of the hills, scarcely sufficient rye or barley to support life.

In the natural course of things, there is a strong tendency towards placing the consumer by the side of the producer, and thus diminishing the quantity required of the machinery of exchange; and wherever that tendency does not grow in the ratio of the growth of population, it is a consequence of some of those weak "inventions" by which man so often disturbs the harmony of nature. Wherever her laws have most prevailed, such has been the tendency, and there have wealth and the power of man over the great machine, most rapidly increased. Rent is the price paid for the use of that power, and it increases with every diminution in the quantity required of the machinery of exchange.

In Attica, in the days of Solon and the Pisistratidæ, wealth and population grew rapidly. Cultivation passed from the poor to the fertile soils, and the manufacturer of Athens consumed what was produced by the farmer of Attica. Led, unhappily, to meddle in the affairs of Persia, and thus to employ a portion of their labour upon the more distant soil of Asia, they soon found themselves driven from the better ones of Attica to those within the walls of Athens, there to perish of starvation. Population and wealth diminished, and thenceforward we find them cultivating the lands of distant and subject cities, through the medium of their citizens: substituting weapons of offence for machinery of production: and becoming poor and dissolute. Poverty begets tyranny and rapacity, and both beget a love of war. That of the Peloponnesus follows. Attica is ruined, and Athens passes gradually from poverty to starvation, and at last to ruin.

Sparta begins with the poor soils. She refuses to permit the growth of population or of wealth. She assassinates her slaves, while employing their masters on the distant lands of Attica, or of Asia; working the apparently rich, but speedily exhausted, soil of plunder, and neglecting the rich soils at home. Poor and rapacious, perfidious and tyrannical, she continues ever weak and contemptible, and passes out of existence, leaving as her sole bequest to posterity, the record of her avarice and her crimes.

Rome, in the days of Servius, cultivated the fertile soils, and population and wealth grew rapidly, with a diminishing necessity for the machinery of exchange, as towns and cities grew in extent, filled with men engaged in fashioning the products of the earth, in exchange for the portion of those products required for the satisfaction of their wants. His successor preferred the distant soils, and employed his subjects in carrying arms and plundering their neighbours; and in building up great works that were to immortalize him with posterity, but which developed none of the powers of the great food-producing machine. The product of labour diminished, and the proportion of the few increased, while that of the many diminished. Inequality of wealth begot inequality of power, and that, in turn, begot a love of the more distant soils, which were to be cultivated by force of arms. Passing through Italy and Sicily, we find her citizens in Greece; in Africa, Asia, Spain, Gaul and Britain; thus going from the rich soils to the poorer ones, and increasing at every step the necessity for the machinery of exchange; and with each step we find the many becoming poorer and more debased, and the few becoming greater and more depraved; until at length, decayed at the heart, the empire passes away: having existed for almost a thousand years, a model of rapacity, dishonesty, and fraud, and having in the whole period produced scarcely a single man whose name has come down to posterity with an untarnished fame.

The people of Florence commenced their cultivation on the light soils at the head of the Arno. With increasing wealth, the products of the land increased: and as food became abundant, the fashioner came. Wealth and population again increased, and the town became a city: and both again grew. Led to involve herself in the wars of the Church, she is found cultivating the distant soils of Bologna, Milan, and the ghibelline Pisa, and with each remove from home, wealth and population diminish, until at length, impoverished and depopulated, the better soils pass out of cultivation, and the once free and happy people become the slaves of the Medici. She increased her machinery of exchange and diminished its power. Bows, and swords, and muskets became more numerous as spades and pickaxes disappeared, and the product of the former proved to be far less than had been that of the latter.

Spain expelled that portion of her people which used little machinery of exchange, and which therefore had a larger proportion of their time to devote to cultivating the powers of the great machine. Another portion, with arms in their hands, cultivated Sicily, Naples, Tuscany and the Milanese: a third, the distant soil of the Netherlands: and a fourth those of Peru and Mexico: and thus she increased her machinery of exchange while diminishing the product to be exchanged. With each step in the process she became poorer, and men now may starve in Andalusia while the *silos* of Castile are filled with grain, the mere cost of transportation on the backs of mules placing it beyond the reach of the poor Andalusian's purse. Her people are still in a state of barbarism, from having been forced to abandon the rich soils, and take to the poor ones, having used too much bad machinery of exchange.

For more than a thousand years, the sovereigns, nobles, and gentlemen of France, have been engaged in the cultivation of the soils of the Netherlands and Germany, Catalonia and Piedmont, the Milanese and Naples: and more recently they have extended their operations as far as Russia; while Canada and Cayenne, India and Egypt have at various times claimed their attention. The study of that nation has been to increase the machinery of exchange, and diminish that of production. Swords have abounded while spades were rare. Cannon were numerous, while roads scarcely existed. Forts and castles were built by men to whom grist-mills were machines unknown. Ships of war were numerous, but merchant ships were scarce. Camps grew and cities decayed. Gentlemen became more numerous as ploughmen disappeared. The soil they cultivated, however, bore

> "Dead Sea fruits that tempt the eye,
> But turn to ashes on the lips."*

France is poor. She cultivates the poor soils, for want

* "From 1803 to 1815, twelve campaigns cost us *nearly a million of men, who died in the field of battle, or in the prisons, or on the roads, or in the hospitals, and six thousand millions of francs.* * * *

"*Two invasions destroyed or consumed, on the soil of old France, fifteen hundred millions of raw products, or of manufactures, of houses, of workshops, of machines, and of animals, indispensable to agriculture, to manufactures, or to commerce.* As the price of peace, in the name of the alliance, our country has seen herself compelled to pay *fifteen hundred additional millions*, that she might not too soon regain her well being, her splendour, and her power. · Behold, *in twelve years, nine thousand millions of francs*," (seventeen hundred millions of dollars,) "*taken from the productive industry of France and lost for ever*. We found ourselves thus dispossessed of all our conquests, and with two hundred thousand strangers encamped on our territory, where they lived, at the expense of our glory and of our fortune, until the end of the year 1818."—*Dupin.*

The results of this course of operation are found in the following statement by an eminent French engineer:—"I have frequently traversed in different departments, twenty square leagues, without meeting with a canal, a road, a factory, or even an inhabited estate. The country seemed a place of exile abandoned to the miserable, whose interests and whose wants are equally misunderstood, and whose distress is constantly increasing, because of the low prices of their products, and the cost of transportation."—*M. Cordier.*

"The conditions of the poorer farmers, daily labourers, and beggars, are so near akin, that the passage from one state to another is very frequent. Mendicity is not deemed disgraceful in Brittany. Farmers allow their children to beg along the roads. On saints' days, especially the festivals of celebrated saints, the aged, infirm, and children of poor farmers, and labourers, turn out. Some small hamlets are even totally abandoned by their inhabitants for two or three days. All attend the festival to beg. * * The principal cause of misery is inebriety; its frequency among the lower orders keeps them in poverty. The *caburet*, (wine and brandy shop,) absorbs a greater part of their earnings."—*Report to the Commissioners on the Poor Laws.*

of machinery to enable her to reach the better. For a population of thirty-five millions, she raises five hundred and twenty millions of bushels of wheat, rye, barley, oats, Indian corn and buckwheat, and about half that quantity of potatoes. Her wheat lands vary from five to twenty bushels per acre, the average being about ten. Her cattle are few and poor: as are her sheep. Her manure diminishes, and her seed increases. Her horses, her food and her fuel, to a vast extent, she imports: and pays for them in the produce of looms that yield but little, because of the universal poverty that forbids improvement of machinery, or combination of action. Her production of solid food, divided among the whole people, gives the equivalent of three hundred and forty-three pounds of bread, and thirty pounds of meat, per annum, to each individual; while of wine, beer, cider, perry and brandy, the amount is one hundred and sixty pounds per annum, or nearly half as much. The labour that water-drinkers would employ in producing corn, is in France given to producing wine and other liquors; of which the consumption averages twenty gallons per annum, for every man, woman, and child in the kingdom. Of what is the actual distribution of food an idea may be formed from the fact that the average income of more than two-thirds of the population is but six cents per day, yielding twenty-four cents for the support of a man, his wife and two children: and that in a country in which the average price of wheat, from 1816 to 1835, was about $1.20 per bushel, and where the profits of the retailer, and the cost of transportation are large; so that ten pounds of wheat may be taken as the value of the earnings of the whole family. Under such circumstances it is not matter of surprise that ignorance of true economy should so far exist as to render it exceedingly difficult to introduce improvements in the machinery of exchange at home, as has been shown in the case of the ingenious *Jacquard*, whose life was unsafe because he invented a machine of greater power than those already in use. The turbulence of French workmen is in the direct ratio of their poverty, and *that* is exceeding great. France now proposes to transport a portion of her people to Algeria, that they may there raise food to be paid for in the products of the ever-wretched artisans of Lyons and Sedan, who are surrounded by fertile soils that would yield largely, and require no troops to protect their labourers. The effort of that country, from the days of Clovis to the present time, has been to increase the quantity of her machinery of exchange, and to prevent any improvement in its quality: thereby precluding any increase in the quantity of labour that might be applied to the development of the powers of the great food-producing machine. Population doubles in about a hundred and twenty years, and wealth scarcely more rapidly. Those who labour are but little removed from starvation, and those who do not, divide among themselves the great mass of the products. The government takes thirty per cent. of the product of land for taxes on the land itself, and on the registration of deeds, mortgages, &c. Interest on the innumerable mortgages with which the country is almost literally covered, absorbs nearly forty per cent., leaving thirty per cent. to be divided between the producer and the lawyers, who now, as in all past times, are numerous beyond imagination, and live on the endless litigation to which poverty gives rise. Vast machinery and small production is everywhere the characteristic of France, and has been so from the days of Charlemagne. Under such circumstances, the exceeding poverty of the people is not matter of surprise; nor is it extraordinary that wealth and population cannot, and do not, increase. At all periods of her history, her *people* have shown themselves well disposed to honest industry, and *Jacques Bonhomme* has, at times, manifested the possession of all the qualities required in a good citizen: but labour, or the care of labourers, was not the business of gentlemen, *i. e.* of people who carried arms, and who generally owed their place in the world to the fact that their fathers, or grandfathers, had profited largely by the cultivation of the rich soils afforded by the plunder of the cities of Italy or the Netherlands: or who like La Hire, Saintrailles, Dammartin, and Dunois, "the young and brave," had distinguished themselves as *ecorcheurs*, *i. e.* flayers, of the unhappy class at home engaged in preparing the great machine required for the production of food. It was their especial privilege to seek plunder and glory, and to collect taxes for the payment of their assistants in the work: and the payment of those taxes exhausted, as it now still exhausts, the power of the country; and meadows are abandoned, while men cultivate thin soils which yield five bushels to the acre, or about three times the seed.

The insular position of England gave her security from invasion. Security tended largely to promote the growth of wealth and freedom, and comparative freedom tended to facilitate the further growth of wealth. That wealth, however, was not permitted to be applied to the improvement of the great food-producing machine. The Church had an interest, amounting to one-tenth, in all its products, increase as they might; and the owner of the land was unwilling to invest his means in improving property liable to such a tax, while the labourer felt little disposed to exert himself when so large a portion of his products was not to be subject to his own disposition. The owner of the remaining nine-tenths was rarely a free agent. In some cases, his property was entailed, and if he began to cut the timber, his son regarded the act as *waste*, and an injunction followed. If his lands required drainage, he could not pledge the income beyond his life, and it remained undrained. When not entailed, it was burthened with endless settlements, dowers, remainders, life-interests, &c., while lawyers surrounded it with forms so endless that a conveyance was one of the most serious affairs of life. The law of succession gave the whole to the eldest son, who was thus made sufficiently rich to desire to do nothing, while his brothers and sisters were rendered too poor to be able to do any thing for themselves, and were generally thrown on the bounty of the state. Wealth grew rapidly, for internal peace prevailed, but it could not go on the land, and it had to seek an outlet. It sought manufactures and commerce, there to obtain, by aid of expensive machinery, temporary in its duration, a less reward than could have been obtained at home while making the great machine. The consequence was that capital, and ships, and manufactures, and gentlemen, and labourers, were all superabundant, and food alone was scarce. To find a market for manufactures, employment for ships, and poor gentlemen, and labourers, colonies were needed: and then, in order that they might use as much as possible of the machinery of exchange, it became necessary to compel them to send their raw materials to England; and they were prohibited from making even hob-nails, or from effecting exchanges among themselves, except through the medium of English ports and English merchants. Other powers were equally desirous to preserve the power of taxing their colonies, but England deemed it right to resist in others what she practised herself, and her colonists were encouraged to engage in the trade of smuggling the products of the machinery which England was thus determined to use. Smuggling led to wars, and wars gave occasion to freebooters like Drake and Hawkins, to immortalize themselves by plundering and burning towns and murdering their inhabitants. Wars were expensive, and involved a necessity for heavy taxes, but colonies were to be maintained in order that employment might be had for the looms and ships of England; and taxes gave support to the sons of gentlemen who would not permit their shares of the great machine to be improved. Navigation laws drove the ships of other nations from the ocean, while "Rules of '56," and other rules, and later, "Orders in Council" drove them from the sea in time of war. "Ships, colonies, and commerce" were the great wants of England. For these, she has involved herself in endless wars. For these, she has committed enormous crimes: and all because she has pertinaciously insisted upon using the inferior in preference to the superior machinery of production. For these, she has sent embassies at enormous cost to distant nations, and has maintained the most expensive fleets and armies: her sole object being the sale of cloth, and knives, and china ware.* England was to be made the workshop of the world at any cost. France marched with the sword alone. England with the sword in one hand and a piece of cloth in the other. Manufactures were too cheap at home, and food too dear. Manufacturers wanted cheap food, and the landlord gave them corn laws to enable him to waste his capital and still get rents: but he gave them also ships and men to enable them to prevent the world abroad from placing the consumer by the producer, and to compel them to do that which he himself would not do, *i. e.* increase the supply of the raw produce of the earth: to be transported in British ships, wrought in British looms, and re-transported in British ships to the place of consumption.

The necessary consequence of such a course of action has been an unceasing disturbance of the movements of all other countries. Labour was not permitted, in England, to seek employment on the great machine of production, and it was superabundant and cheap. Capital, in like manner, was denied employment, and it too was cheap. Both these were then placed under the control of ship-owners and manufacturers, to enable them to force upon other nations cloths produced by women and children who had little food, and very

* "The history of the colonies for many years is that of a series of loss, and of the destruction of capital; and if to the many millions of private capital which have been thus wasted, were added some hundred millions that have been raised by British taxes, and spent on account of the colonies, the total loss to the British public of wealth which the colonies have occasioned would appear to be quite enormous."—*Parnell.*

little to spare for clothing;* many of whom went in rags, and some absolutely naked,† that other nations might have clothing cheap.

In the natural course of things, the fashioner, whether of wood or of wool, takes his place by the side of the producer of the food he is to consume, because the transportation of food requires the use of a quantity of the machinery of exchange so far exceeding that required for the transportation of all other commodities required by the labourer. The policy of England was opposed to this course of action. She had forced herself into the position of being the great fashioner of the world, and there she was disposed to remain. It was, however, an artificial state of things, and, as is always the case where capital and labour are denied permission to take their natural course, it was liable to perpetual change. The thirst for colonies produced wars, and then her armies consumed foreign food, paid for with manufactures. Peace came, and she wanted no food. The other parties then could take no cloths or knives, and her artisans perished by thousands. Sometimes cloths and knives were dear, because she had found employment for her people and her wealth in war, or perhaps in founding new colonies. Other nations then attempted to place the consumer by the producer. Peace made capital and labour, cloths and knives, cheap, and manufacturers elsewhere were ruined. Prices rose again. Another effort was made. Prices fell, and again were they ruined.

---

* By reference to the report of the Assistant Commissioner charged with the inquiry into the condition of women and children employed in agriculture, it will be seen that a change of clothes seems to be out of the question. The upper parts of the under-clothes of women at work, even their stays, quickly become wet with perspiration, while the lower parts cannot escape getting equally wet in nearly every kind of work in which they are employed, except in the driest weather. It not unfrequently happens that a woman, on returning from work, is obliged to go to bed for an hour or two to allow her clothes to be dried. It is also by no means uncommon for her, if she does not do this, to put them on again the next morning nearly as wet as when she took them off.

† See Parliamentary Report on the Coal Mines of Great Britain.

In India, she killed the cotton manufacturer. The Hindoo then exported cotton. In America, she drove the people to the west to raise food, when they would have preferred to remain at home and consume food, while making cloth. Food was rendered so cheap that the planter abandoned food and went to cotton. Cotton was rendered so cheap that the Hindoo was ruined. The Hindoo, deprived of his two great trades, turned his attention to opium. The Chinese government did not like the trade, and tried to put it down. England made war, destroyed a few thousand lives, and many, very many, millions of property, and thus established the right of her subjects to furnish to the Chinese the means of intoxication. The planters of the south, driven from food to cotton, first ruined the Hindoo, and then were nearly ruined themselves. They now raise food, and make ploughs and other machines required in agriculture, and some of them convert their own cotton into cloth. They are placing the consumer by the producer, and the consequence is, that they are better paid for the cotton they have to sell, having greatly diminished their machinery of exchange, while rendering it more efficient. England now threatens them with the Hindoo as a rival producer of their great staple. Such is the character of the whole system. It is one of endless interference, and it has tended to produce elsewhere other interferences with trade, having for their great object security against its effects. Tariffs of protection are universal; and with every new one has arisen in that country a desire for new colonies, to be governed by laws made at home, by virtue of which she may compel her subjects to use the machinery of exchange she thus insists upon providing for the use of the world. She employs her people in cultivating poor soils in Canada, South Africa, Australia and New Zealand, while the richest soils of Britain are yet undrained: and thus obtains, by aid of the most expensive machinery of exchange, commodities that could be produced at home with half the labour.

The eyes of England have always been turned *from home.* She must and would have ships, colonies, and commerce. To that desire is due the waste of thousands of millions: of more than would have sufficed to cover the island with railroads; to render every field a garden; to provide food in abundance for a population five times greater than now finds subsistence on her soil, and composed of a healthy, hardy race, capable of guarding their own rights, and regulating for themselves the hours of labour, the drainage of houses, the mode and expense of interments, and a thousand other things, in reference to which they are now compelled to claim parliamentary interference: by which is indicated an extreme inability to protect themselves.

The state of things that has existed during the last thirty years is the strongest commentary on the system. It is impossible to look at any work on British agriculture without being struck with its backward state in most parts of the kingdom, when compared with what might naturally have been looked for in a country so abounding in wealth and population. The cry is everywhere that the people are too numerous; yet the best lands in many of the counties are badly cultivated, although wealth so much abounds that it has been made a matter of question whether it might not be too abundant for the prosperity of a nation!* So abounding, it has, however, been almost as often the question where to get it, as how to be rid of it. For the first few years that followed the Congress of Vienna, it was lent to all the arbitrary sovereigns of Europe. In 1825, it was sent throughout Spanish America. In 1835, it was sent to all North America. Between each of these, however, was a period of extreme distress to manufacturers and ship-owners, of starvation to operatives, and of ruin to tenants; and such would continue to be the case were the system to be continued. None was ever devised so well calculated to retard,

* Wakefield's Notes to Smith's Wealth of Nations.

without the aid of war, the progress of a nation. It has succeeded in rendering men and wealth superabundant in a nation that imports food, which yet can, even now, produce it at less cost of labour than any other of the world, America not excepted; and it has also succeeded in causing the waste of hundreds of millions in loans, mines, colonies, &c., of which but a small part will ever return.

A change has come over the system, and England is now making a market at home for labour and capital. She is at present fairly engaged in building up the great food-producing machine, and preparing to bring the supply of the necessaries of life up to a level with the demands for consumption. She is substituting the permanent for the temporary; and, with each step of her progress in this direction, capital and labour are becoming more valuable. A century since consols were at 107. They are now at 80, after having been, quite recently, by one of the disturbances to which we have referred, forced up to par. England is the richest nation of Europe; and she owes that distinction to the fact that she has enjoyed peace at home, although she has grievously disturbed the peace of others abroad. She has, on many occasions, failed, totally, to respect in others the rights she desired others to respect in herself. To these failures is due the anomalous position in which she stands. With fertile lands and immense wealth, her soil is covered with alms-houses. A continuance of the system which is now in course of being pursued, will lead, if even the experience of the last few years has not already led, to the conclusion, that the judicious employment of labour and capital begets a market for both. The railroads that have been made have caused the absorption of a vast amount of both in agricultural improvement, which, in its turn, produces a demand for new roads, and they produce a demand for labour. Wages rise, and houses are wanted, and coal, and lime, and marl, and clothing; and the demand for labour and capital again increases; and thus on and on, each producing, and produced by, the other, with a constantly augmenting wealth, and constant improvement of condition.*

For more than two hundred years from the landing of the Pilgrims, the people of the United States never struck a blow, except in defence of their rights.† Their movement westward was of the most gradual kind; and although occasional difficulties have arisen with the aborigines, the change of occupants has, uniformly, been effected with less trouble, and less effusion of blood, than has been witnessed in any other portion of the world except, perhaps, Australia, where the wretched inhabitants were too miserable to think of resistance. During the whole period, we may trace the natural effort to place the consumer by the side of the producer, and thus to diminish the loss resulting from the use of costly machinery of exchange; and during the whole we see the effort counteracted by the false direction given to the capital and labour of England. Laws were passed prohibiting various species of manufactures in the colonies, while others forbade their trading with each other, and thus North Carolina and Massachusetts were forced to exchange their products through the medium of the ports of England. Twenty-two years of European war produced a great demand for food, and tended to the dispersion of the people for raising it to supply the wants of people who thus preferred the use of swords to that of ploughs. Years of disturbed relations with England tended to produce concentration, and labour and capital were applied to fashioning the produce which otherwise might have been exported in its rude state. Robbery and oppression on the high seas forced them to this effort to place the consumer by the side of the producer. Peace came, and the whole wealth of England was turned to manufactures, while armies ceased to waste food. The farmers

* Such would be the effect of this operation, gently and quietly pursued; but what are to be the momentary effects of a railroad mania, producing efforts to do in three years what should be done in ten, remains yet to be seen.

† We should be glad if we could say the same of the past two years.

and manufacturers of the United States were both ruined, and hence arose the first demand for protection by means of a tariff. A few years passed by, and then the years of "prosperity," so loudly vaunted by the Premier as permanent, were followed by the universal ruin of 1826, in which were swept away a new set of manufacturers engaged in finding a market at home for the supplies of food no longer needed abroad. The consequence was the tariff of 1828, which was followed by the act known by the name of the Compromise (1832); and it would be difficult to find in history an instance of more equitable and quiet adjustment of a difficult question. From the time of its passage until the year 1836, however, capital was steadily accumulating in England, and seeking a vent abroad, as railroads then were scarcely permitted at home. Much of it came to the United States, in the form of iron and cloth, to be applied to the making of roads, or of clothing for the people employed in making them. The roads half-made, the collapse came, and all again was ruin. The Compromise was killed, and the tariff of 1842 took its place. That of 1846 has succeeded it; and now we have another collapse. English factories are closed, and artisans are discharged, and thousands of houses are vacated because of the impossibility of paying rent. Railroads still go on, and furnaces are still employed, but panic is the order of the day, and all may stop: and then the iron-makers of America will be ruined.

It is scarcely possible to study this brief history without seeing that the interferences which have existed have been the result of a natural effort at self-preservation. In the regular course of human affairs, the man who makes the shoes eats the food produced by the man who desires to wear them; and he does so because it is easier for him to bring the awl and the lapstone, by aid of which he may make ten thousand pairs of shoes, than it is for the farmer to carry to him the food necessary for his support while doing it. This tendency struggles incessantly to develope itself, and is seen on every occasion making its appearance, but it has almost invariably been crushed; the effect of which has been that the people of the United States are now far more widely scattered, and far less wealthy, than they would otherwise have been. They have been compelled to use a vast quantity of inferior machinery of exchange, in the form of roads and wagons, in place of the superior machinery of steam-engines and mills: and they have been driven to begin on poor soils in the West, yielding ten bushels of wheat to the acre, when otherwise they might have worked their way down into the rich soils of the river bottoms farther east; portions of which may at all times be bought for far less than the cost of production. Pennsylvania abounds in bottom-land that will be cultivated when the farmer can find a market at his door for milk and cream, and butter; but in the mean time her citizens go west to seek other lands that *may* produce something that will bear carriage to the distant markets of the world. It is now obvious what has been the cause of this, the single case in which the policy of the Union has appeared to depart from the direction of perfect freedom of trade. We have always deemed such interferences erroneous, but are now well satisfied that the error has been with us.

Man *must* everywhere commence with the poor soils, and the richer ones *cannot* be cultivated until the consumer and the producer are brought together. Whatever foreign interference tends to prevent this union, tends to compel men to scatter themselves over poor soils, to prevent increase in the reward to labour, and to prevent advance in civilization: and resistance to such interference is a necessary act of self-defence. The article of chief consumption is food, of which rich soils would yield *larger* quantities in return to *half the labour* required on the poor ones; and half the difference would convert into cloth all the cotton and wool produced, and make the iron used, in the Union. Such being the case, the exports required to pay for English labour are so much absolute loss, while the great machine itself suffers in the loss of labour that would double it in product and in value. It has been an effort of the people to diminish their *necessities*, and to increase their *power* over their own actions. The case is not unlike one that has recently occurred, in which the people of a neighbourhood themselves did what the whole people have partially done in the other. The steamboat fare in a particular case was deemed too high. Opposition boats, at half price, were repeatedly attempted, and as repeatedly run off by reducing the fare so low that opposition could not live. Another was attempted, and the price of the old boat was reduced to one-fourth; but the farmers, wiser grown, taxed themselves the additional quarter and refused to leave the new boat, and after two years of ineffectual contest, the price was fixed permanently at half the original price. The resistance offered by the American tariff tended greatly to produce, if, indeed, it was not the absolute cause of the abolition of the corn laws; and that measure was precisely the one needed for giving the right direction to the capital of England. She will now become more extensively agricultural, and the United States may, at some future time, be enabled to concentrate their population upon the rich soils, instead of scattering so widely as they have heretofore done: and as, by degrees, these two effects shall be produced, the necessity for protection will disappear.

If the view we have thus offered be correct, as we believe it to be, it will be obvious that the people of the United States have done in commerce as they have elsewhere done, and that they have engaged in no war of any description whatsoever, except for self-defence. The consequence of this is, the great fact that the poor and scattered colonists of sixty years since now constitute the wealthiest nation in the world. They have accumulated, within a very brief period, a larger property than is possessed even by the United Kingdom, the wealthiest community of the eastern hemisphere. They make a larger dividend on a larger capital, and that dividend is made among twenty-one millions; whereas, that of the other is the portion of twenty-eight millions. The consequence is, that they are better fed, better clothed, better lodged, better warmed, and better taught, than any other community. Such is the result of peace abroad, combined with abstinence from interference at home. That such should be the case, is the great triumph of freedom of trade. They have had no excise officers, or tax gatherers, to interfere with the exchanges of property within, while the interferences with exchanges abroad appear to have been even less than were absolutely necessary for self-protection. Indeed, so strong is the tendency to abstinence from interference, that it has always been to us a matter of surprise that there should ever have been found a majority of the people to sanction any; yet it now appears that it was the result of an instinctive consciousness of what was indispensable for the improvement of their condition: and that that instinct was a safer guide than the theories of those would have directed them.

To many, the correctness of this assertion of the superior wealth of the Union may appear doubtful, but a little examination will satisfy them of its truth. That of Great Britain appears greater, because more centralized. The government can borrow money more readily; but that it can do so is only evidence that capital is not invested as fast as it is produced: that it stagnates: which it never does except where there is some error in the system. At no period during the last sixty years was she so poor as in 1813; yet at none did the government make larger loans, or more readily. In the history of France, we are constantly struck with the facility of obtaining loans, while the country appears to be in a state of universal misery and wretchedness. That misery was the result of enormous taxation, by which the few were enriched, and *they* were always ready to lend to the party by whose aid *their* taxes were collected. The people were too poor and miserable, and property was too insecure, to permit the existence of a demand for capital; and therefore it was that the government could borrow at five per cent. at a time when failure in the payment of interest was a matter of frequent occurrence. Such, likewise, was the case in Florence, in time of distress. The government could always borrow, and most readily when wars had rendered property so insecure that trade was almost at an end. The little states of Germany now borrow at four and a half per cent. from bankers and others who are enriched at the expense of the labourer and taxpayer; but this is an evidence of poverty, and not of wealth. Of a thousand, or ten thousand men: or even hundreds of thousands: each occupying a farm of fifty acres, scarcely one will have, at any time, a thousand dollars to lend, because each appropriates his profits as fast as earned to the improvement of his farm: to bringing the better soils into operation. Had they a landlord, they would be steadily engaged in laying up that which they would otherwise thus promptly have invested, and on rent-day the proprietor might have $20,000 or $50,000 to lend to government: but the fertile soils would remain inactive unless *he* chose to make them active, and he might not choose it. Had they a debt of hundreds of millions, quarter-day would see accumulated the large sums required for the dividends, and it would then rest with the public creditors to determine upon the mode of investment, and governments would borrow without difficulty; whereas, had no such debt existed, each workman, each labourer, each farmer, and each manufacturer, would have invested for his own advantage, as fast as it was made, the amount that otherwise he would have contributed to this fund. In Great Britain both these causes of disturbance may be found, and hence she appears richer than she is; while in the United States neither exists, and hence they are richer than they appear; and the rapidity of increase where every man invests on the instant, and on *his own* property, his otherwise spare labour, or surplus proceeds of labour, is so prodigious as to defy calculation. They are now the wealthiest nation in the world: and their annual accumulations are at least double those of Great Britain and Ireland, although their average expenditure is greater. They spend more, and yet economize a greater *proportion* of their earnings than any people in the world.

The man who employs his children in robbing his neighbours' barns and hen-roosts, and lets his farm remain untilled: will continue poor. The soil he cultivates is apparently rich, but really barren. Such has been the course of France. The man who builds a mill in which to grind his neighbours' grain, and sends a portion of his children to cultivate distant lands, while employing others of them in building wagons and in hauling home their grain, while his own farm remains untilled, will continue poor. He loses labour and manure. The man who does these things, and half-cultivates a large farm, the profits of which make some amends for losses elsewhere, may grow rich slowly. He loses much labour and manure. Such has been the course of England.

The farmer who minds his own business, and thus attracts around him the miller, the tanner, the shoemaker, the blacksmith, the carpenter, the wheelwright, the hatter, the spinner, the weaver, and the paper-maker, performs all his exchanges with the most perfect and the least costly machinery of exchange; and has almost all his labour and manure to put upon his farm, which yields him daily increased returns to that labour, and increases daily in value. He becomes rich. Such has been, *so far as it was possible*, the course of the United States; and hence their greater wealth.

Such being the case, it may be asked how it happens that several of the States of the Union have been involved in so much difficulty in regard to the payment of interest on the money borrowed for the construction of roads and canals? The cause is, we think, easily explained. The tendency of the English system has been that of forcing manufactures and trade, the consequence of which has been that all other nations have experienced a difficulty in concentrating their population sufficiently to enable them to cultivate the rich soils; and this in the precise ratio of their intercourse with her. The people of the United States have felt this in the highest degree. They have been forced to scatter themselves over the west, that they might raise food to send abroad to pay for clothing; and what they needed was machinery of exchange in the form of roads. Those who did thus scatter were poor, for they cultivated soils that yielded small returns; although surrounded by fertile soils covered with timber that they could not yet remove, or by swamps that they were unable yet to drain.

Pennsylvania still to a vast extent cultivated poor soils, while timber abounded in her river-bottoms: and she still was obliged to depend upon her woods for fuel and fencing, while her lands abounded in iron and coal. She had tried to convert her ore into iron, but had suffered heavily by unceasing fluctuations resulting from the unnatural state of things in England. She had tried manufactures: every thing, in short, tending to bring the fashioner to the side of the producer, and thus diminish the cost of the machinery of exchange. Her people were leaving the coal and the ore, to travel west in quest of other lands on which to raise more of the already superabundant food. To get this food to market, or to render the vast deposits of coal and ore productive, roads and canals were needed: and this was the great want of the whole country from the Hudson to the Gulf of Mexico and the Mississippi, because the policy of England limited them to these as their only machinery of exchange. In this state of things, commenced in that country one of her periodical overflows of capital. It had been most abundant in 1825, and all the world had been ruined in 1826 by the excessive scarcity consequent upon its waste in the mines of Mexico and elsewhere. It overflowed again in 1831, and the change of that year ruined many, and rendered very many others indisposed to encounter the risks of trade. In 1833, it commenced again to overflow, the reason for which was to be found in the fact that the Legislature pertinaciously refused to permit its investment at home. The Liverpool and Manchester Railroad had succeeded, and there was a strong disposition to make other roads; but peers did not approve of locomotives running near their mansions, and charters could not be obtained. Various applications, therefore, were rejected, after great expenditure by the applicants. One of these that we now recollect, the Rugby, spent £160,000, or $800,000, in the mere effort to obtain an act of incorporation, AND FAILED. As it could not be permitted to remain at home, capital sought a market abroad, among the people of Pennsylvania, Maryland, Indiana, and other States south and west, who desired to obtain for themselves better machinery of exchange in the form of roads, railroads, and canals. They had the food, and it could be eaten on the ground; and England was ready to supply the iron for the roads, and the clothing for those who were to be employed in making them. To work they all went; but before the roads or canals were so far completed as to be productive, the usual crash came. Capital became so scarce in England that the Bank was on the eve of stoppage; and traders and manufacturers were ruined by thousands. She now wanted to be paid; but trade was ruined. The downfall there had filled the markets of the world with cloths and iron, and the manufacturers and iron-masters of the Union were ruined by events over which they had no control, and against which they could not have guarded. Mechanics and workmen of all descriptions were discharged, and thousands were compelled to seek employment in agriculture: and this at the moment when the market for agricultural products was so over-stocked that wheat scarcely paid the freight to the Atlantic cities, and corn was almost valueless. The half-made roads and canals produced nothing, and the farmers of the States by which they were made, could command no money with which to pay taxes by aid of which to meet the interest. Coal ceased to be mined, and the canals upon which it had been carried ceased to receive tolls; while those who had invested their fortunes in opening mines were ruined. England had destroyed the market for corn at home, and she would receive none: not even to feed her starving workmen. The interest ceased to be paid, and then arose one universal yell throughout all England at the dishonesty of America: of that America whom she had temporarily ruined. Time, however, rolled around, and when corn could again be sold, all gladly co-operated in the effort to place the several States in a position to perform their contracts. At the first moment when such a thing was possible, Pennsylvania, by a *unanimous* vote of legislators elected by the votes of every man in the State, determined that payment should be resumed, and it was done: and now she is reducing the principal of the debt. Maryland has followed: and Illinois and Indiana, both of which were occupied at the time by a very scattered population, are now preparing to follow in her footsteps. A little while hence, and all will have done so, and none will feel so much satisfaction as *those who pay the taxes.*

Many who have united in the abuse of Pennsylvania and of other States, and of Americans generally, were, doubtless, ignorant of the cause of difficulty; and unaware that it was to the perpetual error of English policy, and the perpetual disturbance of which it was the cause, that the defalcation on that occasion was due: as well as the losses that on other occasions had fallen on their countrymen. It may safely be asserted that five-sixths of all the failures of the Union in the last half century may be traced to these causes. In that period we have seen the revulsions of 1815, 1819, 1825, 1831, 1836, 1839, and 1847, and against such changes no one could guard. Merchants and manufacturers found the markets filled with commodities from abroad, by which their business was destroyed: farmers and miners found their customers ruined: and perpetual failure was the result. In all countries in which peace has prevailed, wealth has grown; and where such has been the case, the people have always been honest: and to this America is no exception. On the contrary, we think it safe to say that it is the only country in the world in which the whole body of the people, from the highest to the lowest: *all tax payers:* could have been found uniting in a determination that the debts of the State *should* be paid. Were such a question submitted to the whole people of England or of France, the one *might* do the same, though we doubt it: but the other assuredly would not. The security for the debt of Pennsylvania is among the best in the world; for those who are to pay it have resolved unanimously that it *shall* be paid.

The gradual diminution of the consciousness of right, or power, on the part of those who administer the government towards the people, and the increase in the sense of duty towards them, that accompanies the growth of population and the cultivation of the better soils, may be traced in England upwards from the closing of the Exchequer by Charles II. to the latter years of the last century, when an exhausting war was diminishing the growth of both wealth and population. From that period, during twenty years, the government paid its debts in paper, sometimes worth but three-fourths of what the creditor had a right to claim. With peace came wealth, and an accelerated growth of population consequent upon the power of obtaining food in greater abundance; and with peace returned the feeling of obligation to comply with contracts: and, since 1819, the public creditor has received his interest in full, as he must continue to do, so long as wealth and population shall increase; and his security will increase with every application of labour to the development of the vast resources contained in the bowels of the earth beneath him; for with every such application the return to labour will increase, and the necessity for armies, fleets, and taxes, will decrease.

In France, perpetually engaged in war and in cultivating the poorer soils, there has been little sense of duty, and great consciousness of power on the part of the government; and hence her history is one of unceasing failure in her duties to the public creditor: first in the refusal to pay interest, and next in the reduction or repudiation of the debt. The most striking case, and only so because the largest in amount, was that of the regent Duke of Orleans. A long period of comparative peace was accompanied by some increase of wealth and population; and the growing sense of duty was exhibited in the proceedings of Necker and Turgot; but the consciousness of power prevailed, and they were dismissed. The Revolution followed, with vast waste of treasure and of life. The strong men perished in the field, and the old, the young, and the feeble, combining their exertions with those of the weaker sex, obtained a miserable subsistence from the poorer soils. The public creditor disappeared. His rights were obliterated, and thus power prevailed over duty. Since that period, his rights have been more or less respected; but the continuance of that respect is dependent upon the growth of population and of wealth. Some are now converting meadows into corn lands, while others are paying the government for the privilege of abandoning altogether their little inheritances. Whole departments are unable to produce a single horse for sale. Cattle and sheep are becoming poorer. Should this process long continue, the sense of power may prevail over that of duty, and the public creditor may again cease to exist.

If the reader will now study the history of the public debt of Spain, and mark the total failure of the government in the payment of interest, at those periods when her people were largely engaged in the cultivation of the distant soils of Mexico and Peru, Italy and the Netherlands, and neglecting the richer soils at their feet: of Austria, for a long series of years: of Denmark and of Holland: and, indeed, of every country of the world: he will find that public faith has grown with the cultivation of the rich solis, and failure has followed their abandonment: and thus may he acquire a standard absolutely infallible for testing the value of every public stock. So tested, the stocks of the American States present the best security in the world, and their values vary among themselves precisely in the ratio of the difference between the soils they cultivate. Massachusetts goes deepest into her hard soil, while Florida still cultivates the light soils, though abounding in river-bottoms and swamps that will at some future period afford great returns to labour. New York, Pennsylvania, Ohio and Maryland, Illinois, Indiana, Michigan, and Mississippi, now occupy various places in the scale; but all are growing in wealth and numbers, and all are gradually cultivating better soils, and all will soon place themselves side by side with the great State, the leader in American civilization.*

The view which we have thus offered of the superiority of the result derived from labour employed in *constructing* the machine for producing food, to that derived from *using* other machines of constantly diminishing power, differs greatly from that of the advocates of Mr. Ricardo's system. Thus, Mr. McCulloch says: "There are no limits to the bounty of nature in manufactures; but there are limits, and those not very remote, to her bounty in agriculture. The greatest possible amount of capital might be expended in the construction of steam-engines, or of any other sort of machinery; and after they had been multiplied indefinitely, the last would be as powerful and efficient in producing commodities and saving labour as the first. Such, however, is not the case with the soil. Lands of the first quality are speedily exhausted; and it is impossible to apply capital indefinitely even to the best soils, without obtaining from it a constantly diminishing rate of profit." All this might be true if man *did*

* "The civilization of New England has been like a beacon lit upon a hill which, after it has diffused its warmth around, tinges the distant horizon with its glow."—*De Tocqueville.*

speedily exhaust the best soils; but, as he is always going from a poor soil to a better, and then returning on his footsteps to the original poor one, and turning up the marl or the lime; and so on, in continued succession: and as he has done so in every nation of the world where population and wealth have been permitted to increase: and as, at each step in this course, he is making a better machine: the converse of Mr. McCulloch's proposition may prove to be true. It is held that there are *no* limits to the capital that may be profitably expended in engines, because all are *equal* to the first; but that there *are* limits to that which may be employed in agriculture, because, the last is necessarily *inferior* to the first. If, however, the last agricultural machine be always, as it always is, *superior* to the previous ones: then capital may be invested in agriculture with *more* advantage than in engines, because the last are *only of equal*, whereas the other is of *superior*, power.

A steam-engine *produces* nothing. It diminishes the labour required for converting wool into cloth, or grain into flour: for freeing mines from water: or for transporting wool, or grain, or coal. The gain from its use is the wages of that labour, *minus* the loss by deterioration of the machine. Labour applied to fashioning the earth produces wages, *plus* the gain by improvement of the machine. The more an engine can be made to yield the worse it will become. The more the earth can be made to yield the better will it become. The man who neglects his farm to employ himself and his engine in the work of fashioning or exchanging the products of other farms, obtains wages, *minus* loss of capital. He who employs himself on his own farm obtains wages, *plus* profits resulting from the improvement of the farm, to the extent that that improvement exceeds the loss from the deterioration of the spades, ploughs, engines, or other machinery that is used.

To test the correctness of this view, we submit two cases to the consideration of the reader. A. and B. have each a horse and cart, and a farm from which they can have three hundred bushels of wheat: or its equivalent. An offer is made to give them each that quantity, but the distance is so great that the hauling will occupy precisely the same time as the raising would do. A. accepts, and B. does not. A. spends his time, and that of his horse and cart, on the road. B. stays at home. When it rains, A. stops in the road-side tavern. B. spends the same day at home, repairing his house. When A.'s horse feeds and rests, his master has nothing to do. B. grubs up an old root, or repairs a fence. A.'s horse deposits his manure in the road. That of B. goes on his farm. A.'s horse hauls every day, and the service performed, nothing remains. B. opens a marl pit, and puts on his land manure for two or three years. At the end of the year A.'s horse and cart are worn out, while B.'s are almost as good as new. The farm of A. has deteriorated, while that of B. is greatly improved. Both have done the same number of days' work, and both have received the same compensation, yet A. is poorer and B. richer than at first. Every diminution in the quantity required of the machinery of exchange tends to increase the quantity of labour, both of body and mind, that may be applied directly to production: and such labour is rewarded with an increased return, and an increase in the powers of the machine itself. Such has been the case in all time past, and such will it ever continue to be.

It is by this almost insensible contribution of labour that land acquires value. The first object of the poor cultivator of the thin soils is to obtain food and clothing for himself and his family. His leisure is given to the work of improvement. At one place he cuts a little drain, and at another he roots out a stump. At one moment he cuts fuel for his family, and thus clears his land; and at another digs a well to facilitate the watering of his cattle, and thus keep his manure in the stable yard. He knows that the machine will feed him better the more perfectly he fashions it, and that there is always place for his time and his labour to be expended with advantage to himself.

A piece of land that yields £100 *per annum* will sell for £3000. A steam engine that will produce the same, will scarcely command £1000. Why should this difference exist? It is because the buyer of the first knows that it will pay him wages and interest, *plus* the increase of its value by use. The buyer of the other knows that it will give him wages and interest, *minus* the diminution in its value by use. The one takes three and a third per cent., *plus* the difference: the other ten, *minus* the difference. The one buys a machine that improves by use. The other, one that deteriorates with use. The one is buying a machine produced by the labour of past times, and to the creation of which has been applied all the spare time of a series of generations: and he gives for it one-third or one-half of the labour that would be now required to produce it in its present state, were it reduced to its original one. That of the other is bought at the actual price of the labour that it has cost. The one is a machine upon which new capital and labour may be expended with constantly increasing return; while upon the other no such expenditure can be made. We have now before us an account of the operations at Knowsley, where an expenditure of £7, 10*s*. per acre for draining has been rewarded by an increase of 20*s*. in rent, or more than thirteen per cent. In another case, where land had been abandoned as totally worthless, labour to the amount of 40*s*. per acre has been attended with a gain of 10*s*. per acre to the owner, and 10*s*. to the tenant, making fifty per cent. per annum: without taking into consideration the gain to the labourer in the increased facility of procuring the necessaries of life. Lord Stanley, who furnishes this statement, says, and we are sure most truly, that although he and his father have for several years laid a million of tiles per annum, they feel that they had only made a beginning.* We believe that they have, even yet, scarcely begun to think upon the subject. They are only beginning to waken up. We have also before us an account of a field so completely worn

* Thirty years since, all the tiles laid in the United Kingdom amounted to but seventy-one millions per annum.

out that it produced, with manure, but five hundred weight of turnips, but which, by being treated with sulphuric acid and bones, was made to yield two hundred and eighty-five hundred weight; and another, which gave to coal ashes and coal dust but eighty-eight hundred weight, gave to the acid and bones, two hundred and fifty-one hundred weight. Such profits are not to be found in any other pursuit: and yet England has been wasting her energies on ships, colonies, and commerce, having at her feet an inexhaustible magazine asking only to be worked.

The improvement above described is remarkable, only because concentrated within a short space of time. Had the land described by Lord Stanley been cultivated by the owner, and had he felt that agriculture was a science worthy of his attention; the drainage would have taken place gradually, and the improvement would have been marked by a gradual growth in the power to pay better wages and more rent. We have before us a notice of land rented for nine hundred pounds, at the close of a long lease at one hundred and thirty pounds. During all this time, its owner has had interest on his capital, and at the close of the lease, his capital has increased seven times. His investment was better than it would have been in steam-engines at ten per cent., because *his* engineer paid him for the privilege of building up his machine: whereas, the steam-engineer would have required to be paid while wearing the machine out. Everybody is content with small interest, and sometimes with no interest, from land, where population and wealth are rapidly growing, because *there* capital is steadily augmenting without effort. The house in which we write has greatly augmented in value, while we have had interest in the use of it. Instead of six per cent., we have twenty per cent., and this is the experience of all men who own landed property where population and wealth are *permitted* to increase: for they *will* always increase if not prevented by interferences like those which have existed in England, and to a still greater extent in France. The great pursuit of man is agriculture. There is none "in which so many of the laws of nature must be consulted and understood as in the cultivation of the earth. Every change of the season, every change even of the winds, every fall of rain, must affect some of the manifold operations of the farmer. In the improvement of our various domestic animals, some of the most abstruse principles of physiology must be consulted. Is it to be supposed that men thus called upon to study, or to observe the laws of nature, and labour in conjunction with its powers, require less of the light of the highest science than the merchant or the manufacturer?"* It is not. It is the science that requires the greatest knowledge, *and the one that pays best for it:* and yet England has *driven* man, and wealth, and mind, into the less profitable pursuits of fashioning and exchanging the products of other lands: and has expended thousands of millions on fleets and armies to enable her to drive with foreign nations the poor trade: when her own soil offered her the richer one that tends to produce that increase of wealth and concentration of population which have in all times and in all ages given the self-protective power that requires neither fleets, nor armies, nor tax-gatherers. In her efforts to force this trade, she has driven the people of the United States to extend themselves over vast tracts of inferior land when they might more advantageously have concentrated themselves on rich ones: and she has thus delayed the progress of civilization abroad and at home. She has made it necessary for the people of grain-growing countries to rejoice in the deficiencies of her harvests, as affording them the outlet for surplus food that they could not consume, and that was sometimes abandoned on the field, as not worth the cost of harvesting; instead of being enabled to rejoice in the knowledge that others were likely to be fed as abundantly as themselves. Her internal system was unsound, and her wealth gave her power

---

* Wadsworth's address to the New York Agricultural Society.

to make that unsoundness a cause of disturbance to the world: and hence she has appeared to be everywhere regarded as a sort of common enemy. The tendency of her navigation laws was greatly to increase the quantity required of the machinery of exchange: and the resistance thereto was an instinctive effort at self-protection. That resistance was led by the United States. American ships were not permitted to do what English ships might, and they therefore rendered it impossible for English ships to do certain things that American ships might do. For a brief time English ships came in ballast and went home loaded, and American ships went to England in ballast and brought home cargoes: and thus two ships were doing the work of one. The result was, that all were put upon a footing, and the quantity required of the machinery of exchange was so far diminished that exchanges were performed with far less labour than before; the consequence of which has been that exchanges have increased greatly in number, while the loss by friction: or the cost of exchanging: has fallen, and the work is better done.*

It would seem as if the general resistance to English shipping and manufactures had been the necessary effort for the establishment of perfect freedom of trade, and for securing to the world at large, eventually, the most perfect efficiency of exchange: while reducing the quantity of machinery required for the purpose. England could produce food and machinery at less cost of labour than any other country of the world, and every step in that direction would have tended to render production more and more easy. Other countries wanted machinery to enable them to concentrate their population and to consume their food at home. She refused ma-

---

* "Various devices were fallen upon to counteract the navigation system of the Americans, without in any degree relaxing our own: but they all failed of their object; and at length it became obvious to every one that we had engaged in an unequal struggle, and that *the real effect of our policy was to give a bounty on the importation of the manufactured goods of other countries into the United States*, and thus gradually to exclude our manufactures and our shipping from the ports of the republic."—*McCulloch.*

chinery, and sent cotton and woollen goods which they would have preferred to make; and she fixed her prices high or low, as suited her own convenience: the result of which was, that with each successive effort they were ruined. So with ships. Sometimes she would furnish them at low prices, and at other times they were high. If she was at peace she had ships to spare. If at war, they were scarce, and freights were high. The whole system of that country, in past times, has been marked by a desire to force her own capital and labour off in a wrong direction: from the profitable to the unprofitable: and every step she is now making exhibits a tendency in the right one. Wiser grown, she now looks to home, and is experiencing, at every turn, the wonderful effect of self-cultivation. She is investing vast wealth in railroads, but it grows with the expenditure; for she is now building up the great machine to produce food and raw materials of every description for which her climate is suited. She is expending, as we believe, an equal amount of labour in draining and clearing lands; but her wealth grows with every step in this direction, for the great machine is producing the food and the clothing that are used in building it. While pursuing agriculture with a spirit heretofore unknown, she is furnishing machinery to almost all Europe: a consequence of all of which is that her exports of cotton goods are no longer what they were. Every steam-engine she sends to the continent tends to produce a demand for railroad iron; and every railroad makes demands for engines, and for finer commodities in lieu of the coarser ones she was before accustomed to export. Every new soil that is improved at home tends to produce a demand for engines, and every engine tends to increase the power of producing new and better soils. The interests of all are ultimately to be promoted by perfect freedom of trade, and such has always been the case: but the persistence by a nation so wealthy as England in a course so adverse to the growth of civilization at home and abroad, tended to produce discords calculated to render its establishment absolutely impossible, and a long time may yet be required for its accomplishment.

The PAST says to the landlord of the PRESENT: "I have erred. I have driven labour and capital from the soil, to be wasted on armies, and fleets, and colonies. Your lands are far less valuable than they might have been made, and your children are forced to seek employment abroad, when they might be more prosperous and happy at home. Take warning by my example. Avoid war, and preparations for war, and your wealth will rapidly increase."

To the labourer it says: "I have erred, and you have suffered. Food has been high, and wages low. Labour to prevent war, and preparations for war. Your wages will then increase, and you will acquire power over your own actions, and may stay at home."

To the manufacturer it says: "I have forced labour and capital into trade and manufactures, and the result has been universal unsteadiness. Study to promote economy and the growth of a home market, which will be more steady and more profitable than any foreign ones. The people abroad who eat their own food and make their own coarse clothing, will be better customers than they are now; for when you shall have ceased to disturb the world, you will see perfect freedom and perfect steadiness of trade."

To all it says: "Labour to acquire power over the land that has been given to you, and with each step the feeling of *necessity* will diminish; while with each the consciousness of *power* over yourselves, your feelings, thoughts, and actions, will increase."

CHAPTER IV.

WEALTH AND LAND.

The first cultivator occupies such spots as his small means will permit him to use. He has yet acquired no power to compel the land to yield him what is needed for his comfortable subsistence. With the acquisition of the spade he turns under, and thus expels, the wild grass: substituting for it the oats, or the barley, or the rye, as he deems one or the other best fitted for his purpose. In the outset he requires much land, because but small portions can be made to yield to his demands any return whatsoever. With the growth of his wealth: with the acquisition of axes and ploughs: other portions, however, become productive; and, by degrees, he finds, on a few acres, more continuous employment for his time than, in the outset, was found upon a thousand. His family, too, has grown. If all continue to cultivate the whole quantity, there will be great waste of labour. The territory he has occupied covers several square miles; and the time required to walk to and from their work will be so much deduction from that which should be given to the cultivation of the soil, or of their own physical and mental powers. Each takes his share, and each builds himself a house. Each cultivates his own land; and each calls upon his brothers for aid in harvest: or in building a barn: or rolling logs: or quarrying stone. All are separate, but all are therefore interested in making roads by which all may be enabled to unite. While all lived in the same house, their labours were wasted in bringing home the fruits of the field, and they had no leisure for making roads. Now that all work separately; that each man eats on his own land the rye or the oats needed for his support; each feels more and more the advantage tc be derived from increasing the facility of obtaining the aid that may be required: and thus the division of land consequent upon the increase of wealth in the form of spades and axes, tends to produce increase of wealth in the form of roads: thus increasing the *power* of union, while diminishing the *necessity* therefor. Each labours on his own land, and each labours faithfully, because labouring for himself. Each makes, or procures from elsewhere, some machine calculated to increase the powers of himself and his neighbour; and all combine, at times, to procure those things which, important to all, are beyond the means of any.

If we look to Attica in the days of her prosperity, we see a tendency to the division of land, and the union of men. If we look to her in the days of her lowest poverty, we see Herodes Atticus universal proprietor, and universal builder, while union among men has ceased to exist. If we look to Rome in the days of Servius, we see a vast body of smal. proprietors enriching themselves by the cultivation of theii own land. If we look again, we see universal poverty: the numerous little and prosperous propri'etors being replaced by Scipios and Pompeys, owning vast tracts and overwhelmed by debts, while disunited men have become slaves. So, again, if we look to Gaul, or Africa. Everywhere throughout the world, the tendency to division of land and combination of action among men has grown with the growth of wealth: while poverty has produced its concentration in the hands of a few proprietors, and disunion among its occupants. We see this now exhibited on a large scale in the south of Spain, where a few grandees have replaced the honest, industrious, and enlightened Moors, who combined their exertions for bringing into activity the best soils of their own land, and for fashioning their products: thereby enriching their country and themselves.

The great business of mankind is the production of food, and the raw materials of commodities and things necessary to nable man to enjoy the conveniences, comforts, or luxuries of life. That he may do this, the Deity has given him the command of a great laboratory, in which exist all the elements of production, waiting only the application of the physical and mental powers with which he has been endowed, to render them available for his purpose. The gift was accompanied with the command to labour, that he might have food for himself and his children: to labour, that he might have clothing and shelter: to labour, that he might acquire knowledge: to labour, that he might enjoy leisure and repose. It is a great workshop, in which combination of effort yields largely, but can scarcely have existence when men cultivate the poor soils. To combination division is essential, and where that does not exist, the progress of cultivation is always slow. Hence the wretched condition of all commons, and of all lands upon which exists the partial right of common, as on most of those of France, under the system of *vaine pature*. Starting from the point of absolute barbarism, when all land is held in common, it will be found that the cultivation improves with every approach towards absolute ownership. Thus, it is better now in every part of England than in any part in the days when men were serfs, and had in land no property whatsoever. It is better where short leases exist than where all are tenants at will. It is better where long leases exist than where they are short, and the highest cultivation is invariably found where the owner and occupant are one and the same, and where there exists every inducement to the most perfect economy of time and labour. Thus it is better in Cumberland, where heads of families are generally proprietors of a few acres, than in Wilts or Dorset, where it is held in large masses, and cultivated by hired labourers. This may again be seen in the high cultivation of the peasant proprietors of the valley of the Arno; in the rich fields and the neat and comfortable houses of the small landholders of Belgium; and in the high prosperity of the same class in Norway. The division of land, and its cultivation by the owner for his own profit, are the necessary consequences of the growth of wealth; and with each step in this direction agriculture becomes more and more a science, furnishing employment for minds of the highest order, and yielding the largest returns to their exertions. It ceases to be the labour of the slave, and becomes the refined and elegant occupation of the gentleman, who gives to the direction of a small estate all his faculties, and obtains a liberal reward for permitting a portion of its proceeds to be applied to its improvement; while to those who execute with their hands what he plans with his head, large wages are afforded: and he finds in this employment greater happiness than was enjoyed by those of his predecessors whose thousands of acres were scratched by serfs to enable them to pay the ransom to his captor on the field of battle.

Such is the tendency of things when wealth and population grow. War and waste produce a reverse effect, and land concentrates itself in fewer hands. Hence it is that the age of barbarism, dignified with the title of that of the Feudal System, has been seen to inflict upon the world the right of primogeniture, another of the weak inventions by which man endeavours to set aside the great laws of nature: but over which she invariably triumphs when men remain at peace. The views of M. de Tocqueville in this respect are widely different. He says:

"When the legislator has once regulated the law of inheritance, he may rest from his labour. The machine once put in motion will go on for ages, and advance, as if self-guided, to a certain point. When framed in a particular manner, this law unites, draws together, and vests property in a few hands—its tendency is clearly aristocratic. On opposite principles its action is still more rapid: it divides, distributes, and disperses both property and power. Alarmed by the rapidity of its progress, those who despair of arresting its motion, endeavour to obstruct it by difficulties and impediments: they vainly seek to counteract its effect by contrary efforts: but it gradually reduces or destroys every obstacle, until by its unceasing activity, the bulwarks of the influence of wealth are ground down to the fine and shifting sand which is the basis of democracy."

In no part of Europe has the law of primogeniture been more firmly established than in England; yet in none in which it has existed has there been seen a stronger tendency to the division of land, as has been shown by the numerous shifts and contrivances invented to bar entails, and to remove other obstacles to the division and sale of landed property: the result of which is seen in the fact that she possesses now more than 200,000 proprietors. Down to the commencement of the recent great war, such was the invariable tendency; but during the period of its continuance the poverty of the people and consolidation of land returned together. The few became greater, and the many smaller; and had the war been continued on the same scale for another period of twenty years, that country might have exhibited to the world princes like those of Esterhazy, wearing coats covered with diamonds and surrounded by serfs in rags. With the long-continued peace, a different state of things is gradually arising. Mechanics are purchasing freeholds, and landlords are forming cottage allotments; a small beginning, it is true, but one that shows the tendency of the time. Tenants are claiming longer leases, and landlords are beginning to perceive that short leases and large rents cannot exist together. They themselves have already taken a perpetual lease, at a fixed rent, from the Church. Tenants are now claiming of them the right to be paid for their improvements, perhaps the first step towards perpetual leases, and eventual proprietorship. Each step in this direction is but the preparation for a new one. Railroads raise wages. Drainage raises wages for labourer and tenant, and both acquire the desire to cultivate their own land for their own profit. With each such step the *proportion* of the owner decreases, although his *quantity* of rent increases: and with each there is a tendency to a rise in the standard of living, and to equality of condition. The ability of the non-labourer to hold large tracts of land becomes less when compared with the ability of the labourer to buy it: while the inducement to the latter to obtain a piece of land that he can cultivate after his own fashion, tends daily to increase. The wages of skill and knowledge have risen: and the reward of mere wealth has failed, and must necessarily fail, to keep pace therewith. The great proprietor must work. He now does work, and he finds in the enjoyment of occasional leisure that happiness which a life of idleness and ennui had failed to afford. It is, we think, impossible to look to any part of England without seeing this operation either commenced, or about to commence. In some portions of it, every acre of land has been sold within the memory of persons now living. In the north, where wealth grows rapidly, and the best soils are cultivated, the tendency to division is greater than in the south: and it is far greater in the neighbourhoods of rapidly-advancing Liverpool and Manchester, than in those of declining Winchester and Bristol. In the one direction we see a daily increasing tendency towards harmony and union between the owner of the land and the man who cultivates it: while in the other we see universal discord and disunion, marked by perpetual barn-burnings, poaching, Rebecca-riots, and trials for arson and for violations of the game laws: all tending to show a very demoralized condition of society. When wealth grows, men unite, morally and physically: and the more they tend to unite, the faster it grows, and the greater is the tendency towards division of land. When wealth diminishes and population declines, it invariably concentrates itself in fewer hands.

In France, always at war, wealth could not grow. Men cultivated the poor soils, with the worst instruments. Property concentrated itself in the hands of the church and the great nobles. The Revolution came, and it annihilated both. To prevent the future concentration of land, it was enacted that at the death of the owner it should be divided among his children, excepting, however, a very small share that he might, if he thought proper, bequeath *beyond the limits of his family*. The confiscation was bad. It was a violation of the rights of property, and such measures are always bad: always impolitic: because nature remedies all grievances, when permitted to act. It was, however, done, and nothing now was needed but to permit labour to be applied to compelling the land to yield up its rich treasures, and thus to cause wealth to grow: and that wealth would have been applied to the further improvement of the land, increasing the product and enabling a constantly increasing population to obtain larger supplies of food in return to the labour employed in producing, and in fashioning, on the ground and in direct contact with the producer, the various products of the soil.

Such, however, was not the policy of the rulers, or of the gentlemen, of France. They preferred Italy, Germany, Spain, and even Russia, to their own soil, and they exhausted the population and the wealth of the Empire, in vain endeavours to obtain from abroad what at home nature courted them to accept. With the battle of Waterloo closed a period of exhaustion; but, since that time, repeated revolutions and attempts thereat have prevented the growth of any feeling of security, while the maintenance of immense armies and fleets: expensive palaces: and kings and princes: and a body of officials, whose name is legion: have prevented and still prevent the growth of wealth and population, without which the better soils cannot be cultivated. The consequence is, that there is no demand for labour, and the process of division goes on. More than two and a half millions of proprietors have incomes of $10 or less. Almost a million have between $10 and $20, and seven hundred and thirty-seven thousand have between $20 and $40. Between $40 and $100, there are seven hundred thousand: while the whole number of families whose revenue exceeds $2000 is under seven thousand.

Properties are in many cases, so subdivided that men are

willing to *abandon* them to the government, but even this they cannot do, except on payment of a tax of about forty cents, and until that shall be paid they must remain responsible for the taxes on the land, averaging twenty cents per acre. If they attempt to *sell* them, the tax is equivalent to two years' rent. Under such circumstances, it is not extraordinary that the land should be almost literally shingled over with mortgages, notwithstanding the enormous charges for fees of registration, &c., by which the interest is not unfrequently doubled, and sometimes raised even to a higher point. Interest and taxes swallow up, as we have already said, seventy per cent. of the rent, and the balance is squabbled for between the poor proprietor and the neighbouring lawyer. A century since, the families that lived by the law were thirty thousand in number, and the business was *immensely* lucrative. Since then the number has, we believe, greatly increased, and we can hardly doubt that the amount divided among them has also increased. The whole system of France tends to remove property out of the control of those who have laboured for its production, and to give it to those who have not laboured: and tending thereby to produce that grinding down "into the fine and shifting sand which is the basis of"—not democracy but—turbulence, anarchy and slavery. Throughout her whole history it has been seen forcing men to live in villages while cultivating land at a distance, thus diminishing greatly the productiveness of labour: and now, we see there two millions of poor proprietors, with their little bits of garden, pasture, and arable land, and vineyards, scarcely ever lying together; but here a little and there a little, some in the valley and some on the hill, by which any improvement is rendered impossible. The foreclosure of mortgages, therefore, comes, and the real owners—the mortgagees—take possession. How far such is the tendency may be seen from the fact that in the ten years from 1826 to 1835, thirty per cent. of the whole territorial property changed hands by sale, exchange, and forfeiture, being about as much as changed by means of inheritance and gift. Such is the necessary consequence of the present state of things.

In the Netherlands, the power of division exists in its full extent, yet there the son does not claim his part merely because entitled to it. Wealth increases because men cultivate fertile soils, and a demand for labour consequently exists in other employments. The consumer and producer are near neighbours to each other. If the piece which the son may claim be not sufficient to afford him support, he lets or sells it to his brother: and thus the tendency to division is counteracted by the power of the owner to judge for himself as to the most advantageous mode of disposing of his time. So in Norway, distinguished for the industry and economy of its people, both wealth and population grow, and the tendency towards grinding down the land has no existence. Properties there remain undiminished for centuries.

In the United States, the right of primogeniture existed. It disappeared as wealth and population grew. In no part of the world does the democratic tendency exist so much as in Massachusetts and generally in New England, and in none are the forms used in the conveyance of land so simple, yet there the tendency to minute subdivision has no existence. M. de Tocqueville himself informs us that the "laws of the United States are extremely favourable to a division of landed property: but that a cause which is more powerful than the laws prevents property from being divided to excess." He adds, that "the law has abolished the right of primogeniture, but that circumstances have concurred to re-establish it under a form of which none can complain, and by which no just rights are impaired." The reason for this is, simply, that wealth and the demand for labour and skill grow more rapidly than population. No one will cultivate a piece of land that will not afford him full wages, and hence we find, invariably, that when too small for advantageous division, one son takes the property, paying to the others their share, to enable them to apply, with advantage to themselves, their labour, or their skill, in Lowell, or in Providence. In no country is the tendency to perfect individuality and freedom of action so great; in none is the tendency to union so universal: and in none is the power of man over land so complete.

Perfect individuality, and the tendency to union, keep pace, invariably, with the growth of wealth and the division of land. The land of the great noble of the middle ages was bound to give him a certain amount of rent, and for this his serfs were jointly bound. Unlimited liability—*solidarité*—was the universal rule. If one failed to work or pay, others must make up the deficiency. The serf was nameless. He was merely *a serf:* one of those who were to do the work. So we find it, even now, in India, where villages are assessed *en masse;* and when some of the unfortunate ryots abandon their little properties in despair at their utter inability to comply with the unceasing demands for rent claimed by the Company's government, the rest are held liable for the deficiency. So again, in France, where the people of provinces, and towns, and villages, were all held liable for the taxes; and when the *dragons* of Louvois had expelled the laborious and economical Huguenots, the Catholics who remained were held bound to make up the full amount.

With the growth of population and of wealth, land becomes divided, and individuals make contracts to pay fixed rents; and thus every man acquires power to determine for himself what shall be the extent of his liability: and this tendency is always greatest where men cultivate the richest soils, as may be seen in England. The tenant in Dorset or Hampshire has no rights. His landlord's game consumes his crop, yet must he pay the full rent; whereas in Lancashire or Lincoln, the rights of all are strictly defined. In the one, poor men, who live in mud hovels, still cultivate the poor lands first occupied. In the other, they live in houses, and cultivate the rich soils that two centuries since were swamps and forests.

This tendency to freedom of individual action in the making of contracts for other purposes keeps pace with that in relation to land. Throughout Europe, the right of men to associate has been at all times limited, through a jealousy of every thing like tendency to union among the people, which induced sovereigns and those by whom they were surrounded, to insist upon continuing in relation to them the principle of unlimited liability. Exemptions from it have always been obtained as matters of favour: by aid of royal charters. These exemptions are more or less numerous as population and wealth increase rapidly or slowly, and as the better or poorer soils are cultivated. In France, they are granted invariably as favours, and applications therefor, unsupported by powerful interest, are useless.* In England, they were granted only to a few powerful companies, to enable them to monopolize certain branches of trade: and even so recently as the latter part of the last century, the formation of joint-stock associations with transferable stock, for any purpose, was absolutely prohibited. With the gradual increase of wealth and population, and with the cultivation of the better soils, we see a gradual relaxation of the system of *solidarité*, and charters are now granted to railroad companies, because without them roads could not be made. They are, however, still refused to associations for most other purposes.

In the United States, we can see this tendency to perfect freedom in the making of contracts, whether for the rent of land or for other purposes, steadily increasing as we pass from those States in which they cultivate the poor lands to those in which they cultivate the rich soils of the river bottoms. In the south, men work in gangs, and each man is individually liable for the performance of the

---

* The reader who desires to understand the restrictions on Commercial Association in France, will find them fully explained in the *Revue des deux Mondes*, for July, 1845, in an article by *M. Coquelin*, translated and republished in the Merchant's Magazine for May and June, 1845.

whole work. No contract for rent is here made, and here it is that we find the greatest hostility to exemption from the same principle in regard to all other of the pursuits of life. In the new States of the west, where population is small and scattered, and the rich soils are untouched, the same state of things is found. Union among themselves is difficult, and jealousy of unions exists. In Pennsylvania, much of whose richest lands is yet uncleared, the same jealousy has always existed; but as the various soils: the lime, the coal, and the iron-bearing soils: are coming into activity, it tends gradually to pass away. In no part of the Union has there existed the same tendency to the concentration of *land* in the hands of a few persons, nor has there been elsewhere exhibited so forcibly its effect in preventing the union of *man*. The first has been always, to a great extent, held in masses, and corporations have been formed for the purpose of so continuing to hold it. This latter state of things is found chiefly in the coal region of the Lehigh river, which while possessed of every advantage for a great trade, has ever been unable to contend, because of the monopoly of land, with the Schuylkill region, in which the lands were divided among numerous owners, and were frequently passing from hand to hand. In the first, the union of man has no existence, and wealth grows slowly. In the second, it is seen everywhere, and wealth and population grow rapidly, producing a demand for the products of the earth tending to bring the more fertile soils into full activity.

As we pass north from Pennsylvania, we find land more divided, population more dense, and a greater tendency to perfect individuality, accompanied by an increasing tendency to union, and an increasing power to unite on such terms as may be deemed best for the parties who contract. These things are found to a greater extent in New York than in Pennsylvania: but as we approach Massachusetts and Rhode Island, where men devote themselves most assiduously to bringing into activity all the powers of the earth, we find individuality, the tendency to union, and the power to unite, in a greater degree than in any other portion of the world. There, all have property. There the rights of person and property are most strictly defined and best maintained: and there it is that large capitalists and little shopkeepers; large farmers and little labourers; large manufacturers and little spinners and weavers; widows and orphans, clergymen and doctors, editors and authors, and lawyers; are found uniting for the building of factories, the making of railroads, and every other of the various modes in which wealth can most advantageously be applied to increase the productiveness of labour.

If we desire now to find the cause of the rapid advance of the poor and scattered colonists of the United States towards wealth and power, we must seek it in the division of the land. Every man lives, or, if he will, may live, in his own house and lot, or on his own farm. He works, or, if he will, he may, in his own shop. He drives his own wagon, and commands the ship, of which he is owner in whole or in part. The ship carpenter builds the ship of which he is to be part owner, and the iron founder makes engines for the factory in whose stock he has purchased shares. The female operative works in the mill of which she is part owner, that she may gather means to furnish the house of which she is to be sole mistress: and the coal miner looks forward to the time when he can work his own vein of coal, and pay wages to men that are following in his footsteps. All these phenomena, although some of them are apparently unconnected with land, are the natural results of its division. The landlord who collects large rents patronises his own farmer, his own agent, his own shopkeeper, his own lawyer, his own doctor, and his own carpenter, and these men have all what is termed a valuable "connection." All this is fully exhibited in the Lehigh coal region of Pennsylvania. Great companies prefer great tenants, and little men cannot rent mines. Great tenants keep great shops, at which the little men must make their exchanges, for competition is rendered impossible. Great companies and tenants patronize their own lawyers, and doctors, and carpenters, and bridge-builders, and road-makers; the consequence of which is an universal dulness and stagnation. The miner lives in the company's house, and works company land; and his daughter is idle, for there is no demand for labour. With wealth unlimited beneath the surface, the houses upon it wear all the marks of poverty; the quantity of lime needed to improve even the exterior appearance of their houses being deemed a luxury too great to be afforded to their occupants.

If, now, we pass westward, a few miles, to the Schuylkill region, where land is divided, and where each man looks after his own property, we see a totally different state of affairs. *There* patronage cannot exist. Every working miner seeks to have his own house and lot, and each looks to the time when he may work for himself, either as tenant or owner. Every man selects his own shop with which to trade; his own lawyer with whom to consult; his own doctor; and his own carpenter, when he would build. The consequence is universal activity and energy, and universal demand for labour. The daughter finds a demand for her services in making dresses for her thriving neighbours; and she can marry, because she can aid in furnishing the house; while her husband, the journeyman carpenter, or iron-founder, becomes himself a master, having his own shop, and living in his own house, occupied by his own wife and children; and that house is built on his own lot, within which he cultivates his own garden in his hours of leisure.

If, now, we substitute England and America for the Lehigh and Schuylkill coal regions, the same picture will answer. The first is filled with great land-owners, great farmers, great merchants, great bankers, great lawyers, great architects, great manufacturers, great ship-owners, and great corporations, all living in palaces; while the people cultivate the lands of others; live in the houses of others; work in the factories or the mines of others; tend the shops of others; command the ships of others; and, as a necessary consequence, a vast portion are obliged to eat the food of others. Patronage is universal. The great do not need to work, and the small work without spirit. The first are idle, for want of disposition to work; and the second are often so, for want of work to do. The first waste, because they may. The second do not economize, because they want confidence in the future.

In America, from north to south, we find the state of things that has been described as existing in the Schuylkill valley: greatest in the north, and gradually diminishing as we pass south and west. Every man is working for himself, and anxious to have his own house and lot: or farm: or shop. Those who have houses and lots, and farms and shops, have *in them* their own little savings' banks, in which they deposit all their spare hours and half hours: their spare dollars and half dollars: and thus there is made, almost insensibly, an addition to the wealth of the community, the amount of which, could it be ascertained, would be deemed incredible. Those who have not yet houses and lots, or farms, or shops, have at hand the little factory, or the little bank, owned in shares: the savings' bank of the neighbourhood: in which they make their deposits, there to remain until they shall have enough to buy the house or the farm, or to set up the shop. Wealth thus accumulates rapidly, and produces a constant demand for labour. Every one feels that he *can* "go ahead" if he *will*, and everybody, therefore, does; the necessary consequence of which is, that those who are "ahead" must work to keep so. If they pause but for a moment they are left behind; and this is equally true, intellectually and physically. Every man *will* educate his children, and *will* have his own newspaper, and *will* have portraits, whether in oil or daguerreotype, of his family; and *will* invent his own machine; and the rich must study books, and newspapers, and pictures, and machinery, if they would maintain their position in the world.

To this state of things is due the vast productive power of

the Union, far exceeding that of the twenty-eight millions composing the population of Great Britain and Ireland: and not to the abundance of land, upon the poor soils of which they have been forced to scatter themselves; expending upon them, and upon distant roads and canals, labour that would have been thrice more productive if employed upon the river bottoms of the older States: upon the marl and the limestone, the coal and the iron: all of which would long since have been done, could they have concentrated themselves as they would naturally have desired to do.

To this it is due, that while they are the greatest producers and the greatest consumers, they are the greatest accumulators of the world. *Every man has, in his own home, his own saving fund:* in his own farm, or house, or shop: and each is desirous of making his deposits as large as possible. Therefore, each dislikes taxes. Taxes come with wars. Therefore, each dislikes wars. The question of peace or war rests always with himself, and others like himself, who cultivate their own land and pay their own taxes; and who, having their own houses, and lots, and shops, and mills, and factories, to look after, have no need to seek employment in the work of robbing and plundering their neighbours. Therefore, he and they prefer peace. With peace grow wealth, and strength, and the power of self-protection, whether by means of armies and fleets: if needed: or by means of laws for restraining their neighbours who desire to compel them to use their ships, or to wear their cloths. They are too rich to quarrel with; and therefore it is that causes of quarrel, whether in regard to boundary lines; or indemnity for spoliations on the ocean, or restrictions on their commerce; or interference with the personal rights of their citizens; disappear. They prefer peace, and therefore it is that they have it. They need, therefore, neither fleets nor armies.*

* War with Mexico could never have arisen had it been left to the people to declare it. Mexico commenced it, and battle and victory were the result. Their representatives accepted the defiance; but had it been left to the people to decide the question, the decision, even then, would have been for peace.

If, now, to the great accumulations resulting from the existence of these millions of savings' banks, small and great, we add those resulting from the absence of taxes for the support of ruinous wars: and for preparations for war in time of peace: which latter, on the scale of those of England, would consume a hundred millions a year: we may readily account for at least *five hundred millions* now annually invested, in addition to what would be invested were land held by great landholders: by men who sought in the maintenance of colonies, requiring fleets and armies, the means of providing for themselves and their dependents. These five hundred millions add annually to the productive power at least one hundred millions. If the reader will calculate the result of such an investment, and such a return, he will be enabled to account for the fact that the United States are now the wealthiest country of the world; and the result at which he will arrive will be that it is due to the division, and not to the quantity, of land.

This estimate of the excess of the power of accumulation is equal to twenty-four dollars, or five pounds sterling, per head. A very large portion of this sum may be accounted for by the greater diligence of men who apply their labour on their own property; but much is the result of other causes. England persists in relying upon the poor soils of Poland, Canada, and other parts of the world, for a portion of her supply of food, which she might obtain from her own rich ones; and that is now obtained by the aid of the most cumbrous machinery. It is a rule in mechanics, that the more directly power is applied, the less is the friction and the greater is the effect: and that with every increase in the quantity of machinery, friction increases and power diminishes. So is it here. The friction is great, and hence it is that food is high, and that wages are low. In many parts of England, the agricultural labourer has but nine shillings per week, while the ordinary price of wheat is not less than fifty shillings per quarter, and it is frequently more. The labourer has for his week's work, therefore, but about a bushel and a quarter, or a bushel and a third per week, *for all purposes*, and he can accumulate nothing. Throughout the United States, the labourer has about seventy-five cents per day, which will not vary materially from the average price of a bushel of wheat: which would give six bushels as the price of a week's work. He can, therefore, *consume* more than the English labourer *receives*, and still lay up more than half his wages. That he does this is every day seen. In tens of thousands of cases, the unmarried labourer has from a hundred to a hundred and twenty dollars per annum, and his board. His clothing costs him little, and nearly the whole amount of his wages remains in the hands of his employer, or is temporarily invested: afterwards to be employed in the purchase of a little farm. The large capitalist profits in a similar manner from the cheapness of food, and the result of such accumulation by the two classes is prodigious. Again, no capital need remain idle, or even but partially productive, where the habit of combined exertion exists in so great a degree as in the United States, and where capital is active, labour is rendered productive. In England, on the contrary, the former often stagnates, and the latter is often unproductive.

The waste in that country is almost incredible. The *city* of London,* has vast estates, *chiefly Irish confiscations*, that

* The income of this corporation is as follows:

Trust estates - - -	£360,000
Local rates - - -	230,000
Coal duties and street and market tolls	200,000
Freedom and livery fines - -	50,000
Port of London - - -	60,000
	£900,000, or $4,320,000.

And this with a population of 129,000. The number of officers is two hundred and sixty-three, with salaries varying from £100 to £8000 per annum, and these offices are filled invariably by friends and relations of aldermen and common council men. The private extortion of the body, individually and collectively, adds greatly to the above amount. The consequence of all this is, that "the prudent fly to escape extortion, *but the pauper remains*"—and the poor yield above £300,000 per annum, most of which is squandered; while poor taxes are heavy, and the provision for education is very bad. A single entertainment has cost $120,000, and a single officer receives nearly $40,000 per annum. The salaries of the legal staff amount to nearly $200,000, and the whole amount of salaries exceeds half a million of dollars. Large estates, here as elsewhere, beget habits of great expenditure and great waste, and thus the leaks are almost incredibly great. Massachusetts, with a population of 800,000, expends about $2,000,000, or less than half of what is expended by the city of London: yet, out of this sum, she appropriates $300,000 to the support of infirm and aged poor, and about *seven hundred thousand dollars* for the maintenance of public schools. There men manage their own affairs: because land is divided, and man united.

The admirable effect of the division of land, consequent upon the growth of population and wealth, is fully shown in Prussia, by the result of the abolition of leases in perpetuity, and their conversion into freeholds, with compensation to the owner of the land, at the rate of twenty-five years' purchase of his interest. The great landholders were encumbered with debts, and their estates were loaded with mortgages which prevented improvement. In Pomerania alone, the encumbrances amounted to $24,000,000. The peasant holdings were freed at once, on payment of the stipulated sum; and the small landholders enjoyed a credit that to the great ones had been denied. All other impediments to the free disposal of land by sale, gift, or will, were also abolished; and the result is seen in the fact that wealth and population are now advancing in Prussia at a rate unknown to the rest of continental Europe: and that she is now at the

rates amount to £90,000. Here we have, in miniature, a perfect representation of the whole system of England. The reader who desires to understand both, will obtain the knowledge he seeks by reference to the Westminster Review, vol. 45, p. 193.

head of the great commercial union of northern Germany, throughout the whole extent of which exists perfect freedom of internal trade. Here, as elsewhere, the division of land has been attended with the union of man, and the extension of cultivation over the fertile soils.

The PAST says to the landlord of the PRESENT: "If you desire that your lands become valuable: yielding large rents: labour to promote the maintenance of peace."

To the tenant it says: "If you desire to become the owner of the land you cultivate: labour to promote the maintenance of peace, and to prevent the waste of wealth on fleets and armies."

To the labourer it says: "If you desire to own your house, and lot, and garden, your own shop, or your own farm: to have your own wife and children: to read your own books and newspapers: to go to your own church: to send your children to your own school: and to see them prosper in an active world, where rapidly increasing wealth gives increased wages to a rapidly increasing population: labour to promote the maintenance of peace and economy."

To the nation: "If you desire to acquire, individually and collectively, the power of perfect self-protection: avoid war and preparation for war."

CHAPTER V.

MAN AND HIS STANDARD OF VALUE.

The man who cultivates the poor soils, barters the commodity he produces for the one he wants. His production is small, and consists chiefly of food, most of which is needed for himself and his family. His exchanges are few and small. As population and wealth increase, and as the more fertile soils are brought into cultivation, food becomes more abundant, and he has more to spare to be exchanged for such other commodities as he is now enabled to consume, and we find him gradually adopting a standard of value to be used in his exchanges. In some places cowrie shells pass as money. In others prices are measured by tobacco, the legislator being paid for his services by the delivery of a certain number of pounds: while other quantities are fixed as the price of other services, and of the commodities most commonly in use. Tobacco is, however, bulky and liable to injury by time, and forms a standard of a very inconvenient kind. Wealth and population still further increase, and men are found adopting as standards for the measurement of values, silver and gold: both constantly in demand for various purposes in the arts; both representing in a very small compass a large amount of labour; both free from all danger of injury from rust; and therefore termed the precious metals. Those who desire to part with other commodities now sell them for money, and those who purchase, deliver, or contract to deliver, money, which becomes the universal currency, and the habit of bartering commodities passes gradually out of use.

He now cultivates other and better soils, and as the productiveness of labour grows, exchanges grow in number and amount: and more and more of the precious metals, termed money, are required for the purpose of effecting those exchanges. Representing so large an amount of value, and being themselves of so little bulk, they are, more than others, liable to be lost or stolen; and their possessors: those who hold portions of their capital uninvested, and waiting for the opportunity of re-investment: desire to place them in security. At first, we find them placed with traders called goldsmiths, and afterwards with bankers: or in banks. In some places, banks merely hold them for the owners, to be returned, or to be transferred on books kept for that purpose; but as exchanges become more numerous, checks or drafts are devised, by means of which the property therein is transferred without the trouble of visiting the bank. With another step, we find the machinery of exchange still further improved. Banks now furnish certificates for given sums, large and small, by aid of which transfers are made with a facility before unknown; and thus the machinery for the exchange of property from hand to hand is perfected.

As the better soils come further into action, and labour becomes more and more productive, the fashioner and the producer come more and more together. Communities now arise, in each of which are to be performed numerous exchanges, and in each are men whose capital is at one moment invested in merchandise, and at another uninvested: taking the form of money, and while remaining in that form yielding no return. In each of these communities, a shop is needed for facilitating transactions in the commodity now used as currency. One man desires to lodge his little stock for safe keeping. Another, to obtain an order for money to be paid at another place: and a third, to have bank notes that he can use in the performance of his exchanges, and thus be relieved of the necessity for carrying silver or gold, which although far less bulky than tobacco, are far more bulky than the note.

With each step in this course, we find a great saving of labour, and an increase in the quantity that may be applied to the work of production. The man who has a thousand dollars, or pounds, places it in the bank, and the bank pays it out in ten, twenty, or fifty small sums, of the precise amount desired: and thus the owner is saved the time of counting his money and of carrying it about with him, as well as the risk of loss. In the outset we find bankers charging a commission for the facility thus afforded, but by degrees, they are seen performing these important services, and affording the still greater facility of bank notes, free of all expense to those who use them. The machinery of exchange becomes therefore less costly as it becomes more perfect: and wealth accumulates with increased rapidity.

In the various smaller communities now growing up, are numerous little capitalists preparing for the purchase of houses and lots, or little farms, or for the opening of shops: while among them are some larger ones, that occasionally have their means disengaged. To all of them, *interest* is desirable, while it is in the highest degree advantageous to the community that the accumulations of the tailor and carpenter; the little fortune of the widow or the orphan: and the savings of the doctor or the clergyman: should be kept in active operation, facilitating the application of labour to production. By the combined effort of these little capitalists, a shop is opened for the purpose of lending out their money, and that of affording to the people of the neighbourhood a secure place of deposit for such portions of their respective capitals as may from time to time become disengaged. The stock therein is held in shares, transferable with little trouble: and thus the shoemaker, when ready to buy his house, sells out to the tailor; and the clerk, when ready to open a shop, parts with his interest to the clergyman. The joint capital is security to those who trade with it for the safe return of their money, and now each man having a place of safe deposit, he no longer finds it necessary to hide or bury his little stock: nor even his larger amounts of disengaged capital. The little bank, thus organized, aids the farmer in his purchases of manure; the shopkeeper in obtaining a larger supply of goods; and the builder in obtaining bricks and timber; and thus the little savings of the neighbourhood are always actively employed on the spot on which they have been made. The management of the little machine, though inexpensive, constitutes a deduction from the interest received: and to pay these expenses, the bankers must either make a charge for the accommodation they afford in receiving, guarding, and paying out again at the pleasure and in the sums that suit the convenience of their owners, the small amounts that they are accustomed to keep for their daily business; or the larger ones that pass among them as one or another buys or sells a house, or a piece of land: or they must pay themselves with the interest derived from lending out the moneys thus placed with them for security. The facility of investment is perfect. Land in large and small lots; and houses, and stocks in little institutions for insurance, or manufactures; or shares in ships and railroads, and turnpikes; may always be bought: and therefore but little capital accumulates in banks, to be used for their own benefit; and their profits therefore just suffice to pay their expenses, and to enable their owners to receive the same rate of interest that they would have if their money were lent on mortgage. The advantage derived by them from the existence of the bank, is the facility with which small sums may be temporarily invested, and recalled: while the community profits by the fact that all wealth is actively employed. If the labourer did not *lend* his fellow labourer his horse, he could not *borrow* his cart, and then two horses and carts would be needed where the work was perhaps insufficient for even one: and if the owners of little sums of money kept them in old stockings, they might themselves find it difficult to borrow when occasion required it. The money-shop now constitutes a little savings' bank for disengaged capital: as lands, lots, and houses constitute little savings' banks for the otherwise spare labour of their owners. As the fertile soils come more and more into cultivation, and as with the growth of population and wealth the fashioner takes more and more his place by the side of the producer; the tendency to concentration increases, and is accompanied with a constant diminution in the quantity required of the machinery of exchange used in passing commodities from hand to hand; because the farmer exchanges directly with the tanner and the shoemaker, and the hatter with the dealer in sugar and coffee, the balances alone being paid in money: and is also accompanied with a constantly increasing facility of investment, tending to diminish the quantity of money idle in the hands of its owner, and seeking employment. The diminution in the amount of capital invested in the machinery of exchange from hand to hand, equally with the diminution in that required for its transfer from place to place: the one called money and the other wagons: tends to enable men to apply more labour to production, and thus to bring into activity the more fertile soils, with increased return to both labour and capital: and towards the production of this result the establishment of the little money-shop greatly contributes.

The owner of uninvested capital: money, or currency: keeps some of it in his pocket-book, and some of it in the bank. The former is called circulation, and the latter is known as deposits. The proportion which the former bears to the latter, depends upon the proximity or remoteness of the money-shop, or bank. If it be near, he will keep very few notes on hand, because he can have more at any moment, and his check will always answer in their stead; but if it be at a distance of several miles, he must always have with him as many notes as will answer his purpose for a week, at least. Every increase in the facility of obtaining the description of currency that is needed, tends therefore to diminish the quantity kept on hand, while it tends to facilitate exchanges and promote the growth of wealth. With the growth of wealth and population, there is a tendency to increase in the number of shops trading in money, or banks; to increase in the facility of obtaining the machinery of exchange, called money; and to diminution in the proportion which money, whether gold, silver, or bank notes, or in any form other than that of credits, transferable by checks or drafts, bears to the operation of trade. The proportion which the coin, or the bank notes, used in London or New York, bears to the trade of those cities, is vastly smaller than that of Paris or St. Petersburgh, and less in all than in Mexico or Lima. The circulation of London is not probably greater than that of communities whose trade is not one-hundredth part as great: nor does that of New York exceed in amount what is required by counties of fifty thousand inhabitants. The more perfectly the number of banks is in accordance with the amount of business to be done, the less is the quantity of circulation that can be maintained; and thus the power of banks to profit by aid of that circulation tends to diminish, as with the division of land and growth of trade the facility of investing capital is increased: and they are thus forced more and more to look to their own capital for the profits of business. With each such step, their action becomes more uniform and steady, and they themselves become more safe. Their insecurity results always from unsteadiness. Unsteadiness results always from over-trading. Over-trading can take place only by aid of deposits or circulation. Freedom of action tends to limit both, and by so doing to prevent over-trading, and thus to produce steadiness in their action and in the value of money.

All this is perfectly exemplified in the freeest system that exists. Rhode Island, with a population of about 100,000, has sixty-five banks, with capitals varying from $20,000 to $500,000: and the combined capital is above $10,000,000.

Every village has its shoe-shop, its smith-shop, and its money-shop. Every man has at hand a little saving fund, or bank, owned generally by people like himself: men who work: and in this bank he deposits his little savings, buying first one share, and then another, until at length he is enabled to buy a little farm, or open a shop: or commence manufacturing on his own account: when he sells out to some one of his neighbours who is following in the same course.* The bank derives, from the use of its deposits and from its circulation, sufficient profit to pay its expenses, and no more; because when the trade in money is free, the quantity of idle capital remaining in the form of money, whether real or imaginary, will always be small; as will be the quantity of circulation required. In no part of the world is the proportion which coin and notes bear to the amount of trade so small as there, and in the other States of New England: yet in none do there exist such perfect facilities for furnishing circulation. In no part does the individual banker so little appear. In none does the bank trade so much upon capital,

* The following statement of one of their banks shows the mann[illegible] in which the small institutions of New England are owned :—

Females,	2,438 shares.
Mechanics,	673 "
Farmers and labourers,	1,245 "
Savings' banks,	1,013 "
Guardians,	630 "
Estates,	307 "
Charitable institutions,	548 "
Corporations and State,	157 "
Government officers,	438 "
Mariners,	434 "
Merchants,	2,038 "
Traders,	191 "
Lawyers,	377 "
Physicians,	336 "
Clergymen,	220 "
Total,	11,045 shares

It would be difficult to imagine any thing more democratic.

and so little on credit. In none, consequently, are banks so steady and so safe.

Perfect freedom in the employment of capital: the only true regulator: never has existed anywhere, to its full extent, except in the beautiful system under which that State has flourished, and has been enabled to maintain a currency less subject to fluctuations than any other that the world has yet seen. Of all the communities of the world, it is the one that can boast of the greatest number of banks, and greatest amount of capital therein invested, in proportion to its population; and it can show that its banks, *because of the perfect freedom there enjoyed*, and *because of the free exercise of the right of association for banking and other purposes*, were enabled to pass through the calamitous period from 1835 to 1842, with no alteration in their loans, to the extent of even *three per cent.* of their amount. They cannot expand improperly, because the power of competition is complete, and rival institutions would follow such expansion: and they are thus shown to be governed by the same law which forbids the shoemaker and the tailor, by charging exorbitant prices, to afford inducements to other tailors and shoemakers to come and "push them from their stools." Not having the power of undue expansion, they cannot be compelled to contract, and thus both they and those who trade with them exercise in full perfection the power of self-government. Contractions not being required, their customers do not fail, nor do they fail themselves: as is shown by the fact that in the last thirty-eight years of war and commercial convulsions, the failures have been but two in number, and their joint capitals were less than $50,000. There, the machinery of exchange from hand to hand is more perfect, and less costly than elsewhere in the world: and simply because, there, man and land, and wealth, are least fettered by regulation.

The system of Massachusetts stands next in the order of freedom and security. It is less free, because banking capital is subject to a tax of one per cent., which limits competition to that point at which banks can make out of their circulation and deposits two and a half per cent. in addition to the six per cent. earned by their capital; whereas, in Rhode Island, the average excess of loans over capital is but little over twenty-five per cent., yielding seven and a half per cent. of gross profit, one and a half per cent. of which goes to the payment of losses and expenses, and to the gradual accumulation of surplus funds. Competition produces great economy, and the losses would be very small, had the other states, its neighbours, the same free system. The fluctuations of New York and Pennsylvania often ruin the traders of Rhode Island, whose banks have to bear losses of which they are not the cause, but they nevertheless divide six per cent. from a business exceeding their capitals less than thirty per cent. The banker receives the same rate of interest that the trader pays: neither more nor less. There is little friction to be paid for. The machine moves with a steadiness and regularity unknown in the world: yet every other state and kingdom might have one equally perfect, were they to adopt the same means for obtaining it.

As we pass south and west from New England, we find the population becoming more and more scattered, and more and more employed in cultivating thin soils, while surrounded by forests and swamps covering rich soils: and with each step in our progress we find the trade in money becoming less and less free, the quantity of the machinery of exchange increasing, and its quality becoming depreciated.

New York has had a vàriety of systems, all involving care and supervision on the part of those charged with the business of government, the natural consequence of which is, that her system is less advantageous to the community than those of Massachusetts and Rhode Island, where the people protect themselves. Under her present system, banks are made by individuals, and the saving fund character, by which they are distinguished in New England, has disappeared, and the local investment of capital is thus prevented.

Pennsylvania is the favoured land of banking and landed monopolies. Large banks are permitted to exist while small communities throughout the state are denied the privilege of opening money shops for themselves. Capital is forced from the country to the city, where it accumulates, somewhat as it does in England, and flows off to the south and west, there to be dissipated in wasteful enterprises: while the little farmer and trader of the interior are unable to obtain the temporary loans necessary to enable the one to purchase manure, and the other to increase his stock of axes and spades, shoes and coats. Her policy is suicidal. She abounds in the raw material of wealth, and she expels the wealth and the labour required to bring it into activity.

Passing further south, as men become more scattered, and cultivate poorer soils, land is less divided, and the facility of investment is diminished: and therewith we find freedom of trade gradually decreasing, and States becoming bankers, with the usual results of great instability, enormous loss to the owner of the bank, and ruin to those who trade with it. Passing west, we find on the outer edge of civilization the least freedom and the worst machinery of exchange. The State of Missouri can have but one bank, and that bank will not furnish more than a given quantity of circulation, be the increase of population and trade what it may. It would have been quite as judicious in the framers of the constitution had they determined that but one railroad should ever exist in the state, and that that road should never have more than a certain number of engines and cars. The bank note facilitates the transfer of property from hand to hand, and the railroad car its transfer from place to place. The one is as useful as the other, *and quite as harmless:* as much so as the shoe-shop.

In England, the investment of capital has been at all times impeded by land. In many cases, nine-tenths of the latter have been owned by persons having but a life-interest therein, and liable to be impeded in their actions or contract, by remainder-men. In many others, mortgagees and other parties have had interests at variance with those of the nominal owner. In most others, the owner of the remaining tenth would not permit a drain to be dug, or a tile to be laid, unless he were permitted to take a tenth of the whole product of labour and capital; while paying no wages to the man employed in the work of improvement or cultivation. In some, great landlords owning turnpikes wanted large tolls; while in others steam-engines were held to be nuisances; and railroad makers were regarded as enemies, to be kept at a distance unless they would consent to pay largely for the privilege of doubling the value of the land through which their roads were to be made to run.

The necessary consequence of this has been, that the machinery of exchange has been very abundant, and of very inferior quality. All facility for local investment has been denied, and capital has been forced from the land into great towns and cities filled with starving operatives living in filthy cellars, whose labour was to be employed in converting cotton produced in India or America, into cloth to be sent to America or Australia; to be there exchanged for corn or wool, that could have been produced at half the cost at home: while their employment therein would have tended towards perfecting the great machine given by the Creator for the production of food and wool. To ensure the continuance of the power thus to waste labour and capital, colonies have been founded and maintained; and the flag of England has been enabled to disport itself over barren rocks in the Mediterranean, wild lands in Canada, and wilder lands occupied by wretched tribes in Australia and New Zealand, Southern Africa and Honduras: at the cost of thousands of millions that would have made of the United Kingdom a garden, occupied by a hundred millions of the best fed, best clothed, and best educated people in the world.*

The machinery of exchange used for the accomplishment of these objects has been as costly as it has been bad, and it has absorbed eight hundred millions of the savings of the people, in addition to the thousands of millions raised by taxes. The owners of those eight hundred millions require dividends; and the fleets and armies, which constitute a part of this vast system of bad machinery, require pay: and to provide for all these charges, fifty millions a year are required. The collection of the taxes required for these purposes produces a demand for a vast quantity of inferior machinery, intermediate between the producer and consumer, in the form of tax-gatherers: and the payment of these contributions tends to render necessary another large quantity of machinery, in the form of managers of almshouses, poor law commissioners, &c., who take the produce and divide it among those who desire to consume, but cannot find employment: and they cannot do so because the spades and picks that should be employed in making roads and trenches at home, have been sent to Canada, the Cape of Good Hope, or Australia, to be there employed in the cultivation of the thin soils of the hills, while rich soils at home remain unimproved and valueless.

The necessary consequence of all this is a tendency to cause the centralization of wealth in places in which it is not produced: and in the hands of those who have not laboured for its production: and thus to cause waste. Added to this is the fact that the mass of the people do not own the land they cultivate. Capital accumulates in their hands from the commencement to the close of the year, to be distributed by the landlord, who gives back to the soil a small portion of its product, or not, at his pleasure; and when he

* The colonies of England are forty-four in number, and their annual cost, exclusive of fleets and armies kept on foot for their protection, exceeds three millions, while the whole exports to them are only ten millions. From this statement of costs and trade, India is excluded.

chances so to do, he calls it an investment of capital on land; thus charging all and crediting nothing to the great machine. A further consequence of all this is, that the quantity of the machinery of exchange required, in the form of money, is large: being considerably more than double the amount, per head, that is required in New England, although under other circumstances it would be less.

To add to the stagnation and centralization thus produced, the habit of local union among the little communities throughout the kingdom is, as far as possible, restrained by law, for the benefit of the larger unions in the metropolis; and for that of the larger capitalists, bankers, manufacturers, and traders there and in the principal towns. Centralization is the rule. The law fixes the manner in which men may be permitted to unite for the purposes of trade, and what shall be the relation of the partners towards each other, and towards the world: and no effort at self-government can enable the parties to avoid that law. But recently, the formation of joint-stock associations, with transferable shares, was prohibited *on any terms.* Twenty years since, not more than six persons could associate for opening a place for dealing in money, even if all were liable for the debts of the concern: and all this was for the benefit of a large association to which had been granted exemption from the restrictions imposed by previous laws. About that time, however, men were permitted to associate in larger numbers for the formation of banks, but on the sole condition that *each* associate should be liable for *all* the debts of the concern: thus maintaining in full force the barbarous system of unlimited liability: *solidarité:* that had descended from olden time. The maintenance of this involved a thousand other regulations, and hence arose a necessity for various new laws to determine the relation of the parties to each other: yet they remain to this day in a condition so little satisfactory, that parties who desire to associate are forced to resort to various contrivances with a view to procure some approach to safety. The necessary consequence of all this is, that prudent men take no part in such institutions. They deposit their money for safe keeping, receiving *no* interest, while the bankers lend out both it and their own very little capital, and thus are enabled to divide *double* interest.

The result of all this may be seen by the following comparison of the system of Rhode Island, and that of the joint-stock banks of London, the great centre of the trade of the world.

The sixty-five banks of Rhode Island have a capital of about - - - - - - - - - - $10,300,000
The amount of their investments is usually about 13,000,000

Their dividends are about six per cent., affording the same rate of interest as could be obtained from loans on mortgage security, as there is no liability to be paid for.

The five joint-stock banks of London have a nominal capital of - - - - - - - - - - - - - - 55,000,000
Of which there is paid up - - - - - - - - 11,700,000

Each shareholder being individually liable for all the debts, it is attempted to free him from the responsibility by making him and his brother shareholders subscribe for £100, of which but about £20 is called in: and thus, instead of a capital of a million, we find one amounting to £200,000, while the remaining £800,000 consists of *promises to pay;* but these promises involve liabilities, for which the givers expect to be paid. They, therefore, trade to as great an extent as if they had the whole million. Their deposits amount to about £10,000,000, nearly the whole of which vast sum is lent out, liable to be reclaimed whenever any change takes place in the state of affairs; and thus while the actual capital of the five great banks is little more than is found engaged in the money trade of the little State in which banking is most free, the amount of their loans is four times as great, being probably £11,000,000,—$53,000,000. Their dividends are from six to eight per cent., in addition to the sums that are appropriated to the increase of their capital: whereas mortgage loans yield but four per cent. Of the depositors, some receive a small interest, and some have none, they having thus to contribute towards the dividends of the men who take large risks in hopes of receiving large profits: of those who prefer the uncertain profits of the gaming-table to the certain ones of regular employment. Were those banks freed from barbarous liabilities, the whole amount of their capitals would be at once paid up, as depositors would gladly convert their almost unproductive capital into bank shares paying four per cent. To yield such dividend would require a business not exceeding their own means by more than thirty per cent.: and their shares would then, because of the perfect safety of the institutions and perfect certainty of dividend, constitute a security of the highest order. Were chartered banks once to be formed under a general law, it would soon be seen that institutions with large capitals and small liabilities were safer for their owners, because steadier in their action: and safer for those who trade with them: than such institutions as those which now exist, and which resemble an inverted pyramid, *all top and no bottom;* and the latter would soon pass out of existence, for no one would trust them.*

Under such a system, joint-stock banks are held in little favour, and private banks abound; and here we see in full force the effect of regulation. We have shown that in Rhode Island, out of sixty-five banks, but two failed in thirty-eight years, including the periods of war and of the great revulsions of 1815, 1825, 1836, and 1839: whereas, in England, from 1839 to 1843, both inclusive, a time of pro-

* "The year 1836 marked the widest spread and extremity of the [joint-stock bank] system, and nothing has since been able to revive it, so as to make it a favourite object of public patronage, although, as we believe, joint-stock banks were, on the whole, never in so sound and satisfactory a condition as they are at this instant of time. This want of power to compete for public favour with the other new thing, the railway system, *is no doubt owing to the unlimited liability of shareholders, in banks,* and the absence of that obnoxious principle in railways."—*Bankers' Circular*, January 8, 1847.

found peace, eighty-two private bankers became bankrupt; of whom forty-six paid *no dividends*, twelve paid under twenty-five per cent., twelve under fifty per cent., three under seventy-five per cent., and two under one hundred per cent.: leaving seven yet unascertained.

Under the one system capital is promptly invested where it is accumulated. It falls gently as the dew, and it diffuses life and animation everywhere around. Every village having its money-shop, owned in the neighbourhood, the little capitalist is not compelled to send his money to Boston, or New York, for investment. The consequence is, that every farmer and mechanic who wishes the aid of a little capital can have it, provided his character entitles him to claim it.* In England, on the contrary, there is a constant tendency to the centralization of capital in London, because of the difficulty attendant upon investing it at home. Of the 3,013 shareholders in the five joint-stock banks of that city, 1,106 reside at more than fifteen miles from it. The natural tendency of capital is to accumulate in towns, and to be from thence distributed over the country, equalizing the rate of interest to all portions of the nation; and such would be the case in England, were banking free: but the tendency of the present system is to force capital from the country to the city, and to increase the inequality that would naturally exist. It is offered in London at one and a half to two per cent., when in parts of the country it is almost unattainable at any price. The same state of things exists in many parts of the United States. In Pennsylvania, because of the refusal to permit the establishment of local banks, large sums

*The little bank of the little town in which we write, with its capital of $50,000 has about a hundred and fifty stockholders, embracing all the little capitalists farmers, and lawyers, and widows, and orphans, and tailors, and shoemakers of the neighbourhood. It divides six per cent.—precisely what the borrowers pay—and its stock is at par. Each owner profits by the local application of his capital, in the increased demand for labour and merchandise that is thereby produced: and each participates, through directors with whose characters he is acquainted, in the management of his capital. Such institutions produce unmixed good: and such would be the character of all were banking once set free from the control of politicians.

are remitted to Philadelphia, to be employed in building up great banks: while farmers, and mechanics, and traders, can scarcely borrow at any price, because they have no money-shop within fifty miles of them. The capitalist receives less than he would otherwise do, and his property improves slowly, because his neighbours cannot obtain the means to improve *their own* little farms; to increase their machinery; or to augment their stores of goods. Capital accumulates in the city, and the rate of interest falls. Large investments are then made in distant banks or railroads, and after a little time he finds that his means are gone: that the great banks and himself are ruined together. Such is precisely the case in England. Capital is forced, by means of *regulation*, into the city, there to be managed by the great bank, and to be by it expelled thence to Spain, Mexico, Peru, Chili, Indiana, and Illinois; whereas, had the currency been left to take care of itself, and had land and trade been relieved from restriction, employment for it would have been found at home. There would then never have arisen the necessity for threats of interference on the part of the ever-belligerent Secretary for Foreign Affairs, to compel the re-payment of money which would not have been lent but for the meddling of legislators and politicians with the affairs of individuals.

Under such a system, steadiness in the value of the commodity used as the standard for the measurement of the values of commodities, was impossible; but instead of perceiving that unsteadiness was produced by restriction and regulation, it was erroneously attributed to the excess of freedom, and a new system was established by the celebrated Bank Restriction Act of 1844. To the movements of the one great bank have mainly been due all the violent revulsions in trade throughout the world, whose effects upon the United States we have already described. What have been the causes of the extraordinary changes that produced those revulsions we propose now to show: as well as to inquire how far the new system tends to prevent their further recurrence.

Under the old charter of the Bank, great inconvenience and loss were experienced by the mercantile world from the extraordinary fluctuations in the supply and value of money. At one moment it appeared to be so abundant as to be almost valueless. Vast sums remained in bank at the credit of individuals, yielding them no return; and the bank itself was soliciting applications for loans, at low rates of interest. It was then forced out in loans to all the poor sovereigns of Europe. A few months passed by, and the bank was charging almost double the usual interest on the best paper, and forcing out the securities which it had laboured to monopolize. By those who had securities of the first order, money was to be obtained with exceeding difficulty; while, by those who held such as were of the second order, it was unattainable at any price. A little time elapsed, and trade was paralyzed. Money was then again cheap, and it was sent to the mines of Mexico; and then again a little time, and it was dear. Again cheap, it was sent to make roads and canals in Illinois, and banks in Mississippi and Alabama. Again dear, the bank was seen labouring to save itself from ruin, and *sauve qui peut* was the order of the day.

On the verge of suspension, in 1836, and escaping only by the adoption of measures that involved in ruin a large portion of the trading world at home; it was seen, as early as 1839, enlarging its loans in the face of a steady drain of bullion, indicating an already existing excess in the currency, and thus involving itself in difficulty so serious as to compel resort to measures of severity far exceeding those of the former period. Hosts of shopkeepers and mechanics, merchants and manufacturers, were ruined; operatives, in countless thousands, were deprived of employment and reduced to starvation; and the best of the foreign customers of England so seriously injured, that for a time trade seemed almost at an end. Severe as were these measures, the desired effect was not immediately produced; and the great bank, the regulator of the monetary concerns of the greatest mercantile community of the world, was seen to be forced, on bended knees, to solicit the aid of its great neighbour and rival, the Bank of France, to save it from absolute bankruptcy.

The frequency and extraordinary extent of these changes, induced a proper feeling of doubt as to the capacity of those to whom had been intrusted the management of the currency; and a strong disposition was felt to ascertain by what laws, if any there were, the institution was governed. A Parliamentary committee was appointed, and numerous sittings were held. Witnesses were examined, for and against the bank; and a huge volume of evidence was printed, much of which was strange enough certainly, as coming from men who might have been supposed to know some little of the laws of trade. With all the evidence, the committee failed to discover the law that was desired. The only conclusion at which it was possible for it to arrive was, that the institution was administered without reference to any principle whatsoever: that its movements were invariably those of momentary expediency: and that the dangers and difficulties which had occurred were likely to be repeated at the first favourable moment. Such having been clearly shown to be the case, even by the evidence of the governor of the bank himself, it was deemed necessary, on the renewal of the charter, to endeavour to subject its action to some certain law: thus fitting it to become the regulator of the action of others: and hence the Bank Restriction Acts. Those acts are not yet three years old, and the same scene is renewed. A period of frightful speculation is followed by universal panic. Consols, but recently at par, are now at 80. The government is forced to pay five per cent. for money. Railroad stock has fallen, in many cases, twenty to thirty per cent. The best paper cannot be negotiated at less than ten to fifteen per cent. per annum. Bank notes cannot be obtained even for silver bullion. Dealers in corn, and cotton, and bullion, are again proscribed. Deputations from Liverpool and Manchester claim of the minister a suspension of the law, and he is assured that large orders remain unexecuted, because of the impossibility of obtaining the means necessary for their execution, while operatives are starving for want of employment. The bank itself, with bankruptcy staring it in the face, is compelled to enlarge its loans when it would contract them; and thus is exhibited, for the third time within little more than ten years, the spectacle of a great regulator utterly unable to control its own movements. It has hopes, however, in aid from the Russian autocrat. He has already saved the regulator of France, and he promises to do as much for that of England. The great community of Britain see, in the promised aid of *two millions*, a prospect of relief! The bank becomes "more liberal in its discounts." "The screw" is not so tight. They think they see that the regulator may save itself without utterly destroying them; and bright hope gladdens the face of thousands, in reflecting upon the idea that the Czar is enabled, by means of the issue of bank notes, adapted for the purposes of small traders as well as large ones, to dispense with the use of gold to such an extent as to enable him to become a creditor of their own government; and to entitle himself to an annual remittance of £60,000, in payment of interest on the promised loan: whereas similar action on their own part would render available a much larger amount of their own capital, free of all demand for interest, thus lessening the cost of the machinery of exchange, and increasing the power of production.

A brief interval of expansion is followed by another contraction. At one moment, interest is reduced to five per cent., and at the next it is raised to nine. At one, exchequer bills are in favour. At the next, they are proscribed. From hour to hour the system changes, and universal ruin is the result.

Such is the condition of the people of England under the control of its great bank. They are dependent upon the chance measures of a body of gentlemen, no one of whom has ever yet, so far as we have seen, been able to explain the principles by which they are governed in the administration of the vast machine subjected to their control.

The Bank Restriction Act has failed to produce the effect desired. It has given no steadiness to the value of money. By one party, the fault is attributed to the law itself; while by another, it is asserted, that if the bank had acted "in the spirit of the law of 1844," the difficulty would not have occurred. Such are the words of the author of the law, who attributes the pressure to the extraordinary spirit of speculation that has recently existed; to the scarcity of corn; and to other causes: and who, as might have been expected, is willing to see it in any cause but the real one, which is to be found in the radical defect of his own measure. It professed to regulate the action of the bank; and, had it done so, the directors would have found themselves *compelled* to act in accordance with its letter and its spirit: and then there could have been no such speculation as that we have recently witnessed. Had it done so, the difficulties naturally attendant upon short crops would not have been aggravated, as they now are, by the total prostration of trade, the discharge of workmen, and the impossibility of obtaining wages to be used in the purchase, at any price, of the necessaries of life.

The trade in money requires no more law than that in shoes. It requires, on the contrary, perfect freedom, because it is so vastly greater in amount* that interference to the extent of one-half of one per cent. is there more felt than in the other would be one amounting to a hundred per cent. The tendency of gold and silver to steadiness in value is the great recommendation which they possess, entitling them to claim to be used for measuring the value of all other commodities; and were the trade in money perfectly free,

* Every contract for the purchase or sale of any commodity, or property, involves a contract for the delivery of a quantity of money equivalent to the price. The trade in money is therefore equal in amount to the sum of the prices of all commodities, and properties, and labor, sold.

they would constitute standards almost as perfect as does the yard-stick as a measure of length, or the bushel as a measure of capacity. On an average, the whole quantity of corn, and cotton, and sugar, in market, in any year, is consumed in the year, and a failure of crop may make a change of fifty, or even of a hundred, per cent. in the price; whereas, the quantity of gold and silver always in market—and which can be kept there because they are not subject to rust, or decay—is more than a hundred times the quantity required for a year's consumption: and a total failure of the year's crop should not affect it to the extent of even one per cent. Nevertheless, such are the penalties, prohibitions, liabilities, and other restrictions, to which traders in money are subjected: so numerous and powerful are the monopolies established for their *regulation:* that of all trades that in money is the least steady: and of all commodities, money is the most subject to sudden alteration in supply, and consequently in value, as compared with other commodities. It is a yard-stick, of perpetually changing length: a gallon measure, that contains sometimes three quarts, and at other times six, or even twelve. The *regulation* of the currency is held to be one of the functions of government, because, in past times, all sovereigns have found it to be a convenient mode of taxation. Philip the Fair changed the coinage thirteen times in a single year, and more than a hundred times during his reign. Louis X., Charles IV., Philip V. and VI., John, and their successors, almost to the Revolution, followed the illustrious example. In England, similar changes have been made, but to a much smaller extent, France having been, at all times, distinguished among the countries of Europe for frauds of that and other kinds. All the governments of Europe, great and small, have, at various times, done the same thing; and hence their claim, still maintained, to execute, either by themselves or their deputies, the same profitable office. That of England transfers the duty to the bank, which institution performs it in such a manner that at one time money is cheap, and the State is enabled to compel the owners of three and a half per cents. to receive three per cents. in exchange, and thus to effect a large saving of interest: while at another time money is dear, and the owners of the new stock find they have been juggled out of their property. We do not desire to say that such is the object sought in the production of these extraordinary changes, but such is certainly their effect: and good reasons can always be given for them. At one time, it is the enormous import of stocks from the continent; at another, the influx of South American shares and stocks; at a third, the vast loans to the United States; and at a fourth, the deficiency of the crops; but stocks would not come if money were not made too cheap, and corn might be deficient without producing any material change in the value of money, except as regarded corn itself. If the supply of sugar were small, the price of sugar itself would rise, and there would be somewhat less money to be exchanged against cloth, the price of which would slightly fall; and so, if the supply of grain were short, there would be less money to be exchanged against sugar; but in no case would a deficiency in one commodity materially affect the prices of other commodities, were the currency let alone. The true reason is, that the task of regulation is committed to one great institution, whose movements are totally unregulated. It monopolizes securities at one time, and produces an apparent excess, and consequent cheapness, of money. It forces them back upon the market, when much of this apparent excess has found employment in new enterprises, to which resort would not otherwise have been had, and now the scarcity is equal to the previous abundance. It is a great fly-wheel in the midst of an infinite number of little wheels, all of which are compelled to go fast or slow as the master-wheel may direct. If its own movement could be rendered uniform, all would work harmoniously; but if it must continue to be, as it has heretofore been, subjected to perpetual jerks, and to changes from backward to forward motion, and *vice versa*, from forward to backward, the inevitable consequence must also continue to be the destruction of many of the little ones: and eventually, perhaps, it may be that of the great one. These little wheels are the bankers, and merchants, and manufacturers of England: of the United States: and of the world: who have been for a long time engaged in studying the law which governs the motion of the great fly-wheel, but with so little success, as yet, that we hazard little in asserting that there is no man in England, in or out of the bank, that would commit that law to writing, and stake his fortune on proving that it had been operative during any one period of twelve months in the last twenty years. In despair of arriving at any comprehension of the laws of its action, all resign themselves blindly to its influence, and the error of the great regulator is propagated throughout the whole system. Joint stock and private banks expand when it expands, and contract as it contracts; and an error of a single million in Threadneedle-street thus produces error to the extent of tens of millions in the money transactions of the kingdom. Hence the necessity for subjecting it to fixed and positive rules. The currency needs no such regulator, but if such an one must continue to exist, its action should be rendered perfectly automatic: leaving it then to the proprietors of the little wheels to use such gearing as would enable them to attain as much or as little speed as they might respectively require. It should be *acted upon by the community*, instead of acting itself upon them, and then it might be consulted with the same confidence as the thermometer. The law that should produce this effect, would not be that of 1844, which, with all its machinery of banking department, and department of issue, has totally failed to answer the end proposed. It has failed, because it was framed with a view to changes in the amount of *currency in use*, which are ever slow, and small in amount: while it contained no reference to changes in the *currency seeking employment*, which have always been rapid, and great in amount.* It made the bullion of the bank dependent upon the circulation which is in constant use among the great body of the people, and cannot be materially increased or decreased, without a great change in the state of trade, or in

* It is curious to see in the evidence of eminent bankers the reasons adduced for thinking that deposits—convertible on the instant into notes or gold—are not as much currency as notes or gold themselves. One among the most learned of the bank directors, thought that they could not be so considered, for the owner "could not pay his laborers with them," nor could he do with them "whatever he could do with sovereigns and shillings." He thought, however, that they possessed "the essential qualities of money in a very low degree." The "essential quality of money" is that of facilitating the transfer of property, and that quality is possessed in a higher degree by the bank note than by gold and silver; and in a still higher degree by the check than by the note: for the owner of money on deposit draws for the precise number of pounds, shillings, and pence required, and transfers them, without the trouble of handling or counting even a single penny. It is curious, too, to remark the strong tendency existing in the minds of many of the witnesses, distinguished in the monetary circles of London, to confound notes of hand, and bills, with currency. A note is a contract for the delivery, at some future day, of a given quantity of money, or currency. Its value, in money, depends on the proportion between the money and bills in market, and is just as much liable to variation as that of sugar or coffee. If money be plenty, and bills, or coffee, or sugar scarce, the price of the article in which the deficiency of supply exists, will be high; but if sugar, or coffee, or bills, be abundant, and money be scarce, the price of the superabundant commodity will be low. Notes may be *bartered* for merchandise, as is done in England to a great extent; but an increase in the supply of notes in the market, although it may materially affect the *credit* price of commodities: or the price in *barter* for promises to deliver money at some future day: will make no change in their money prices, unless there exist a facility for converting the notes into money. In time of severe pressure, there is great facility in bartering merchandise for notes; but want of confidence induces the holders to fix the prices very high, with a view to cover the cost and risk attendant upon the conversion of notes into the commodity that is needed, which is money, or currency: the thing with which they must redeem their own obligations. The term currency means *money on the spot*, and in England, with the exception of the silver coinage for small payments, nothing is recognised as money but gold, which passes from hand to hand, either by actual delivery of the coin, or by the transfer of the property in a certain portion of that which exists in the vaults of banks and bankers: by means of private drafts, or checks, or by that of obligations of the bank itself, called bank notes. A contract for the delivery of flour at a future day might, with the same propriety, be called flour, as a contract for the delivery, at a future day, of a certain quantity of the commodity which is current for the payment of debts, and which we call money, can be called money, or currency, itself.

The difficulties of the bank result from the fact that, whenever speculation the feelings of the people; instead of making it dependent upon the deposits of unemployed capital, the property of the few, which are liable to increase or decrease by every change of weather, and by every speck that appears in the political or commercial horizon.

By the new charter, the quantity of bullion to be held is made dependent entirely on the state of the circulation; a sovereign, or, to a certain extent, its equivalent in silver, being required to lie in the vaults of the bank for every pound of its notes that is in the hands of the public beyond the sum of £14,000,000. An examination of the operations of the bank, shows the circulation an almost constant quantity, amounting, since the date of that charter, to £20,000,000; and so long as the public shall insist upon keeping it at that point, £6,000,000 of bullion must remain in the bank, not to be used under any circumstances whatsoever: and of little more value to the community, while they so remain, than would be an equal weight of pebble stones. How far the circulation can claim to be treated as a constant quantity, we propose now to inquire. In doing so, it is necessary to bear in mind that trade is more active at certain seasons of the year than at others; and that, as more exchanges are to be performed, more notes, or machinery of exchange, are required in the active than in the dull season; and that, therefore, if we would compare one year with another, we should take, in all cases, the same months of the

---

is rife, and men are anxious to make contracts for the future delivery of money, she facilitates their operations by taking their notes freely, and becoming responsible for the delivery of the money on demand: by which means her debts, called deposits, are largely increased. If she has the money, all is well; but if she has not, she thus swells the imaginary amount of the currency, and prices rise. When the time arrives for payment, it commonly proves that both parties have been trading on their credit. The bank must be paid, or she cannot pay, and must become bankrupt. She seduced the poor debtor to over-trade, by assuming to do that which she could not have done if called upon. and she now ruins him for having yielded to her solicitations. She escapes by lucky accident, and speedily re-exhibits what is called "an increased liberality" in her accommodations; *i. e.*, she again runs largely in debt for the purchase of securities.

year. Following this rule, we now give the circulation of April and October, for the years from 1832 to 1840 :—

	April.	October.
1832	£18,449,000	£18,200,000
1833	17,912,000	19,823,000
1834	19.097,000	19,107,000
1835	18,507,000	18,216,000
1836	17,985,000	18,136,000
1837	18,365,000	18,876,000
1838	18,872,000	19,636,000
1839	18,326,000	17,906,000
1840	16,818,000	17,221,000

The year 1840 was a year of utter prostration. In that and the following year, trade was at an end, so far as the ruin of the customers of England: and particularly the people of the United States: by the extraordinary movements of the bank could accomplish that object. Nevertheless, under these untoward circumstances, the circulation remained above £16,000,000; and we shall now find it gradually attaining a point higher than it had been at for many years :—

	April.	October.
1841	£16,533,700	£17,592,000
1842	16,952,000	20,004,000
1843	20,239,000	19,561,000
1844	21,246,000	

NEW LAW.

	April.	October.
1844		£21,152,000
1845	£20,099,000	21,260,000
1846	19,865,000	21,550,000
1847	19,854,000	

From this we see that in the first period embracing the nine years from 1832 to 1840, both inclusive: and including the crisis of 1836–7: the variation in the month of April, above and below the medium point of £18,500,000, is under three per cent.; while that of October, above and below the point of £18,900,000, is but little over four per cent. until we reach the close of 1839, and commencement of 1840; when the bank had been compelled to trample in the dust all that were in any way dependent upon it, thereby almost annihilating the trade of the country, and that of all countries intimately connected with it.

In the second period, it attains a higher point than in the first. Private and joint-stock banks have been ruined by the extraordinary revulsion of 1839, and confidence in their notes has been impaired: and the bank now profits by the ruin which it has caused.

From 1844 to the present time, the variations are under two per cent. There is, however, a material difference between the average amount of the first and third periods, and a permanent increase appears to have taken place. In the time that has elapsed, there has been a great increase of population, wealth, and trade, and an increase of the machinery of trade might have been calculated upon; yet no real increase in the circulation has taken place, and the change that is above shown is only apparent, and offers a new proof of the tendency to constancy: despite all legislative interferences: to which we desire to call the attention of our readers. Previously to 1844, there were no limits to the circulation of the private, joint stock, Irish and Scotch banks, which averaged, between 1833 and 1839, about £20,000,000. By the new law, they were limited to about £17,800,000, which is almost the precise amount at the date of the latest returns. The vacuum thus made had to be filled by notes of the Bank of England, which have, therefore, risen from £18,000,000 to £20,000,000. The average of the total circulation from 1833 to 1839 was £37,838,000; in January last, it had reached £39,400,000; in April, it was £37,819,000.

Small even as are these variations, they are still to a considerable extent only apparent. It is well known that when money is very plenty and cheap, bankers and banks retain on hand a larger amount of each others' notes than when it is scarce and high; and a note in their vaults is just as much out of circulation as if it remained in those of the issuing bank itself. In the above table it is shown that the highest April was that of 1835, when the bullion in the bank was £10,673,000, the securities below £26,000,000, and the market value of money but three per cent. The highest October was that of 1833, when the bullion was nearly £11,000,000, the securities £24,000,000, and the rate of interest also but three per cent. It was a period of recovery from recent excitement that had been followed by depression and loss. The next highest October was that of 1838, when trade was paralyzed: unemployed capital abundant: the stock of bullion near £10,000,000: and the rate of interest three per cent. In 1842–3–4, the apparent circulation was greater than in any of the years of the first period, yet the bank was unable to extend its business, which was scarcely equal to the amount of its circulation and surplus. In all these cases we find precisely the circumstances calculated to produce an accumulation of Bank of England notes in the vaults and chests of private and joint-stock bankers: while the *lowest* April and October, until we reach the total prostration of 1839–40, were those of 1836, when the loans of the bank had reached the *highest point*, and when, according to the theory of the bank restriction act, the circulation should have been highest.

Under the new law, the highest April was that of 1845, when the bullion had reached the enormous sum of £16,000,000; and the highest October, that of 1846, when it had just re-attained that amount. In view of these facts, we doubt if the variation above or below the medium point, in the real circulation, from 1833 to 1839, ever equalled one and a half per cent.; a proportion so small, that for almost all purposes it may be regarded as being a constant quantity.*

* "We have shown, by unanswerable arguments, that under no circumstances will more circulation be retained in the hands of the public than is just sufficient to perform the functions of a medium of exchange for the internal transactions of the country. No man retains more money in his possession

That such has been the case, has not been due to any efforts of the bank for that purpose. On the contrary, none have been spared that could have tended to increase and decrease the amount. Between 1833 and 1839, it increased its securities from £22,000,000 to £31,000,000, and thus forced up the amount of unemployed capital at the credit of its customers, from £8,000,000 to £18,000,000, *for all of which they were entitled to demand notes*, if they would; and it had diminished its investments from £31,000,000 to £21,000,000, thereby enabling the owners of unemployed capital to invest at low prices, the effect of which was shown in the reduction of deposits from £18,000,000 to £7,000,000; yet the circulation neither increased nor decreased materially. Under the new law, we find it purchasing securities and contracting debts, until the former rise from £22,000,000 to £36,000,000, and the latter from £12,000,000 attain to £24,000,000: and again diminishing, the first to £25,000,000, and the second to £16,000,000: and all this with no change worth notice in the circulation. The transactions of the whole period have shown that scarcely any power can be exercised over it, for its increase or decrease; and yet this almost invariable quantity is made the measure of the bullion to be retained in the vaults of the bank: the result of all which is, that it has a circulation of £20,000,000 that it cannot compel the people to return upon it for redemption, and that it is, nevertheless, obliged to keep £6,000,000 out of these £20,000,000, in bullion; while the whole commercial community is thrown into an agony of despair by the total refusal of accommodation, because the amount of bullion is reduced to £9,000,000. Had the law provided that £6,000,000 should be packed up and stowed away, never

---

than he requires for immediate use, but either places it in a bank, or employs it in the purchase of commodities on which he expects to obtain a profit, or securities which will yield an interest. As a rule, therefore, the circulation is at all times confined to the lowest sum which is sufficient to conduct the transactions of the country."—*Economist.*

again to be opened or removed for any purpose whatsoever, it would have been quite as useful for the maintenance of any thing like equality in the value of money; and far more useful in that it would not have lulled the people into a belief that safeguards had been provided, when safety there could be none. It may be said, however, that panics might arise when people would bring the notes for redemption. Panics follow violent changes of action, like those of 1825, 1836, and 1839, by which great losses are produced, threatening the existence of the bank; and nothing could be better calculated to produce them than the institution of a system that professed to afford security when it gave none. The directors thought they were safe if they obeyed the law, and the people relied on the law for security. It has been obeyed: yet security to bank or individuals has not been attained, nor can it ever be by aid of that law.

The power and the discretion of the people: their capacity for self-government: in regard to the regulation of the circulation, have been fully manifested. They want no aid from the law, which is just as useful as if its object had been to fix the number of shoes, hats, or coats, that should be kept by the manufacturers of those commodities; with a view to provide against any man claiming to purchase a hat, and not being able to find one. Should such an one ever be passed, many men will be found going without hats, shoes, or coats; for the supply of those articles, whenever it shall come to be regulated, will be as unsteady, and their prices will become as variable, as we now see to be the case with money. The people do require, however, protection against the exercise, by the bank, of the vast power confided to it, by means of which it is enabled to purchase securities, passing the amount to the credit of their owners, and calling them "deposits:" by which operation prices are forced up, the rate of interest is diminished, capital is made to appear superabundant, and a speculative disposition is produced. That institution has a monopoly of the power of trading as a banking corporation. Had it not, the persons, whose capital is there locked up, unproductive to themselves, while the bank is increasing the amount of its securities with a view to the making of large dividends; might demand bullion for their deposits, and open banks themselves, lending out their own money for their own profit, and thus curbing the bank: but this they could not do, prior to 1844, because every association for banking purposes was subjected to heavy penalties, in the form of liabilities, which forbade that any prudent man should take part in their formation; and since the new law, the formation of them, even coupled with the principle of unlimited liability, requires permission from the government: and as if utterly to prevent people of small means from taking part in them, the price of a share is fixed at a hundred pounds, of which one-half must be paid in. Thus is restriction loaded on restriction, to produce steadiness! The effect is similar to that which would be obtained by adding a ton of iron to the top hamper of an already overloaded coach.

For the benefit of those who have not traced the operation of an expansion, we propose to show the manner in which it acts. Let us suppose, first, a state of affairs, in which every thing is at par. Money is easily obtained for good notes, at a fair rate of discount, and for mortgages, at the usual rate of interest; while all those who have disposable capital, can readily obtain good securities that will yield them the common rate of profit; the daily supply of money and securities being about equal the one to the other. In this happy state of affairs, the directors of the bank, feeling themselves very easy, fancy that it would be profitable to take another million, and forthwith their broker is desired to purchase that amount of exchequer bills, or other securities. At once the equilibrium is disturbed. A demand for securities exists, exceeding the ordinary amount of supply. Prices rise, and some unhappy holder is tempted to sell, in the hope that there will be less demand to-morrow, and that then prices will fall, and he may buy in again with a fair profit. At the close of the day, his bills have become the property of the bank, and he: or all those who have united to furnish the the desired million: is creditor to the bank, either directly or through his banker, for the whole amount. His capital is now uninvested, and he appears in the market on the next day as a purchaser. Unfortunately for him, however, the bank, too, makes its appearance, for the second time, in the same capacity. The first experiment has been attended with vastly fortunate results. Its "deposits" have grown with the increase of its investments. Such success emboldens it to repeat the operation, and another million is purchased, with similar results. It obtains the bills, and the owners obtain credits on the books of the bank, which thus runs in debt, and the more debt it contracts, the more means it appears to suppose itself to have at command. With the second million, prices have risen; and with the third, they rise still higher; and so on with each successive million. *Capital* appears superabundant, because the former owner of these millions of securities is seeking for profitable investments; when the real superabundance consists only in *debts* which the bank has incurred. Prices advance from day to day, and a speculative disposition is engendered by the growth of fortune among the holders of stocks, and next it becomes necessary to manufacture new stocks for the purpose of employing this vast surplus capital. New railroads are therefore projected and subscribed for: vast contracts are made: boundless prosperity is in view. Men who should be raising corn, are breaking up the old roads to replace them with new, or building palaces for the lucky speculators. Immense orders for iron, and bricks, and timber, are given. Prices advance. England becomes a good place to sell in, and a bad one to buy in. Imports increase, and exports decrease. Bullion goes abroad. The bank has to sell securities. Prices fall. Business is paralyzed. The roads are half made, and cannot be completed. The people are ruined, and the bank escapes with difficulty from the ruin she herself has made, congratulates herself on the dexterity she has shown, and prepares to repeat the operation at the first opportunity. Such is the history of 1825, 1836, and 1839, at all of which periods, the bank manufactured "deposits" by monopolizing securities, and was then itself misled into the belief that the increase of its own debts indicated an actual surplus of capital. Whenever that institution purchases a security: which is always the representative of some already existing investment: the person from whom it is purchased will unquestionably use the means that are placed at his command for the creation of some new species of investment, as no man willingly permits his capital to lie idle. If it make this purchase with the money of others, the inevitable effect must be to raise prices, and stimulate the late owner to increased activity to provide the new investment; and whenever it shall be provided, he will, either directly or indirectly, demand payment in gold, and then the security must be parted with to provide means for the payment; at which time prices will as inevitably fall, because the creditor of the bank has been labouring to invest capital which had no real existence in any other form than that of a railroad, or canal, or some other public work, or debt, already created, and which could not be used for the formation of other roads or canals:—and thus, while the one party has been trying to invest his funds, the other has been holding the evidence of their being already invested, and drawing interest for their use. A double action has thus been produced, causing inflation and speculation to be followed by panic and ruin.

The course of the bank, in the late railroad speculation, appears to have been precisely the same as was, in the great land speculation of 1836, that of the banks of the west, established among a scattered people who still cultivated poor lands: and who *borrowed* money to make the banks. A man purchased a section of land, and paid the amount to the treasur r. The treasurer deposited the money in the bank. The bank lent the man his money, on his note. He paid it again to the treasurer, who again deposited it in the bank, which again lent it to the original owner, who again bought land, and again paid the treasurer, repeating the operation until, with a single thousand dollars, he became the owner of tens of thousands of acres. At the end of the operation, the government had parted with vast bodies of land, and had, in exchange, a vast amount of bank credits: and the bank held the notes of the speculator.

For a series of years, every species of difficulty had been thrown in the way of those who desired to make roads, the effect of which had been to cause an unnatural accumulation of uninvested capital: to lower the price of money: and to produce enormous speculation in railroads *to be made*. All England was engaged in it, from the highest peer to the smallest shopkeeper; for the desire of gain by speculation is always in the direct ratio of the difficulty of obtaining a living by honest industry. It is universal in France: and far greater and more universal in England than in the United States.* The consequence was, that early in the last year a large amount of money was required to be paid for deposits on account of roads for which charters were to be obtained. The difficulty was supposed to consist not in the *matter* of capital, but in the *manner* of payment. All the bullion in the bank would not accomplish it. The very fact of the vast sum required in that early stage of the business should have been sufficient to induce great doubt of the propriety of the operation, and had the bank not interfered, very many doubtful speculations would have fallen to the ground. Ever ready, however, to foster a speculative tendency, she

* In France, speculation in stocks by women in high life is a matter of daily occurrence. In England, it is less frequent, but it does occur: as the papers of the day furnish ample evidence. In both countries, ladies make bets on the results of horse-races: small ones, it is true, but small as they are, they are evidence of the speculative tendency. In the United States, such things are unknown.

was not found wanting on this occasion. She took the money, and lent it out as fast as paid in; and thus enabled the same thousand pounds to pay the deposits on thousands of shares, precisely as did the western banks with the funds of the land speculator. In the latter case, there was one advantage, which the railroad speculation did not possess. No further payments were there to be required; whereas, here, the loan was only to facilitate the first payment, which was to be followed by an almost endless series of instalments. In February, 1846, the bank had become debtor to its depositors—the principal of whom was the accountant who received those deposits, or, in other words, a state treasurer —£18,000,000, and it held £36,000,000 of securities, £23,000,000 of which were private; and thus it had afforded to the railroad speculators of England precisely the same facility that the western banks granted to the land speculators of their respective vicinities. Had no such interference taken place, and had subscribers to roads been compelled, as they should have been, to find money instead of giving notes; thus affording evidence of the existence of the capital required; many ruinous schemes would have been crushed in the outset: fewer persons would have been employed in building roads, and more would have been engaged in cultivation: prices would not have been so high: more manufactures would have been exported: and the corn required to make amends for deficient crops would have been less in quantity, and paid for with manufactures, or with bullion, that might have been spared without causing the slightest disturbance in the monetary world of Britain: but the proprietors of the bank would have received no *bonus*, in addition to their usual half-yearly dividend, the object sought for in fostering speculation.*

* So long as the bank lent out the means which properly belonged to it, as was the case throughout a large portion of 1845, manufactures were exported with profit; and they continued to be so until the expansion had to

Among the assets of the bank are three quantities that may be regarded as constants. These are—

1. The rest, or surplus capital - - - -	£4,000,000
2. The circulation - - - - - -	20,000,000
3. The public deposits, to the extent of - - -	2,500,000
Total - - - - - - -	£26,500,000

With all the excitement of the last two years, the average amount of securities held by the bank, is but about £30,000,000. That excitement has been produced by using the capital of others, placed in her hands, while those others were trying to use it themselves. Had the law limited her to the use of the above items, which may be regarded as almost the same as her own capital, and by the use of which she interferes with nobody: and had the amount of her securities never exceeded the sum of those quantities: no excitement could ever have been produced; no panic could ever have followed; vast losses would have been avoided; bank stock would not have fallen, in two months, from 205 to 189; and England would now be in the enjoyment of high prosperity, notwithstanding the failure of her crops.

During the period from 1832 to 1839, the amount of those items varied but little from £23,000,000. We will now show the state of the securities of the bank, taking that sum as a *par*, and marking as plus +, or minus —, the variations that occurred, with their effects. In November, 1831, securities had been greatly in excess, and there was considerable speculation. In January, the bank was reducing her

time to produce the effect of making England a good place to sell in, and a bad one to buy in. We take the following from the *Bankers' Circular* of March 19, before the crisis had arrived. After stating that, for about two years after the passage of the Charter Act, manufacturers had been able to sell to advantage, while the prices of imports were not remunerative, the writer goes on to say, that "no manufactures exported, and none sold at home, have left a fair profit to the manufacturer since July last; on the other hand, almost all the imported commodities, above enumerated, (cotton, silk, hemp, tobacco and indigo, coffee and sugar,) except silk, have risen in value, and yielded a fair profit to the importer."

loans, and money was scarce, and worth on first-rate bills 4 per cent.*

1832—April +	£1,300,000.	Bullion going abroad. Excitement diminishing. Interest 3¼ per cent.†
July +	600,000.	Reduction. Great losses in trade. Little demand for money. Interest 3 per cent.
Oct. +	1,000,000.	Trade paralyzed. No demand for money. Interest 2¾ per cent. Bank again extending itself, and forcing up the amount of unemployed capital left with it on deposit.
1833—Jan. +	200,000.	No demand for money. Bullion and deposits increasing. Continued paralysis. Interest 2¾ per cent.
April +	1,300,000.	Bank monopolizing securities, and thus increasing the deposits. No demand for money. Interest 2¼ per cent.
July	Par.	Deposits fall with the diminution of securities held by the bank, and capitalists now obtain 2½ per cent.
Oct. +	1,200,000.	Business reviving. Increased demand for money. Rate 3 per cent. Bank has bought £1,200,000 of additional securities, and the unemployed capital has consequently advanced £1,000,000.
1833—Dec. +	500,000.	Bank has diminished securities, and deposits have fallen therewith. Interest is now 3½ per cent.; showing an increased demand for money, and increased facility for investment, with the diminution of bank securities.
1834—April +	2,600,000.	Great expansion, producing increase of deposits. Interest has consequently fallen to 3 per cent. Tendency to purchase foreign securities, as those of England are being monopolized by the bank.
July +	4,600,000.	Further expansion. Increase of deposits. Foreign stocks remitted to England for the absorption of the large apparent surplus capital. Bullion going abroad. Interest 3¼ per cent.

* The perpetual jerks to which this great concern has always been liable, are well shown in the few months prior to April, 1832—In August, 1831, the securities were £25,900,000; in October they had fallen to £20,750,000; in November they had risen to £24,450,000. In February, 1832, they were £25,550,000; in April £21,900,000. With such a fly-wheel, the only wonder is that any of the little wheels escape destruction.

† The rates of interest here given, have reference to first class paper in London.

1834—Oct. +	£5,600,000.	Further expansion. Prices rise. More stocks imported,* and more bullion going abroad. High profits of speculators have raised the rate of interest to 3¾ per cent.
Dec. +	3,200,000.	Reduction. Deposits diminishing, and price of money maintained. Bullion going abroad.
1835—April +	3,500,000.	Increase. Deposits rising, and bullion still in demand. Interest still 3¾ per cent.
July +	2,700,000.	Reduction. Deposits falling therewith. Bullion still in demand. Money less abundant for speculation, and interest 4 per cent.
Oct. +	5,000,000.	Great increase of securities and of deposits. American stocks coming to absorb the great surplus capital. Great speculation. Interest 3¾ per cent.
Dec. +	8,700,000.	Great increase of deposits, and heavy import of stocks. Large contracts for present and future payments thereon. Great speculation, and interest 3¾ per cent.
1836—April +	5,400,000.	Reduction of securities and of deposits. Interest still 3¾ per cent.
July +	4,150,000.	Reduction of securities and of deposits. Money much wanted for payments on contracts for stocks, and interest rises to 4 per cent.
Oct. +	6,300,000.	Increased securities. Large payments for foreign stocks.† Export of bullion. Great distress. Interest 5 per cent. Crushing of American merchants.
Dec. +	6,600,000.	Distress greatly aggravated. Bank forced to expand in the face of diminishing bullion. Interest 5½ per cent.
1837—April +	6,300,000.	Bank, having lost all command of its own actions, is still obliged to keep itself expanded. Continued export of bullion. Distress continues. Interest 5½ per cent.
July +	4,000,000.	Bank enabled at length to contract its business. Small return of bullion. Distress somewhat diminished. Interest 4½ per cent. No confidence.

* "From November, 1834, to March, 1835, there was an enormous speculation in the prices of South American stocks, which caused an advance to a great extent, and brought a large import of foreign stock from all parts of the continent."—*Mr. J. H. Palmer*, *Report on Banks of Issue*, p. 106.

† "The loss of bullion by the bank, between 1st of April and 1st of September, 1836, I believe to have been occasioned by the excess in the American securities."—*Ibid.* p. 115.

Date	Amount	Remarks
1837—Oct. +	£3,500,000.	Continued contraction. Trade very dull. Deposits and bullion increasing. No confidence. Interest 3½ per cent.
Dec. +	600,000.	Great reduction. Trade very dull. Large imports of bullion. Interest still 3½ per cent., notwithstanding the heavy amount of deposits, because of continued want of confidence.
1838—April —	200,000.	Decrease of securities, with constant increase of unemployed capital, and of deposits of bullion. Trade paralyzed. Interest 2¾ per cent.
July —	650,000.	Diminution of securities. Bank exports bullion, having no demand for money at home. Trade very dull. Interest 3 per cent.
Oct. —	200,000.	Small increase of securities. Trade slowly reviving. Import of bullion at an end. Interest 3 per cent.
1838—Dec. —	2,000,000.	Great diminution of securities and of deposits. Amount of unemployed capital still large, and American stocks coming for sale. Interest, however, rises to 3½ per cent.
1839—April	Par.	Increase of securities, paid for with bullion, which falls to £7,000,000. Import of American stocks, and interest rises to 3¾ per cent.
July +	900,000.	Increase of securities. Heavy payments for foreign stocks. Great diminution of deposits. Heavy drain of bullion. Severe distress. Interest 5½ per cent.
Oct. +	2,860,000.	Large increase of securities in the face of heavy drains of bullion. Bank unmanageable. On the verge of ruin. Interest 6½ per cent. Soon after, forced to apply to the bank of France for aid.
Dec. —	500,000.	Bank escapes bankruptcy. People ruined. Business at an end. Extreme distress. Interest 6½ per cent.
1840—April +	100,000.	During the whole of this year, trade continues prostrate. Money is scarce and high, interest being about 5 per cent. on the best paper, while on second rate, it can scarcely be obtained at any price: yet the bank is totally unable to afford relief. The ruin of trade has diminished her circulation and that of all other banks. Deposits are smaller, and the bullion tends rather to diminish than to increase, because she has ruined the people of the United States, Canada, India, and others of the best customers of England, who are no longer able to be purchasers of manufactured goods. Distress is universal abroad, and poverty and starvation equally so at home.
July —	600,000.	
Oct. —	200,000.	
Dec. —	600,000.	

1841—April —	£700,000.	Presents precisely the same features as 1840. The bank, always able to promote speculation and to produce ruin, is now, as always before, utterly unable to afford aid. There is no confidence. Interest is about 5 per cent. for the best paper, and enormously high for any but the best. The few grow rich upon large interest, and the many are ruined.
July —	700,000.	
Oct. +	400,000.	
Dec. —	200,000.	

With 1842, the circulation of the bank rises to £19,500,000, which, added to "the rest," and £2,500,000 of public deposits, would give a trading capital of nearly £25,000,000, which may be taken as the *par*, but there is no demand for money. The nation is paralyzed, because its customers have been ruined.

1842—Oct. —	£2,500,000.	During this period, the bullion grows from £9,000,000 to £16,000,000, and interest falls from 3 to 1¾ per cent. The bank is unable to use its own means, even at the lowest rate of interest; and she now loses all that she had gained by over-trading and high interest, in the previous years, *and more*. Had her loans remained steadily at *par*, she would have exhibited a larger amount of "rest," than she was able to do after all her exertions; while the nation would have saved the vast sum that was forced abroad and lost.
Dec. —	4,500,000	
1843—April —	1,400,000	
July —	3,500,000	
Oct. —	2,800,000	
Dec. —	4,000,000	
1844—April —	2,800,000	
July —	2,500,000	
Aug. —	2,000,000	

Throughout the whole of this calamitous period, no difficulty existed but that which the bank itself had made. It forced capital to seek investment abroad, by monopolizing securities at home; whereas, had it confined its investments to the amount of its permanent means, retaining, in the form of bullion, the capital of others intrusted to its care, increasing or decreasing in amount, as its customers thought fit to deposit or to recall it; *the whole business of the institution would have been regulated by the community, it being itself a perfectly automatic machine.* While the amount of its securities was determined by the quantity of circulation in use, the amount of its bullion would have been determined by the

17 *

deposits of capital not in use; and they, like the circulation, would have been nearly a constant quantity, fluctuating, perhaps, between six and eight millions, instead of rising to eighteen, and falling to six millions.*

We will now briefly show the working of the proposed system. Let us suppose that, on a given day, the bank has a circulation of £20,000,000, for which she holds securities: and deposits to the amount of £10,000,000, for which she has bullion: that, in the course of the following week, she nas returned to her notes to the amount of £200,000, to be placed to the credit of depositors; and that, in the next, £200,000 are withdrawn in bullion for exportation. The following is the state of affairs, at these several periods, *under the existing system*:—

	Circulation.	Securities.	Deposits.	Bullion.
1st, - - - -	£20,000,000	£20,000,000	£10,000,000	£10,000,000
2d, - - - -	19,800,000	20,000,000	10,200,000	10,000,000
3d, - - - -	19,800,000	20,000,000	10,000,000	9,800,000

* Previously to the passage of the present law, a memorial was presented to Parliament, signed by many of the principal bankers and merchants of London, remonstrating against the restriction on the bank issues, on the ground that circumstances might arise that would render necessary some extra expansion, with a view to the preservation of merchants, bankers, and traders, from ruin; but the Minister resisted the application. He had seen the directors, in 1825, 1836, and 1839, increasing their loans, with ruin staring them in the face; and he desired to prevent the recurrence of such a state of things, by making it imperative on them to reduce as the bullion passed out of their hands. How little such has been the effect of the law, may be seen from the fact, that, in April last, when the bullion had fallen to £10,000,000, the amount of securities was greater, by £4,000,000, than it had been in December, when the bullion was £15,000,000. In all these cases, the bank found itself unable to control its own action. It had set the ball of speculation in motion, and it did not dare to stop it. A review of the proceedings of the institution cannot fail to prove to the satisfaction of every one capable of understanding them, that no case, appearing to require such interference as was desired by the petitioners, has occurred within the last thirty years, except when produced by the over-trading of the bank itself; and that by taking away the power to produce speculation, and thus striking at the root of the evil, would be obviated all necessity for interference with a view to remedy its consequences; even had experience shown that it was in the power of the bank to afford any remedy, which has not been the case. It has always exhibited herself as powerless to relieve the community from the consequences of disturbance, as it has been powerful for its production.

The fact of the return of any part of the circulation, is evidence of the existence of an excess in that portion of the currency, requiring correction, which correction is now being made by the public. Its conversion subsequently into gold for exportation, is evidence of the existence of an excess in the currency generally. To re-issue the notes thus returned, would be to re-produce the excess, and with it a necessity for farther correction. As fast as issued, they would be brought back, and gold would be demanded for them: the public thus enforcing the remedy just as steadily as the bank directors were producing the disease. If the latter persisted for any length of time, they would find themselves drained of bullion, in consequence of a constant effort to compel the public to keep on hand a larger amount of notes than they wanted; precisely as they have been on so many recent occasions.

The remedy for an excess of currency is a reduction of the amount. Had the directors, at the close of the first of the two weeks above given, sold £200,000 of their securities, they would have absorbed £200,000 of the unemployed capital of individuals placed with them for safe keeping, and would thereby have re-established the equilibrium; thus preventing any necessity for the exportation of capital in quest of employment. If, on the other hand, deposits were converted into circulation, it would be evidence of a slight deficiency of the latter, and the bank might, with advantage to itself and the community, exchange an equal amount of its gold for securities.

Had such been the system, there would have been no revulsions to alarm the prudent and drive them from trade. On the contrary, steady action and profitable business would have tended to increase the number of persons among whom to select its customers; to increase the permanent value of capital; and to increase the dividends of the stockholders. While the proprietors of the bank were thus benefited, the people of England would have been enabled to avoid losses, to the extent probably of £100,000,000, resulting from the violent revulsions in the United States: Canada: South America: India: and in almost every other part of the world: produced by the extraordinary unsteadiness that has been manifested. The directors, on their part, would have avoided the anxiety resulting from the existence of large liabilities accompanied by small means, and they would have been spared the humiliation of seeking aid from the continent. All would have been benefited.

It is usual to attribute the difficulties of the institution to a necessity for importing corn; but a moment's reflection will satisfy the reader, that if it retained in its possession, in bullion, the whole of the unemployed capital of individuals: *with which alone could foreign corn be purchased*, except so far as manufactures would be received in payment: it would be entirely unimportant whether the owners thereof withdrew it, or left it in its vaults. If corn were needed, the owners of bullion would exchange their commodity for the one they wanted, and the bank would have no occasion to feel that any such transaction had taken place. It would have the same amount to invest, whether the bullion in its vaults were £1,000,000, or £16,000,000. Corn would rise in price, and sugar would fall: but the rate of interest, or the price of money, would be scarcely at all effected. Not having availed itself of the depositors' capital, to force down the rate of interest, the withdrawal thereof would not compel it to raise that rate. Perfect steadiness in the currency is entirely consistent with variations in the crops. They have no necessary connection with each other.

It may be asked, why the use of the money of individual depositors should be more calculated to produce unsteadiness than that of the £2,500,000 of public deposits above referred to? The answer is, that to that extent the public appear never to seek to use the funds in the hands of the bank; whereas, individual depositors never willingly permit their capital to lie unproductive, and are always seeking the means of investing it. The man who has £1000 in his desk, and is seeking to employ it, produces a certain effect upon the market; but if, while thus engaged, he places it for safe keeping with a man who uses it, a double effect is produced. His £1000 is invested, while he is in the market seeking for an opportunity to make it yield him interest. Prices rise in consequence of this double action, which does not take place in regard to the small amount of public deposits to which we have referred.

In regard to those deposits, we have had abundant evidence of the injury that may result from permitting them to be employed to an unlimited extent. The excess of receipts, in 1835 and 1836, was chiefly at New York, and at the land offices of the West. As fast as it was accumulated at the first, it was lent out to the merchants to enable them to extend their importations, and thus increase the surplus revenue. In the West, it was lent to land speculators, who paid it to the government on one day, and on the next borrowed it from the bank to buy more land. The government parted with its land, for which it held the engagement of a deposit bank, and the latter held the note of the land-jobber. In the same way, the surplus of the British revenue being lent out to the merchants of Liverpool and London, has a tendency to promote importation and to stimulate improperly the increase of the public revenue: and consequently to increase the surplus to be left at the disposal of the bank.

Much disturbance is now produced by the accumulation of the public moneys during the quarter, to be lent by the bank, and then called in, to be paid out in dividends: the consequence of which is, that money is always higher before, and lower after quarter-day, than the average. Were the bank deprived of the power of *lending* those moneys, a mode would probably be devised of *paying* them in advance: and thus a cause of disturbance, now existing, would be removed. The mass of the public debt is held by institutions and individuals that intend to keep it, and that desire to re-

2 C

invest the interest at the most favourable moment. Were the bank to arrange to anticipate the dividends on all stock deposited with them, the owners would soon find that their interests would be promoted by receiving them in anticipation of the general payment, and investing when money was least abundant, rather than by waiting until it was most abundant: and by degrees the business of paying dividends, instead of being crowded into a few days, would be distributed throughout the year; to the benefit of the bank and the receivers of dividends. The one would receive interest for the time anticipated, and the other would invest with more advantage from being able to obtain them at any moment: while the community would gain, because the interval between the accumulation and investment of capital would be lessened.

England is now the great market for the gold and silver of the world, and there is, consequently, towards it a constant stream of those commodities. They are arrested on their way from the place of production to that of consumption, and pass from hand to hand for a short time; but their tendency to the crucible of the goldsmith is constant, and their arrival there inevitable. That country has thus far been to the monetary world, what the ocean is to the physical: and the tendency of water to the one is not greater nor more steady than would have been that of bullion to the other, had the level been preserved as steadily. The slightest increase in the supply of water, in any quarter, is marked by an increase of that tendency; while with every diminution in the supply its movements become more sluggish. Were the ocean to change its level forty, fifty, or a hundred feet at a time, as does the currency of England, not only would the flow be arrested, but we should see established a counter-current, producing ruin in all parts of the earth. Precisely such is the effect produced by England, when she compels the export of bullion to any part of America: a trade as unnatural as would be the export of cotton to India, or of tea to China. With the United States, the export of the precious metals is a proper branch of trade. They are one of the channels by which the products of Mexico pass to the place of chief consumption, and silver flows from thence as naturally as do cotton and corn.

It may be said, that even were the bank regular in her operations, she could not control the movements of the other banks. Such is not the case. She has been unable to regulate them in time past, because, from her own irregularity of action she has been unable even to control her own movements. With *perfect steadiness* on her part, every change in every part of the kingdom would be as readily observed as are variations in the temperature by the nicest thermometer; and the check to every attempt at excess would follow instantly on its discovery. The people themselves are competent to this, as will be shown whenever they shall have afforded them the means of discovering the existence of such excess, but that is not afforded by the law of 1844, which makes the blind leaders of the blind.

We think that a careful examination of the facts we have submitted must tend to satisfy our readers that it is possible to establish a system of such perfectly steady action that the movements of the world may be measured by it. Perfect freedom of action would be far preferable; but as it is highly unlikely that the bank will be, for some years to come, divested of the monopolies she enjoys, we have desired to show that she might exercise her privileges in a manner that would prevent all further injury: and that she might do this, not only without loss to her stockholders, but with positive advantage to them. She has a monopoly of the right of furnishing the only species of currency that circulates throughout the kingdom, and she has likewise a monopoly of the public deposits. She should confine herself to the employment of the capital thus placed at her disposal, and not enter into competition with the owners of unemployed capital placed with her for safe keeping; but leave them to determine for themselves whether they will use it or not, and whether they will themselves superintend its management, or associate with their neighbours to open shops for that purpose. If there be a legitimate demand for money, they have a right to the enjoyment of the interest paid for the use of their own capital. If there be not: and they are quite as competent to judge of this as the bank directors: it is injurious to them to have a competitor in the market, offering to lend their money, when they themselves cannot find persons willing to employ it: and thus forcing down the rate of interest, and compelling them to seek abroad for means of investment. Were she to abstain from such interferences with individual interests, she might reconcile the community to the continuance, for a little further time, of the monopoly she now enjoys, and she would certainly obtain a higher average rate of interest than now: do as large an average amount of business: and make quite as good dividends: particularly if competition should induce a little economy in the management, which now does not exist. What is true of her, is equally true on this side of the Atlantic. Our banks have been led away by the idea of privileges for which they have paid, and which they have desired to use: and the consequence has been that their dividends have been less than they would have been under a system of perfect freedom of competition. All the banks of Pennsylvania divided, for a quarter of a century, from 1815 to 1840, *less than six and a tenth per cent.*

The average of the dividends of Massachusetts and Rhode Island, where freedom has been almost perfect, has been nearer the value of money in those states than it has been in the other. Over-trading produces a necessity for under-trading; and not only is the excess of gain then lost, but there is accumulated a mass of bad debts, tending for a time to deprive the stockholders of dividends altogether; as we have so recently seen to be the case. The receiver of eight per cent. in one year has nothing in the next, and is obliged to congratulate himself, if his capital, though unprofitable, prove yet whole. Throughout the country, it is seen, that the monetary systems of the States are steady and profitable to the owners and the community, in direct proportion to the freedom that is granted. The greatest of all regulators is perfect liberty of action, securing unlimited competition, whether by individuals or associations: leaving to the latter to arrange with the public the terms on which they will trade with each other, whether of limited or unlimited liability.

We have said that banks were as harmless as shoe-shops. Both are subject to precisely the same laws. The one is a place to which shoemakers bring their products, with a view to enable each person in want of shoes to obtain such as will exactly fit his feet. If no such place of exchange existed, men with large feet would be travelling one street, and encountering men with only small shoes for sale, while in another street, would be found men with large shoes meeting men with small feet: the result of all which would be that many would have corns from wearing shoes that were too large; while of the rest, the chief part would be suffering with pinched toes, bunions, and other results of shoes that were too small. The quantity of shoes in market would be always greater than would be needed if there existed a place of exchange, and the loss of time by both buyers and sellers would be exceedingly great; and withal nobody would be fitted, and there would be no steadiness of prices. The shoemaker would be enabled at one moment to insist upon more than he had a right to claim, because possessing the only pair that would suit the man to be fitted; but at another, when half a dozen with the same sized shoes chanced to meet with the single customer, the price would be as much below the mark. Where trade is free, shoe-shops exist in the quantity necessary for the business to be done, and their number tends to increase in a proportion rather below that of the increase of the population and wealth of the community; and with every step in this progress, men are enabled more readily to supply themselves with shoes: while the quantity required to be kept on hand by the shoe-dealer, tends steadily to decrease in its proportion to the quantity sold, and the price becomes daily more and more uniform. There is a diminution in the number of shoes idle for want of feet, and of feet idle for want of shoes.

A bank is a shop belonging to the owners of disengaged capital: money, or currency: who club their means for its formation, and then divide the same into such sums as suit the wants of the various persons who desire to obtain the aid of capital: thus making shoes to fit the feet of their customers. One hundred very small capitalists, thus associated, may, in one place, grant aid to the great manufacturer; while, in another place, may be seen half a dozen large capitalists, owners of the bank, granting aid to a thousand farmers, mechanics, small traders, &c.* Where no such shop exists, the farmer may want aid to purchase seed or manure: the mechanic may suffer for want of a steam-engine: and the manufacturer for want of ability to keep on hand a sufficient supply of materials: and all may seek for a long time before finding a person that has the precise sum they wish to borrow, and is willing to receive the security they have to offer; while at the same moment, other persons who are able to afford the desired aid, and would be willing to receive the security, are seeking in vain for persons willing to employ their capital. The money-shop here performs the same duty as the shoe-shop. It fits the labourer with capital, and the capitalist with labour; and the less interference the more perfect is the fit. Were the trade in money free, the number of money-shops would, like that of the shoe-shops, increase in a ratio somewhat less rapid than that of wealth and population; and with every step in this progress, there would be increased facility

* Where land is divided, and trade free, large capitalists do not buy bank stock; because their capital, otherwise invested, yields larger returns. No better evidence need be desired of unsoundness in any system, than the fact that such men hold bank stock, to any extent, as a permanent investment. anks should, and would, if let alone, be only larger savings' funds.

for promptly investing capital, and increased facility on the part of the labourer in obtaining the aid he desired. The amount of capital unproductive to its owners for want of labour, and remaining on deposit to their credit, would diminish; as would the power of banks to trade upon borrowed capital: and thus every increase of freedom would tend to give increased steadiness in their action.

The banks of Rhode Island, and of New England generally, trade largely on capital, and little on credit, because capital can be invested promptly and freely. In England, it is directly the reverse. Restrictions throw the trade into the hands of the few; and banks of all kinds, from the great one in Threadneedle street, down to the smallest private banker in the kingdom, trade upon credit rather than upon capital. Joint-stock banks are bolstered up by long lists of what are termed "a wealthy proprietary," who are frequently only great speculators; for men who are really wealthy will not assume the liabilities to which owners of bank stocks are subjected.

The object sought to be obtained by aid of the several bank restriction acts is directly the reverse of what has been described as existing in Rhode Island. They prohibit the formation of new associations for the opening of shops at which the owners of disengaged capital can meet the owners of labour that need its aid, while they maintain in full force all the previously existing penalties and liabilities; and thus tend to increase the quantity of capital idle in the form of deposits: to increase the power of banks to overtrade: and to produce speculation, to result in the destruction of their customers and themselves.

They tend also to diminish the facility of obtaining circulating notes, and thus to increase the quantity kept on hand by individuals: thereby enabling banks to overtrade by means of their circulation, to an extent greater than could exist were they not in force. Every provision of those acts tends to increase the power of the bank to produce disturbance, by overtrading at one time, followed by undertrading at the next. Every part of them tends to increase restrictions, and to produce increased unsteadiness in the supply of money, and inequality in its price. Every part tends to enable the few to enrich themselves at the cost of the many. Every part is in opposition to the spirit of the age. Freedom of trade, whether in money or in cotton, goes hand in hand with civilization. The bank restriction acts are a step, and a serious one, towards barbarism. They are in keeping with the system of tithes, settlements, and entails, by which the improvement of the land is prevented; and with that which compels men to be still using turnpikes where they might have had railroads: thereby preventing them from combining the lime with the clay, and compelling them to cultivate poor soils for 9*s*. a week, with corn at a high price; when they might be now cultivating rich soils at 12*s*. a week, and raising food that could be sold cheaply, and yet pay better rents than at present. They tend to prevent the local application of capital; and to force it into London, to be driven abroad: when, if used at home, it would yield twice the return. They are not in keeping with the time.

In regard to money, the policy of France has been the same as in all others of the machinery of exchange, *viz.* to increase its quantity and deteriorate its quality: and thus to prevent the application of capital or labour to production, and to compel men to continue to cultivate the poor soils. She has silver in abundance; but she has few spades, ploughs, horses, cattle, or steam-engines. Every thing is forced to centre in Paris; and the government borrows at four per cent., while the poor cultivator pays in interest, taxes on registration of mortgages, and law expenses, more than half the product of his little property. The *government* cultivates Algeria, and *he* abandons the meadow to seek the hill-side; or, in despair, flies from his land and turns soldier: preferring to eat the bread raised *by* others, rather than to raise bread *for* others, while eating himself the miserable compound of chestnuts, a little flour and water, that falls to his share. In regard to currency, as everywhere, the rule of France is, and has always been: great means for small ends.

Closely connected in trade with England, the people of the United States have known little of self-government in regard to the machinery of trade known as *money*. At one moment capital stagnated in London, and States and individuals were solicited to take it at low interest; and canals, and roads, and factories, and furnaces, were commenced. At the next, capital was dear in London; and their markets were filled with cloths and iron, to be converted into money, to be transmitted to England; and then prices fell, and manufacturers and iron-masters were ruined. The whole system of that country has been, and is, unsound and irregular; because she has surrounded land and capital with restrictions that forbid the existence of regularity. For a series of years she forbade the investment of capital in roads, and forced it out to Illinois and Michigan: and soon all was ruin abroad and at home. Now she is forcing it into roads, and all is ruin at home. Happily for the people of the United States, no loans were made to them, or they too would be ruined; but how far they will escape remains yet to be seen. She has commenced the habit of looking towards home; but many years have yet, we fear, to elapse before she will fairly apply her wealth and labour to the production of food; cultivating her own rich soils instead of the poor ones of Australia and Canada: and until she shall do so, her system must continue to be unsound and irregular, unprofitable to herself, and dangerous to those intimately connected with her in trade; and of this no further evidence need be desired than is furnished by the events of the present year.

With each step in the passage from the poor to the rich soils, population and wealth tend to increase more rapidly; and with each step in their progress, there is increased demand for both: giving to the labourer an increased proportion of a larger product; and to the owner of capital an increased return from a diminished proportion: and affording to all increased power of accumulation. The value of land increases with the development of its powers, and that development results from the application of labour and capital. Every measure tending to restrict the amount applied, tends to lessen the wages of the labourer, and the profits of the capitalist, both of whom *can* seek elsewhere the employment denied to them at home: and tends in a still greater degree to affect the interests of the land that *cannot* fly. The landowner is therefore, most of all, interested in the abolition of every regulation and restriction that tends to the expulsion of either; and especially interested in the repeal of every law that tends to prevent local unions for the formation of banks, insurance companies, manufacturing associations, and all other modes of combination tending to enable the fashioner to eat his food on the spot on which it is produced; and thus to improve the quality and diminish the quantity of the machinery of exchange. With each step in the diminution of the *quantity* required for use, the *quality* improves, and fluctuations tend to cease. With each step, banks become more useful and more safe; with each, man acquires increased power to command the aid of wealth; with each he obtains increased reward to labour; with each, the precious metals become less *necessary* as a part of the machinery of exchange; and with each he acquires increased *power* to command the use of them for other purposes tending to improve his taste, and to promote his enjoyment of life.

The PAST says to the sovereign of the PRESENT: "If you would reign over a numerous, wealthy, and prosperous, people: diminish the machinery of exchange between the producer and the consumer, by reducing the demand for money to pay taxes, thus diminishing the necessity for tax-gatherers; and increasing the number of the producers."

To the capitalist: "If you wish large returns to your capital: labour for the abolition of laws tending to restrict you in regard to the modes of its employment."

To the landlord: "If you wish large rents: oppose all measures tending to the export of wealth and population, and labour to remove restrictions on the land."

To the labourer: "If you wish large wages: seek union with your fellows; labour and economize; promote the growth of wealth; and wealth will give you power."

To all: "Avoid war and waste!"

CHAPTER VI.

MAN AND HIS FELLOW MAN.

THE early cultivator has no means of self-defence. He may be enslaved by any one stronger than himself. His neighbour is distant, and they are separated from each other by forests and swamps. The strong man constitutes himself proprietor of their persons and their lands, the proceeds of which he receives, allowing them what he pleases in return. He is the lord, and they are serfs or slaves. They cultivate the poor soils, whose small returns scarcely afford sufficient food for themselves: but of this small quantity the lord takes a large proportion. They *raise* wheat and hogs, but they *eat* bread made of oats and acorns. Voluntary union being here impossible among the many, the few have power to compel union; and men work together in gangs, to build forts or castles for their masters: to murder the subjects of his neighbour lord: or to burn their houses and ravage their little farms. Sometimes, we find them associated together in larger masses for the building of palaces, the erection of pyramids, great cathedrals, and magnificent tombs; or for the cutting of canals through fertile lands, whose pestilential air sweeps them off by hundreds of thousands: and again, similar masses are found plundering rich cities; ravaging kingdoms; fighting battles by sea and land; or building pyramids of human heads: the object of all these operations being to hand down to an admiring world the names of a Tamerlane, Bajazet, Scipio, Frederick, Louis, or Napoleon, who are held to be *great*, because of the infinite littleness of the people over whose destinies they rule.

In all cases of involuntary union, the principle of unlimited liability: *solidarité:* is seen to exist. The lord wants a certain number of men, and they must come. He loses a portion of his subjects in battle, and he calls on the balance to make up the deficiency. He wants a certain amount of annual contribution, and those who can pay must make up for those who cannot. The Hindoo who remains at home pays the taxes of those who fly to seek in plundering others, satisfaction for having themselves been plundered. By the conscription laws of France, under the Empire, and perhaps even now, the family is bound for the services in the field of its members; and if the elder son desert, the second is bound to take his place. The nation is held bound to supply the demands of the army, and when the boys of eighteen are exhausted, the conscription is anticipated and those of sixteen are taken to fill the ranks. Nero would have the people of Rome with but one head, that he might take it off. Towns and cities are held by conquerors bound for the conduct of all their citizens, and history is filled with cases of their utter destruction, accompanied by the murder of the men, and the violation of women, in satisfaction for the error, or the crimes of individuals. With the growth of population and wealth, the better soils are cultivated, and men are enabled to live closer to each other: and voluntary union tends gradually to supersede the involuntary. Ceasing to labour in gangs, they cultivate pieces of land for which they pay rent: and thus individuality grows with wealth, while union tends to give them a self-defensive power, by aid of which they obtain a gradually increasing proportion of the product of their labour.

The fashioner needs the service of the labourer, and he is willing to protect him in leaving the service of his lord, to come to him in the little town. The lord looks with jealousy upon all voluntary union, as tending to lessen his powers of government: and at first he seizes his slave, carrying him back to the land from which he had escaped. By degrees, however, the town grows and becomes strong to defend itself and the runaway serfs who seek refuge within its walls. This state of things having arrived, it becomes necessary for the lord to content himself with a smaller proportion of the proceeds of labour, that he may retain a portion of his serfs. To make amends for this, he must devote more of his income to the improvement of his land: that the amount of his rents may grow, even if his proportion diminish. New soils are brought into cultivation, and the returns are larger; but with each step in this progress, there arises an increased power of consumption on the part of the people, and a more rapid increased demand for labour in the towns: and thus the competition of landlord and manufacturer tends to enable the labourer to have a continually increasing power to determine for himself where he will labour, and what shall be his share of the proceeds. With the increase of his power over the materials of the land, he thus gradually acquires the exercise of the right of self-government.

His proportion thus increasing with the growth of wealth, he is incited to exertion: and with the increased power of determining for himself the manner in which his labour shall be applied, it becomes daily more productive. His habits are inexpensive, while those of his lord are not. He accumulates, while the other dissipates. He improves his style of living, and the other is compelled to do the same. He can afford it, while the other cannot. He buys land, which the other is forced to sell. He then cultivates his own land and keeps the rent himself, applying it to cultivating the better soils. There is thus a constant tendency to the division and transfer of land and power, as wealth and population grow: and to the establishment of individuality, and of perfect equality of physical, moral, intellectual, and political condition.

If we look to England in the days of the Saxons, we see immense bodies of land held by Earl Godwin, and other great lords. In the days of the Conqueror a single individual held seven hundred manors. Later, the county of

Norfolk numbered but sixty-six proprietors. If we look to Scotland, we find the number of proprietors increase as we come downwards in point of time, in all those counties in which population and wealth grow rapidly, and the better soils are cultivated: while it diminishes as we recede from the rich soil of the Lothians, until we find the whole of the poor county of Sutherland the property of a single individual, busily engaged in expelling all the small people whose families have for ages exercised rights over land, guarantied originally by word, but unhappily not *by deed*. If we look to France, we see vast properties continuing for centuries undivided because of the slow growth of wealth and population, and so remaining until the general confiscation of the Revolution. Till then, the lord was still lord, and exercised the *droit de poursuite* against the person of his absconding serf who sought employment in the towns: which were, because of their universal poverty, incapable of affording him protection. In Spain, and Mexico, and Sicily, and India, and Hungary, we see immense bodies of land in the hands of individuals. In all those countries, war has prevented the growth of wealth and population, and the poorer soils are still alone cultivated. The reward to labour is small. The labourer has a small proportion of a small product, and is a slave, or little better: while the land-owner has a large proportion, with but little revenue where his possessions are not immense. If thence we pass to the Netherlands, we find the better soils carefully cultivated, the return to labour larger, the condition of the people better, and the power of the lord diminished. There, the tendency to an increase of wealth, population, and freedom, was at one time greater than in any portion of continental Europe: but the oft-repeated invasions of French armies made of that unfortunate country a great battle-field, and drove a large portion of the most useful population to seek elsewhere the security denied to them at home. Progress has been, therefore, slow, but with the continued peace of thirty years, we see gra dually advancing the power of the labourer over the products of his labour, and therewith a steadily increasing tendency towards perfect self-government.

The rent of land in England is estimated at £30,000,000, and the proportion which it bears to the product is supposed to be one-fifth, which gives £150,000,000 as the total amount. The number of proprietors is estimated at 200,000, giving £150 as the average rental of each. The total product in the days of the Edwards could scarcely have exceeded one-fiftieth of this amount, or about £3,000,000. Of this, the lord claimed probably two-thirds, or £2,000,000. The number of freeholders recorded in Domesday-Book is twenty-six thousand, but most of these must have been very small, as individuals had whole counties: while the manors held by others varied from two hundred to almost eight hundred. In the calamitous times that followed the Conquest, and particularly during the contest which preceded the accession of the Plantagenets, the mass of the small freeholders were swept away, and land concentrated itself in fewer hands; and we think it doubtful if the number at this period, who were really proprietors of freeholds, could have exceeded two thousand: with an average income of £1000.*

The population being about two and a half millions, of whom at least two-thirds could have had little employment but in agriculture, and the remaining million of the product being divided among them we have 12*s.* per head for each member of the family, or 2*l.* 8*s.* for a man and his wife and two children. That this is not very wide of the mark, is obvious from the fact that the oxherd of this period has but 7*s.* per annum, and the shepherd 10*s.*, in addition, perhaps, to a very small quantity of very bad food, without clothing, or any other perquisite. A quarter of wheat is sometimes

* In regard to this and other estimates which follow, it will, we presume, be obvious to the reader that strict accuracy is not important, even if it could be obtained. They are given with a view merely to illustrate the principle.

2*s*. and sometimes 24*s*., and frequently much more. If, therefore, we estimate the annual wages at one quarter of wheat, or eight bushels, it is probably above the truth: and this is all that he receives for his own clothing and for procuring a supply of food and clothing for his children; supposing his wife to support herself.

The product of land at the present time being taken at £150,000,000, of which one-fifth goes to the landlord, there remain £120,000,000 to be divided; and if the persons dependent on agriculture be three times as great as in the former period, this gives £24 per head. There has arisen, however, since then, a large class of persons engaged in various operations connected with agriculture, intermediate between the land-owner and the labourer; who absorb, perhaps, one-half of this amount, leaving the remaining half to be divided among the labourers: and giving £12 per head, or £48 for the support of a family, consisting of a man, his wife, and two children. This amount is perhaps too great. The latest estimate we have seen is £40, and this will not, we think, vary much from the truth.

The average rent of the landlord at the close of the fourteenth century being taken at £1000, and the average amount received by the labourer's family at £2, 8*s*., it follows that the landlord's income of this period is sufficient to enable him to pay almost four hundred men: while the average of our day being £150, and the labourer's family requiring £40, the average power of the representatives of land is not equal to the pay of even four labourers. The ability, in the early period, to pay so many men enables land to command their services for the maintenance of its power, and the lord is, therefore, always surrounded by hosts of men ready to do his bidding: whether for the collection of rents from his own tenants, or the plunder of those of his neighbour. He is supreme legislator, exercising his powers *Dei Gratia:* and to question his right is treason against the state, *i. e.* against himself.

By degrees, however, wealth and population grow, better soils are cultivated, and forests disappear. Roads are made, and the little territories of the lords being thus brought into communication with each other, towns and cities grow: and the people obtain power to take to themselves a larger proportion of the proceeds of their labour: now become doubly productive. Out of the little and scattered territories grows a kingdom: and the towns and cities, and the labourers, feel the benefit of increased wealth and union in the gradual diminution of the thousand oppressions under which they have thus far laboured. The right of the landlord to the enjoyment of the tenant's wife: and his right to pursue his labourer, and inherit his goods: die away. Population, and wealth, and union, increase still further. With each step man rises in the scale until at length he comes to be consulted in regard to affairs of State, and the payment of contributions. The people are becoming strong, because they work and economize. The landlords are becoming weak, because they hunt, and feast, and make war. From that time to the present, such has been the course of affairs. With every step in the growth of wealth and population, we see evidence of an increasing tendency to union among the people, because of the constant augmentation of the means of production, intercourse, and exchange: and freedom follows union. With every such step, the power of the labourer over the product of his labour, whether in the distribution between himself and the land as represented by the lord: or between himself and the government as represented by the lords assembled in Parliament: has increased, while the power of the land and its representatives to control the movement of society, has diminished. With the more equal division of property, the class interested in maintaining the security of person and property has increased in numbers and power: while the class possessing power to disturb the public peace has diminished in relative wealth and strength. Security at home, and comparative peace abroad, tend now to facilitate the production of wealth, and population tends rapidly to increase as better soils come into cultivation : and with each step we see a diminution in the power of the few to control the action of the many. The right to make laws in virtue of descent from lords of olden time is no longer, in regard to questions of general interest, exercised in opposition to the wishes of those who hold their power from the people. Thirty years since, the House of Commons still, in a great degree, represented land. Even then the poor soils continued to be cultivated. Wealth grew, and better soils were brought into activity: and man and his interests acquired power in that house, at the cost of land. Fifteen years have since rolled round, and man has even at this moment acquired a stronger representation than ever before. He has obtained a vast accession to his power over his actions, and all at the cost of land.

The value of labour and of talent is daily rising. The value of mere brute-wealth, unaided by mind, is daily falling. The time seems to be at hand when every man must work, if he would maintain his position in society. The direction of affairs has fallen somewhat under the control of mind, and has been, to a certain extent, rescued from that of mere matter. That this process is still going on, is every day more obvious. The men of our day are the representatives of a considerable portion of the popular mind. The measures of Sir Robert Peel and Lord John Russell differ little, because they are the decrees of a larger portion of the people than has heretofore controlled the management of their own affairs. With another step the whole people will take part therein, and then steadiness of action will begin. These results, too, are the direct consequence of measures to which the representatives of land are, and have been, prompted by a desire for the advancement of their own material interests.

In all countries power has gone with the ownership of land, and hence it is that where poor men cultivate poor soils, the few appear so great. With the growth of wealth and population the land becomes divided, and the many acquire power over themselves and their actions, in accordance with the decree of the great Creator, who made all men equal.

The progress has been, as yet, comparatively slow, because landlords have been the makers of laws: and large armies, and great fleets, and vast church establishments, and numerous colonies, have afforded opportunity to provide for their children out of the public purse. With the increasing desire for peace that in all countries accompanies the growth of wealth and the habit of self-government, these tendencies are passing away, and wealth grows more rapidly than ever: enabling the labourer and the mechanic, whether employer or employed, still more rapidly to improve their condition: while the land tends daily more and more to be compelled to provide for the families of its lords, heretofore supported out of taxes on beer, sugar, tea, and coffee. With the arrival of the time when fleets, and armies, and colonies shall cease to exist, and it seems likely soon to arrive, the division of land will proceed more rapidly than ever before: and the necessity for the exertion of their powers, whether mental or physical, will be more than ever felt by each member of the community, from the lowest to the highest.

Until recently, the land, as represented by the landlord and the Church, preyed upon the tenant. The latter made improvements by which he *might* profit during the lease, as the former *certainly* did at its close. Recently, the landlord has taken a permanent lease from the Church at a fixed rent. Now, the tenants are demanding long leases, with "tenant right"—or a right to be paid for improvements. From that point to perpetual leases, the distance is not great: for as the power of man over his labour goes up, wealth increases more and more rapidly, and the power of land over man goes down. Every new soil brought into cultivation gives power to the tenant, while diminishing that of his lord.

Every railroad that is made: every engine employed in drainage: every tile kiln that is built: every newspaper that is printed: and every monopoly that is abolished: tends to improvement and equality of condition. They are inseparable, and those who would prevent the last, can do so only by retarding the progress of the first.

Such has been the tendency in every country in which growing wealth and population have facilitated the cultivation of the better soils, and have enabled men to live in closer connection with each other; while the reverse has been the case in every one in which they have declined. They may be seen increasing in the happier days of Rome, when Latium was filled with populous and prosperous towns which made treaties of commerce with Carthage: and the tendency to freedom was then great. Wealth disappeared as Rome declined towards the barbarism of the days of Scipio, of Marius, and of Octavius. Population diminished, and the best soils went out of cultivation. The free labour of the Roman citizens was replaced by that of slaves, and the pauper population of the city was fed by contributions levied upon Sicily, and Africa, and Egypt. With growing poverty land acquired a daily increasing power, and the habit of self-government disappeared; the internal history of the State, almost from the days of the elder Brutus, being but a record of contests for power by *parvenus* nobles on the one hand, and nobles by descent on the other: and yet the triumph of a plebeian demagogue in securing for himself and his fellows a share in the general plunder of the people of the State, abroad or at home, is marked in the story books which pass for histories even in our days, as a triumph of the people themselves.

With the diminution of wealth in Gaul, we see arise the great land owner, with square leagues of territory, and surrounded by hosts of slaves. He is seen, too, in Attica and in Sparta, as Greece declined.

The prudent and industrious man grows rich and strong.

He can enforce his rights, because he respects those of others. The man who fights and drinks, closes his career in the poor-house, having lost all power of self-government. So is it with nations. In the history of none can we find this more thoroughly illustrated than in that of France, which presents a record of selfishness, rapacity, and weakness, scarcely paralleled among nations claiming a place among civilized communities. Her kings have plundered princes, and nobles, and people. Her nobles and princes have plundered each other, and have been ever ready to combine with foreign nations against the State. From the days of Charlemagne to the present time, there has been, as formerly in Rome, an unceasing contest between the plebeian aristocracy that owed its wealth to the plunder of the last war, civil or foreign: and the more noble aristocracy which derived its title thereto by descent from the heroes of that which next, or next but one, preceded it: and the sole question between them has been as to who should now exercise the right of plunder, at home and abroad. The government has been one of wealth derived from the spoils of war; from taxation, oppressive beyond imagination; and from the spoliation of men who were sufficiently advanced in civilization to desire to apply their faculties to the purposes of trade, or sufficiently enlightened to think for themselves in matters of religion. Both factions: the new nobles and the old: have exerted their energies in plundering and murdering the people, and the people have done the same by them. In her external relations, we find the same universal selfishness and rapacity miscalled "love of glory." The consequence has been universal feebleness. The people have been unable to assert their rights against princes and nobles, while princes and nobles have been equally powerless against kings and ministers: and the whole nation has exhibited at all times, from the days of Rollo to that of Waterloo, an almost total incapacity for self-defence. French armies have been, time after time, defeated in Holland, Germany, Switzerland, Spain, and

Italy: while foreign armies have repeatedly, unresisted, traversed France for hundreds of miles, and her severest defeats have been on her own soil. Turbulence and rapacity, vanity and feebleness, are the characteristics which distinguish her history beyond that of any nation of Europe. Under such circumstances, self-government could have no existence.

By no people have the rights of others been so much respected as by the people of the English colonies of America, now the United States. In their progress west, they have encountered decaying tribes of savages, whose vanity has sometimes produced war. In their progress south-west, they have encountered the half-civilized people of Mexico; and there, again, the vanity of the barbarian has produced a war that we could wish had been avoided. With these exceptions, they have never fired a musket but in self-defence. Peace has given wealth and strength to the people and to the nation. Every man determines for himself what he will do with his time and his talents; selling them to the best advantage: and every one participates in determining the amount of contribution that shall be required for the service of the community of which he is a member.* Self-government exists to a degree never before known; and increasing wealth and population, the results of peace, give strength to the nation among the community of nations. The largest producers of the world, they are the largest consumers, and their trade is valuable: a fact which is due to the use of spades and ploughs in preference to that of swords and pistols. Without fleets and armies, they exercise a self-defensive power unknown to nations who employ important portions

---

* "If he be a subject in all that concerns the mutual relations of citizens, he is free and responsible to God alone for all that concerns himself. Hence arises the maxim that every one is the best and sole judge of his own private interest, and that society has no right to control a man's actions, unless they are prejudicial to the common weal, or unless the common weal demands his co-operation. This doctrine is universally admitted in the United States." —*De Tocqueville.*

of their people in carrying muskets and burning powder, and require from other portions heavy contributions for their support while thus employed. France employs thousands of labourers in fortifying Paris, while New York, at one-tenth of the cost, and in little more time, places twelve hundred thousand volumes in her district-school libraries. France expends hundreds of millions and wastes a hundred thousand lives, in subjugating Algeria, while the people of the Union, at one-fifth of the cost and without the loss of a life, cover their vast territory with a network of railroads. The one acquires strength that enables her quietly to settle, with honour to herself, every question in which she feels an interest, and to defend every right: while the other tyrannizes over the weaker powers in her neighbourhood, and is set at defiance by those which are stronger. Restless weakness characterizes the one: and quiet strength the other.

In no portion of the population of the Union are the beautiful effects of peace and rapidly augmenting wealth better illustrated than in the comparative progress and condition of their negro population and that of the West Indies. Imported into the latter, and there involved in ruinous wars, retarding the growth of wealth: we find that race at the date of emancipation, a few years since, numbering fewer souls than had been imported. If we desire to trace the cause of this, we must look to those countries in which population tends downwards, and there we shall find the labourer badly fed: badly clothed: and over-worked: while his children perish of famine and disease. That such was there the case is obvious from the fact that from the date at which importation ceased, their number steadily declined, and was far less on the day of emancipation than it had been twenty years before.

In 1817, the slaves of Jamaica numbered 346,000. In 1829 they were reduced to 302,000, although the manumissions had been only 4000. What was the number emancipated, we do not know, but it was probably considerably less than in 1829. In the same period of twenty years, in the United States, their number would have increased to about

600,000. In Jamaica, labour was rendered unproductive by wars, restrictions, heavy taxation, and interferences with the right of property. The value of the labourer was reduced, and his owner had no interest in improving his condition: the consequence of which is seen in the total absence of increase of numbers. More slaves were imported into this one island than into the whole American Union. The one now presents to the world a very poor population of 300,000 recently redeemed from slavery: the other one of more than 3,000,000, rapidly redeeming themselves.

In the United States, on the contrary, wealth has grown rapidly, and the demand for labourers has consequently been great. The return to labour has been large, and the labourer, white or black, has had his share. Well fed, well clothed, and well housed, because valuable to his owner, the three or four hundred thousand barbarians have grown to millions of comparatively civilized men. Still slaves, and liable to be sold, they are yet exempt from the dangers of conscription, which, to the separation from parents, wives, or children, might add exposure to the dangers of war: to perish among the snows of Russia, or the sands of Africa; or to return with the habits of the camp, and unfit to resume the peaceful duties of civilized life. Still slaves, they are exempt from the dangers of being impressed and dragged from their families to spend long years upon the ocean, engaged in the work of plunder and of murder, to return perhaps with the loss of a leg or an arm: and to find that their wives have died in the almshouse, and their daughters have been driven to seek by prostitution the means of a wretched subsistence. They are still slaves, yet they have before them no dread of invading armies, resembling those which have carried rape, murder, plunder and desolation throughout Spain, Germany, Italy, Holland, the Netherlands and France. They are still slaves, but their labour is valuable because aided by the machinery of rapidly growing wealth: and their masters, unlike those of the unhappy people of Ireland, would feel it a serious sacrifice were they compelled to ship them off, stowed almost in bulk, on board of ill-found and ill-provisioned barques and brigs; to have the horrors of the middle passage repeated in these enlightened days. They are still slaves, yet their masters feel that they consult their own interests in feeding, clothing, and lodging them well, because wealth increases more rapidly than population, and their labour becomes daily more valuable. Still slaves, and liable to be sold, they consume a larger *proportion* of the proceeds of their labour than falls to the lot of half the people of Europe who claim to be considered free; and they are daily improving in their physical, moral and intellectual condition, preparatory to becoming: as they will at no very distant day, and that without violence, free citizens and proprietors of the States they inhabit: the few miserable barbarians having become a numerous, happy and civilized people, because of the maintenance of peace and consequent growth of wealth: and ready then to unite with their white fellow-citizens in the great enterprise of carrying civilization into the heart of Africa, and thus perfecting the work already so well begun. In no other country has the race increased its numbers, because in no other have wealth and the demand for labour, and the price of labour, increased so rapidly. In few, if indeed in any, of the countries of continental Europe, have the mass of the people exercised the rights of self-government in regard to the application of their time, their labour, and its proceeds, in as great a degree as have the negroes of the southern states: although still slaves, and liable to be sold. Had it been otherwise: had they furnished as many soldiers, and endured as much suffering as the people of France, Italy, Spain and Germany: their numbers would have remained as nearly stationary. Wherever wealth and population have been *permitted* to increase, freedom has invariably followed in their train: and evidence that such will be the case may be found in the anxiety of so many of the owners of slaves in relation to every measure, originating even among themselves, tending in that direction. That slavery yet endures is due to the fact that concentration is difficult, because of the constant error of the English policy, which forces men to scatter themselves over the thin soils of new states, while leaving untouched the rich soils of older ones. With concentration labour will increase in value, and land will become divided, and will be found far more valuable when well cultivated by free blacks, working for themselves and bringing into activity the better soils, than are now the lands *and* the slaves who scratch the superficial soil, while leaving untouched those more valuable which lie beneath. Slavery is one of man's weak "inventions," and it cannot endure in a country that enjoys the blessings of peace, of light taxation, and general freedom of action.

M. de Tocqueville saw the tendency to self-government, but he feared it. He did so, because he had not studied the causes of its rise, or the phenomena which mark its existence, and promote its extension. He speaks uniformly of France and the United States as the democratic states. His test of democracy is the division of land, not that of the exercise of the right of self-government. In France, division is *compulsory*. The people are poor, and the little farm of ten acres which has given a miserable support to one family, is divided into two, three, or five, by the sons: and each mortgages his share to obtain the assistance required to enable him to support a miserable existence. Land, there, still governs the man. In the United States, the system consists in letting every man judge for himself to whom he will leave his property: but if he leave behind him no directions, the law supplies his place, and says that all children have equal rights. In the one case, self-government is complete. In the other, it is nowhere seen.

The habit of voluntary association is the essential characteristic of self-government. Without that, it can have no existence. In the United States, the type of the whole system is found in "the bee:" the union of the old settlers to put up a log-house for the newly arrived family. Starting from that point, it may be found in every operation of life. The logs are to be rolled: the roof of the barn is to be raised: or the corn is to be husked. Forthwith, all assemble, and the work which to the solitary labourer would have been severe, and often impossible, is made "a frolic" of, and an hour or two of combined exertion accomplishes what otherwise might have required weeks, or months. Does the new settler want a horse, or a plough, or both? One neighbour lends him the first, and another the last, and he soon obtains a horse and plough for himself: whereas, without such aid he might have toiled in poverty for years. A place of worship is needed, and all, Methodists, Episcopalians, Baptists and Presbyterians, unite to build it; its pulpit to be occupied by the itinerant preachers of the wilderness. The church brings people to the neighbourhood, and promotes the habit of association, while the lesson taught therein promotes the love of order: and in a little time the settlement is dotted over with meeting-houses, at one of which Baptists, and at another Presbyterians meet each other, to listen to the man whom as their teacher they have united to select. Is one of these houses burnt, the congregation find all others of the neighbourhood placed at their command until the loss can be repaired. Next, we find them associating for the making of roads, and holding meetings to determine who shall superintend their construction and repair, and who assess the contributions required for the purpose. Again, we find them meeting to determine who shall represent them at the meeting of the county board, or in the Assembly of the State, or in the Congress of the Union. Again, to settle where the new school-house shall be built: and to determine who shall collect the funds necessary for the purpose, and select the books for the little library that is to enable their children to apply with advantage to themselves the knowledge of letters acquired from the teacher.* Again, they are seen forming associations for mutual insurance against horse-thieves or fire ; or little savings' funds, called banks, at which the man who wishes to buy a horse or a plough can borrow the means necessary for the purpose. Little mills grow up, the property of one or two, and expand into large ones, in which all the little capitalists of the neighbourhood, shoemakers and sempstresses, farmers and lawyers, widows and orphans, are interested: little towns, in which every resident owns his own house and lot, and is therefore directly interested in their good management, and in all matters tending to their advancement; and each feels that the first and greatest of those things is perfect security of person and property. The habit of association is seen exercising the most beneficial influence in every action of life, and it is most seen where population and wealth most abound: in the states of New England. There, we see a network of association so far exceeding what is elsewhere to be seen as to defy comparison. The shipwright, and the merchant, and the more advanced and less active capitalist, unite with the master in the ownership of the vessel: and all unite with the crew in the division of the oil which is the result of the cruise. The great merchant, the little capitalist,

* "It is not impossible to conceive the surpassing liberty which the Americans enjoy; some idea may likewise be formed of the extreme equality that subsists among them; but the political activity which pervades the United States must be seen in order to be understood. No sooner do you set foot on the American soil, than you are stunned by a kind of tumult; a confused clamour is heard on every side; and a thousand simultaneous voices demand the immediate satisfaction of their social wants. Every thing is in motion around you; here, the people of one quarter of a town are met to decide upon the building of a church; there, the election of a representative is going on; a little further, the delegates of a district are posting to the town in order to consult upon some local improvements; or in another place the labourers of a village quit their ploughs to deliberate upon the project of a road or a public school. Meetings are called for the sole purpose of declaring their disapprobation of the line of conduct pursued by the government; whilst in other assemblies the citizens salute the authorities of the day as the fathers of their country. Societies are formed which regard drunkenness as the principal cause of the evils under which the state labours, and which solemnly bind themselves to give a constant example of temperance."—*De Tocqueville.*

20

the skilful manufacturer, the foundry-master, the engineer, the workman, and the girl who tends the loom, unite in the ownership of the immense mill: and millions of yards of cloth are furnished to the world by this combined effort on the part of individuals who, if they worked alone, could not have supplied thousands. The property-holder of the city, and the little capitalists, are everywhere seen combining their exertions for the construction of roads and the building of steamboats, by the use of which the habit of union is increased. In every relation of life, the same tendency to combination of action is seen to exist. Everywhere, man is seen helping, and governing himself.* That he may do this effectually, wealth is necessary: for men cannot live near each other while forced to cultivate the worst soils. Wealth thus produces union, which is seen most to exist where wealth most exists: more in the east than in the west, and more in the north than in the south. Union in turn produces wealth, which grows more rapidly in the north and east than in the west and south: and thus wealth, combined action, and power of self-government, with a constant increase in the respect for laws which they themselves have made: manifested alike by individuals and by States whose population counts by millions:†

* "The citizen of the United States is taught from his earliest infancy to rely upon his own exertions, in order to resist the evils and the difficulties of life; he looks upon the social authority with an eye of mistrust and anxiety, and he only claims its assistance when he is quite unable to do without it."—*De Tocqueville.*

"The small number of custom-house officers employed in the United States, compared with the extent of the coast, renders smuggling very easy; notwithstanding it is less practised than elsewhere, because everybody endeavours to repress it. In America, there is no police for the prevention of fires, and such accidents are more numerous than in Europe; but in general they are more speedily extinguished, because the surrounding population is prompt in rendering assistance."—*Ibid.*

† "When the clerk of the court advances on the steps of the tribunal, and simply says: 'The state of New York *versus* the state of Ohio,' it is impossible not to feel that the court which he addresses is no ordinary body; and when he recollects that one of these parties represents a million, and the other two millions of men, one is struck by the responsibility of the seven judges whose decision is about to satisfy or disappoint so large a number of their fellow citizens."—*De Tocqueville.*

and corresponding increase in the return to labour, are seen constantly advancing; each helping and helped by the other.

Such is democracy, but of all this what exists in France? Nothing! The habit of voluntary association has no existence, except for revolutionary purposes.* No meeting can be held without the sanction of government. No church or school-house can be built without that sanction. The government pays the clergy and the teachers. It builds the roads and bridges, and it makes libraries: supports theatres: sells tobacco and salt at its own shops: grants or refuses permission to the labourer to stay or to quit the Capital: dictates the terms upon which he may offer to sell his labour: regulates elections: fixes the amount of contributions to be spent in making wars, in building hospitals for the wounded, or in pensions to men who have produced the necessity for these wars: prohibits all meetings for the discussion of its measures: interdicts such discussions in the newspapers:† opens private letters:‡ and finally surrounds the capital with cannon sufficient to lay it in ruins, if the people should talk too loudly. The democracy of France and that of her old ally against the Christians of Italy, and Germany, and Spain, are of the same character. Turkey has been ruled by pashas, who, after being allowed to gorge themselves, have been squeezed by the government. France has always been, and is, ruled by farmers-general with various titles: always squeezing the people, and sometimes squeezed. The reader who

* "In America, public opinion acts by elections and decrees; in France, it proceeds by revolutions."—*De Tocqueville.* "In countries where associations are free, secret societies are unknown. In America there are numerous factions, but no conspiracies."—*Ibid.*

† Six journals have just been seized for exposing government abuses, viz.: the Democratic Pacifique, the Estafette, the Gazette de France, the Union Monarchique, the Charivari, and the Reforme.

‡ A secret department exists in the French post-office, in which suspected letters are broken open and read, by order of the government. An *employée* who officiated in this department before the revolution of 1830 is now [1847] reinstated, at a salary of ten thousand francs per annum. This, it is alleged, affords a clue to the extensive robberies of the mail. Charges of corruption are made against thirty or forty officers of government.

would desire to see the type of the administration of France, should study the history of Fouquet. *Solidarité*: unlimited liability: is there the rule. Exemptions, therefore, by persons desiring to exercise the right to associate, are obtained with difficulty so great that to do so may be deemed almost impossible; and hence the absence of the habit of association which exists always in the ratio of the growth of wealth and population. Self-government is there unknown.*

In England the habit of association has always, to a great extent, existed. It may be seen developing itself with every step in the growth of population and wealth; and now with greater rapidity than ever, as witness the union of effort for the construction of her system of railroads. It has been, and is, however, restrained by an infinity of regulations and liabilities, relics of a barbarian age, tending to produce monopoly of power in the hands of individuals: great agriculturists: great bankers: great merchants: great manufacturers: and great politicians: always the cause of great disturbance among the little people by whom they are surrounded. Hence the frequent combinations of workmen, and the ruinous "strikes," by which trade is interrupted for weeks, and the progress of wealth is impeded. Hence the incendiarism, machine breakings, assassinations, vitriol throwing, and other acts of outrage of so frequent occurrence.† Hence, too, the tremendous contests in past times for seats in parliament: hence the wars, the large armies and fleets: and hence the

* "It is evident that a central government acquires immense power when united to administrative centralization. Thus combined, it accustoms men to set their own will habitually and completely aside; to submit not only for once or upon one point, but in every respect and at all times."—*De Tocqueville.*

† "Incendiarism, machine breakings, assassination, vitriol throwing, acts of diabolical outrage, all have been perpetrated for intimidation or revenge."—*Gaskill, Artisans and Machinery.*

"An engineer, who has contributed largely to benefit society by his inventions, tells the writer of this book that he has completed several machines which he considers of general utility, but which he dares not bring forward in the present state of the popular mind."—*Results of Machinery.*

necessity for penal colonies, appropriately designated "hells upon earth!" like Norfolk Island. The tendency to self-government has there existed in a degree unknown to any other part of Europe; for there wealth and population have grown with some rapidity, and there men have been most enabled to associate. It grows now more rapidly than ever, because of the great increase in the facility of communication and intercourse: and the result is increased harmony. Men can now differ in opinion without fighting. They begin now to recognise the right of their neighbours to worship God after their own fashion: and to vote for protection, or free trade, as they please, without being mobbed or stoned; as has been shown in the late election: a great triumph of the principle of self-government. The hustings of London and Manchester, and of England generally, have been almost as quiet as the election grounds of the United States have always been. The voters felt that they had rights to defend, and duties to perform: not masters to serve. In many places they went to the work seriously and gravely, like the Puritans of old; and such men do not need to fight at elections. The more earnestness, the more quiet, the more union, and the more strength.

The events of the last thirty years of peace contrast most forcibly with those of the previous twenty years of war, waste, and ruin. During the whole of that period, land was strengthening itself against man. Properties were enlarged, and property-owners became too great to look after their own affairs. Little farmers were expelled, to make way for great ones. The little ones went to the poor-house, and the great ones were ruined by making improvements on short leases; although, during the whole time, land was making laws to limit the supply of food, and keep up rents. The power of the people over their own actions rapidly diminished during the war, and its close found the mass of them reduced to pauperism, and subject to all the insolence of little tyrants directly or indirectly representing the land. Such were the results of a diminution in the proportion of wealth to population. The results of an increase in that proportion we are now witnessing.

The effect of a long period of peace in promoting the growth of wealth and freedom was first exhibited in Prussia, in the removal of all impediments to the free disposal of land by sale, gift, or will. Next, we find the emancipation, with compensation to the lord, of the small free proprietor: the tenant in perpetuity: previously subject to the most barbarous and absurd regulations. Again, we meet with the associations of land-owners, large and small, for the institution of provincial mortgage banks, whose operations have since grown to a vast amount, and have increased the power of cultivating the deeper and better soils, which before could not be reached because of the inferiority of the machinery in use. Labour has become more productive, and population and wealth have grown with great rapidity; and with them, the habit of peace and the tendency to union: and the ability to demand control over the power of taxation, and the administration of the public affairs. Hence the new constitution: an important step towards self-government.

In her exterior relations Prussia has afforded signal evidence of the tendency of growing wealth and population to produce peace, in the establishment of the great Commercial League of Northern Germany. France has always made deserts between her and her neighbours: in the Palatinate: in the Netherlands: in Piedmont and Savoy: and in Catalonia. Her policy has been that of glory and isolation: and such is it now. Prussia, on the contrary, labours to convert deserts into farms, intersected by railroads. The one advances rapidly. The other scarcely at all. England is now pursuing, in that respect, the policy of Prussia. Self-government and the disposition to union with her colonies on terms of equality, and with foreign nations, are growing by degrees; yet impeded everywhere by monopolies of land and capital, producing unsteadiness, and exercising a strong repulsive power. She repeals her corn-laws, but other nations cling more closely to their tariffs; feeling that the union between the producer and consumer at home is more profitable than union with nations abroad, and disunion at home. The United States, however, advance most rapidly in wealth and population: and their tendency to union is proportionably great. State after State has been added to the Union, silently: but it was reserved for Texas to prove the extraordinary attractive power of superior wealth. That State was settled chiefly by men who had opposed the protective policy; and among the leaders were found some of those who had most warmly advocated the Nullification Law of 1832. Ten years later, the tariff of 1842, held by them to be equally objectionable, was passed. Texas had then established herself as an independent power, recognised by the principal powers of the earth: yet she gladly sunk that independence, and became a State of the Union, adding another star to its flag. Had war been the policy of the people, they would have remained poor; and Texas would still be a wilderness: or, if a State, she would have remained an independent one. Again, if we desire to see the effect of self-government in producing habits of order and union, we may turn to the settlers of Oregon; and see them quietly forming a constitution for themselves, electing township and county officers, members of the little legislature, and governor. The whole machinery of government is there, self-existent. The people knew what they wanted, and they made it. They wanted no essays on government: no great men to teach them. At home they had practised respect for the rights of others: and when abroad they proved that they had not forgotten the lesson.

According to several eminent writers, there exist various races of men: and some of the most eminent of the writers of our time have been disposed to attribute to the antipathy of those races many of the phenomena to which we have referred. A more careful study of history might, however, as we think, satisfy them that although men are of various colours, white, red, brown, and black, there have existed from the creation to the present time but two races, to wit, the great race and the small one: the race of the few and that of the many: the race that lives by the labour of others, and that which lives by their own: the race of the plunderers and that of the plundered.*

When population is small, and poor men cultivate poor soils, the great race abounds; but as wealth and population increase, and rich men cultivate rich soils, the great race becomes rare. *Parmi les aveugles, les borgnes sont rois:* and this is equally true whether we consider man physically, morally, intellectually, or politically.

Throughout Africa, kings and ministers abound, and kings and ministers make *razzias*, carrying off and selling for slaves the inoffensive subjects of their neighbour kings: first perhaps mutilating them that they may better serve the purposes of their masters. Throughout Asia, the great race is numerous. Kings and kings' sons, ministers and their dependents, zemindars and other officers, down to the mundils and potails of villages, plunder the poor people by whom they are surrounded: each to be plundered in turn by those above. In Mexico, too, the great race is numerous, for there the whole people cultivate the poorest soils. Daily revolutions produce a daily supply of men ready to manage the property of others, and to enrich themselves by the profits of management. Armies are mainly composed of generals, colonels, and majors, all ready to give orders, but none ready to obey.

If we follow the history of Athens, we can see a gradual increase in the numbers of the great race, until the whole

---

* "The human species, according to the best theory I can form of it, is composed of two distinct races, the men who borrow and the men who lend. The infinite superiority of the former, which I choose to designate as the *great race*, is discernible in their figure, port, and a certain instinctive sovereignty. The atter are born degraded. 'He shall serve his brethren.' There is something in the air of one of this caste, lean and suspicious, contrasting with the open. trusting, generous manners of the other."—*Lamb*.

people became masters of the lives and fortunes of the inhabitants of a thousand subject cities; and every man claimed to be fed, and clothed, and amused, out of the products of their labour. Greatest among the great, we find Miltiades and Cimon: Pericles and Alcibiades: followed by troops of members of the military aristocracy, all hungry for their shares of the spoils. Athens then cultivated the poorest soils, and great men were numerous: shining conspicuously among the little men by whom they were surrounded. In Italy, when towns and cities were filled with prosperous inhabitants, and men cultivated the most fertile soils, great men were rare; but as by degrees those soils were abandoned and slaves took the place of freemen, the great race became more and more numerous: so numerous at length that it became necessary to diminish their number, and hence the wars and proscriptions of Marius and Sylla: Pompey and Cæsar: Anthony, Octavius, and Lepidus. With the decline of the empire, we may see the great race steadily increasing, until at length the number of those who lived by the labour of others came to exceed those who lived by their own. With the gradual revival of Italy, we may see in the kingdom of Lombardy a thriving people with few great men: but France came, and desolation marked her footsteps. The fertile soils went out of cultivation, because the little race were employed in building castles for their masters. In Florence, when wealth and population grew and man cultivated the rich soils, great men were rare. Perpetual wars brought poverty and the great race; until at length those who laboured but little exceeded in number those who did not. In France, the great race have always been numerous. To that country Europe was indebted for the Feudal System: the system of the great race. Every petty leader had his castle, and all were at all times ready to plunder such of the little race of merchants and travellers as came within their grasp.

Throughout her history, that race so abounds that it is

with difficulty we can distinguish those who might be entitled to claim pre-eminence. Philip the Fair distinguished himself by his robberies under the name of alterations of the coin: but John and various of the names of Charles and Philip almost equalled him. He plundered the Jews and the Italians, on various occasions: but in this he was fully equalled by numerous others. He burned the Templars and confiscated their property: but Louis XIV. did as much by the Huguenots. He squeezed the people: but in this even he was excelled by Anjou, Berri, and Burgundy, who farmed the kingdom during the minority of Charles VI. France has been at all times the land of great men. Princes, dukes, marshals, constables, nobles, and gentlemen financiers, revenue farmers, and tax-gatherers, have always abounded: the consequence of which has been that a very poor people has always cultivated, as they still continue to cultivate, the worst soils of the kingdom.

England abounded in great men in the days of the Conqueror and his immediate successors, and they were surrounded by little men who cultivated poor soils. With time, great men became more rare, and the little men became greater. The wars of the Roses produced "the Last of the Barons," and many other great men. The number diminished from that period to that of the great rebellion, when the few became greater, and the many less: and so it continued during the rest of that century. From that time the number diminished until near the close of the last century, when commenced again the era of great men followed by troops of officials: civil, military and naval: some employed in impressing seamen, and others in commanding ships and fleets: some engaged in crimping soldiers, and others in leading armies: some in imposing taxes and dividing among themselves a large share of the proceeds, and others in collecting excise duties on salt, beer, tobacco, and all other of the commodities used by the little men: and lastly, another large body in collecting means to support in poor-houses starving labourers, their wives and mistresses, their children, legitimate and illegitimate. The few became greater and the many less. For the last thirty years, the great have been becoming less numerous, and less great, while the little have been becoming greater; but England still abounds in great men; railroad kings, who dictate what roads shall be made, and how they shall be made: bank directors who make money plenty or scarce, at their pleasure: Ministers who grant or withhold millions to starving Irishmen: East India directors who support armies and make dividends out of the proceeds of taxes on salt and other necessaries of life used by the half-starved labourers of India: private bankers who fail and make no dividend: great lawyers, and doctors, and merchants, and manufacturers; grooms of the stole, equerries, generals, admirals, colonels, and captains; and county magistrates intent upon enforcing the game laws: while the little people who labour are forced, not unfrequently, to content themselves with mud hovels and eight shillings a week: filthy cellars in Liverpool and Manchester: or rags and nakedness in coal mines.

The United States, happily for themselves, have had few great men. The number varies, however, as we pass from old Massachusetts where the powers of the earth are most fully developed, towards Florida and Arkansas, where the richest soils are still covered with forests: or are a mass of swamps. The good ship Mayflower brought with her, happily, no great men, and no little men. All were equal, and all willing so to continue. From that time to the present, that State, and those of New England generally, have had no great men to manage their affairs, the consequence of which is that they require little or no management.* They have had no great bankers, but banking is there more extensive

* "All the domestic controversies of the Americans at first appear to a stranger to be so incomprehensible and so puerile, that he is at a loss whether to pity a people which takes such arrant trifles in good earnest, or envy that happiness which enables it to discuss them."—*De Tocqueville.*

and more perfect than elsewhere in the world: no great merchants, but the most perfect merchants in the world: no great ship-owners, but the best ships: no great mechanics, but the most perfect machinery: no great manufacturers, yet they send their products to the British possessions, and pay duty while those of Britain are free: no railroad kings, yet they have made more railroads than any similar number of people in the world: no great schools or teachers, but the best schools and the best educated people in the world:* no army, no navy, no great lawyers or conveyancers, yet in no country is the secure enjoyment of the rights of person and property so complete.†

As we pass from New England, south and west, population and wealth diminish, and men cultivate poorer soils: great men increase in number, and the village politician becomes more distinguished; while the little become less. Arriving in South Carolina, we find a diminishing population cultivating worn-out soils: and there we find greater men than elsewhere in the Union, while the little there become least.

The wolf is great amid a flock of sheep. The "medicine man" is great among the savages of the Rocky Mountains. The Sultan of Delhi is great among his poor subjects. Blackbeard was great among inoffensive and defenceless merchantmen. Drake was great among the poor

---

* "There is no other region in Anglo-Saxondom, containing 750,000 souls, where national education has been carried so far."—*Lyell.* "In no subject do the Americans display more earnestness than in their desire to improve their system of education, both elementary and academical."—*Ibid.*

† "In the United States, the democracy perpetually raises fresh individuals to the conduct of public affairs, and the measures of the administration are, consequently, seldom regulated by the strict rules of consistency or of order. But the general principles of the government are more stable, and the opinions most prevalent in society are more durable than in many other countries. When once the Americans have taken up an idea, whether it be well or ill founded, nothing is more difficult than to eradicate it from their minds. The same tenacity of opinion has been observed in England, where, for the last century, greater freedom of conscience and more invincible prejudices have existed, than in all the other countries of Europe."—*De Tocqueville.*

people of Carthagena. Locke and Bacon were greater than is now Herschel, who to all they knew adds vast treasures of knowledge. Saints were numerous when Christianity scarcely had an existence, and when the test of orthodoxy consisted in the belief or denial of the doctrine of the immaculate conception. Elizabeth, to her parliament and her people, was a greater queen than is now the occupant of the throne; and the poor Duke of Newcastle was a far greater man than is the existing Chancellor of the Exchequer. Men are thus great, or little, precisely in the ratio of the greatness or littleness of those by whom they are surrounded: and the true test of a nation is to be found not in the size of their great, but in that of their little, men. Where all are informed, distinction in letters is difficult. Where all are religiously disposed, few can claim canonization. Where all exercise power over themselves, few can interfere with the happiness or property of others. Complaints are made of the *decline* of science in England, accompanied, perhaps, with reference to the brighter days of Newton, Locke and Bacon: when tens of thousands possess all the knowledge of the three combined, and add thereto an intimate knowledge of sciences whose names even were unknown, and whose existence was unsuspected in those "good old times."

Greatness and goodness rarely travel in company, for where great men exist, the little men are weak, and their masters are profligate. Demosthenes thundered out his Philippics while pocketing the bribes of Philip: Cicero displayed equal eloquence in defence of Crassus and in the impeachment of Verres: and Mirabeau was by turns the partisan of the Revolution and the Throne.

The great man: lord of the little man who cultivates the poor soils: pays himself for performing the duties of government, and leaves little for his slave. The man who cultivates the rich soils pays his servants for attending to his affairs, and keeps much himself.

Throughout India. the great man revels in luxury, while

the little man perishes, not unfrequently, of famine. The general has large pay: but the soldier, who executes the orders, receives little, and must pay himself by plunder. The high officials are paid, and pay themselves in addition. The lower ones receive little pay, and they too pay themselves. Such, too, is the case in Russia, Spain, Mexico, Egypt, and other countries in which the poorest soils are cultivated, and where men are least free.

In France too such has been the universal rule. Kings, princes, lords, gentlemen, bishops and archbishops, farmers-general, and financiers of all kinds, paid themselves. Soldiers and tax-collectors received little pay, but paid themselves by living on the people. Such is still the case. Those who administer the government take openly sixteen hundred millions a year out of a gross product of seven thousand millions: and with this palaces are maintained: galleries established: fêtes and entertainments given: soldiers and sailors, and equipages, and wives, and mistresses supported. To this is to be added the prices, privately paid, for licenses for the building of opera-houses, and for concessions of railroads and public contracts: and thus all pay themselves.* The poor subordinate receives less than is required for his support, and he too pays himself. The wretched conscript, torn from his family and friends, receives five dollars a year, in addition to poor clothing and little food, and he too must pay himself.† The miserable payer of taxes continues necessarily to cultivate the worst soils, for he alone *cannot* pay himself.

* The proceedings in the case of M. Teste throw much light on the system.

† The pay of a common soldier is forty-eight centimes, [or nine cents] per day. From this pittance ten centimes are withheld as a provision for the linen and stockings he may require, and for the small articles necessary to his dress and cleanliness; thirty centimes are withheld for his food, and he is supplied with one pound and a half of tolerable bread in addition; eight centimes, (about one and a half cents,) are given to him for pocket money. * * * The soldier has two meals a day. * * * The first is composed of soup, and a quarter of a pound of boiled beef; the second of a small portion of vegetables, generally of potatoes or beans, with a quarter of a pound of mutton or veal. The only drink given is water.

In England, too, great men pay themselves: and hence the enormous salaries of a country whose production is less than that of the United States. Bishops accumulate vast fortunes, and chancellors become "leviathans of wealth." Ministers and ambassadors, to great private fortunes, add the emoluments of office, varying from $30,000 to $60,000 per annum. Viceroys and governors-general have princely revenues, and chancellors' sons exist on salaries of $20,000 a year: while noble clerks sell to the government the privilege of suppressing their useless offices, for pensions varying from $6000 to $10,000, and even more. Lords, ladies, chancellors and judges, whose name is legion, figure on the pension list, while sinecures abound. Meanwhile, the poor subordinate, who does the work: the letter-sorter and the tide-waiter: starve upon miserable salaries: and hence the dangers that attend the transmission of money by the post,* and hence, too, the bribery of custom-house officers, and the frauds upon the revenue. With the thirty years of peace, and the consequent growth of wealth and population, some change has been effected, and the great are somewhat less paid, while the subordinate receives somewhat more: but the fact that land still pays itself is made obvious on all occasions.

If we look to Attica, we may trace the gradual rise of this state of things from the days of Solon to those of Pericles, who involved his country in war in preference to producing his accounts: and thence to Herodes Atticus, who paid himself so abundantly as to incur the displeasure of a master well versed in the payment of himself and friends. So in Rome, as cultivation diminished, we may trace the growth of the habit of self payment from the days of Cincinnatus,

* Colonel Maberly, the deputy postmaster-general, stated some years since that the losses were terrific. In the United States, on the contrary, with 14,000 post-offices, and with more remittances of money than all the world beside, the losses are so trivial as to be estimated at only the two-hundredth part of one per cent.

who tilled his own little farm, to those of Scipio whose accounts were not producible: to those of Pompey and Cæsar, whose debts were counted by millions; and those of Commodus, who, in his brief reign, squandered the accumulations of his father and found the vast revenues of the empire insufficient for the gratification of his beastly appetites. With each step in this progress, we find population and wealth diminishing, the fertile lands abandoned, and the people becoming more and more slaves.

In the United States, the people pay their servants, and all are paid according to their services. In the New England states, the people govern themselves, and their servants have little to do, and therefore receive little. The people have, therefore, self-government, good government, and cheap government. As with all other machinery, it becomes less costly as it improves in quality. The friction on a railroad is small, and therefore goods are cheaply carried. The turnpike gives more friction and more cost. As we pass south from New England we find less self-government: less good government: and more costly government. The people who cultivate inferior soils are obliged to content themselves with turnpikes, and with governors to whom they pay high salaries. In the government of the Union, the president receives a salary that is large in proportion to the business that he has to do, yet moderate by comparison. The chief officers of government are reasonably paid, but the inferior ones are always fully paid.* The custom-house officer has full wages, and hence the small amount of frauds upon the revenue. The letter-sorter receives full wages, and hence it is that the transmission of money through a country with fourteen thousand post-offices is attended with risk so

* "The mean of American salaries is much superior to ours. When the Federal or State governments want capable men, they do as American merchants do, they pay them. * * * In the Treasury Department, of one hundred and fifty-eight persons employed, there are but six who have less than $1000; but it is equally true that there are only two who have more than $2000."—*Chevalier.*

small as scarcely to be estimated. The common soldier has high wages. Labour is always in demand, and he must have the market price. Wars, therefore, are expensive and undesirable: while in France they constitute cheap pastime for the great, who take large salaries themselves and give the poor soldier almost nothing in return for his time.

Where wealth and population grow, the price of labour rises, and soldiers and sailors must have higher wages to secure their services. As the better soils are cultivated, wars, therefore, become more and more expensive: and thus while the habit of union and peace tends steadily to increase, the costliness of war tends in the same direction. In every way, therefore, does wealth tend to promote the further growth of wealth, and the development of the rich treasures of the earth.

If now we inquire, what is the service rendered by those who thus pay themselves, we find it to resolve itself into the one word, government; and by this is meant the management of the affairs of others. The minister governs all: the general governs soldiers, and the admiral governs sailors. The people govern nothing, not even themselves and the products of their labour. Of that they are relieved by the class of the great, who pay themselves for their trouble, and whose trade is war: for in time of war the spoil of friends and foes is largely distributed, and they direct the distribution. If we seek to find other services rendered in return for the large pay that is received, we shall find none. The great write no books. They furnish no ideas. They invent no machines. Bacon and Locke: Shakspeare and Milton: Arkwright and Watt: Washington and Franklin: benefactors of the human race: came from the ranks of the little men, as has every man to whose labours society has been indebted. Great men and governments *patronize* authors and artists, to the destruction of taste in literature and art: and authors and artists starve under their patronage. With the growth of wealth and population authors and artists are found contributing to supply the wants of the large class of little men, and then taste improves: and then authors and artists grow rich. Doing little good themselves, and being thus the cause of little good in others, the class of great men is one with which we may readily dispense ; and the most rapid advance in civilization will invariably be found where, and when, it is least numerous.

With the increase of population and wealth the better soils come into cultivation, and men acquire the power of self-government in regard to thought and action, and in regard to the disposition of their labour and its proceeds; and with each step in this progress towards perfect individuality there is an increasing tendency to union, peace and harmony; tending to promote the further growth of wealth, and the further extension of cultivation, and to increase the power of man to associate with his fellow man on terms of strict equality.

The PAST says to the sovereign of the PRESENT: If you would reign over a great nation: avoid war, and labour to promote the growth of wealth.

To the representatives of the land: If you would have your properties increase in value: avoid wars and labour to promote the growth of population and of wealth.

To the people: if you would acquire the power to think and act for yourselves: to determine how you will employ your faculties of body and of mind, and what shall be the disposition of the proceeds: labour to prevent war, and waste.

CHAPTER VII.

MAN.

The savage lives in constant dread of starvation. He draws his supply of food from the poorest soils. The lonely cultivator of the almost desert land is forced to depend upon the thin soil of the hills for support, and is in constant fear for his life, and for the safety of his little property. In every stranger he sees one poor as himself: one to whom his little stock of wealth, trivial as it is, would be a treasure: or if, perchance, the stranger come from distant and civilized lands: from among a people who cultivate the rich soils of the earth: the lonely man sees in the nails and beads, and other treasures of his visitor, what "would make him rich indeed;" and avarice seizes on his soul. His labour, severe as it is, scarcely yields him food, and he has no means with which to buy. He murders his visitor, and seizes on his goods. Here we have combined, fear, rapacity, treachery, and cruelty: and such are, uniformly, the characteristics of the men who are forced to rely on the poorest soils of the earth for the means of subsistence.

The man who cultivates the rich soils is animated by Hope. He finds his labours blessed with large returns, and he sees in the underlying marl or lime, and in the inexhaustible supplies of coal and iron by which he is surrounded, the means of adding to his power over the comforts, conveniences, and luxuries of life. His neighbours are men who, like himself, have property, and who, also like himself, could fight in its defence should occasion make it necessary: but both he and they feel that in their union there is strength, and they know no fear. In the future they feel perfect confidence, and from that confidence spring feelings of liberality and benevolence.

By many of the teachers of Mr. Ricardo's doctrine, it is held that man works because he fears starvation. By others, taxation is held to be a strong stimulus to exertion.* Fear, the characteristic of the slave, is in their estimation the great moving principle in man: and the whip, in the form of taxation, is held to be useful in compelling him to extract from soils of "constantly increasing sterility" the means of support, and the rent required by his lord. That such should be their estimate of the character of man is not extraordinary. Mr. Ricardo makes him, throughout, the victim of a sad *necessity* that precludes the existence of hope. He is destitute of *power* over the land, or over himself, and he *can* have no confidence in the future. The machine he uses *must* deteriorate. *He* may escape, but *his children must pay the penalty* he has incurred by aiding to increase the numbers of mankind, and thus compelling resort to less productive soils.

How far such views are in accordance with facts, we propose now to examine. If man *does* commence with the fertile soils, and proceed downward toward the poor ones, we must find, with the growth of population, a constantly increasing tendency towards the vices of the slave: fear, cruelty, rapacity and treachery. If, on the contrary, he commences with the poor soils, and if, with the growth of population, he is enabled to pass to better and ultimately to the best soils, we must find him constantly animated by hope, and prompted to new exertions for the improvement of his own condi-

* "To the desire of rising in the world, implanted in the breast of every individual, an increase of taxation superadds the fear of being cast down to a lower station, of being deprived of conveniences and gratifications which habit has rendered all but indispensable, and the combined influence of the two principles produces results that could not be produced by the unassisted agency of either."—*McCulloch.*

tion and that of his fellow-men: and with every step in that direction the vices of the slave must disappear, to be replaced by the virtues of the freeman.

"Hope springs eternal in the human breast,"

and she is the mother of liberality and benevolence, of kindness and gentleness. Without her, they can have no existence.

If we trace the history of the people of Athens, from the days of her prosperity, prior to the Persian wars, we can see the gradual growth of the vices of the slave. Fear prompts them to the atrocious butcheries of Corcyra and of Mytilene. Rapacity is shown in the seizing of the common treasure: in the unceasing growth of taxes; in the perpetual increase of their own pay as judges and legislators; and in the appropriation of the tribute to the maintenance of theatres from which the tribute payers were excluded. Universal tyranny: universal indolence: and universal pauperism: accompany extended dominion.

In Laconia, we find a people that cultivated the poorest soils for the benefit of their Spartan masters: and there we find, at home, fear of the poor Helot prompting to acts of treachery and cruelty, while abroad we see fear of Athens exhibited in the starvation of the prisoners of Sicily: in the cold-blooded massacre following the battle of Ægos Potamos; and in the history of the thirty tyrants. With each step in their downward progress we see land concentrating itself in fewer hands, until at length nearly the whole becomes the property of a single individual: and at each we see avarice and all the vices of slavery more and more abounding.

In Rome, we can see increasing fear manifested in the murder of Pontius: in the cold-blooded destruction of all prisoners of distinction at the close of every triumph: in the ruin of Carthage: in the proscriptions and massacres of Marius and Sylla, and of the successive triumvirates: and in those of Tiberius, Nero, and their successors: and with each step in their progress, we can see land more and more concentrating itself: the fertile soils more and more abandoned: and slaves more and more taking the place of the free people of the days of Servius. With each step, those within the walls become more and more pauperized; and with each, rapacity, cruelty, and perfidy become more and more the distinguishing characteristics of the whole mass: rich and poor: nobles and plebeians: warriors and politicians.

For centuries in the history of Naples and of modern Rome, we may see indolence increasing as poverty compels the abandonment of the more fertile soils, and produces fear of starvation: while rapacity, treachery, cruelty, and jealousy, gradually come to pervade every order of society. In Florence, they may be seen advancing steadily, as wars and desolation force men to cultivate the poor soils of the earth, and substitute poverty for wealth. Perpetual fear is manifested by unceasing poisonings and open murders: and Tuscany at large presents a scene of rapacity, treachery, and cruelty, fitting it for the birth-place of the principal actor in the massacre of the St. Bartholomew. If, again, we trace the history of the same beautiful country during the last hundred years: from the accession of the present race of sovereigns: we may see population and wealth gradually increasing: land becoming divided: and cultivation extending itself over the fertile soils: while hope is seen taking the place of fear; and justice and benevolence becoming substituted for the universal rapacity and tyranny which had driven population and wealth from the land, and had compelled its inhabitants to fly to the poor soils of the hills for safety.

If we look to Spain, we may see perpetual fear manifested in the proceedings of the Inquisition, and of the government, whether in Naples, or Milan, Sicily, or the Netherlands. It may again be seen pervading her whole colonial system. If we desire to meet rapacity, cruelty, and jealousy increasing as depopulation and poverty compel the abandonment of the most fertile soils, we may find it in every page of her history.

In France, perpetually at war, we see in the people almost constant fear of starvation: in the church, perpetual fear of liberal ideas, manifested by the atrocious burnings at slow fires of miserable heretics of both sexes; by the persecutions of the unfortunate Vaudois; and by the *dragonnades* of Louvois: in the lawyers, by unceasing intrigues against the nobles, and in the nobles, by corresponding intrigues against the upstart nobility of the gown: in the class of nobles and gentlemen, perpetual fear of insurrection, manifested by the building of forts and castles, and by the unceasing prohibitions of the use of even the most simple arms by the unhappy people: in princes, perpetual fear of assassination, as shown in thousands of instances, but most strongly in the barricades of the bridges of *Montereau*, and of the *Sevre:* and in kings, by a system of *espionnage* unparalleled in the world for baseness and meanness.

If we desire to see rapacity and cruelty, we may find it in every page of her history, at home and abroad; in the plunder and destruction of the Albigenses; in the wars of the *Bourguignons* and *Armagnacs;* in those of Louis XI. and the bold Charles; those of the League, and of the *Fronde.* If we look abroad we may find it at every period in her intercourse with unhappy Italy: with Germany, Spain, the Netherlands, and Holland. If we desire to find jealousy, it will be met in the unceasing invasions of Guienne and Normandy; and in the perpetual succession of the puerile wars of Francis I. and Henry II. It will be found again in the fomenting of the unceasing wars of Germany and Italy, the object being the depression and ruin of her neighbours, in the vain hope of thereby raising herself.

If we seek for perfidy, it may be found in the thousand-times repeated abandonment of her Italian allies; in her conduct towards the unfortunate house of Savoy; in her treatment of the people of Catalonia; in the tiger-like attacks of

Louis XIV. upon the people of the Netherlands and Holland; in the ruin of Franche Comté, to whose neutrality she had in her hours of distress and danger been so repeatedly indebted; in her conduct on various occasions to the Swiss; in her perpetual violation of the rights of the people of Guienne, and Normandy, and Roussillon, and of each successive province added to the kingdom; in her negotiations with the Turks, her allies against Austria and Italy: in short, at every step of her progress from the days of Charlemagne, and in every page of her history, internal and external.

Even now, we see fear in the fortifications of Paris; in the enormous armies maintained throughout the kingdom in a time of general peace; in the censorship and perpetual persecution of the press; in her system of passports; in her system of *espionnage;* in the opening of private letters; and everywhere in her jealous interference with her unfortunate neighbours of Switzerland, Italy, and Spain. We see rapacity unequalled, in the collection of sixteen hundred millions of taxes, and their distribution among countless officials, embracing the families and friends of all connected with the government.*

If we seek cruelty, we may find it in the suffocation of hundreds of unfortunate Moors in their last remaining place of refuge; in the *razzias* of Algeria; and in the recent proceedings at Tahiti. In every movement we may see jealousy of England. That power is so unfortunate as to have a great marine and numerous colonies, and France is unhappy that she has them not; and that she may have them, she wastes hundreds of millions on worthless Algeria.

England has a great trade with the East, employing labour

---

* The whole number of officials appointed and paid by the government liable to removal, and susceptible of promotion, and annuitants or pensioners; is 931,977, and the amount of their salaries and pensions is 397,000,000 of francs, or nearly 80,000,000 of dollars! To this must be added 400,000 soldiers and 60,000 sailors and marines, making a total of 1,392,000 persons receiving pay from that portion of the nation which styles itself "The State."

and capital that could be better employed at home; and France, to rival her, expends millions on embassies to China, and expeditions to Japan, with little to send to either, and with little reason to hope that they will find in her a market for their products.*

Poverty and wretchedness: the necessary consequence of misgovernment: exist in every part of that great country; and where they are found, the habit of union can have no place.† Society is divided into two great classes, separated by an impassable gulf: those who labour to produce and may not enjoy, and those who enjoy without producing. In such a state of things, fraud and deception: the habit of robbery and plunder: become habitual.‡ Confidence in the future can have no existence, and without that, feelings of liberality and benevolence can find little place in the heart of man.§

* "I have always thought and said that the alliance of France was an advantage for which all the powers of Europe would contend, so soon as she should have established her government on a solid foundation, and abandoned that system of policy which consists in an unceasing repetition of the assertion that the whole world, envious of her glory and jealous of her power, is leagued against her; that they threaten her independence, and would destroy her institutions, but that she has only to raise her voice, to affright the sovereigns and liberate their subjects: '*she, the first, the most enlightened, the bravest, and the only free, of all the nations.*' This stupid and antiquated system can result only in wounding their feelings, extinguishing their ancient sympathies, and causing them to call in question her glory, her genius, and her power. It tends to produce weakness and isolation."—*Girardin.*

† "The citizen is unconcerned, as to the condition of his village, the police of his street, the repairs of his church, or of the parsonage; for he looks upon all these things as unconnected with himself; and as the property of a powerful stranger whom he calls the government."—*De Tocqueville.*

‡ According to the *Journal des Debats,* many parts of France now exhibit a state of things resembling that which existed in Wales but a short time since. That paper says:

"Bands of mendicants continue to spread terror in the whole of the Bocage. These individuals, dressed in gray blouses, their faces smeared with soot, six or seven or more together, obtain grain and money, uttering the most horrible threats against those who venture to make any observation to them. Similar scenes have taken place in the district of Parthenay."

§ In France, "without the walls of the prison, religious ardour is met with in the ministers of religion only. If they are kept from the penitentiary, the influence of religion will disappear: philanthropy alone will remain for the

More than any other nation in Europe, England has enjoyed peace at home, yet has her policy been marked by many and serious errors. She has looked abroad, and ships, colonies, and commerce have involved her in ruinous wars, while her own richest soils have remained uncultivated. War, and preparation for it, have produced here their usual effects, in a degree corresponding with the extent to which war has been her trade. We see, here, fear exhibiting itself in the maintenance of a standing army: in the prohibition to the people of Ireland of the right to carry arms: in the revival in that country of the system of the curfew: in the opening of private letters:* in the trials for high treason that marked the early years of the late war: in the Manchester massacre: in the barbarous punishments of soldiers: in the collusion between high officers of the government and officers charged with summoning juries for the trial of state prisoners:† in the Rebecca riots: in the throwing of vitriol and various other modes adopted for inflicting personal injury: in the proceedings of the Luddites: in the constant resistance to the introduction of improvements in agricultural and manufacturing machinery: and in various other of the modes of action

---

reformation of criminals. It cannot be denied that there are with us generous *individuals*, who, endowed with profound sensibility, are zealous to alleviate any misery, and to heal the wounds of humanity: so far their attention, exclusively occupied with the physical situation of the prisoners, has neglected a much more precious interest, that of their moral reformation. * * * But these sincere philanthropists are rare; in most cases philanthropy is with us but an affair of the imagination."—*De Beaumont and De Tocqueville.*

* "Let us begin by acknowledging that the case attempted to be made out against the present government, as guilty of something worse in the shape of post-office *espionnage* than their predecessors, has not hitherto been sustained. * * * The moment the Marquis of Normandy stated in the House of Lords that he had opened letters while in office in Ireland, it became evident to all impartial reasoning men that the two parties were upon an equal footing."—*Westminster Review*, 1844.

† Direct interferences have been proved "to have taken place between the solicitor of the treasury and the officer whose duty it was to have maintained an impartial position between the subject and the crown," by means of which the crown has been enabled to pack the juries on trials of high treason. See *Westminster Review*, vol. 45, p. 210.

adopted by individuals, and by those charged with the duties of government. Here, as elsewhere, fear has been accompanied with cruelty, as shown in her mad-houses, the horrors of which have, until recently, almost exceeded belief: in her monstrous system of impressment; in the prodigious extent to which capital punishments have, until recently, been carried: in the *excessive* overworking of young and feeble operatives: in the harshness exercised towards the class of unfortunate people who, from ill health, or inability to obtain employment, are thrown upon the public for support; as shown in the recent poor-law system, so merciless that it could not be enforced in reference to some of its most important features: in the horrible treatment of pauper lunatics:* in the maintenance of places of exile like that of Norfolk island, the "hell upon earth:" in the punishment of poachers:† in the expulsion of the Highlanders; and, more recently, in that of the people of Sutherland:‡ and both cruelty and rapacity are fully shown in the taxation of India, where duties are imposed upon all the necessaries of life, and salt is monopolized for the benefit of proprietors of India stock. Through-

* "Examples of the most horrifying description have been recorded by the poor-law commissioners, who, in their published reports, have given innumerable instances of the grossest barbarity. The portion of the domestic accommodation usually assigned to these unfortunates is that commonly devoted to the reception of coals, &c.; namely, the triangular space formed between the stairs and the ground-floor. In this confined, dark, and damp corner may be found at this very time no small number of our fellow-beings, huddled, crouching and gibbering with less apparent intelligence, and under worse treatment than the lower domestic animals."—*Westminster Review*, vol. 45, p. 192.

† In Buckinghamshire, with a population of 237,000, there were of summary convictions in 1839, 363; 1840, 370; 1841, 407; 1842, 511; and 1843, 466. Game law convictions in 1839, 89; 1840, 99; 1841, 125; 1842, 134; and 1843, 178. Proportion per cent. of game law to summary convictions in 1839, 21.5; 1840, 26.1; 1841, 30.7; 1842, 26.1; and 1843, 31.8. Proportion of game law convictions to 100,000 of male population in 1839, 118; 1840, 130; 1841, 163; 1842, 174; and 1843, 230. Increase per cent. 95.2.

‡ Three thousand families were expelled from their little farms on the Sutherland estate, and their villages *burnt*. Two acres *per family* were allowed them elsewhere, to be held on short leases, on payment of a rent of two shillings and six pence per acre. Nearly the whole race of Highlanders has been expelled in a similar manner, and their habitations destroyed.

out England, Hope does not, as a rule, prevail. The "uneasy class" is large. Every man looks with anxiety to the future for himself, or his children. The avenues to employment are blocked against those whose means are insufficient to command "connection," and therefore is it that great sums are paid for "good wills;" for shares in established houses; and for appointments to office. The necessary consequence of such a condition of affairs is the existence throughout society of power on the one hand, and of feebleness and servility on the other. The labourer must vote as he is ordered, or he may be ejected from his cottage: and he must be grateful in the highest degree for the allotment of a quarter of an acre that he may cultivate on payment of an exorbitant rent. The operative must submit, for employment is scarce. The clerk must bend, for clerkships are not abundant.

She is now, however, turning her attention homeward. She is making railroads, and bringing into cultivation better soils: and each step in that direction will tend to give to the labourer increased hope in the future, while to the landlord it will give increased confidence that it rests with himself alone to secure not only a continuance of the present income from his property, but a steady and rapid increase. With each step, we shall find man more and more acquiring power over himself, and greater self-reliance, essential to the extension of those feelings of liberality, benevolence and kindness, by which portions of British society have been so honourably distinguished.

By no portion of the human race has peace been so steadily maintained as by the people of the United States, during the sixty years which followed the recognition of their independence, and in no country have wealth and population so rapidly grown. In none, therefore, does man exercise so much power over himself. In none prevails so universally confidence in themselves, and in the future.* Hope ani-

* "Society says to the poor man in America, labour! and at eighteen years you will earn more, labourer as you are, than a captain can do in Eu-

mates all to industry, and stimulates the faculties for the invention of machinery for increasing the productiveness of labour,* while prompting all to union for the promotion of works of public usefulness, of charity and benevolence.† In none is there so little religious jealousy, for there are no spoils to be divided. In none so little jealousy of station, for all feel that they themselves can rise. In none so little jealousy of property, for all have or can obtain it.‡ In none does there exist a recognition so universal of the superior claims of talent, for all read. In none so little deference

---

rope. You will live in abundance, you will be well clothed, well lodged, and you will be able to accumulate capital. Be assiduous, sober, and religious, and you will find a devoted and submissive companion; you will have a home better provided with comforts than that of many of the employers in Europe. From a workman you will become an employer; you will have apprentices and domestics in your turn; you will have credit and abundant means; you will become a manufacturer or great farmer; you will speculate and become rich; you will build a town, and give it your name; you will become a member of the legislature of your state, or alderman of your city, and then member of Congress; your son will have the same chance of being president, as the son of the President himself. Labour! and if the chance of business should be against you, and you should fall, you will speedily rise again, for here failure is not considered like a wound received in battle; it will not cause you to loose esteem or confidence, *provided you have been always temperate and regular, a good Christian, and faithful husband.*"—*Chevalier.*

* "Tall, slender, and well-made, the American appears built expressly for labour. He has not his equal in the world for rapidity of work. None so readily fall into new modes of practice. He is always ready to change them, or his tools, or even his trade. He is a machinist in his soul. * * * There is not a countryman in Connecticut or Massachusetts, who has not invented his machine."—*Chevalier.*

† "The Americans have great *earnestness of character.* * * * Only let them fully apprehend the importance of an object, and you will see them move to it with a directness of mind, and a scorn of sacrifices, which would surprise weaker natures. * * * I know of no country where there are more examples of beneficence and magnificence. The rich will act nobly out of their abundance; and the poor will act as nobly out of their penury."—*Visit to the American Churches.*

"In no country in the world do the citizens make such exertions for the common weal; and I am acquainted with no people which has established schools as numerous and as efficacious, places of worship better suited to the wants of the inhabitants, or roads kept in better repair."—*De Tocqueville.*

‡ "In America, those complaints against property in general, which are so

to authority, for all think.* In none does there exist so universally the feeling of self-respect.† In none is avarice so rarely seen.‡ In none are the contributions of money and service, in aid of literary and scientific, religious and charitable institutions:§ of schools, colleges, libraries, hos-

---

frequent in Europe, are never heard, because in America there are no paupers; and as every one has property of his own to defend, every one recognises the principle upon which he holds it."—*De Tocqueville.*

* "The inhabitants of the United States are never fettered by the axioms of their professions; they escape from all the prejudices of their present station; they are not more attached to one line of operation than to another; they are not more prone to employ an old method than a new one; they have no rooted habits, and they easily shake off the influence which the habits of other nations might exercise upon their minds, from a conviction that their country is unlike any other, and that its situation is without a precedent in the world. America is a land of wonders, in which every thing is in constant motion, and every movement seems an improvement. The idea of novelty is there indissolubly connected with the idea of amelioration. No natural boundary seems to be set to the efforts of man, and what is not yet done, is only what he has not yet attempted to do."—*De Tocqueville.*

† "The mass of the American people are more fully initiated than the mass of European population, in what relates to the dignity of man, or at least, in regard to their own dignity. The American workman is full of self-respect, which he manifests not only by an extrême susceptibility, and by his repugnance to use the term master, which he replaces by that of employer, but also by much greater good faith, exactitude, and scrupulousness in his transactions. He is exempt from the vices of the slave, such as lying and stealing, which are so frequent among our labourers, particularly those of our cities and factories."—*Chevalier.*

‡ "It might be thought, that among a people so profoundly absorbed by the care of their material interests, misers would abound. Such is not the case."—*Chevalier.*

"The universal moving power with an American is the desire of wealth, but it would be to deceive ourselves to suppose that he is not capable of pecuniary sacrifices. He has the habit of giving, and he practises it without regret, more frequently than ourselves, and more largely also; but his munificence and his gifts are governed by reason and by calculation. It is neither enthusiasm nor passion that opens his purse."—*Chevalier.*

§ "There is no village in the United States without its church, no denomination of Christians in any city without its house of prayer, no congregation in any of the new settlements without the spiritual consolation of a pastor."—*Grund.*

"Whatever may be the actual use of the means to be found in this country, certainly those means, as they contribute to supply the church with a well-trained and efficient ministry, excel any thing which we have at home. The student for the sacred calling gets a better classical and general education than he would get in our dissenting colleges, while his professional education is not inferior; and he gets a theological education unspeakably better than pitals, asylums for the deaf, the dumb, the blind,* the youthful and the adult criminal;† so great: because in none is land so powerless, and in none is man so strong or so united.‡ In none does there exist so strong a tendency towards bringing into activity all the vast treasures of the earth; because in none is the capitalist, large and small, so free to invest his accumulations at his pleasure. In none is the labourer so free to select his employer. In none is the employer so free to discharge his labourer. In none is the reward of labour so great. In none are fleets and armies so small: and in none does there exist so strong an inducement to the application of all the powers of body and of mind, in the manner deemed likely most to contribute to the advancement of physical, moral, intellectual, and political condition.§

Oxford or Cambridge would afford him, though his classical advantages would be less."—*Visit to the American Churches.*

"I have seen a list of bequests and donations made during the last thirty years, for the benefit of religious, charitable, and literary institutions, in the State of Massachusetts alone, and they amounted to no less a sum than $6,000,000, or more than £1,000,000 sterling."—*Lyell.*

* "It appears doubtful whether the education of the blind has ever been carried so far as at present in the United States; and there is one set of particulars, at least, in which we would do well to learn from the new country." —*Martineau.*

† "In America, the progress of the reform of prisons has been of a character essentially religious. Men, prompted by religious feelings, have conceived and accomplished every thing which has been undertaken; they were not left alone; but their zeal gave the impulse to all, and thus excited in all minds the ardour which animated theirs."—*De Beaumont and De Tocqueville.*

"A multitude of charitable persons, who are not ministers by profession, sacrifice, nevertheless, a great part of their time to the moral reformation of criminals."—*Ibid.*

‡ "In no country does crime more rarely elude punishment. The reason is, that every one conceives himself to be interested in furnishing evidence of the act committed, and of stopping the delinquent. During my stay in the United States, I witnessed the spontaneous formation of committees for the pursuit and prosecution of a man who had committed a great crime in a certain county. In Europe, a criminal is an unhappy being who is struggling for his life against the ministers of justice, while the population is merely a spectator of the conflict: in America, he is looked upon as the enemy of the human race, and the whole of mankind is against him."—*De Tocqueville.*

§ "In spite of the constant influx of uneducated and pennyless adventurers

We are told, that "God hath made man upright, but he has sought out many inventions." Man *was* made upright, and man *is* upright, when permitted so to be. Throughout the world, he is disposed to labour for the maintenance and improvement of his condition, wherever he sees that such improvement follows labour: but unhappily there has existed at every period, and in every portion of the world, a class to whom labour was disagreeable, and who preferred living on that of others, paying themselves for performing the duties of government. In some cases, they exercise greater, and in others less, power over those by whom they are surrounded; and in all cases, the vices of the slave are found existing in the precise ratio of that power: while with its diminution we find them invariably becoming replaced by the virtuous habits of freemen. England has increased more rapidly in wealth and population than the rest of Europe, and, therefore it is that there those vices are found least existing: while France has remained almost stationary, and, therefore it is that in that country hope scarcely exists, while fear, and jealousy, and cruelty, and avarice so much abound.

That such is the case is not the fault of the people but of the government, which deprives them of the power, and the hope, of improvement. Great numbers of Frenchmen have crossed the Atlantic to settle in the United States, where they have manifested the possession of all the qualities requisite for excellent citizens, and so would they do at home, had they hope to animate them to exertion. The Union possesses no class of citizens more orderly, industrious, and respectable, than those derived from France. The same, however, may be said of the natives of every clime. The Englishman brings with him the habit of strikes, turn-outs, and combinations, but it passes gradually away,

---

from Europe, I believe it would be impossible to find 5,000,000 in any other region of the globe whose average moral, social, and intellectual condition stands so high."—*Lyell.*

as he finds that he has rights, and has also the power to maintain them. The German labours and thrives everywhere. The Irishman brings with him his party feuds: and Catholic and Orangemen maintain, for a time, the cordial hatred engendered by long years of oppression on one hand and unquiet endurance on the other: but in time this, too, passes away, and all become Americans, the causes of hate forgotten. So would it everywhere be, were men permitted to cultivate the land in peace, and to enjoy the fruits of their labour; but so long as large armies and fleets are to be maintained: so long as the major part of the produce of the land shall continue to be consumed by those who do not labour: and so long as men shall be compelled to cultivate poor soils when they might have rich ones: virtue and happiness cannot increase. The people, everywhere, love peace, and everywhere they desire to unite with each other. Their rulers, everywhere, love war, and preparation for war.

The PAST says to the landlord of the PRESENT:—If you would desire to see your property increase in value: strive for the maintenance of peace, that population and wealth may grow; and that habits of union, and feelings of benevolence and kindness, may prevail throughout the society of which you are a member.

To the labourer it says: If you would acquire the power of union with your fellows for the promotion of feelings of mutual kindness and benevolence: if you would acquire confidence in the future: if you would be animated by hope: strive for the maintenance of peace.

CHAPTER VIII.

MAN AND HIS HELPMATE.

THE savage derives his subsistence from the poorest soils. He roams abroad, and shoots the deer: but leaves to his unhappy helpmate the task of carrying it home on her shoulders, and that of preparing it for his consumption. He helps himself, and when there is sufficient for both, she may eat. When it is otherwise, she may starve. She is his slave, ever ready to prostitute herself to the stranger for a mouthful of food, a bead, or a nail.

The man who cultivates the rich soils of the earth sees in woman the source of his greatest happiness. The companion of his hours of enjoyment, he turns instinctively to her for solace in the hours of affliction. He labours, that she may rest. He economizes, that she may enjoy the comforts and luxuries of life: while she regards him as the chosen partner of her existence, and the father of her children; and, as such, entitled to exclusive possession of her affections.

If we trace the history of woman in Athens, we may see the gradual decline of her influence as incessant wars brought poverty and depopulation, and as the cultivation of the fertile soils was more and more abandoned ; until we meet, on the one hand, the *Hetæræ*, constituting an important element of society: and, on the other, the female slave, engaged in the severest labours, and not unfrequently perishing for want of food: while abroad, women and children are involved with husbands and fathers in the atrocious punishments that follow resistance to the orders of a rapacious military aristocracy, eager to divide among themselves the plunder of subject cities.

If we look to Rome in the prosperous days when the fertile lands of Latium, cultivated by their free owners, gave food to numerous cities, we may see woman respected, and respecting herself. If we seek her in the days when population had declined, and cultivation had been abandoned to slaves, and when Italy had ceased to afford food for her greatly diminished numbers, we find her type in Messalina and Agrippina, Poppœa and Faustina.

In modern Italy, with the decay of population and of wealth, we see thousands of women, who have witnessed the massacre of their husbands and their sons, driven abroad, to perish of starvation, or subjected to the last outrages by hordes of wandering barbarians: Franks or Germans: while in Lucrece Borgia, or Beatrice Cenci, we find the type of woman in the higher ranks of life. In the poorest parts of Italy: those in which land is least divided: may now be found the wealthiest women: while the wife of the poor serf slaves in the field to obtain a small allowance of the poorest food. Increasing inequality of condition, and increasing crime, are thus the invariable attendants of poverty and the abandonment of the fertile soils of the earth. If we desire other evidences of this, we may turn to France in the terrific days of the Merovingians: and there we find the sex a slave to the worst passions of men, the subjects of female barbarians occupying thrones, who are known to history by the names of Fredegonda and Brunechild: women almost unmatched for crime.

Exhausted by wars of conquest under Charlemagne, we find France a prey to invasion from every side, by barbarians who respected neither age nor sex. The cultivation of the land was abandoned, and the people who escaped the sword perished of starvation. Poverty and depopulation gave birth to the barbarism of the feudal system, for which the world stands her debtor. With each step in its progress men were forced to resort to poorer soils: and with each we see the poorer freeman gradually losing control over his actions, and becoming daily more and more the slave of his lord. With each, we see the honour of his wife and daughter becoming less and less secure; until at length we find the *droit de jambage et de cuissage* universally asserted, and so generally exercised that the eldest born of the tenant is held more honourable than the others: it being probable that it was the child of the lord. Concubinage becomes universal, and bastardy ceases to cause any feeling of disgrace. Dissolute queens provide mistresses for their husbands: while princes, styled "the good," or "great," number their concubines by dozens: and *bâtards* and *grand bâtards* fill the highest office of state, and monopolize the great dignities of the church: or distinguish themselves as *ecorcheurs*, or flayers of the unfortunate peasant, whose wife perishes of starvation while they accumulate vast fortunes, and take rank among the good and great. Later, queens find in the easy virtue of their maids of honour, security for the adhesion of their partisans: and *gentlemen* find in rape one of the inducements to the invasion of the unfortunate lands of Italy or Spain, Germany or the Netherlands. Cities and towns are sacked: and nobles and gentlemen gorge themselves with plunder, while women and children ask in vain for food. Titled prostitutes next direct the affairs of state, and women suffer at the stake for errors of opinion: while wives and daughters of the poor serfs labour in the field, seeking in vain from the miserable soils they cultivate the means of supporting life. Unceasing wars and universal poverty are accompanied by excessive inequality, and by the dissoluteness of manners that invariably attends the absence of all control on the part of the *many*, and the consciousness of the possession of unlimited power on the part of the *few*. Duchesses now publish to the world the histories of their amours, and princesses of the blood are honoured by the notice of Montespans. Queens and kept mistresses are *compagnons du voyage*, and *Brinvilliers* furnishes poisons to enable amorous wives to change their husbands. Thus, by degrees, we reach the period when incest ceases to be a crime, and the representative of majesty takes his mistresses indifferently from among the daughters of others, or his own. The *parc aux cerfs*, or royal academy for prostitutes, maintained at the cost of millions collected by taxes on salt and all other of the necessaries of life, next occupies the time and mind of the sovereign: while a *du Barri* holds the helm of state. Arriving at the period of the Revolution, we see *poissardes* heading insurrections, while queens, princesses, and duchesses, are dragged to prison, preparatory to being made to feel the weight of the revolutionary axe: and indiscriminate murder: *noyades* and *fusillades:* sweeps off by thousands miserable men, whose wives and daughters, reduced, perhaps, from affluence, are forced to beg their bread from door to door, or seek a refuge from starvation in the horrors of public prostitution.

In nothing is the brutalizing effect of perpetual war more fully exhibited than in the total want of respect for female life or honour, that is shown in every portion of the history of France. The "*bons bouchers*" of Charles the Bold spare neither women nor children. The *Bourguignons* and *Armagnacs* spare none. The Turkish allies of France sweep off the women and children of Italy by thousands into captivity. On the other hand, Diana of Poictiers is more conspicuous in history than her royal, and more youthful, lover: and the head of the house of Bourbon is rarely mentioned but in company with his mistress, *la belle Gabrielle:* while thousands feel for the sorrows of the unhappy La Fayette, who would find it difficult to bestow a thought upon the unfortunate women of Milan, Mantua, or Naples, Ghent, or Bruges, whose husbands and sons are mowed down by thousands; while they themselves are made to endure the last indignities to which their sex is liable, and their daughters are forced to seek in prostitution the means of obtaining food. The history of that unfortunate country is one of perpetual poverty; and a record of total inability to resort for support to any but the poor soils: and the man who derives his subsistence from those soils is always a barbarian: and not the less so because he chances to wear a cocked hat and feathers. Extreme inequality in the condition of the different portions of the female sex, is one of the characteristics of barbarism: and in every portion of the history of France is exhibited the same inequality that is now shown in the poor girl who, unable to purchase fuel, sleeps in the day and works by night in the stable that she may derive from the proximity of animals a supply of heat, on the one hand: and the vast fortune of the *Duchesse de Praslin*, on the other.*

If we look at the condition of the sex in the present day, we see the results of perpetual war, in the fact that women still labour in the field: in the aversion to marriage on the part of the men: and in the absolute necessity for the *dot.* An unportioned woman has no chance of marriage: while those who have portions see their husbands but for a moment, before forming a connection that is intended to last for life. *Marriages de convenance* are universal, and frequent adultery is the necessary consequence: while tens of thousands of women see no immorality in the formation of temporary unions. Foundling hospitals enable them to dispose of their offspring, to perish by hundreds in the hands of hireling nurses paid out of the proceeds of taxes imposed upon the honest and virtuous labourer, whose unremitted exertions are insufficient to enable him to procure a miserable subsistence for his wife and his children: and who lives on, a creature without hope, while mistresses and female stock-gamblers, titled and untitled, have boxes at the opera, and sport their gay equipages at the *fête* of *Longchamps:* while queens and princesses have palaces that count almost by dozens, and young ladies, just married, and become *enceinte*, publish the fact through

* "The *trousseau* of Mademoiselle Martignon, who is going to marry the Baron de Montmorenci, is to cost a hundred thousand crowns ($110,000). There are to be a hundred dozen of chemises; and so on, in proportion."—*French Newspaper.*

out the kingdom, to be received as cause for rejoicing by the poor man who sees his wife or daughter dying for want of food. Under such circumstances, it is not extraordinary that in meeting three young Parisians, we should have reason to feel assured of the middle one being a bastard: that being the proportion of illegitimate to legitimate births.

In England, the position of the sex has been widely different. More than any other portion of Europe has the soil of that country been exempt from the horrors of war, the effect of which is seen in the fact that the cottage of the labourer figures in every portion of the English landscape, affording the strongest evidence of the long existence of internal peace. The husbandman has been there exempt from the necessity of seeking protection within the walls of the town. There he has, more than in almost any part of Europe, been enabled to economize the machinery of exchange by living on the land that he cultivated, and thus has saved the cost of transporting himself to his work, and that of transporting the products of his labour to his place of residence: and, still more important, he has had a place upon which he might bestow those hours and half hours that in France are necessarily wasted. He has had A HOME of his own, and having the thing, he has made the word to express the idea.

In no part of Europe has the feeling of perfect individuality existed to the same extent as in England, and that it has there existed has been due to the fact that there, more than elsewhere, has internal peace existed, permitting man to place himself on the spot upon which his labours were to be applied. The home of the individual man required a mistress, and the choice of the man was influenced, necessarily, by the fact that she was to be his companion in his home, distant perhaps from the homes of other men, and that he was to be *dependent* upon her kindness and affection for the happiness of his life, and for the care of his children. Peace and the growth of wealth tended therefore to give to the weak woman power over the strong man: whereas war has, in all ages, tended to render her his victim.

With each step in the progress of wealth and population, we may see an improvement in the condition of woman, from the day when powerful barons contested the rights of the heiress of Henry I., and the poor Saxon neif was sold to slavery in Ireland; and that when the daughter of Torquil Wolfganger presided over the revels of Front de Bœuf; to those in which the throne was filled by the masculine Elizabeth: but with the following century came a long period of internal war and waste, to be followed by one of extreme demoralization; that of the reigns of Nell Gwynn and the Duchesses of Portsmouth and Cleveland. Royal and noble bastards then abounded. From the Revolution of 1688, until we approach the close of the last century, wealth and population gradually increased, and the people were better fed, better clothed, and better lodged than in any former period: the effect of which may be seen in the improved condition of the sex. Many of the abominations which marked the early years of the century had passed away before the commencement of the great war. Kings ceased to have mistresses to aid in the management of the affairs of state, and fleet marriages became less common. With that war and its enormous waste, we find, however, a new state of things. The *few* now become immensely rich, while the *many* become poor. The price of corn rises, and that of man falls. Landholders become too great to manage their own affairs, and they must have great tenants, with great farms. Cottages disappear, and almshouses become filled. Labour ceases to yield food, and women seek to have bastards that they may obtain allowances, *and thereby obtain husbands*. Indiscriminate intercourse becomes so common as in some degree to arrest the growth of population;* while

* It was stated twelve or fifteen years since by a clergyman: we think the Rev. Mr. Cunningham: that the morals of his parish were improving; and the reason given for this belief was, that bastards had become more numerous, from which fact he inferred that indiscriminate intercourse had become less common.

thousands of children perish of neglect and want of food. Great club-houses, and houses of prostitution increase in a ratio corresponding to each other, and thus we find that each step in the progress of war and waste: necessarily accompanied with growing inequality: is attended with a deterioration of the condition of the sex.

With the long continued peace and the consequent growth of wealth, there has been a gradual improvement in the condition of the sex, in England, but *bondagers*, *i. e.*, female field-labourers, still figure in the leases of Northumbrian landholders; half-starved women are yet conspicuous among the habitués of gin-shops: sales of wives with halters round their necks have not yet disappeared: women and girls still labour in coal mines, and sometimes in a state of perfect nudity: and adultery is not unfrequently the consequence of marriages in which property and not inclination is consulted. A state of society in which exists inequality to the extent to which it is found in England, is not favourable to female honour. Heavy taxes tend to produce poverty, and mischievous regulations bar men from finding employment, and hence marriage is far less universal than it ought to be. Taxes and regulations tend to produce a large class with money to spend, and with no employment for time, and hence a disposition for gallantry that would not otherwise exist. The steady and regular application of time or talent is the best security for morals, and that is invariably seen most to exist where labour yields the largest reward. All men would marry, if all could do so with safety to themselves. In such a state of things, the exceptions are only sufficient to prove the rule. The universal possession of property is the best guarantee for the security of property; and the universal possession of wives and families is the best security for morals; for husbands and fathers are interested in the repression of every thing tending to promote immorality.

In Scotland, improvement would appear to be less certain.

There, entails increase in number. There, sheep have taken the place of men whose cottages have been burned, and who have been compelled to seek refuge within towns and cities: and with their homes the sex has been compelled to lose the pride of female honour. Glasgow presents a scene of wretchedness rarely equalled among civilized men, and houses of prostitution exist in the ratio of one to twenty-eight! Such are the results of the increasing power of land, and diminishing power of man.

Perpetual peace abroad and at home has given to the United States constantly increasing wealth, and every man has been thereby enabled to feel that he may marry without hesitation. All, therefore, do marry; and hence the rapid increase of population: and hence the general morality. Bastardy is rare. If we seek to find it, it must be among the people who cultivate the poorer soils. Thirty years since, it abounded among the Germans of Pennsylvania, who raised small crops from the heavy clay; and then women laboured in the fields: but it has gradually diminished as population and wealth have grown, and as they have been enabled to combine the inferior lime with the superior clay, and have thus obtained a better soil. Receding gradually, it may yet be found in the counties more distant from the city, where a scattered population still obtain small crops from poor soils. It may be found in all those counties in which poor farmers sell all their hay, and buy no lime. In general, however, it exists to a very small extent; and the sex, respecting themselves in a higher degree, are respected, in a degree unknown to other portions of the globe. Dowry is rarely thought of.* *Marriages de convenance* scarcely

* "We buy our wives with our fortunes, or we sell ourselves to them for their dowries. The American chooses her, or rather offers himself to her for her beauty, her intelligence, and the qualities of her heart; it is the only dowry which he seeks. Thus, while we make of that which is most sacred a matter of business, these traders affect a delicacy, and an elevation of sentiment, which would have done honour to the most perfect models of chivalry."—*Chevalier.*

exist. The marriage tie is held sacred,* and all because each man has, or can have, his own home, within which he is sole master: except so far as he defers its management to its mistress, whose control, within doors, is most complete; but there she stops.† Everywhere is manifested towards the sex: old and young: rich and poor: high and low: a degree of deference elsewhere unthought of.‡ They travel, unprotected, for thousands of miles, fearing no intrusion: and encountering none of those discomforts to which they are exposed in every part of Europe.§ With marriage, the task of providing for the family is assumed by the husband; and woman then is left to the performance of the duties of the household, and the care of her children: and everywhere the labour incident to the performance of those duties is lightened by improved machinery.‖ In no part of the Union, however, is she seen to the same advantage as in Massachusetts, where man derives from the cultivation of a naturally sterile soil re-

* "You may estimate the morality of any population, when you have ascertained that of the women; and one cannot contemplate American society without admiration for the respect which there encircles the tie of marriage. The same sentiment existed to a like degree among no nations of antiquity; and the existing societies of Europe, in their corruption, have not even a conception of such purity of morals."—*M. de Beaumont.*

"The marriage tie is more sacred among American *workmen* than among the *middle classes* of various countries of Europe."—*Chevalier.*

† "Not only does the American mechanic and farmer relieve, as much as possible, his wife from all severe labour, all disagreeable employments, but there is also, in relation to them, and to women in general, a disposition to oblige, that is unknown among us, even in men who pique themselves upon cultivation of mind and literary education."—*Chevalier.*

‡ "One of the first peculiarities that must strike a foreigner in the United States is the deference paid universally to the sex, without regard to rank or station."—*Lyell.*

§ "We have allowed the administration of the customs to adopt practices unworthy of a civilized nation. It is inexplicable that they should have imposed upon the French, who believe themselves the most polished nation of the earth, rules, in virtue of which their wives and daughters are personally examined and felt, in filthy holes and corners, by female furies. These scandalous brutalities of the agents of the treasury are inexcusable, for they produce nothing to the revenue."—*Chevalier.*

‖ "The inventive spirit of the people of New England, and of their descendants throughout the Union, is displayed in the production of machinery for economizing the time and labour of their wives."—*Chevalier.*

turns to labour unknown to those who cultivate the prairies of the West: and where may be seen, congregating in thousands, female operatives among whom bastardy is unknown. The greatest of all the moral phenomena of the world is to be found in the city of Lowell, and the enlightened traveller will find in its examination abundant compensation for a failure of his visit to Niagara.*

With each step in our progress south, men cultivate poorer soils, and the power of combination diminishes; and with each such step the value of female labour, and the power of woman to provide for and defend herself, diminishes, until we find her and her children becoming the property of another. That all may become free, and that woman everywhere may acquire power over her own actions, determining for herself who she will marry and who she will not; that she may everywhere obtain a home in which to devote herself to the performance of those duties for which she was intended; the happy wife becoming the mother of children educated to be useful to themselves, their parents, and society: it is essential that wealth should be permitted to increase. It does increase most rapidly where men cultivate the most fertile soils; and that those soils may be cultivated, combination of action is indispensable. The consumer *must* take his place by the side of the producer. With each step of increase in the density of population, the power of combination increases, the consumer and the producer being enabled

---

* "The factories at Lowell are not only on a great scale, but have been so managed as to yield high profits, a fact which should be impressed on the mind of every foreigner who visits them, lest after admiring the gentility of manner and address of the women, he should go away with the idea that he had been seeing a model mill, or a set of gentlemen and ladies playing at a factory for their amusement."—*Lyell.*

"Morning and evening, and at meal times, seeing them passing in the streets, well dressed, and again, seeing suspended on the walls of the factories, among the vases of flowers, and the shrubs which they cultivate, their scarfs, and their shawls, and the hoods of green silk with which they envelope their heads, to secure them from the heat and dust in walking, I said to myself, This is not Manchester."—*Chevalier.*

more and more to place themselves by the side of each other. Population and wealth increase most rapidly where women are most chaste, and where they are most chaste they are most valued: whereas, where neither population nor wealth is permitted to increase, woman is, and must ever be, a slave and a prostitute; and man a barbarian, cultivating the poorest soils.

The PAST says to the sovereign of the PRESENT: "If you desire that woman should occupy the position for which she was intended by her Creator: cultivate peace."

To the landlord it says: "If you desire that your lands shall become valuable: avoid war, and permit wealth to increase, that woman may be chaste and population grow."

To the labourer it says: "If you desire that the honour of your wife and daughter be respected: labour to promote the maintenance of peace."

To woman it says: "If you would be a happy wife, mistress of your own home, and surrounded by your children: love those who cultivate peace."

CHAPTER IX.

MAN AND HIS FAMILY.

The savage, deriving from the poor soils a wretched and precarious subsistence, and compelled to change his place from day to day, sees in the birth of a child but an addition to his burthens, and but for the affection of the mother, few, particularly of the weaker sex, would live a single day. The child, in turn, arrived at maturity, sees in the parent but a useless consumer of the small stock of food, and leaves him to perish in the desert; or exposes him on the river bank, there to die the lingering death of starvation, or to become food for tigers: or, more mercifully, buries him alive, and thus terminates at once a life of tyranny over others, that has been productive of little but wretchedness to himself.

The man who cultivates the rich soils of the earth rejoices in the birth of his child. The great machine in the preparation of which he is engaged, yields to his labour a daily increasing recompense, and with each addition to his family he finds a more rapid increase of his wealth. Food increases more rapidly than mouths to consume it: and with each addition to their number, he finds himself enabled to devote more and more of his attention to the study of their characters and the formation of their minds, with a view to making them good sons, preparatory to their becoming good and useful citizens. He unites with his neighbours for the establishment of schools, and colleges, and libraries; and he economizes his own expenses, that they may want none of the training required to enable them to fill, usefully to themselves and beneficially to the community, the station, be it what it may, in which they shall be placed. The child, in turn, desires to aid the parent. Arrived at manhood, he remembers that in his youth his feelings and his rights had been respected, and he now pays the debt incurred in infancy, respecting in his parent the rights that, in his turn, he would have respected in himself.

By nothing is the progress of mankind in population and wealth made more manifest than by the change in the relation of parent and child. In the infancy of cultivation the one is a tyrant and the other a slave; but with each step in the progress of civilization, we find a tendency towards equality of condition, each learning more and more to regard the other as a companion and friend, differing in age, but equally labouring for the common good: the father granting to the son the benefit of his experience, while the son contributes as far as in his power lies, to the performance of the labours required for the great object of maintaining and improving their common condition.

The Spartans lived on the produce of the poor soils, cultivated by slaves. The child, if unfit to become a warrior, was destroyed. If saved, it was the property of the State. The parent acquired no claims upon the affections of his son, and the latter, arrived at maturity, felt that he had no debt to pay.

In the earlier and happier days of Rome, men drew large supplies of food from the rich soils, and then fathers and children were friends; but with tyranny abroad comes tyranny at home, and the fierce warrior is seen exercising over his son the power of life and death. With the gradual progress of decline, family hatreds grow, and husbands and wives, fathers, and sons, and daughters, are seen engaged in deadly strife. With each step land becomes more and more consolidated, and man becomes more weak: and with each is seen the growth of family hatred. Constantine murders his son. Constans, Constantius, and Constantine contend for the empire of the world: but as that empire diminishes in extent, we see mothers murdering sons, and brothers deposing and blinding brothers, the bitterness of hate growing with the abandonment of the fertile lands, and the increasing worthlessness of the prize.

Throughout the eastern world, where poor men cultivate the poorest soils, we see a perpetual series of family discords. Fathers are deposed and blinded by their sons: sons are murdered by fathers: and brothers are assassinated by brothers. In the lower walks of life, we may see the poor Hindoo, old and unable to labour, exposed upon the banks of the Ganges by order of sons who, anxious to prevent increase in the number of useless mouths, destroy their own children: although surrounded by the most fertile lands, waiting but for the growth of population and of wealth to yield ample supplies of food and of all other of the necessaries of life.

In modern Italy, with the diminution of population and of wealth, and the abandonment of the rich soils of the Campagna, we see nunneries innumerable, filled with unwilling daughters forced to undergo a living death for the benefit of sons who indulge themselves in uncontrolled license among the unfortunate women of plundered towns and cities, driven to prostitution for the support of life. There, too, we find murders and poisonings among fathers, brothers, sons, and nephews. Poverty produces everywhere repulsion and hate, and where it exists family affection can but rarely find a place.

In the rapidly growing Holland, and in the Netherlands of the middle ages, we meet a better state of things. There, increasing wealth facilitated the cultivation of the various soils, and the producer and consumer were enabled to place themselves side by side. Population grew, and with it the demand for labour. The parent saw in the child the future support of his age, and the child, grown to manhood, remembered the debt contracted in his youth.

France, always at war, and always poor, has restricted herself to the cultivation of the worst soils. Her men were ever in the field, engaged in the duties of their vocation: in the Netherlands, Germany, or Hungary: in Spain, Piedmont, the Milanese, Naples, or Sicily: while at home their wives were the prey of bands of *ecorcheurs*, and of robbers of every nation, invited alternately by the *Bourguignon* and the *Armagnac:* the Leaguer and the royalist: the sovereign and the rebellious noble. Of the children who were born, a large proportion perished in their infancy. Wealth and population were sometimes stationary, while at other times they went backward. At others, they advanced, yet slowly: and the result of a long series of ages is, that she presents still to view a scattered population engaged in cultivating the poorest soils. The feeling of "home" has had no existence. The foundling hospital repeats the story of Sparta. Few children are born, and of them but one-half attain maturity, then to be taken from their parents, to seek, in the fields of Germany, of Russia, or of Algeria, the means of subsistence: and that at the moment when the habits of life are to become fixed. The parent hopes little from the son, whose first duty is to that portion of society which governs the rest, and calls itself "the State." He does, therefore, little for him. He gives him hard work, and no instruction.*

* "Frugality in Nantes, with the labouring classes, is the effect of necessity more than virtue. Drunkenness is common, and temperance is almost a stranger to them. In the country it is nearly as bad; nine out of ten of the little farmers who come to this market, Wednesdays and Saturdays, and particularly at the fairs, return home in a state of intoxication. The life led by them when on military duty, from the age of twenty to twenty-eight, most certainly demoralizes them. * * To prevent the increase and lessen the state of disorder into which the greater part of the labouring class and mechanics of Nantes has fallen, a number of master tradesmen and proprietors of factories will not employ those men who do not agree to allow a certain sum weekly to be retained from their wages for the use of the wife and family The example spreads, and will, no doubt, become more general; but this circumstance also shows forth, in strong colours, the immoral state of the working class in France."—*Report on La Loire Inferieure, by H. Newman, H. B. M. Consul, to the Commissioners on the Poor Laws.*

The son, in turn, remembers the lessons of his youth. He neglects his parent, and tyrannizes over his child.* As a natural consequence, crime in families abounds. Poverty instigates to murder, and parents perish by the hands of children by descent or marriage: wives by those of husbands, and husbands by those of wives, to an extent unknown in the other countries of Europe: the natural result of unceasing war and waste. It is not, however, to the lower sphere of life alone that we must look for such events. Extreme inequality of condition tends to the production of crime among the highest as well as among the most lowly. The starving wretch seeks food on the highway, while the marshal seeks in the plunder of cities the means with which to indulge his passion for display. Both are equally criminal, and both equally the offspring of war. The world now rings with the *Praslin* tragedy, but thousands of cases less patent to the world, might be produced to show how small is the extent to which the feeling of attachment to home, or family, exists throughout the population of France. The system forbids its existence.

England has grown rich and populous. She has cultivated far better soils, and there has the feeling of attachment to home and family been more fully exhibited than in most other portions of Europe. Nevertheless, the provisions for maintaining the concentration of land, by which the progress of cultivation has been so much arrested, have equally tended to discourage the growth of harmony in families. The father feels himself a life-renter, and he is jealous of the rights of his son. The son watches the movements of his father, and a chancery injunction stays the parent engaged in the com-

* "Experience proves that most workmen, who are fathers of families, *will only consent to send their children to school during the years when they can earn absolutely nothing*, and that they are withdrawn as soon as their weak arms will enable them to earn a few *centimes*, and that it is to this deplorable abuse of paternal power, goaded by poverty, that we should attribute the moral and physical weakness that is here exhibited at all stages of life."—*Report of the Prefect of the Department of the North.*

mission of acts of waste. Younger sons see in the elder brother a rich man, made so by the accident of priority of birth, and they feel themselves to be poor and dependent on his bounty. Wives become poor at the death of husbands, while sons are made rich. Mothers of great sons spend their last years in the great almshouse for decayed nobles, Hampton Court.* The system retards the development of the powers of the earth, and the growth of intellect: and prevents the existence of family affection: and all because it tends to the maintenance of inequality of condition. To that inequality it is due that we see so great a body of the "uneasy class" of younger sons side by side with vast wealth. Thence arises the general thirst for office among men whose abilities would qualify them to work with advantage to themselves, their families, and their countrymen, were a way opened for them; but who are compelled to solicit favours at home, or to seek in the cultivation of the poor soils of Canada or of Australia that support which would be afforded in vast abundance by the rich, but undivided and therefore undeveloped, soils at home. Still more strongly is this the case in Scotland. There, entails abound. Throughout half the kingdom the rich soils lie unimproved, while poor men cultivate the poor ones. Scotchmen emigrate in shoals to Canada; some of their own motion, but thousands at the order of their landlords, in whose hands accumulate immense estates, while impoverished daughters and sisters, reared to affluence and unable to work, hide their diminished heads in poor villages, thankful if their little allowances suffice to preserve them from starvation. Family pride abounds: but there, as everywhere, the affection of the family is in the inverse ratio of its pride—or vanity.

Throughout Great Britain, restrictions on land have tended to render man superabundant, and to compel him to seek

* Such was the case with the lady who was mother to Lords Wellington, Wellesley, Mornington, and Cowley.

employment from manufacturers whose markets were uncertain, and whose wages were not unfrequently altogether suspended. Labour has overflowed, and wives have been compelled to abandon the care of their families, and to seek support in factory and colliery work: while children have been taxed far beyond their powers, to produce wages to be expended in dissipation by their parents. The history of both wives and children, as developed in the recent reports to Parliament, is an awful one, and tends to show how absolutely the feelings of family affection may be blunted by the working of an unsound system. Throughout the whole island, there is now an universal demand for more wages and less work: and Parliament, which has already interfered to compel the parents to do that which parental affection has failed to prompt them, is now called upon to interfere between the employer and the employed, of all ages; while the former sees ruin in the prospect of any reduction in the labours of the latter. That such interferences should be needed is evidence abundant of the unsoundness of the system to which it owes its rise. Were man permitted to develope the powers of the earth, he would acquire power over his own actions, and would then determine for himself the hours of labour, without the aid of Parliament. Every step towards perfect freedom in the actual possessor of land is a step towards freedom in man. The fruits of the tree of Scotch and English entails are agricultural paupers, starving operatives, overworked children, and "uneasy" ladies and gentlemen—younger brothers and sisters.

In the United States, where all marry, all see the increase in the numbers of their families without alarm. The growth of wealth so far exceeds that of population, that the demand for labour is constantly in advance of the supply. In addition to the natural increase the immigration from abroad grows with each successive year, and the demand advances with its growth, for each producer is a consumer: and each makes himself a market for much of the products of his own labour, while consuming a portion of the products of his neighbours. Such is even now the case, but it would have been at all times still more strongly felt had not the erroneous policy of England forced men to seek the west who might have been so much more advantageously employed in the east. With each step in their progress, men cultivate better soils, obtaining increased returns to labour: and hence the steady increase in the quantity of the comforts and conveniences of life at the command of the labourer, accompanied with a steady increase in the inducement to the exertion of the physical and mental faculties. The father works that the children may be clothed and educated, and when the proper time arrives they work for themselves, but not till then. How great are the exertions of parents for the education of their children may be seen from the fact that in the public schools of New York may be found one-fourth of the whole population of the state: while in the libraries belonging to those schools may be found twelve hundred thousand volumes, accumulated in about a dozen years, and now accumulating at the rate of a hundred thousand in each year: and were concentration on the rich soils possible, the number would soon be doubled. How small is the labour required from children of immature years may be seen in the fact that in the mills of Lowell, there are none below twelve, while but seven per cent. are below seventeen: whereas in England, before the late interferences, no less than thirty-six per cent. were below the latter age, while many were of such exceedingly tender years as to render their long continued employment in the manner described destructive of all power of development; and hence the numerous cripples. Such, likewise, is the case in France, in some of whose manufacturing departments, almost two-fifths are exempted from the conscription because of bodily ailments.*

* "The paupers are described as consisting of weavers, unable at times to support their families, and wholly chargeable to public or private charity in case of illness, scarcity, or discharge from work; of workmen, ignorant, improvident, brutified by debauchery, or enervated by manufacturing labour, and

If we compare with the coal mines of England those of Pennsylvania, we see similar differences. In the first, we see girls and boys, sometimes of very tender age, and sometimes working together in a state of absolute nudity: whereas, in the second, we see few boys, and none but those that are fully competent to the labour at which they are employed. In no part of the world, therefore, are children so soon fitted to provide for themselves, because in none is the parent in so great a degree the companion of the child; and consequently in none are the faculties of the latter so early developed. In the relation of parent and child there exists, therefore, the strongest tendency to harmony, while in that of the children with each other there is little room for cause of difference. In the eye of the law, all are equal. If there be property to be divided, any inequality of division must be a consequence of favour on the part of the parent, whose control over that property is, as it should be, absolute: and all have therefore reason to cultivate his good opinion. Throughout the whole country, there prevails, however, a feeling of independence, and a consciousness of ability to rise, which forbid that sons should vegetate while waiting for the division of the father's land: and there is, consequently, less of what is sometimes termed "waiting for dead men's shoes," and less wrangling about the partition of estates than in any country of the world: although the amount now annually divided is fully equal to that of the United Kingdom, if not even greater.

With each step in the passage from the poor to the fertile soils, man acquires more power over his own actions, and a more perfect consciousness of his rights, accompanied by a corresponding sense of his duties. As the power of concentration and of combination of action increases, labour is

habitually unable to support their families; of aged persons, prematurely infirm, and abandoned by their children; of children and orphans, a great number of whom labour under incurable disease or deformity; and of numerous families of hereditary paupers and beggars heaped together in loathsome cellars and garrets, and for the most part subject to infirmities, and addicted to brutal vice and depravity. See *Villeneuve: Economie Chretienne.*

more largely paid: and each step is marked by an increase in the *power* of the parent to perform his duties to the child, and a diminishing *necessity* on the part of the child for the performance of those duties, in case of death or accident to the parent: while each is marked by an increasing *power* on the part of the child to aid the parent, and a diminishing *necessity* on that of the latter for depending on such aid. Their union becomes more and more voluntary, and is, therefore, on both sides, more and more marked by the performance of duties, and the respect for rights.

The PAST says to the parent of the PRESENT: "If you desire to do justice to all your children: strive for the maintenance of peace. With peace come wealth and the cultivation of the more fertile soils: and with them comes the division of land, by aid of which your sons and daughters will be enabled to marry and settle near you, and you will be surrounded by happy families of children and grandchildren."

To the children it says: "If you desire to remain with your parents, and to have your children, in turn, remain with you: strive for the maintenance of peace."

To all it says: "Family affection is inconsistent with war, and preparation for war: for with these come taxes, and poverty, and dispersion over the poor soils of the earth."

CHAPTER X.

CONCENTRATION AND CENTRALIZATION.

THE people of the Happy Valley commenced the work of cultivation on the sides of the hills by which it was shut in from the world. Could we have had a view of them in the early stages of the settlement, we should have seen a few families on the various sides, north, south, east, and west, cultivating the thin soils, and deriving from their labour a slender subsistence, while below the rich soils were covered with magnificent trees, through which rolled a beautiful stream. Intercourse between the families must have been impossible, except by keeping round the sides of the hills, themselves very frequently indented by ravines also filled with trees, and hence all intercourse must have been attended with severe labour. By slow degrees we find them, however, working downward, and all looking inward toward the banks of the little stream. Population increases and cultivation extends itself, and the young people desire to meet together; and marriages take place; and exchanges arise; and places of exchange are needed; and farmer's sons become blacksmiths and tanners, and shoemakers, and tailors, and hatters, and carpenters, and masons, and weavers; and thus, by degrees, a town arises: and now we see a little community perfect in itself, and capable of advancing in civilization were it to have intercourse with none other in the world.

If now we enter the home of one of these happy farmers, we find him also turning his eyes inward. His wife, his children, his farm, his cattle, and his house, stand first in his thoughts. In these it is that he finds his happiness. We should, however, greatly err if we supposed the man whose thoughts are thus concentrated upon his home to be incapable of associating with his fellow men, or to be in any degree incapacitated for so doing. On the contrary, it is because of his combination with them that he is enabled to exercise the power of concentration. The miller is near him, and he is not obliged to travel abroad with his grain when he desires to have it converted into flour. His near neighbours are the tanner, the shoemaker, the hatter and the butcher, and he is in the habit of daily intercourse with them. He discusses with them and with others of his fellow-citizens, the laying out of roads; the arrangements of the little and growing town; the building of churches; the institution of schools and little libraries for his children, and the formation of a library for their own joint use: and he combines with them in all the arrangements for the maintenance of perfect security of person and property; for the settlement of differences that may arise among their fellow-citizens; for the collection of the contributions required for the making of roads and for other purposes; and for a vast variety of other matters interesting to the community at large. Combination tends to promote security and the growth of wealth, and wealth enables him daily more and more to concentrate his thoughts upon his home, and its occupants: and this concentration, in its turn, promotes the growth of wealth, by enabling him daily more and more to reflect upon the measures necessary to the advancement of the common good: to devote his leisure in aid of those less fortunate than himself: to acquire knowledge by the study of nature, or of books: and thus still further to advance the interests of the society of which he has the happiness to be a member. The labours incident to the performance of the general business of the society are light, for they are divided among all; and they cost little, for they are performed by the men who have themselves to contribute towards its payment. All work and all pay, and hence the work and the pay fall lightly upon each.

With each step in the extension of cultivation over the fertile soils towards the foot of the hill, the return to labour increases, and means are obtained for carrying the work of cultivation upwards towards the hill-top. Rich lands, whose soil is the accumulation of centuries, furnish pasture for fine herds of cattle. Manure abounds, for the consumer has taken his place by the producer. The miller, the blacksmith, and other mechanics, exchange their products with the farmer, whose horses are rarely on the road, but almost always at the plough: and thus, from day to day, and hour to hour, the power of man over land, and over himself, is seen to grow, and with each step grows his love of home.

If, now, we place ourselves on the hill-top, we may look down into other valleys like the first. In each the work of cultivation has commenced on the hill-side: and in each we see the eyes of its inhabitants turned downwards towards the rich lands that occupy the centre of the little settlement. In each we see the attention of all turned inwards towards their homes, and their common home. In each we see the growth of wealth marked by the extension of cultivation upwards, and in each we see the gradual advance of roads towards the hill, or mountain, top: and among all the communities of all these little valleys, we see a tendency towards the establishment of communication with each other, for purposes of trade, and for facilitating operations of common interest.

If, now, we take a bird's-eye view of these various communities, we shall see in each an infinite number of little pyramids, with heights proportioned to their breadth and depth. With the extension of the breadth of cultivation we have seen it rising in its height until it has advanced far up the steep hill-side; and on all sides we see it rising higher as it sinks deeper into the fertile soils of the valley below. In each we see a variety of schools surmounted by an academy for the more advanced: and *that*, as wealth and population shall increase, and academies shall become more numerous, and as the love of knowledge sinks deeper into their souls, to be itself surmounted by a college. In each we see the little associations for purposes of general interest to the various sections of the valley, surmounted by a general one assembled in the little town, the common centre of attraction to the whole people.

With the establishment of intercourse among these little communities, the tendency to union, so well begun in each, is seen to spread. Each grows in wealth and population, and intercourse becomes more frequent; and next we find them all combining for the making of roads, or canals, the founding of colleges, and other works calculated to promote the common good. The union becomes more complete: and rules are adopted for the determination of the relations of the several communities, and of those of the members of each, with each other: and thus by degrees a government is formed. General laws now embrace the whole of the various societies constituting this new pyramid, which now surmounts the whole.

If we now look down again into the several societies, we shall see that to their members the importance of these laws diminishes with distance. First stands *the* home. Next, the common home of the original community: and, lastly, the general home of the several communities. In the first, each finds his chief source of happiness. In the second, he finds means of augmenting that happiness, by combination with his neighbours for the maintenance of the roads in daily use by himself and them: for the support of schools required by his children, the library required for himself, and the church required by his family. In the third, he combines with more distant neighbours for the maintenance of roads which he sometimes uses, and for the regulation of affairs of general interest, by which he may at times be affected: whereas in the regulation of those of his own little community he has a daily and hourly interest: and in those of his own home, one that ceases neither day nor night.

General laws are formed, but local regulations remain untouched: and thus each little community preserves its perfect individuality, rendered more perfect by union with its neighbours; for the union of all adds to the *power* of each for the maintenance of the perfect security essential to the growth of wealth and population, and the further extension of cultivation. Each has now its own government for all matters appertaining to its members, while each submits to general rules for the conduct of their people towards those of the adjacent communities. The base of each widens, and their relations with each other become more intimate, as better soils are taken into cultivation: and with each step their power of union and their strength increase; yet concentration within the limits of each becomes more and more complete. Each now has churches of various denominations. Each has high schools, and preparatory schools. Each has the fashioner and the producer by the side of each other. Each sees to its own roads and bridges, and each has its local court for the settlement of differences among its people. The machinery of all this is simple, and the cost is light; for those who look to the affairs of the community do so in the intervals of their own employments: and as the people determine for themselves whom and what they will pay, they desire to have little waste. In time, twenty, thirty, fifty, or a hundred of these little communities, at first scattered over the land, and separated by broad tracts of forest, and deep and rapid rivers running through the most fertile lands: or by hills and mountains: are brought into connection with each other: and these numerous little pyramids now form a great pyramid, or State. Perfect concentration, however, still exists. Local rules still govern local interests, and local judges decide local differences. Local roads and bridges are made under the direction of local officers: and local mills, and shops, and factories, furnish the producer with mouths to consume on the ground the various products of the earth. The State, thus formed, is neighbour to another little State:

and with the further growth of population and wealth intercourse arises, and a new union is now formed; each, however, still preserving its local organization and its laws, so far as regards the interest of its own people, but adopting such as may be deemed equitable in relation to those of their own State with those of the other. Each grows again: and within each the little pyramids rise, increasing in height, and breadth, and density: and again arise new unions with other and more distant little States; and with each step wealth and population advance more rapidly. The great union acquires strength from the increasing strength of the various parts of which it is composed; and the little unions acquire it, because of the perfect concentration of their local concerns, by means of which each is left to determine for itself what to do, and what to omit doing, in regard to its own business: and to do it by persons selected by themselves, and to do it economically. With each step in their progress of wealth and population, there is in each little community an increasing number of persons possessing each *his own* land, and *his own* house, upon which he concentrates his exertions for *his own* physical improvement; and *his own* wife, and *his own* children, in whom centre his hopes of happiness: and for the promotion of whose ease, and comfort, and enjoyment, he is at all times anxious to exert his physical and intellectual faculties. The machine is simple. It moves of itself, for each man moves his share. The work is done, yet it is difficult to see by whom. The labour is light, for it is done by many. The strength is great: for it has the form which all matter tends to take, and which is, consequently, the most natural. Its power of resistance is great. Its power of motion is small, and hence its tendency to peace.

Such is concentration. Opposed thereto is centralization. The one looks inward, and tends to promote a love of home and of quiet happiness, and a desire for union; facilitating the growth of wealth and the preparation of the great machine of production, and enabling man acquire a love of books and a habit of independent thought and action. Here each man minds his own business, and superintends the application of the proceeds of his own labour. Centralization, on the contrary, looks outward, and tends to promote a love of war and discord, and a disrelish for home and its pursuits, preventing the growth of wealth, and retarding the preparation of the great machine. Under it men are forced to move in masses, governed by ministers, and generals, and admirals: and the habit of independent thought or action has no existence. Here no man is permitted to mind his own business, and no man controls the application of the proceeds of his labour. The State manages every thing, and the State is composed of those whose profits are derived from managing the affairs of others.

Throughout the world has existed a tendency to the concentration of man, as may be seen by studying the progress of Attica and of Greece generally: of the cities of Latium: of those of the Netherlands, and of India: but in the early periods of the history of man, he is seen uniformly to have been exceedingly poor, and compelled to depend for subsistence on the poorest soils; as witness eastern Argolis, so early abandoned: and hence the perpetual contests in Greece for the possession of little tracts of land capable of yielding food. In this fact may be found the cause of the difficulty of general association, seen invariably in the early periods of society: and to this may be traced the existence of power on the one hand, and that of slavery on the other. Individual power over bodies of men has been, at all times, and in all nations, attended by contests for the exercise of that power. Poverty tends thus to produce foreign war, to increase poverty, and to produce the concentration of land: and this, in turn, tends to produce civil war, to augment poverty, and to increase the appetite for foreign wars; as is shown in the histories of all countries, but especially in those of Greece, Rome, and France. It was reserved for later times, when wealth, material and intellectual, more abounded; and when men *could* occupy better soils than those of Attica and the eastern slope of Argolis, to exhibit the gradual formation of a community in a manner perfectly natural, and almost undisturbed by foreign or domestic wars.

France has never, from the days of Clovis, exhibited any material tendency to the concentration of man, or of wealth upon land: or of the affections of man upon either wife or family. In the early period of her history, we find barons innumerable, engaged in collecting men and taxes, for the purpose of carrying them forth from their territories, to spread ruin among their neighbours. For a brief period, we find nobles and sovereigns granting charters to cities and towns, to enable them to acquire power to become centres of their various neighbourhoods, and thus to bring the consumer to the side of the producer. Perpetual war and desolation enfeeble the towns and they gradually lose the few privileges they have obtained, and the consumer and producer are again separated. Great nobles and kings are next seen gathering together all of men and wealth that can be commanded, and carrying them forth into Italy and Spain, Germany and the Netherlands: there to be employed in the acquisition of power over the wealth of other men. The great city of Paris: great because alone capable of affording the slightest protection to person and property, and therefore the resort, from all parts of the kingdom, of those who had been plundered and desired to plunder in turn: fares like the rest, and loses its privileges. If the reader desire now to see and understand the process by which poverty has been maintained in France, and the causes why she still continues to cultivate poor soils, he may study the history of that city in the reigns of Charles VI. and VII., and then satisfy himself what must have been the condition of the lesser cities of Amiens and Beauvais, Aix and Thoulouse. The rights of the people have had no existence. The right to labour, even, was deemed to be held of the crown, and crown and nobles made themselves the conduits by which the population and wealth of the kingdom were passed to foreign countries. With the exception of a feeble attempt to establish local courts in opposition to the parliament of Paris, we meet, for centuries, with no attempt at the local concentration of either man or power in any portion of the kingdom. Every thing had to go forth from the place of production in payment of the *taille*, and the thousand other taxes: and the people were *corvéeable à volonté*, to make the roads by which it was to pass out. With the Revolution was swept away the very shadow of local administration. From that moment, every thing went forth, to every part of Europe, and on the seas and oceans by which it was surrounded.* Conscriptions were anticipated, and boys of sixteen were torn from their mothers' arms. None remained at home but the blind, the halt, and the lame, and the stunted; and thus was France exhausted. The little pyramids had never risen, and the great ones could not rise. Paris and the Emperor stood alone, columns in the desert, and on the first attack both toppled over.

From that hour to the present every thing has continued to go forth from the land to Paris, there to be distributed and exported by means of armies and fleets; or in the payment for luxuries consumed by kings, and princes, and nobles, and gentleman, and financiers, and all others of the class who live by managing the business of others. Seventy per cent. of the whole revenue of the land-owner in this manner goes forth in the payment of taxes and interest; and hence it is that the kingdom exhibits throughout a dreary flat, occupied by a poor people who scratch the poorest soils, and who pretend to the exercise of no single right: being still, *in fact*, though not in theory, *tailleable et corvéeable à merci et à miséricorde*. Prefects, and mayors, and deputies, and deputies' assistants: all are provided for them. If the bridge requires to be rebuilt, it is to be done, or not done, for, and

* "But France got drunk with blood to vomit crime,
And fatal have her saturnalia been
To Freedom's cause, in every age and clime."—*Byron.*

not by, them. If the road requires repair, orders therefor must come from Paris. If the mine proprietor desire to open his coal, he must solicit permission at Paris, and pay for it. If the baker desires to open a shop, he must seek permission, and pay for it. Local institutions have no existence. Local expenditure has none. Local manufactures, or local unions, or local action of any kind, have none. They *can* have none, for the whole product of the kingdom, except what is needed for the absolute support of life, is swallowed up by officers of the crown, to pass by every channel to Paris, that thence it may be forced out to Algeria for the subjugation of Abd-el-Kader; to Spain, to promote intrigues in which the people have no interest; to Egypt and elsewhere, to procure knowledge of olden times and of hieroglyphics, while the people at large are unable to read or write their own language; to create picture galleries for a people, one-half of whom are forced to obtain bread-tickets to save them from starvation: and, in short, by every means that can be devised to drive it forth from the land, and to prevent the concentration of man or of wealth in any portion of the kingdom. The system grows with what it feeds on. Under the government of the Restoration, a thousand millions sufficed. Gradually it rose to twelve, thirteen, fifteen, and now even sixteen hundred millions are insufficient; yet at this moment, when people pay for the privilege of abandoning lands they have not means to cultivate, we see complaints that the sovereign *has not yet* been enabled to provide the proper retiring pensions for ministers. Such being the system, we feel disposed to believe with *M. Rubichon*,* that the government must eventually become proprietor of the whole soil of France. That time arrived, and it seems likely soon to arrive, the whole kingdom will present a dead level of serfdom, preparatory to the recom-

* Editor of the Statistics of France, recently published by order of the king.

mencement of troubles similar to those which marked the close of the last century.

Louis Philippe is called the Napoleon of peace. His only claim to the title is that he has not himself made war in Europe. The French *people* do not desire war, nor have they ever desired it. The peace of Europe has been perpetually disturbed by sovereigns of France, who have ruined the people over whom they presided. Louis Philippe has not made war in Europe, but around him everywhere he has promoted war; and he is now exhausting France, and rendering her poor and turbulent, preparatory to becoming revolutionary. He has restored to the people no one right of which they had been deprived; but he has deprived them of rights, and of the power to protect themselves, by increased demands for men and money to go forth from France. The thing which is called in France centralization is the reverse of concentration. The latter tends to enable men to cultivate better soils, and to unite for the purpose of governing themselves. The former, to compel men to abandon good soils and fly to poor ones; and to submit to being governed by others. Some little concentration exists in Paris, and hence the necessity for bringing it under the control of cannon.

Peace at home, and the consequent growth of wealth and population, have tended to produce local concentration in England; but that tendency has been, and still is, neutralized by a thousand opposing influences. Towns and cities have corporations, with privileges exercising strong repulsive tendencies. Parliament centralizes the power of England, Scotland, and Ireland, within the walls of St. Stephen's, that it may devote itself more advantageously to the management of the affairs of the world, and thus expel the population and the wealth that might be advantageously employed at home. The bank centralizes the money power, that it may promote the expulsion of the wealth that escapes the government, in loans to Russia and Mexico, Indiana and Illinois: in making banks in Australia, and railroads in France and India. The bar centralizes legal power in London, that a few may acquire large fortunes, to be invested in government loans that are applied to the maintenance of fleets and armies. The manufacturers centralize capital in Manchester and Stockport, that they may supply cheap cloths to foreign countries, that would benefit themselves and England much more largely were they permitted to place the consumer and the producer by the side of each other. The land-owner centralizes his rents, to be expended in London, Paris, or Italy; when, if they were expended where they had been produced, they would have given more and better food to his tenants, and more rent to himself. He centralizes the road-making power in the hands of himself and his fellows, that he may sell his land at high prices to the road-makers.

Every thing tends to centralize itself in London; and hence it is that picture-galleries are created, while nothing is given to the great work of placing the whole people in a condition to read and think for themselves. Hence it is that so much care is bestowed upon the relations of the people of Syria, Portugal, and Italy, with each other, and so little upon those of the people of England among themselves. Hence, too, it is that bishoprics are established abroad, while to the labourer's child at home is scarcely taught the existence of a Deity. Hence, too, the care bestowed upon the negro slave in America by a people surrounded by starving operatives and half-clothed labourers.

The tendency of centralization in England, as in France, is to cause men to mind the business of others, and to neglect their own; to cause them to look *from home:* and hence it is that "ships, commerce, and colonies" is the motto of England. She is now turning her attention towards home; and men are finding that if they would continue to have rents they must make roads and improve their lands; and that every such investment yields twice or thrice the rate of interest afforded by other modes in which labour can be employed. Even this, however, is done in a manner tending to concentrate wealth in a few hands. Iron masters, railroad kings, and great landlords, grow rich: while the mass of little capitalists are ruined by a speculation that owes its origin to the centralization of power in the hands of great bankers, and great legislators. Concentration is, however, taking the place of centralization, and cotton mills are closed as railroads are made. Food will become cheaper, and clothing less cheap; and other nations may be permitted to place the consumer by the side of the producer. When that time shall arrive, we shall see the termination of the system of government commissions for the centralization of power in the hands of the few, who charge themselves with the management of the affairs of others: paying themselves largely for the work.

In the growth of the United States, we have the exemplification of the natural system. At first we find a few scattered settlements gradually approaching each other; they form states, and the states at length form a union, growing from year to year by the addition of new states; yet towns, counties, and states preserve each their local administration and government, managing their own affairs in their own way: and leaving to the general association little more than the management of the affairs of the whole body with other bodies beyond their limits.

In Massachusetts, the oldest of the States, this exemplification is by far the most complete. Concentration of man, of wealth and power, and of the human affections, exists to a degree unequalled in the world: and hence the small amount of business that devolves upon the public servants. Wealth tends to stay at home, and to be invested where it is produced; and hence the rapid advance in prosperity. Passing south and west, we find diminishing concentration: diminishing power in the people to assert their right to manage their own affairs in their own way: and increasing power in their deputies to compel them to manage those affairs in the way dictated by others. In no part of the world, however, do the people do so much for themselves, and in no part is it so well and so cheaply done, as in the United States at large.*

The result of the three systems is as follows:

The product of the thirty-five millions of the people of France is about $1400,000,000, of which those charged with the administration of the affairs of the nation take almost *a fourth*, or ten dollars a head. That of the twenty-eight millions of the United Kingdom is about $1800,000,000, of which those charged with the management of affairs of Church and State, take about *a sixth*, or ten dollars a head. That of the twenty-one millions of the people of the United States exceeds $2000,000,000, of which the various governments, local and general, county and city, take about *a forty-eighth* part, or two dollars a head.† The product and division per head are, therefore, as follows:

	Product.	Labour and Capital.	Government
France	40	30	10
Great Britain and Ireland	64	54	10
United States	95	93	2

In the first, the people leave all to the government, which is largely paid, and nothing is done for them. In the second, the people do much, but much is left to the government, and

* "Of all nations this is perhaps the one whose government affords the least scope for glory. None has the burden of directing her. It is her nature and her passion to go by herself. The conduct of affairs does not depend upon a certain number of persons; it is the work of all. The efforts are universal; and any individual impulse would only interfere with the general movement. In this country political ability consists not in doing, but in standing off and letting alone. Magnificent is the spectacle of a whole people moving and governing itself;—but nowhere do individuals appear so small."—*De Beaumont.*

† The taxes were thus estimated by *M. Chevalier*, ten years since, for the State of New York:

Federal taxes	$1 40
State taxes	19
County tax	31
Local school-tax	9
	$1 99

This may be taken as a fair average for the Union, and the variation from hat time to the present is not material.

something is done. In the last the people do almost every thing, and leave little to the government, which is slightly paid, and every thing is done. The first looks altogether abroad, and cultivates the worst soils at home. The second looks very much abroad, and cultivates a vast amount of poor soils at home. The third concentrates its energies at home, and passes as rapidly as it can from the poor to the better soils, and labour is every day more largely rewarded. With concentration, the production would be greatly increased, while the *necessity* for government would be lessened: because the *power* of self-government would be increased.

The great prosperity of the people of the United States is uniformly attributed to their abundance of fertile soils. They have been supposed to be receiving wages for their labour, *plus* the excess that elsewhere would be absorbed as rent. Forced, however, to squander their labours over the poor soils of the west, and to use a vast amount of the inferior machinery of exchange, they appear to have been receiving only wages *minus* the profits of the capital which has been wasted in subjecting to cultivation poor soils, when fertile ones were at hand waiting the demand for their products. The rich meadow-lands of Pennsylvania and of various other States have remained covered with timber, while thousands have sought the west, there to commence the work of cultivation on dry prairie-land upon which trees will not grow; and to obtain from an acre of land thirty or forty bushels of Indian corn that must be converted into pork before it can reach a market, distant thousands of miles: whereas, by the careful cultivation of the better soils of the older States, their labour might have been blessed with returns far greater. An acre of turnips in England is made to yield twelve or fourteen tons. Acres of potatoes yield frequently almost as much; whereas an acre of prairie-land yields but a ton of Indian corn, the most productive of all grains. The meadow-land of Pennsylvania is not worth the cost of clearing, because the market for its products has no existence: and until the consumer shall place himself side by side with the producer, it can have none. Place him there, and then nothing will be lost. The rich soils will give forth their products, and the refuse will remain on the spot, to go back into the ground: and thus the produce of the rich will fatten the poor ones. The land round cities is valuable, because the soil gives forth its produce by tons: not bushels. An acre of potatoes will outweigh a dozen acres of wheat, and its refuse will fertilize an acre of poor soil; but from the produce of an acre of wheat sent abroad to be exchanged, nothing goes back upon the land. We see everywhere that when furnaces are built, coal mines opened, or mills established, land in the immediate vicinity becomes more valuable: and it is because that, when the consumer and the producer come together, man is enabled to compel the rich soils to exert their powers in giving forth the vast supplies of food of which they are capable, and to pay them back by giving them the whole refuse: and until they do come together, nothing can be done. To render the meadow land worth the cost of clearing, the farmer must have a market on the ground for his milk and cream, his veal and his beef. If compelled to convert the milk into cheese, giving the refuse to his hogs; and to drive his lean cattle to market: sending also to distant markets the food they would have consumed in the process of being fattened, and thus losing altogether the manure: the land is but little more valuable than the prairies of the west, always to be had at the minimum price of a dollar and twenty-five cents an acre: whereas to clear the trees and stumps and level the ground might cost twenty dollars: and hence it is that men fly from rich soils to poor ones. The people of the United States are now scattered over a million of square miles, and over that vast surface they have been forced to make roads, and to build court-houses, schools, and churches: whereas, had they been permitted to follow the bent of their inclinations they would not, at this time, have passed the Mississippi. The tendency of man is to combine his exertions with those of his fellow men; and when we find him doing otherwise the cause will be found, invariably, in the existence of some essential error in the course of policy. Self-interest prompts him to this union. He feels that two, ten, or twelve, acting together, can accomplish that which would be impossible to a thousand men, each acting alone: yet is he seen flying off to the wilderness, abandoning his home, his parents, and his friends, while meadows uncleared exist in unlimited quantity, soliciting his acceptance of their gifts. To produce an effect so contrary to the laws of nature, a powerful repulsive force must exist. It does exist, and the extent of its power may be measured by an examination of the condition of the adjacent province of Canada. Concentration therein is impossible. The man who should undertake there to establish a work of almost any description, would inevitably be ruined by the perpetual fluctuations of the English system.

But a few months since, the prices of cotton cloths were high. Now, the mills are closed, and a single town exhibits twelve hundred houses unoccupied. The cotton manufacturer of Canada would be ruined. Three years since, the price of iron was low, because peers would permit but few railroads to be made. Now, it is high, because they have permitted the formation of roads innumerable. A month hence railroad building may stop, and then the world will be flooded with iron, and foreigners will be ruined. Against such revulsions, the product of a system that is to the last degree unsound, the people of the British provinces have no protection. Ministers are omnipotent: Parliament is omnipotent; and the Bank is omnipotent. They make war or peace: grant or refuse railroads: make money abundant or scarce, at their pleasure; and the poor colonies must bear all: and hence the utter worthlessness of land, as is shown by the occurrences of every day.*

* "By describing one side of the frontier, and reversing the picture, the other would be described. On the American side, all is activity and bustle.

Railroads and canals are made with government assistance, but they are almost unused, and so must they continue to be, until the people shall acquire the power of self-protection: or until England shall have learned to obtain her own food from her own rich soils, and to permit those who occupy the other portions of the earth to consume, on the ground on which it is produced, their own food, returning to the soil its refuse: and thus facilitating the construction of the great machine, and the development of all its wonderful powers.

From first to last we may see in the great fathers of the country a full belief that the proximity of the consumer and the producer was essential to the promotion of agriculture.

The forest has been widely cleared: every year numerous settlements are formed, and thousands of farms are created out of the waste; the country is intersected with common roads, &c. * * * On the British side of the line, with the exception of a few favoured spots, where some approach to American prosperity is apparent, all seems waste and desolate. * * The ancient city of Montreal, which is naturally the capital of Canada, will not bear the least comparison, in any respect, with Buffalo, which is a creation of yesterday. But it is not in the difference between the larger towns on the two sides that we shall find the best evidence of our inferiority. That painful but most undeniable truth is most manifest in the country districts through which the line of national separation passes, for a distance of a thousand miles. There, on the side of both the Canadas, and also of New Brunswick and Nova Scotia, a widely scattered population, poor, and apparently unenterprising, though hardy and industrious, separated from each other by tracts of intervening forests, without towns or markets, almost without roads, living in mean houses, drawing little more than a rude subsistence from ill cultivated land, and seemingly incapable of improving their condition, present the most instructive contrast to their enterprising and thriving neighbours on the American side. * * * Throughout the frontier, from Amherstburgh to the ocean, the market value of land is much greater on the American than on the British side. In not a few parts of the frontier this difference amounts to a thousand per cent. * * * The price of land in Vermont and New Hampshire, close to the line, is five dollars per acre, and in the adjoining British townships, only one dollar. On this side of the line, a very large extent of land is wholly unsaleable even at such low prices, while on the other side property is continually changing hands. * * * I am positively assured that superior natural fertility belongs to the British territory. In Upper Canada, the whole of the great peninsula between Lakes Erie and Huron, comprising nearly half of the available land of the province, is generally considered the best grain country of the American continent."—*Lord Durham.*

They had seen the effects of provincial government. They had been in the situation in which Canada now is placed, and they had felt its hardships. The people of that province are poor, and so must they remain pending the existence of the system: because, while it lasts, they must continue to scatter themselves over the poor soils. *There* great men are numerous. They are busily employed in governing the poor and scattered little men, and paying themselves: as they will continue to do, so long as the power of concentration on the rich soils shall continue to be denied. The abundance of land is said to be the cause of American prosperity, but Canada has land in greater abundance, and yet she is too poor to make a road: too poor to keep her own people, who are now deserting her capital to open houses of trade in New York: too poor to keep the unhappy immigrants from Ireland: while the ever-growing wealth of the Union, blessed as it has heretofore been with peace, has furnished means of employment for all that came direct from the British Isles and from Europe at large, and all that overflowed from Canada; and having received them, has placed them at once in a situation to obtain, if they would, houses, lots, and lands: *homes of their own.*

The right of resistance to wrong is inherent in every man: and every man and every nation may be at times compelled to resort to war in self-defence. War is an evil, and so are tariffs of protection: yet both *may* be necessary, and both *are* sometimes necessary. But for universal resistance, the corn-laws would still exist, and the land-owners of England would not yet have felt the necessity of looking towards home. Concentration is now advancing in the United States because the interferences of England are diminished, and thus we see mills slowly rising throughout the Southern States, filled with black operatives. Planters now raise the food required for their hands, and ploughs and other agricultural implements are made at home: and hence it is that the overcharged markets of the world are relieved of the surplus cotton, and that the planter obtains for a crop of two millions more than could have been yielded by one of three millions. With a large crop freights are high, and the machinery of exchange absorbs a large proportion of the small price obtained abroad. With a small crop, freights are low and prices abroad are high; and the planter obtains a large reward, enabling him to clear and drain his rich soils. He is placing the consumer by the side of the producer, and with every step in this course he will obtain increased returns from a diminished surface. With each, he will improve his own condition, while the labour of those by whom he is surrounded will become daily more valuable: and with each, there will be seen an increasing tendency to improvement in their physical, moral, intellectual and political condition. If we now turn our eyes to Pennsylvania, we see the same results. To bring into activity the coal mines of the eastern portion of that State, has required an expenditure of $50,000,000, by aid of which they now send to market three millions of tons of coal, worth $6,000,000: all of which is expended on the spot, in payments to labourers employed in mining coal, constructing engines, and building houses. Small as is, as yet, the result, it has doubled the value of every farm, over hundreds of thousands of acres. The farmer has now a market for his timber, and he clears his rich lands with profit to himself from furnishing wood to be used in propping mines, building boats, laying railroads, and building houses. He has a market for his cabbages, his turnips, and his potatoes; his veal and his beef; and he is thus gradually acquiring power to force out from the great treasury of food what nature intended it should give forth: and that power is consequent upon the fact that men have come to eat it. Close the mines, and he must raise wheat to compete with the product of the dry lands of western prairies: and at once must his lands decline in value. To accomplish thus much required a vast sum. but, as we have already seen, in every operation connected with the fashioning of the great machine, the first cost is the greatest. The land that yields coal yields also iron ore. A hundred furnaces would produce five hundred thousand tons of iron, worth, at the price in England, $12,000,000, or twice as much as the present yield of coal: and yet these hundred furnaces, that would bring to the producer twice as many mouths as does now the coal, would cost but $3,000,000. Why, then, are they not built? Capital abounds for every purpose, and iron which should be sold for fifteen dollars, commands thirty dollars: and yet furnaces are built but slowly. The reason is to be found in the fact that every species of manufacture is a lottery, and will so continue while the policy of England remains unchanged. The furnace-builder must calculate upon paying himself in a year or two, and so much time may not be allowed him. Even at this moment, the increasing difficulties of the times may have caused the abandonment of great lines of roads, diminishing the demand for iron, and lessening the price one-half: and if so the furnaces and rolling-mills of Pennsylvania may be closed. Pending the existence of this state of things in a nation possessing the power that is wielded by England, all operations of trade or manufacture requiring large expenditure, must continue to be mere gambling; and, as a necessary consequence, they must continue to be monopolized by the few who can afford to incur large risks for the chance of large profits: and those are not the men who work most economically. When the manufacture of iron shall become safe, it will fall into the hands of working men: and then iron will be cheap. While such fluctuations shall continue, all operations in agriculture must likewise continue to be attended with great vibrations, consequent upon the changes of English action. At one time, cabbages and potatoes will find a market on the ground, as in parts of the country now they do. At another, they will rot in the ground for want of a market, as some years since they did.

The tendency of the whole system of the United States,

is that of taking from the great machine all that it will yield, and of giving nothing back: and that tendency flows necessarily from the want of power over their own actions. Concentration is natural, and dispersion is unnatural, yet dispersion flows naturally from the absence of that power. The farmer of New York raises wheat, which exhausts the land. That wheat he sells, and both grain and straw are lost. The average yield per acre, originally *twenty* bushels, falls *one-third.* Had he a market on the ground for wheat, and milk and veal, he could cultivate rich soils, and the same labour that now yields ten bushels would yield him forty: and with each year he could clear such soils, for increasing population would produce demand for timber, and stone, and clay for bricks; and with each the great machine would yield forth more largely the treasures with which it is charged. He sows his wheat early and it is killed by the fly. Had he a market on the ground, for the produce of the rich soils now covered with timber, he could so improve his land as to sow it late, and then it would escape the fly. He sows his wheat on bottom lands, and it is killed by frost. Had he a market on the ground for veal and beef, he could enrich his higher lands with the manure produced on the lower ones, and then he would escape the frost. The farmer of Ohio raises wheat on thin soils, and it is killed by drought. He tries raising corn and wheat on the river soils, and it is drowned out, or destroyed by rust. He obtains ten bushels to the acre, which he must sell: and the produce of his land diminishes with each year. Were the consumer near him, his lower lands would be appropriated to meadows for his cattle, whose manure would enrich the poor soils of the higher lands, and drought would not then materially affect them. Another obtains thirty bushels of Indian corn from rich land, that, under a proper system of drainage, might yield a hundred bushels: but while he wastes his labour and manure on the road, no drainage can take place. Thirty-two tons of corn, sown broad-cast, have been obtained from an acre, in Massachusetts. That acre was enriched with the manure yielded by western corn, consumed in the rich State that has already placed the consumer by the side of the producer. When Ohio shall make a market for such crops, she will have them.

The Kentuckian exhausts his land with hemp, and then wastes his manure on the road, in carrying it to market. Had he a market on the ground for corn and oats, peas and beans, cabbages, and potatoes, and turnips, he might restore the waste: but the rich bottom lands must remain undrained until he can place the consumer side by side with the producer.

Virginia is exhausted by tobacco, and men desert their homes to seek in the west new lands, to be again exhausted: and thus are labour and manure wasted, while the great machine deteriorates, because men *cannot come* to take from it the vast supplies of food with which it is charged. Thousands of acres, heavily timbered with oak, poplar, beech, sugar-tree, elm and hickory, are offered at about the government price, or a dollar an acre, and on long credit, but they are not worth clearing: and they cannot be cleared, until there shall arise a demand for lumber for the construction of houses, mills, and railroads: and that cannot arise so long as men shall continue to be limited to the use of the worst machinery of exchange; wasting on the roads the manure yielded by the products of their poor soils, and the labour that might be applied to the clearing of the rich ones. An acre of wheat has been made to produce a hundred bushels, and such will, at some future day, be the produce of these lands: but the consumer and the producer will then be near neighbours to each other, and all the manure produced by the land will go back again to the great giver of these rich supplies. She pays well those that feed her, but she starves those who starve her: *and she expels them.*

The cotton planter raises small crops on thin soils, and he, too, is ruined by drought. He tries rich soils, and rains destroy his crop, even to the extent of more than two hundred thousand bales, worth many millions of dollars, in a single season. Were he near neighbour to consumers of food, vegetable and animal, he could raise large crops of grass and food on rich lands, and manure the poor ones: and then he would suffer little from drought or rain. He would have always at hand, aid in harvest, and his cotton fields would yield him larger crops from smaller surface.

South Carolina has millions of acres admirably adapted to the raising of rich grasses, the manure produced from which would enrich the exhausted cotton lands: but she exports rice and cotton, and loses all the manure, and must continue so to do until the consumer of veal, and beef, and corn, shall take his place by the side of the producer of cotton. When that time shall arrive, her wealth and population will both increase: but until then both must continue to diminish.

The sugar planter raises large crops, but they too are drowned out: or, if they escape the loss from rain, they perish with the frost. Had he neighbours who would consume food produced from rich land, he might raise his sugar on lighter soils while draining his heavier ones; and he would have at hand supplies of labour to aid him in his harvest. He now prays for the appearance of the cotton worm, as the farmer of Ohio prays for the potato-rot in Ireland. The one wants hands to make his crop, and the other mouths to eat it. Both are thus compelled to wish their neighbours ill, and for the same reason: because the consumer of food cannot take his place by the side of the producer. The direct effect of the dispersion of man is to cause vast loss of labour and manure, and to prevent the growth of those feelings of kindness that are found where men possess the power to concentrate themselves, and to combine their efforts for the general good.

The prosperity of the people of the United States is *not* due to the abundance of land. It exists despite of the necessity that has been forced upon them, for squandering their labour over the surface of hundreds of millions of acres of poor soils, leaving untouched the rich soils that lie beneath. It exists, despite of the necessity for living apart, when they might have lived in communion with each other, combining their exertions for the establishment of better schools, larger libraries, better houses and gardens, and all of the thousand aids to the development of intellect, of taste, and of the affections. It is, in despite of these obstacles, that they have schools where every man is educated:* that they have colleges and libraries fitted to produce men like Prescott and Bancroft, Kent and Story, Irving and Cooper, Norton and Robinson, Anthon and Pickering: that mind has been developed in the construction of machinery,† enabling them to establish with the mistress of the manufacturing world a competition that, more than any thing else, has tended to produce the abolition of restraints upon agriculture; and which in its turn tends now to produce a total change in her system and that of the world, by aid of which the machinery of exchange will be diminished in quantity and perfected in quality: the consumer of Germany, Italy, Canada, the United States and India, taking his place by the side of the man who produces the food he is to eat. With each step in the progress of this change, labour will become more and more productive: man will learn more and more to concentrate his thoughts and affections upon home: he will learn more and more to unite with his fellow man, and will acquire daily increasing power over the land and

* "In New England, every citizen receives the elementary notions of human knowledge; he is moreover taught the doctrines and the evidences of his religion, the history of his country, and the leading features of its constitution. In the States of Connecticut and Massachusetts, it is extremely rare to find a man imperfectly acquainted with all these things, and a person wholly ignorant of them is a sort of phenomenon."—*De Tocqueville.*

† "The Americans possess a quicker mechanical genius than even ourselves—as witness their patents and improvements for which we are indebted to individuals of that country in mechanics, such as spinning, engraving, &c. We gave additional speed to our ships, by improving upon the naval architecture of the Dutch; and the similitude again applies to the superiority which, in comparison with British models, the Americans have, for all the purposes of activity and economy, imparted to their vessels."—*Cobden.*

over himself: and he will become richer and happier, more virtuous, more intelligent and more free.

That the people of the United States should have acquired power thus to affect the movements of the world, has been due to the fact that they have abstained from war, and preparations for war, while other nations have wasted millions of lives and thousands of millions of treasure on useless fleets and armies, and in wars of desolation. That they have to so great an extent remained at peace, has been due to the fact that the war-making power rested with the whole people: with the men who paid the taxes, each one of whom had in his house and lot, his farm, his shop or mill, a little saving-fund in which he could deposit his time and money; and a home occupied by his wife and children, the depositaries of his affections. For them to go to war is difficult, because with them alone rests the power to declare it; and before such declaration can take place, a majority in favour of such a measure must be obtained. Among them is an infinite variety of interests. Some produce corn, and some cotton: and others tobacco, or rice. Some manufacture wool: others wood or cotton. Some own ships: and others steamboats. All these people *may* lose by war, and few *can* gain much. Under such circumstances, before a majority can be obtained, much discussion is needed in and out of the newspapers; in and out of the halls of Congress. Time is gained. The arguments for and against the war are read abroad as well as at home. The cost of war is discussed on both sides, and the value of the trade at risk is brought into view: and the result is a settlement of the difficulty. Such is the history of the Oregon and Maine boundary questions. Slow action is safe action; and where a nation takes the form of a pyramid, with a great base and very small top, the motion is slow, and appears devoid of energy: whereas, in one like that of France, where the pyramid is inverted, the movement is rapid, and energy appears to exist; but here, as elsewhere, the amount of power exerted is in the inverse ratio of the time employed.

It may be suggested that concentration might have a tendency to prevent the expansion of mind consequent upon the existence of the present system, and that men would think too much of home, and become selfish. Directly the reverse is the effect that is produced in private and in public life. The prudent man that is fond of his home, his wife, and his children, has leisure to read and to think. The voluptuary and the spendthrift have leisure for nothing that tends to the expansion of mind. Such we see to be the case in France. Every speech in the chambers, and every newspaper, abounds in selfish views. If we look back through her history, among sovereigns, nobles, leagues, and leaguers, the whole presents a picture of selfishness not to be exceeded in the world. If we look at the people, it is the same. Expansion of mind and liberality of feeling cannot exist where men cultivate the poorer soils, for communication is slow and difficult; and man must mix freely with his fellow man, or he remains a barbarian.

In the course of England we find far less selfishness than in that of France; but it invariably appears during long periods of war, like those of India, and that long one which closed with the battle of Waterloo. Each step in the progress of the latter was marked by growing disregard of the rights of man abroad and at home, until neutrals were driven from the ocean, and the people of England were driven, almost *en masse*, to the poor-house. If we trace the progress of feeling from the days of the Edwards to the present time, we may see growing liberality with increasing population. If we look at the kingdom now, we may see the intensity of selfishness in many of the highest, and very many of the lowest orders: the one owners of extensive and ill-cultivated lands, looking to corn laws for support: and the other *habitués* of the gin shop. If we desire to find liberality of feeling, it may be met in abundance among the middle class of people who rejoice in the comforts of home.

We have shown that in no country does there exist the same tendency to concentration of affection, of feeling, of action, and of wealth, as in Massachusetts: yet *there* may be found liberality of feeling in the highest degree. How, indeed, could it be otherwise, when every boy, however poor, has in the little library of the town school, towards which his father pays his little contribution, and in which the son feels himself as much at home as the sons of the wealthiest, books that enlighten him in regard to the modes of thinking and acting throughout the world: and may now, or soon will, read in the morning's penny newspaper the history of the proceedings of *the previous evening* in every principal town in the Union, from New Orleans and St. Louis to the very extremity of Maine? With every diminution in the quantity required of the machinery of exchange, whether of things or ideas, we find expansion of intellect, liberality of views, and the disappearance of selfishness. Concentration, by means of which the consumer and the producer are brought together, has the same effect in nations as in families; and if we desire to see improvement in moral feeling, in habits of kindness, and in the disposition to make exertions for the common good, we shall find it as we look more and more inward, and endeavour more and more to render pleasant that home in which we are placed: in which, but for the interference of the laws of man with those of the Deity, there might in all time past have existed a degree of happiness, of which, in most nations, its inhabitants have had but little idea.

Passing southward from Massachusetts, eldest born of the family of States, we find, from north to south, and from east to west, a tendency in the same direction: but diminishing as men become more and more scattered, and the fertile soils are seen more and more unoccupied. Throughout the whole system exists, in a greater or less degree, the tendency to concentration of feeling and affection, as is best shown in the existence of twenty-two hundred newspapers, each giving to its readers the history of the proceedings of the neighbourhood; and in the universal tendency to have in every little settlement, schools where the young can meet for instruction; and places for the worship of the Deity, where all, young and old, can meet. The *home* stands first; and where that is the case, there will be found in the highest degree the power of obtaining knowledge relative to things *distant from home.**

Were France to turn her regards inward instead of outward, and dispense with fleets and armies, and foreign missions, and the numerous other absurdities that characterize her system, the expenses of her government need not exceed those of the United States. That done, wealth would increase; and her people would cultivate the rich soils instead of the poor ones: and population would then advance. The United Kingdom contains less than a hundred millions of acres, occupied by twenty-eight millions of people, and the machinery of government that is needed is less than in the United States, where twenty-one millions occupy six hundred millions of acres; for where people are concentrated they protect themselves: whereas, where they are scattered they require protection. Were the expenditure of England reduced to five millions of pounds wealth would grow rapidly; for everybody would work, either with his head or his hands: and the experience of every day in that country goes to show

---

* "I travelled along a portion of the frontier of the United States in a cart which was termed *the mail.* We passed, day and night, with great rapidity, along roads which were scarcely marked out, through immense forests. * * * From time to time we came to a hut in the midst of a forest, which was a post-office. The mail dropped an enormous bundle of letters at the door of this isolated dwelling, and we pursued our way at full gallop, leaving the inhabitants of the neighbouring log houses to send for their share of the treasure. * * * *It is difficult to imagine the incredible rapidity with which public opinion circulates in the midst of these deserts. I do not think that so much intellectual intercourse takes place in the most enlightened and populous districts of France.*"—*De Tocqueville*

the rapid improvement of the higher orders, since it has been discovered that if men would maintain their places in society they must contribute towards its well-being, as the world gives nothing for nothing. In no part of the world do all classes, from the highest to the lowest, so uniformly labour for the advancement of the interests of the society in which they are placed, as in Massachusetts: and in none do men who have acquired fortune exert so much influence: and simply because, with all their fortunes, they continue to work almost to the close of life. They are always ready to unite in what is needed to be done, and to contribute both time and money to its accomplishment: and society respects them, because they promote the good of society. In less enlightened parts of the Union, men of wealth do little for the promotion of the interests of those around them, and the latter take no interest in them. All this may equally be seen by comparing the rapidly growing Liverpool with the stationary Bristol. Concentration tends to promote activity of mind, and that activity will exhibit itself more usefully abroad in the precise proportion that it manifests itself usefully at home. The nation that keeps itself poor by efforts in behalf of "the liberties of Europe," exhibiting to the world a whole people in the almshouse, does far less for the extension of freedom than it would do were it to mind its own business, and exhibit the beneficial effects of freedom in universal prosperity and happiness. The Parliament that occupies itself with the affairs of Spain and Italy, and India and Canada; and reports on coal mines, and drainage, and interments, exhibiting a near approach to barbarism; does less for liberty than a Congress whose attention is turned exclusively homeward, leaving the liberties of the world to take care of themselves. The influence of the United States upon the world is now greater than that of England, because it maintains little army or navy; and its people increase in numbers, and grow rich by minding their own business. True grandeur goes with peace and prosperity, and the cultivation of the rich soils of the earth. Littleness and selfishness are the invariable accompaniments of war and the cultivation of the poor soils.

The highest degree of security for the rights of persons and of property that exists in the world is to be found in Massachusetts: and it is there obtained at the smallest cost, because there the people do most for themselves; and those charged with the duties of government do least. As we pass from that State and from New England generally, south and west, security diminishes, and the cost increases. In every part of the world security diminishes with the increased cost of government. The latter is greater in France than in any other portion of Europe: and hence it is that the government builds fortifications, and that every man feels that he is sitting on a volcano that may burst forth at any instant. In that country *centralization* is carried to the highest point: while in Massachusetts is shown the perfection of *concentration*. In the one, man's *necessities* are great: while in the other, his *powers* are greatest.

The PAST says to the landholder of the PRESENT: "If you desire that your property increase in value: labour to promote the growth of wealth, and the concentration of man for the purpose of eating the food where it is produced."

To the labourer it says: "If you desire a large return to your labour; to live in your own house, or on your own farm, eating your food on the ground on which it is produced: labour to promote the growth of wealth."

To all it says: "If you would be free, and happy, and rich: labour to promote concentration, whose companions are peace and wealth; and avoid centralization, whose companions are poverty and war, followed by the dispersion of man over the poor soils of the earth."

CHAPTER XI.

COLONIZATION.

Look to it from what quarter we may, we see the human race descending from the great centre of the eastern continent, the plateau of Asia, and seeking in the lower lands the means of obtaining increased supplies of food; those first cultivated having been, invariably, possessed of the smallest quantity of the food-producing properties. Emigration is, therefore, in strict accordance with the laws of nature. From that point the first people proceed to occupy the land given for their use. At every stage of their course we see them arresting their march, and stopping to apply themselves to the cultivation of the upper and poor soils, and by degrees bringing into action the more productive ones. In the infancy of the stately tree, its roots are short and just beneath the surface; but with each day of its growth we find them spreading in all directions further from the trunk, while the great tap root descends deep into the lower soils, and both unite to give stability to the beautiful mass of branches and foliage. Next, we find lateral roots sending up suckers, which, like their parent, derive their earliest nourishment from the superficial soil: but which, with age repeat the operation exhibited in the first, and thus establish new centres of attraction for the various elements provided for the support of vegetable life. The first still goes on, and as its height increases the great root sinks deeper, while the lateral ones still extend themselves, and at each step stability is increased. Surrounded by its descendants of various ages, diminishing in height and their roots in depth as they recede from the great centre, it forms a perfect double pyramid.

Precisely such is the course of man. He stops and labours; and wealth begins to grow. He builds houses; and population and wealth increase. He sends forth the little shoots, while the few houses become a town. Wealth and population again increase, and he is enabled to descend deeper into the earth, from which he derives increased supplies. The town becomes a city, whose wealth exerts a force of attraction upon the population around, in the ratio which its own mass bears to the mass to be acted upon. Upon the old and the rich they exert a strong attractive power: but upon the young and the active, it is less, and is not unfrequently counteracted by similar yet weaker forces, acting in an opposite direction; and the latter are seen preferring the poor soils somewhat distant, which with their small means they can cultivate, to the richer soils nearer the centre. The little settlements around become towns, and new roads are made. Roads are wealth, and they give value to the poor and still more distant lands; and thus is counterbalanced the attraction of the towns, and even of that of the great city, whose force is diminished by distance; and here we find the younger and poorer members, whose fortune is in their strength of muscle alone, establishing their abode. Population and wealth continue to grow, and therewith the attractive power of the city tends to increase; but therewith further roads continue to be made, and these constituents of wealth tend to attract in the opposite direction. Man, therefore, like all other matter, once in motion, tends to continue his onward course, but is invariably attracted by wealth: and thus is he subjected to forces similar to those which keep in order the great planetary system: the centripetal and the centrifugal: and find him where we may, he will be seen advancing towards civilization more or less rapidly, precisely in the ratio of the existence and perfect balance of these opposing forces.

The construction of a little log-cabin in the wilderness is a strong inducement to the next settler to take up his abode in the neighbourhood. If its owner possess a plough and a horse, the attraction of wealth is greatly increased, if the new emigrant be less rich. The two combined now attract more powerfully, and the third and fourth follow. With each addition the attraction becomes stronger, and it is greatly increased if these last are enabled to add to the stock of wealth, oxen and horses, ploughs, harrows, and axes. Population increases, and a little store arises, the nucleus of the village now about to appear. At another step we find the church and the school-house, and with these additions to the wealth of the neighbourhood the attraction is felt throughout an increased extent of country, until neutralized by the counter-attraction of other settlements at a distance. That such is the course of things may readily be proved by any one who will trace the growth of towns and cities in the old world or the new, where wealth and population grow.

Such is the natural tendency of things: but man has "sought out many inventions." These "inventions" are seen in the form of wars, producing taxation; and in that of regulation; for he fancies, not unfrequently, that the laws established by the Deity are insufficient; and therefore makes, perhaps with the best intentions, others totally inconsistent with the great natural ones established for his government in his relations with his fellow man. These interferences are sometimes found existing to an extent so great that wealth diminishes: and then increasing poverty is seen to exercise a strong repulsive power, and men are compelled to increase their distances from each other in the hope to obtain from the miserable soils then cultivated, the food necessary for the preservation of existence. Thus, we see the poor Arab occupying countries that in other days afforded large returns to labour, enabling a dense population to obtain abundant supplies of the necessaries, comforts, and luxuries of life. The same course of events may be seen, on a large scale, in the histories of Mexico and India.

At other times, the repulsive forces are found existing in

a degree causing wealth to increase but slowly in its ratio to population, and towns and cities then exerting but little attractive power: while from the small demand for labour, and consequent poverty of the labourer, the mass to be attracted is so small that no movement whatsoever is produced. In this state of things there will exist very sight tendency towards bringing into activity the stronger and less accessible powers of the earth in lands already cultivated; or towards facilitating, by means of roads, the cultivation of newer lands: and men will then be seen vegetating where they are born; doing as their fathers did, and living as they lived: too poor to emigrate, and almost too poor to live at home. Such is the state of things presented by many parts of France and southern Germany, where man's *necessities* are great, and his *power* is small.

Again, we find taxation and regulation, with but occasional war. Wealth does grow, but still slowly. The centres of attraction exert small force, and the bodies to be attracted are generally light, but variable in their capacity to obey its influence. If now, more powerful attraction be elsewhere established: if wealth accumulate more rapidly in a new direction than in the original one: the smaller bodies will be first attracted, and the merely labouring population will be drawn in that direction, provided they possess within themselves the power of motion: for the mere pauper is irresistibly attracted by the spot on which he stands.* If the new force continue to increase and the older ones remain stationary, the larger masses begin to move, and now the mechanic and the small farmer are attracted. Another step in the same direction exhibits moving off, the larger farmer, and the man possessed of capital to employ mechanics: and thus, class after class moves in regular succession. Such, precisely, is the case with Ireland. Twenty years since, the mere labourer, or the young man of some-

* See page 155, *antè*, for the state of things within the limits of *the City* of London.

what better condition, possessed of nothing but the ability and the disposition to work, constituted the only class that fled to America. By degrees, the small farmers came, but with the rapid growth of wealth on one side and its almost stationary condition on the other, each year has witnessed an improvement in the class of immigrants ; and now men with substantial, but moderate, capitals, are seen to traverse the Atlantic with their wives and children : seeking the employment for their time, their talents, and their capital, which in their father-land cannot be obtained. Again, we may see continued peace promoting the rapid growth of wealth and population, and the centres of attraction increasing rapidly and producing a strong attractive force ; neutralized, however, by taxation for preparation for future wars, and regulation by which wealth is rendered stagnant and forced to seek abroad the employment denied at home. The force exerted is not then in the ratio of its mass. In this state of things, railroads, ships, and steamers are constructed, all acting as conductors to any existing opposing force. External attraction being thus added to internal repulsion, a strong centrifugal force is the result. Such is the condition of England in relation to the United States. Her force of attraction should have stood first among that of the nations of the world, but it has, at all times, been diminished by endless taxation for the maintenance of armies ; for the payment of interest upon moneys borrowed for the support of armies and fleets in past times ; and for the salaries of hosts of officers whose services would soon cease to be required were economy to come in fashion : by taxation for the support of an immense church establishment : and by endless regulations that forbid association, and tend to maintain existing monopolies in land, in trade, in banking, and in every other of the pursuits of life. But for them, labour and capital would be attracted to England : whereas they are incessantly being expelled from it.

If we look now to the starting point of European civilization in America, to Massachusetts, we shall find there the equilibrium more perfectly established and maintained than elsewhere in the world. With a soil naturally sterile for all the purposes of agriculture, and destitute of coal, that State supports a population of a hundred to the square mile; better fed, better clothed, better lodged, and better taught than any other in existence: and there wealth grows with a rapidity elsewhere totally unexampled. Perfect freedom to associate has produced the universal habit of association, which is there carried to its highest point, and therefore it is that wealth tends to remain in the places of its accumulation: in the little towns and cities of the State: the result of which is exhibited in the establishment of an attractive power of prodigious force. Her neighbours possess better food-producing soils, and they have coal and iron, while she has ice and granite. Among *them*, too, wealth grows rapidly: for in all may be seen existing, more or less, the same absence of interference to which is due her rapid growth. By them is, therefore, exercised a force of counter-attraction so great that were she by taxation or mischievous regulations to produce a repulsive force within, wealth and population would both rapidly diminish: and she would be placed in the same position relative to them now occupied by Dorset and Hampshire, in relation to Lancashire and Yorkshire. In her the equilibrium is perfect. Labour and capital never emigrate for want of demand at home, but because of a somewhat greater demand abroad that tempts the young to seek elsewhere their fortunes: and hence is it that labour and skill are there so liberally rewarded. They *make* rich soils, for they have power to compel the great machine to answer to their demands; and they themselves grow rich, while the poor emigrant obtains, not unfrequently, little but disease and death from the proximity of soils not exceeded in the world for their power to afford return to labour; which yet he is unable to subject to the plough. *They* place the consumer by the producer. *They* gather the manure yielded by the soils of the west, and by its aid obtain from an acre a hundred bushels of corn: while the emigrant, surrounded by rich soils, obtains but forty, and sees his product diminish yearly, because he returns to the great machine no portion even of the refuse of its gifts. Here we see exemplified, on a great scale, the operation that may, on a small one, be found in progress on the farm of every improving farmer. He begins on the hill-side, and as he works down to the rich soils and abstracts from them their manure, he carries it up the hill to enrich the poor ones. The man of Massachusetts began on the poor soils of his high and rocky land, but he is gradually working his way, by force of wealth, and the power and habit of union, into the richer lands of the south; and carrying up the hill, *to make a soil*, that manure which the farmer and planter of the south and west *cannot* reserve even to such extent as to enable them to *maintain* their soil as they found it: still less to improve it. When the latter shall have acquired the power of concentration, they will keep their manures and improve their soils: but not until then.

By all the advocates of the Ricardo doctrine, the prosperous condition of the people of the United States is attributed to the abundance of fertile land, yet, in all other countries men have been most poor where land was most abundant, and where the inhabitants had, apparently, most the choice of soils. Fertile land, uncultivated, abounded in the days of the Edwards, yet a supply of food was then obtained with far more difficulty than now. It is more abundant, by far, in Mexico than in the United States, yet inferior food is obtained at the cost of far more labour. The whole agricultural product of Mexico, with a population of eight millions, is far less than that of a single American state. It is more abundant in Russia, South America, India, Ceylon and Brazil, yet in all food is far more scarce. The reason why labour is in demand and largely paid is, that peace having been maintained, the whole people have been engaged in the work of production instead of that of carrying muskets and sabres, and therefore wealth has rapidly increased.

Of the correctness of the view we have submitted in regard to the tendency of wealth to attract population, the reader may be fully satisfied by a glance around his own neighbourhood, or over his own state or kingdom, reside where he may. Such an examination will, we think, result in a conviction that the law is universal in its application, as are any of the laws of physics. Having so satisfied himself, he will be prepared to accompany us in an examination of the several systems of colonization now in progress: the English, French, American and African.

That which now chiefly occupies the English mind is the one based on Mr. Ricardo's doctrine of the value of land, and which was first introduced about fifteen years since, in a work entitled England and America. It was there shown, as the writer thought, that the system of the United States tended to scatter population too widely: that land was sold too cheap, and that the people would be more prosperous if the government took from them a larger amount of their capital, by way of facilitating them in the work of clearing the timber and draining the meadows. In that and other works subsequently published, it was also shown that England possessed, in her colonies, a vast quantity of land of the best description, capable of yielding a large return to labour: and that nothing was needed to render it highly valuable but that "a sufficient price" should be put upon it, the proceeds of sales to be expended in transporting labourers to the land. The idea took rapidly, and colonization became the rage. To buy land at from 12*s.* to 20*s.* per acre, and to apply the purchase-money to the transport of labourers, and by this simple process to render it as valuable as that which at home would command a hundred pounds an acre, was abundantly captivating. The "political economists" were highly delighted with it, and books containing the most glowing descriptions of the vast wealth certain to be realized, were published. The only difficulty appeared to be that of determining what was the price at which it would not be too cheap.* High-priced land was deemed most likely to secure high wages to the labourers.† Men of fortune invested their whole means in carrying out colonists and implements of husbandry. Companies were formed for northern and southern, eastern and western, Australia; for New Zealand, north and south; and immense grants of territory were obtained from the government: coupled, however, with the condition that the proceeds were to go to ridding the country of that portion of its population which was held to be surplus; that portion whose *necessities* were great, and whose *powers* were small.

There exists in England a large class that in the United States constitutes the most useful of all classes, and that would be so everywhere, if permitted: but which there occupies a most uncomfortable position. It is the class of small capitalists: men who have time, and talents, and labour, that they would desire to employ; and a small amount of capital that would enable them to render their time and labour profitable to themselves, and highly so to society, if opportunity could be found. Being, however, surrounded by monopolies, some of which result from law and others from custom, while a third and great class results from the concentration of the ownership of land; that opportunity cannot be found, and time, talents, education, and capital, hang heavily on their hands. They are too large for labourers, and too small to be large farmers, and the

---

* "Land in the new colony, instead of being extravagantly dear, would be remarkably cheap at £2 = $9 60, per acre."—*Torrens.*

† "Wages must be higher in the new Australian colony than in the old Australian colonies, as long as waste land shall continue to be sold at a higher price in the new than in the old."—*Ibid.*

land-owner will have none of them. They are too small to become cotton manufacturers by themselves, and the law forbids their association for becoming such, by regulations that tend to destroy the habit of union. They are too small for bankers, and the law surrounds associations for banking purposes with penalties that secure to great bankers and great speculators a monopoly of that trade. They are too large for shopmen, and too small to command what is called "a connection." They are too large for curates, and too small for bishops: too large for apothecaries, and too small for doctors: too large to go before the mast, and too small to obtain a place in the cabin: and this applies to almost every pursuit in life, the consequence of which is that they are known as "the uneasy class" of society. To the difficulty which such men find in obtaining employment for their time and their means is due the fact that heavy *bonuses* are given for employment accompanied with small but certain remuneration; the party thus sinking his capital in exchange for an annuity to be earned by the application of his labour: that such large sums are given for presentations in the church: that good-wills in shops, banking houses, &c., command so high a price: and to this is likewise due the vast amount of business transacted by life insurance offices, whose profits are derived from managing the capital of thousands who, if they were permitted, would manage it far better themselves. Throughout that country abound clever and well-informed men with moderate means, who are willing to abandon all hope of rising in the world, and to sell themselves for life, for small fixed incomes: one of the strongest evidences of unsoundness in the system. The same thing may be found in portions of the United States. Its extent is very limited where population is most dense, and men are seen obtaining large returns from the originally poor soils: but it increases as we pass south and west, towards those parts where land is abundant, and where men obtain a poor subsistence from poor soils, while surrounded by rich ones that they cannot cultivate. The more perfect the power of man over land, the greater is his power over himself, and the less is he disposed to confine himself to the effort towards *maintaining* his condition: abandoning the hope of *improving* it.

To this class, the discovery of the new principle of colonization was a god-send. Their time and their capital were almost unproductive. Instead of three per cent. consols, they could have hundred per cent. lands. Home had many attractions, but their situation, on the whole, was uneasy. They were, in many cases, gentlemen in feeling and character, but at home they could not live as became gentlemen. In Australia, they could have farms consisting of the most fertile lands, with rent-paying tenants, and employ their own time in hunting or fishing, reading or writing; while their wives and daughters could amuse themselves with music and drawing. The prospect was immeasurably attractive, and accordingly the offices were besieged by applicants for land. Clergymen and half-pay officers sold out and invested their little fortunes in certificates that were to entitle them to fertile soils somewhere: but where, they knew, and apparently cared, not. That it was land appeared to be all-sufficient for them. Lawyers and doctors, with small capitals and smaller practice, were eager to settle in this new El Dorado, where they might combine the profits of professional occupation with a little rent-roll, and pass downwards through life in the enjoyment of a good table, garnished with old wine. Farmers threw up their leases, preferring to constitute themselves rent-receivers, and thus becoming gentlemen of leisure, instead of remaining rent-payers. Small traders, mechanics, and men of every class in society, purchased prizes in the new and grand lottery. Ships were laden with furniture, books, pictures, materials for drawing, pianos, music, flutes, fishing tackle, fowling-pieces, and all other of the appliances necessary for the enjoyment of perfect happiness. Delicate and highly educated women, wives and daughters, embarked for Australia, confident that they should find in the enjoyment of perfect repose, ample amends for the loss of the society of the friends of their youth. With their arrival in the colony, the beautiful vision disappeared. The fertile lands were inaccessible, and those which were accessible were worthless, except for sheep-runs. High and dry lands, without trees, were abundant: and bottom-lands, covered with timber that they could not fell, were equally so. Both were to them equally valueless. Labour was scarce and high, for the order of things had been inverted, and the capitalist had gone ahead of the labourer: the true emigrant. Ladies and gentlemen had to wait on themselves. In short, all the troubles, and difficulties, and annoyances, so well described by Mrs. Kirkland in her admirable account of the "New Home," were experienced by these deluded and unfortunate colonists; the only difference being that their's were tenfold greater than her's. They had pianos and harps in abundance, but they required only axes and spades, pots and kettles. The bubble burst, and all that remained was blighted hope, accompanied by a consciousness of having wasted fortune in pursuit of an *ignis fatuus*. They were blind, and they had permitted themselves to be led by the blind.

The whole history of these colonies is one of endless disputes and troubles. The Government *would* take them into its care. Governors who knew little were appointed by secretaries who knew less, and they not unfrequently evinced a total want of capacity for the performance of their own duties, and an equal want of respect for the rights of others. As colonial secretaries had shown themselves determined to be masters, and determined not to permit officers and directors of associations for the promotion of the great scheme to exercise the powers of government, the latter were glad to throw upon the shoulders of the former the burden of failure that necessarily resulted from its own inherent defects; and a scene of wrangling has ensued, resulting in leaving it somewhat doubtful with the public whether the fault was in the projection, or in the carrying out of the scheme. All that is generally known is, that a vast number of people have been ruined by the purchase of farms that are totally worthless: that "accommodation land," as it is termed, *i. e.*, land that was calculated for the supply of beans and peas to towns which never existed, was sold in lots of two, or three, or five acres, at enormous prices by lucky speculators; that the government itself retailed lots, a dozen at a time, at prices worthy almost of Liverpool and Manchester, in towns that scarcely existed but on paper: that those prices were paid because "the original and inexhaustible powers of the soil" were so great that population and wealth must so rapidly increase that it was difficult to tell to what size these towns and cities might not grow; and that, therefore, the government thought it inexpedient to wholesale them. Concentration, too, was the order of the day. Men must not be permitted to exercise the right of self-government so far as to judge for themselves where they would place their houses, or their stores. Land was fixed at so high a price that they might be compelled to remain together, and thus their powers were diminished, that their powers might become greater. Such was the scheme that lured to Australia tens of thousands of accomplished men and women, possessed of moderate competence. Many have died, while very many have returned beggars from this land of promise. The thing is dead, never again to be revived, though many even yet write about it. But few weeks have elapsed since the necessity for a new and grand plan of emigration was urged on the government, and by men standing high in the political and economical world: to the exceeding terror of the poor Canadians, who dreaded to see a repetition of the horrors of Australia.

The number of people transported to the wilderness was great, and the amount of capital sunk in the speculation was enormous. The larger the amount of property sent to the colony, the greater was held to be the profit of the mother country. Tables of exports were printed, showing how large a market had been secured: but imports there were none. It was all pure loss. For some years past emigration has, fortunately for the colonies, wholly ceased. They will now proceed in the natural way, cultivating the lands that are accessible and using others as sheep-walks, by which means they will arrive in time to be respectable members of the British colonial family; and at some future period they may become sufficiently wealthy to attract further emigration, which now they are not.

The scheme failed because it was in direct opposition to the laws of nature: and to the lessons of the past. The wilderness offers little attraction to the labourer and still less to the capitalist, large or small. In all successful colonization, the former is found just ahead of the houses, and towns, and roads of his predecessors, *and if he pass too far ahead, he starves.* He prepares the way for the little capitalist who is willing to pay some one for clearing a little land, and building a log-house; and the latter, in his turn, smooths the way for one a little larger: but all must keep within sight and hearing of their predecessors. No one voluntarily goes upon land that has not already acquired some little value by the application of some labour in the construction of communications. The first settler adds a little to that value by preparing a few acres of land and building the house. The second increases it, and thus it rises in time, from being absolutely worthless, to becoming worth something, and passes gradually from one or two, to six, eight, or ten dollars per acre; but in no case will it exchange for as much labour as it would cost to place it in the same condition, were it again reduced to its original state; and the reason that it will not do so is that with every step in the progress of wealth and population better soils can be obtained with less labour. That which is now required for combining the lime with the clay, is not one-fifth as great as was first expended in clearing and enclosing the poor clay: yet the new soil thus produced is of treble power.

We know of no case in which the emigration of capitalists has been successful. Few men have undertaken the work, possessed of greater advantages for the work than the founder of Pennsylvania, yet he sunk nearly his whole fortune in the operation. He received the grant in payment of a debt of £30,000, and after having, in twenty years, expended £52,000, he had received less than £20,000: leaving him *minus* above £62,000, for which he offered to receive £12,000 from the government, and relinquish his claim. The Swedes and Dutch had preceded him, and thus paved the way for his arrival. Without this, his loss would have been vastly greater. The same experiment has been tried in other colonies, and always with the same result. One of the Peel family, a few years since, undertook the business of colonization, and sunk, we think, about £70,000 in a few short months. At Sydney; in Van Diemen's land; and in that other colony of Norfolk Island, fitly designated as "a hell upon earth," the only title to which it can fairly lay claim; the State has been the great capitalist, and were it now to sell out, it would be found that had it been an enterprise of private capitalists they would have been ruined had they possessed the fortunes of the Barings, the Rothschilds, and Astor, and fifty more such, united. Australia would not now sell, in the market of the world, for one-twentieth of its cost. The difference has been paid out of taxes on tea, coffee, sugar, beer, &c., by which men were impoverished and driven to crime, to prepare them for the new colony fitting for their reception.

Neither is it possible, as we believe, to find an instance of the emigration of people able and willing to labour, to an entirely new country, that has been successful; except where they were animated by something more than the mere desire of wealth: and the efforts of colonists not so animated have always failed, except where supported out of taxation upon the people who remained behind. The French colonies were supported by the government, or they failed. The first emigrants to Oregon would have starved, but for the existence of the settlements of the Hudson's Bay Company. The recent emigrants to California would have been in the same condition but for the existence of a certain amount of wealth, in cleared and cultivated lands, in oxen and mules, and houses, belonging to the earlier settlers. The settlement of South Africa, a few years since, was a failure as complete as was that at the Belize, where many of the settlers starved in view of the richest lands of the world, which they had not means to clear and occupy. The Swedes made no progress, nor did the cavaliers of Virginia, and therefore was it that the latter requires slaves. The South Carolina settlement, planned by Locke, with its caciques and its various absurd machinery, was an entire failure. That such is the case, is the consequence of a great law of nature which forbids that man should profit by the superior soils until he has won them by severe labour, for which they are the reward. The settler in Mississippi cultivates the poor land on the hill in full view of the river bottom, because the scrub-pine is more easily removed than the oak; and because he knows that if it were even in his power to remove the latter, the land on which it is growing is wet, and he has not the means to drain it: and that he should be ruined in the attempt. He obtains a bare subsistence from the poor soil on which he works, because he can sometimes sell his labour to a neighbour, or borrow a plough or a horse, or sell wood to a steamboat: and were he deprived of the advantages thus resulting from the existence of other wealth than his own, he would starve. What inducement, then, can man have to go out of sight and hearing of his fellow man? He is everywhere, when permitted, seen seeking union with him, and deriving aid and comfort from that union. He finds the greatest demand for his labour where that union is rendered possible by the existence of wealth: for without it there can be none. In the wilderness, he finds land, and land only, which is not wealth, and it can therefore exert no attractive power. The more he has of it, the poorer he is. Left to himself, then, man will never seek it, unless the desire of emancipation from tyranny over his thoughts or his actions induce him to submit to the privations incident thereto. That, and that alone, enabled the Pilgrims to endure the horrors of the first winter on the bleak shores of Massachusetts Bay.

The author of this plan of colonization saw, and saw truly, in the tendency of the people of the United States to scatter themselves over the wild lands of the west, a cause of poverty and not of wealth. He saw that concentration was needed, but he erred in regard to the means by which it should be sought. He assumed that man always selected first the rich soils: although he might have seen remaining uncultivated in the old states, millions of acres of rich lands, while men passed westward to cultivate prairie lands, where water is almost a luxury. Had he seen the true cause of man thus squandering his labour in the wilderness of America, he would have found the true remedy for the apparent over-population of Britain; but this he did not see, and therefore was it that he was led to attribute the waste of labour to excess in the exercise of the right of self-government: whereas the true reason was to be found in the almost total absence of the existence of any power to determine for themselves where they would live and where they would not. They would have preferred remaining at home with their relative and friends, but the misdirection of the wealth and labour of England produced a repulsive force, driving them abroad to seek in the wilderness that which home would not afford: and therefore was it that they went west to obtain ten bushels of wheat per acre, leaving behind land, unoccupied, that would have given almost as many tons of potatoes, the manure from which would have enriched the poor soils already in cultivation. These they could not raise because too bulky for transportation, and there existed no market for milk, eggs, veal or beef: and therefore was it that they sought the west where they could obtain Indian corn, which, being converted into pork, might *perhaps* be received by England in payment for shirts and pantaloons.

The author of the scheme saw that concentration was needed on the one side of the Atlantic, and therefore was it that he proposed *de-concentration* of the people of the opposite side, to be followed by forced concentration in the southern hemisphere. Men were to be deprived of the right of selecting for themselves, and to that end land was to be fixed high: and they were to be made to pay twenty or forty shillings an acre for that for which man had done nothing, while for that in the Western States for which man had already done much in the form of communications, the government asked but five shillings. That he should so far have erred is extraordinary: but that so many thousands should have risked their fortunes and happiness on such a scheme is far more so.

The colonial system of England has been, and is, her greatest curse. To acquire, and to retain, colonial subjects: for as equals they have never been regarded: wealth has been expended that would have made of every field in the United Kingdom a garden from which the occupant, enabled by its aid to bring into activity the better soils, would have drawn an amount of food thrice exceeding what the poorer ones have given him. So applied, it would have been attended with a vast increase of wealth and population, and the roads would long since have afforded facilities of communication almost equalling those of the present day. To wars for colonies may be attributed the whole of the present enormous debt with which she is burthened; and by the weight of which she will be distanced in the race she has now to run, with a people who, bone of her bone and flesh of her flesh, have no such load to carry. To retain them now, she maintains an immense army and a prodigious fleet, requiring taxes to an extent that tends to produce repulsion and to drive abroad both man and wealth that should remain at nome.

Were she at once to grant to every colony the right of self-government, a fleet as large as that of the United States would perform all the duties of maintaining the police of the ocean, and no army whatsoever would be needed. She would thus save twelve millions, and in such a case a penny saved is more than a penny gained. That sum is the interest of four hundred millions, or half of her whole debt. The vast sums now wasted on preparations for war would speedily extinguish that debt; and were its reduction once fairly commenced each man would feel himself lightened of a load, while the increase of his productive power would enable him to bear more easily that portion which remained. Wealth would grow with greatly increased rapidity, and its application to agriculture and to the extension of roads and railroads would produce an increased demand for labour, with increase of wages tending to enable the labourer to improve his physical, moral, and intellectual condition. Population would then increase more rapidly, and the demand would grow more rapidly than the supply. Every new appropriation of capital to a road would produce farther demand for capital for engines and cars; for ploughs, and spades, and pickaxes, and tiles, and lime, and marl, and houses, and shops, and saw-mills, and grist-mills: and then everybody, labourer and capitalist, would have reason to be content, for the value of capital would rise with the increased demand at home, resulting from the habit of looking *towards home;* and from the growth of the power of the great food-producing machine. We now see the three per cents., which were for a long time worth 107, selling at 80. With each step in the progress of freedom, mere annuities, whether for the use of capital or labour, would be less sought after, and consols would, and will, fall to 70, and perhaps far less.

Those who doubt this may satisfy themselves by looking to the continent, and seeing at how low a rate money is, and in times past has been, supplied to governments in some of the poorer countries of Europe. When their trade shall become more free wealth will increase more rapidly, and th rate of interest will rise as it has done in England. Governments will then dispense with armies and wars, for both will become more costly. The capitalist will then have larger profits, for he will manage his own capital: and the labourer will have larger wages, for he will manage his own labour. The true interests of both are therefore identical, and nothing can injure one without equally injuring the other. The price of money rose during the long war, but the price of commodities advanced in a more rapid ratio, and the capitalist received less in quantity while receiving more in proportion. The interest of £100 will now purchase twice the amount of comfort that it would have done when consols were at 48.

Freed from the burden of colonies, any and everywhere, she would need no army abroad and she would require none at home, because increasing prosperity resulting from the abolition of taxes, would be attended by increased disposition for the performance of duties, and increased respect for the rights of others, among the whole people. "Strikes" would become less abundant among those who work, because tax-gatherers and receivers; and pensioners, and sinecurists, and admirals,—red, blue, and yellow; the class which prefers not to work: would be less numerous. She would need no army for home defence, for harmony would prevail throughout the whole system, taking the place of existing discord; and millions of men, feeling that they had rights, and possessing over their neighbours the same advantages that enabled a few thousand yeomen, at Cressy and Poictiers, to triumph over the countless mob of princes, nobles, and gentlemen to whom they were opposed, would be at all times ready to defend their homes, their wives and children; while railroads would enable her, at a moment's notice, to place them where their services were needed. Her apparent strength would be less, but her real strength would be far greater; and it would increase with prodigious rapidity. Wealth is strength, as has been shown, time after time, by the people of the Netherlands and Holland, and of the free cities of Germany, in their ability to defend themselves against the invading armies of France: and as would have been shown by Italy, had she not possessed within her bosom, in the Church, a power deriving from abroad its ability to produce division and weakness at home. Wealth results, not from the labour of men who carry muskets, but from that of those who carry spades and pickaxes: and if the former do not give wealth, they cannot give strength, physical, moral, intellectual, or political. Ten millions spent in railroads give more strength: more power of self-protection and advancement: than could be given by all the fleets and armies of the world assembled at a cost of hundreds of millions.

Were the millions now thus spent applied throughout Great Britain to improving the great food-producing machine, the result would be a constant increase in the power to make more roads; to cultivate still better soils; to participate in the advantages of union for the maintenance of perfect security at home, and against interference from abroad; and to unite for the dissemination of instruction throughout the whole body of the people: tending thus to make them feel that they could protect themselves, and that without either fleets or armies. Seeing this, none would venture even to hint invasion. Instead of fort-building, and "great activity in the dock-yards," such as has been seen even within the last three years, forts would be dismantled and their cannon would be melted, while the vast machinery of the dock-yards would be applied to the production of machines destined for the improvement, and not for the destruction, of man. With every step in the progress towards increased wealth and population, causes of quarrel would diminish, while the self-defensive power would be increased. She is now indisposed to quarrel with the United States, because they are populous and rich; but she feels small annoyance at a dispute with the scattered people of Buenos Ayres, who have land in abundance, and therefore cultivate the poorest soils. The people of the United States use spades and ploughs. They dispense with armies and fleets, and hence their self-protective power. Were they to adopt the conscription for land and naval service, and the endless taxation of France, they would soon become as weak as France. That power has always maintained the largest armies in Europe; and she has, with the exception of England, expended most largely on her fleets, and to what purpose? From the days of Rollo to those of Blucher and Wellington, she has shown herself, when the time of trial came, almost incapable of self-defence, whether on her land or on her sea frontier. The tendency of her whole system has been to take from the labourer the wealth that he produced, and give to those who did not labour the disposal of it, and they have invariably disposed of it to suit their own purposes.

Such, too, has been the tendency of the colonization system of England. It has given to secretaries and those who desired to be secretaries; admirals and generals, and those who sought to place themselves at the head of fleets and armies; the disposal of wealth that they had not laboured to produce: and the consequence has been waste, for no man economizes in the expenditure of that for which he does not work. Nor has that been the only mode in which such effect has been, and is now being, produced. Large sums have been forced to the West India islands, to be managed—and mismanaged—by agents. There, wealth did not grow: and population was diminished because of the denial to the slave of the comforts necessary for his physical and moral improvement: and necessary to increase of numbers. Large sums go to Canada, for the construction of canals, forts, &c., to be expended by those who take no part in their production. Large sums have gone to Australia, and those who desire to understand the mode of obtaining small results with great means, may study with advantage the proceedings of several of the governors. Large sums are on their way to India, to make railroads; but those who are to spend them are not those who labour to produce them. The whole system of colonization tends to withdraw capital from the control of its owner, and diminishes in that respect the power of self-government; and by that it may be judged. When wealth is permitted freely to be invested, it stays at home; as is the case in New England to an extent unknown in the world: and it is so, simply because every man has near him a little money-shop, or manufacturing establishment, in which he invests his twenty, fifty, or one hundred dollars, as fast as earned, preparatory to the purchase of a little farm; the opening of a shop; or the establishment of a little factory; and by the very act making a market for his further accumulations: enabling the farmer to sink deeper into the rich soil, to increase his products, and to become a customer to the new store. Wealth, there, drops gently as the dew, and everywhere produces the same effect in affording life and nourishment to all, the little and the great: stimulating the one to exertion that he may become great, and the other to increased exertion that he may maintain his position. If we look to other parts of the Union, we shall see States withdrawing capital from the control of their owners, to be wasted in making canals and railroads that would have been profitable had they been made by the men who laboured to produce the means by which they were made: for then they would have been made economically. Pennsylvania has, by restriction, driven wealth out of the State, to be sunk in banks and railroads in Mississippi: while borrowing the capital which Englishmen were not permitted to use at home to make their own roads and canals. What has been the consequence? Waste, loss, and ruin—temporary at least—everywhere. If, now, we inquire who have been the smallest losers by the calamitous events of the past ten years, we shall find them among the people of New England—the men who cultivate the hardest soil in the Union: that which would appear to afford the least chance for profitable investment: that which produces ice and granite in abundance, but affords no coal. There wealth increases more rapidly than elsewhere in the world; and there it tends most to remain under the direct and immediate control of the owner. Nevertheless, the Yankees are the greatest colonists in the world; and there are none so ready to drive a railroad through New York or Ohio, or to seize on the profits of a speculation in opium, or in bird's-nests: but when they do so, they take care that the men who manage their concerns abroad shall be owners like themselves, directly interested in the result.* The great capitalist needs the aid of the small one who has little but his time and talent to sell; and hence the latter can always find a market for that time and talent, and has always before him the knowledge that he *can* rise if he *will*. He goes abroad, to stay permanently in Illinois, or temporarily in Canton or the Sandwich Islands, not because he must, but because he will. His self-government is perfect, because that of the capitalist is so; and hence it is that colonization,

* "No fact which I have met with has so much surprised me as the extraordinary diffusion of the American commerce, and the great spirit of enterprise manifested by them. In many places, where the British merchants can find no commerce apparently worth their attention, the Americans carry on a lucrative and prosperous trade; and, in half-civilized countries, where the largest profits are always realized, the Americans are so eminently successful, that the British merchant cannot attempt to compete with them.

"This appears to arise from the following circumstance:—The masters of the American vessels engaged in this kind of trade are, in many instances, whole, and, in all other instances, part, owners of the vessel and cargo; whereas masters of English vessels have frequently little or no interest in the vessel and cargo; and are, moreover, frequently tied down by directions from the firm for whom they act. The difference between these two cases is very great. The American can turn every circumstance that occurs to account; he can instantly enter into any speculation that holds out a prospect of success; and can act with rapidity and decision, on his own responsibility. The English master, on the contrary, has usually a prescribed line of duty to fulfil, from which he cannot vary." * * *

"While this port (Mombas, on the east coast of Africa,) was in the possession of the English, but one British merchant vessel arrived there, yet three American vessels entered the harbour. The master of the English vessel was not a part owner—the Americans were all part owners, and carried on a lucrative trade, shipping a large quantity of ivory; whereas the English master was placed in a very unpleasant position; for, owing to the orders he had received from his owners, he had not been able to ship a cargo suited to the market of Mombas; and if Lieut. Emery had not kindly cashed a bill for him, the speculation would have been a total failure."—*Grey's Expeditions in South Australia.*

both of labour and of capital, goes on with such rapidity where the tendency to local investment is so great. In no part of the world are the *necessities* of man so small: in none are his *powers* so great.

Such would become the case in England, were colonies abandoned, fleets sold, and armies disbanded. There would, however, be no more dividends of Indian taxes collected on the principle of Mr. Ricardo, and called rents as an excuse for grinding the poor wretch who is already so reduced by taxation that he cultivates the earth unaided by spade, reaping-hook, cart, horse, or mule; who then divides the produce equally between himself and the collector of rents; then gives half the balance for the privilege of eating a little salt in his bread; and finally pounds the grain with a stone, for want of a mill: yet happy if, after affording him a handful of rice per day, the balance be sufficient to enable him at occasional intervals to purchase a rag to cover his nakedness. Neither would there be so large a number of profitable offices to divide among younger sons of wealthy landowners, but fathers would then see the necessity of providing for the children whom they had begotten for their own good pleasure; and the small landholder, cultivating his own little farm for his own profit, and therefore well cultivating it, would gradually replace the great landholder and his great son, the poor cornet of dragoons, or navy lieutenant, execrating the peace and hoping for war, plunder, and promotion; and that other son who seeks employment in the Church as the best means of advancing his condition in life, and watches eagerly for the death of the incumbent of his father's wealthy parish; or pays a large price for the privilege of participating during the week with the farmer by aid of the forced division of crops which he has not laboured to produce, while teaching on Sunday the great lesson, "do unto your neighbours as ye would that they should do unto you." Rents would then rise rapidly in amount, but the proportion which they would bear to the product would decrease rapidly. The man who worked would produce more and would take a larger proportion of that increased quan tity as the reward of the labour and skill expended: while he who did not work, although receiving more in amount, would find the standard of living rise more rapidly than his means, and would see that if he did nothing—if he stood still while the rest of the earth moved—he would be left behind in the race. The class of great men; and the uneasy class, with good blood in their veins, and little money in their pockets; and the pauper class: all of them, in all ages and nations, the disturbers of the world: would disappear, and the happy and prosperous class; the lovers of peace and harmony; of labour, physical and intellectual; of instruction, secular or religious; of wealth, as a means towards the attainment of a great end, and not as the end itself; of that equality which secures to all men the exercise of those rights which they desire to enjoy themselves,—and secures it in the ratio of their performance of their own duties;—would daily increase in number: and with that increase would England grow for ages in population and wealth: leaving it for future advocates of the Malthusian theory to determine how many centuries were to elapse before it would become necessary to establish what is called "systematic colonization," by which is meant the substitution of the will of the few who administer the government and expend capital which they do not labour to produce, for that of the many who do labour and wish to be permitted to determine for themselves where they will be employed, and what they will do with their wages. Systematic colonization means nothing but the forced export of men who would live at home if they could, and who could do so if taxation and regulation permitted; and its advocates will invariably be found among those who derive their means of support from the proceeds of taxation, regulation, and monopoly.

It is impossible to look at England, or Scotland, without seeing that all this is now going on. The landlord is waking up to the fact that he is losing his place in society, and that if he would keep it he must work, and his capital must work. His rents increase, but the standard of living rises and he must economize, or his rents will cease to grow. The outlet for his sons in the army, and navy, and church, and colonies, is becoming daily less, and children and grandchildren become more numerous, and fewer of them die off. He must provide for them, for the people will not. Wars are not as profitable as heretofore: and the prospect is that in the lapse of a little time they will cease to occur. Cotton manufacturers, and spinners and traders' sons, are now at the head of affairs, and they have small respect for men who are fond of spoil, whether in the form of the plunder of a city, or of a treasureship: or in that of tithes. They are, it is true, the representatives of the past unsound commercial policy, but they are far better than the men who represented her military policy. Both, however, are part and parcel of the same system, and both will eventually disappear. All are learning to work, the consequence of which is that at no time were the better soils so rapidly brought into cultivation; at no time has the reward of labour so rapidly increased: and at no time has there been seen so strong a tendency to the approach of the period when every man would feel that consideration by the world is the reward of service rendered to the world by the exercise of physical and mental faculties: and that if he desire to eat and drink largely, he must work steadily and devotedly: but at no time has the reward of service been so great. The habit of labour brings the habit of peace; the sense of security; the love of literature and art; the happy home, and the leisure for its enjoyment, rendered doubly grateful by the necessity for exertion of the faculties of mind and body at other times and elsewhere. The great landholder no longer vegetates. His wife no longer dies of ennui. Every faculty of mind and body is stimulated into action, and man is now learning to live by helping those around to live. With each step in this pro

29*

gress, the power of man over land, and over himself, will grow: food will become more abundant: and schemes of colonization will tend to disappear.

More than ten centuries have elapsed since France commenced the work of colonization, under Pepin and Charlemagne: substituting the barbarities of the feudal system for the peaceful government of the Lombards, under which northern Italy was then rapidly advancing towards civilization. From that day to the present she has sent colonies throughout Italy, and into Spain, the Netherlands, Holland, and Germany; but they have always consisted of the uneasy class: that of gentlemen whose pride of family forbade that they should work, and whose wealth went little further than was needed for the provision of such weapons of offence as were necessary for the plunder of the rich cities of those countries: in turn, Ghent and Metz, Turin and Barcelona, Milan, Florence and Naples. The consequence has been that they have never taken root, and that the limits of France are now more contracted than when the process of colonization commenced. Even ancient Gaul itself is still divided into several kingdoms, between which there exists the same feeling of antipathy that but a little while since was felt by the Bourguignon and the Armagnac, the Breton and the Norman, the Gascon and the Provençal. War has produced depopulation and poverty, driving the remaining people to the poorer lands to labour by themselves; whereas peace would have produced wealth and population and union: and all Gaul would, *if permitted*, long since have formed one strong and independent state, intersected in every direction by roads and canals, and requiring neither armies nor fleets for the preservation of its independence. The attractive power of wealth has never been permitted to exist, even at home; for the colonists who returned gorged with the plunder of

Italian cities, were always eager for the plunder of Italian merchants and usurers who might, incautiously, venture within their grasp: and when *they* could not be found, they were always prepared to exercise their skill upon their fellow countrymen. Wealthy England and Flanders exercised a strong attractive power and drew largely from France, which thus lost her most industrious people; the men who cultivated the richest soils: and there remained only those who could not fly, and who, limited to the cultivation of the least fertile soils, remained poor, and thus has France itself to this day remained poor.

Poor people cannot emigrate. Voluntary emigration from France has therefore never existed. For centuries has she prosecuted the work of colonization, but always with ill success: for the government has been invariably the leader, and the work has been attempted with the sword, and without the spade. The English colonies in America sought wealth and not power. They moved on gradually, appropriating land as they needed it for cultivation. France allied herself with the savages, and endeavoured to seize on the whole country north and west of the Ohio and the Mississippi. The one prospered and desired peace, while the other was poor and restless: and the result was that the peaceful man expelled his poor and troublesome neighbour, as the only means of preserving peace. The Puritans and Quakers remained: ultimately, perhaps, to combine the whole continent in one great union, while France has scarcely a foot of ground upon it. Thus has the spade triumphed over the sword.

The French ministry were of the Ricardo school of political economists. They thought abundance of land with fine timber and flooded by innumerable streams, meant wealth; and they gladly undertook the settlement of Louisiana, sending thither the rogues and vagabonds, and prostitutes, of Paris, from whose labours large returns were looked for. All the world was eager for a division of the profits; the excitement exceeding that which but recently has prevailed in England, in the precise ratio which the gambling spirit of poor and anti-commercial France, accustomed to set her whole fortunes on the hazard of a battle, was greater than that of wealthy and trading England. The difference between the two consisted, however, only in the extent to which the madness was carried.

Everywhere else the result has been the same. The English colonists of India went partly for the purposes of trade, and England had power to maintain trade. Those of France went to fight, because the power to maintain trade did not exist. France exported chiefly men and arms, and with those commodities the market of India was already overstocked. The merchant expelled the soldier.

She is now colonizing Tahiti and Algeria, as she did Alsace, Lorraine, and Franche Comté: by first converting them into deserts. Algeria is said now to be flourishing, and it may so continue as long as she shall continue to send annually fifteen or twenty thousand men, and some hundreds of millions of money to pay them; but when those supplies shall cease, Algeria will follow the course of all her previous colonies. There are now strong inducements to go there. The man who stays at home pays those who go, and taxes swallow up one-fourth of the whole product of the kingdom. If he go himself, he ceases to be a payer and becomes a payee.

Were the colony this day put up to sale, it would not produce, in the market of the world a single dollar. France has wasted a hundred thousand lives, and many hundred millions of money in buying land possessing no intrinsic value whatsoever, while holding twelve millions of acres of her best soils still in forest: while her coal and iron are yet almost untouched: while her marl and her lime remain where nature placed them, beneath the poor soils now cultivated for want of means to bring into activity the better ones: while meadows remain undrained and untouched by the spade or the plough: while a large portion of her land is held in common: while the product of her agriculture is but five times the seed: while importing corn, and coal, and iron: and while almost destitute of roads or canals by which the little produce of her agriculture might reach a market. She wants wealth, and she buys more land! Such was her policy in America, and we have seen the result. Such will it be in Africa. The people of France are too poor to found colonies, and France is too poor to keep them when founded. If she cannot now, after thousands of years of occupation, with the advantage of the wealth that has been slowly accumulated, cultivate her good soils at home, what hope can there be that she will do so abroad? There is none. We heard of the prosperity of Australian colonies, and we now hear of that of Algeria. The one was, and the other is, supported by taxation upon the people at home, and the prosperity of the one is as factitious as was that of the other. The characteristics of French colonial policy are restlessness and feebleness. That of all successful colonies is quiet energy.

The colonization of the United States differs from that of the two countries we have considered, in the great fact that they desire no subjects. The colonists are equal with the people of the States from which they sprang, and hence the quiet and beautiful action of the system. The poor and widely scattered three millions of 1783: inhabitants of the thirteen provinces: have grown to more than twenty millions, inhabiting thirty states; of whom every man exercises independent action, or is in train soon to do so, even although now deemed and held to be a slave. Population has increased with wonderful rapidity, but wealth has far outgrown it. The two forces—the centripetal and the centrifugal—here balance each other perfectly, so far as regards internal action: but external action increases greatly the centrifugal force, and thus prevents, to a vast extent, the growth of wealth, of comfort, of civilization, and of happiness. Factories, steam-engines, and other articles of wealth attract the labourer towards the place on which he stands. Railroads and canals attract him towards uncleared land: or half-cleared land. On one hand, he sees the little bank: or the manufacturing corporation: saving funds, in which he may deposit the surplus of his earnings until ready to open a store: or buy a little farm: or commence manufacturing on his own account. On the other, he sees the larger farm, of eighty, one hundred and sixty, three hundred and twenty, or even six hundred and forty acres, that may require the unceasing labour of his life to bring into cultivation: but which will be his own, and an inheritance for his children. That is to be his savings' bank. In it he deposits all the spare half hours and quarter hours that, working for another, would be wasted. He has every inducement to economize his time and money, for his farm wants, and will pay for, both. He may be an independent farmer, if he will: and he does will it. Such would, however, more frequently be the case, could he remain at home. Throughout all the old states land is held in quantities far too large for thorough cultivation, and the result is seen in the fact that meadow-lands remain undrained: that men still cultivate clay unable to bring it into combination with the lime: and that vast bodies of wood still cover the most fertile soils; whereas, were concentration permitted, wealth would grow at double pace: land would become more divided: and men would obtain from twenty acres highly cultivated, a reward twice exceeding that which they have from farms in the wilderness ten times as large.

The government facilitates this operation, by purchasing the lands from the poor remnants of the original occupants now fast passing, and necessarily so, out of existence. It pays them well, by granting them annuities far exceeding any value their land could have obtained had not the white man brought with him the love of labour; the habit of order and economy, and the consequent power of accumulating wealth: qualities which they themselves did not possess. By their aid the poor Indian is enabled, at every step of their progress, to acquire food more readily than before, as all may see who will compare the situation of the distant tribes with that of the nearer ones. The habits of the savage are, however, wasteful. He hates labour, and he loves rum and war; and he cannot avail himself of the advantages that are offered to him by civilization.

The price that is paid appears to be, and is, small, yet it is more than they are really worth, and they are resold for less than cost: as we have already shown. They are held in trust, not for Americans alone but for the world. The man of every clime, American or English, Dutchman or Dane, Swede or Norwegian, Frenchman or German, Catholic or Episcopalian, Calvinist or Lutheran, Mohammedan or Pagan, may claim and receive his share in the trust, on payment of a sum that barely indemnifies the community by whom they have been acquired, for the cost of purchase, survey, and sale: and without including a thousand expenses incident to the operation, among which may be included nearly the whole cost of the army, as its chief employment has heretofore been that of providing for the security of the persons and property of settlers on those lands.

Here we may see and trace the true cause of value in land. The millions of acres belonging to the savage are valueless. He starves, surrounded by rich meadows, covered with the finest timber. The white man approaches, and roads are made: and land acquires some value, for which he is paid, although he has contributed nothing towards its production. It is surveyed, and by this simple act it acquires more value. At length it reaches the minimum price, and some of it is sold. Further roads and settlements are made, and more is sold, and when all shall come to be disposed of, the true account of expenditure and receipt will not balance. There will remain a large debit to the public lands, although it will not appear, much of it being charged to other accounts: ana most of it having been paid by individuals in the form of taxes. If land had any intrinsic value, there would be a large profit. As it has none: as it always sells for less than cost: there is a loss.

The first settlement made the wave of colonization rolls on, the poorest emigrant taking the lead and preparing with his small means a little of the poorer land, and a little house, for the better man that is to follow. To him he sells his improvements, pushing on ahead to perform again the same operation. The settlement grows to be a State, and quietly forms for itself a constitution of government, when, of right, it takes a place in the Union. From first to last, self-government is the rule. The colonist goes when and where he pleases, consulting nobody. He and his fellows make their own constitution of government, and elect their own governors, legislators, members of Congress, and local officers.

The beautiful effect of the habit of self-government is fully shown in the recent settlement of Oregon. The people were beyond the limits of any territorial government, and they formed a system for themselves; doing it quietly and perfectly: and now we have the annual message of the governor of the little State as regularly as that of the President of the Union. They have, happily for themselves, no great men among them, and therefore all may become great.

To those familiar with the land system of the United States, it is scarcely necessary to speak of its beautiful simplicity: or of the care with which it guards, so far as law can do so, the rights of the poorer class of settlers, who *squat* upon lands before the time arrives for selling them. In perfect harmony with this simplicity is the quiet grandeur of its results: so widely different from those of the recent settlements in Australia. The one is natural, the other systematic colonization. The one is governed by the practical good sense of men who think and act for themselves, while the other is directed by men who think that their fellow men are not competent to determine what is best for their interests. The one class *know* that men must scatter themselves over the poor lands before attempting the rich ones. The other *thinks* that if land were put at "a sufficient price," men might be compelled to cultivate the rich ones first. The only perfectly successful colonization in the world is that of the United States: and it is successful because its practice is in direct opposition to the theory of Mr. Ricardo and his followers, who cannot find in it, from first to last, a single fact in support of their doctrines.

The system is a good one; but it would be far better were it less needed. The same labour that has been expended in the colonization of Texas, Oregon, and California, would have yielded thrice the results had concentration on the older lands been possible. The man who buys a share in lands already cleared and cultivated, obtains it at far less than cost: while he who goes to the new ones must pay cost, and a large cost it is. Were that, however, the only loss, it would be cause of less regret than now it is, when we see that the acquisition of Texas has involved the country in a war that has already cost perhaps fifty millions, and may result in an expenditure of hundreds of millions. *That war is due to the existence of the repulsive force produced by the misdirection of the wealth and labour of England.* Had the people of the United States been permitted to bring into activity the fertile soils of the older States, concentrating their population, and placing the consumer by the side of the producer, Texas, and Oregon, and California, would have offered no inducement for settlement: labour would have been more productive: wealth would now be far greater: and the country would be still at peace. The universal thirst for land results from the necessity for occupying much land, to be badly cultivated by men who remain much poorer than they need be. Were concentration now rendered possible, that thirst would disappear, for men would obtain large returns from smaller surfaces, and become rich: and peaceful habits would come with wealth.

Lastly, we come to the colonization of Africa, undertaken with the most benevolent motives, by men who thought they saw in that vast and almost unoccupied land, with its abundance of the most fertile soils, an outlet for the negroes of the south: but who have long since found that the poverty of Africa exercised small attractive force when set against that of the wealth of the Union. There, as elsewhere, men have had to commence with the poor soils, and to enable them to do so and prosper, constant contributions have been and will continue to be required. The process will, nevertheless, be continued, and by it civilization will be carried into the heart of Africa: and thus will that quarter of the globe be made to participate in the benefits resulting from the peaceful policy and growing wealth of the United States.

African colonization has been opposed by many who fail to see that when men remain at peace and permit wealth to grow, the great laws of nature invariably triumph over the weak and pitiful inventions of man. They would have immediate, unconditional, emancipation, result how it may. We propose now to show what has been the course of southern colonization, with a view to show how perfectly the facts observed have been in accordance with the views submitted to the consideration of our readers; and, as we hope, to satisfy them that here as everywhere slavery came with poverty, and that freedom comes with growing wealth and population: that here, as everywhere, the latter are companions of peaceful and quiet action: and that if they would free the slave with most advantage to himself, they must act with, and not against, the man to whom the laws have guarantied the right of property in that slave and in his children. Well understood, the interests of all are in perfect harmony with each other, and point, as we believe, invariably towards the same course of action.

Raleigh's first settlement in Carolina was that of a man seduced by the idea of speedy wealth to be derived from the cultivation of fertile soils. It was made on the Island of Roanoke, described as the paradise of the world, for the luxuriance of its vegetation, the plumage of its birds, and the brilliancy of its skies. The soil was too rich, and his people perished. Upon these attempts, he wasted £40,000, for those days a vast sum: and it was a total loss, the result being to him even worse than that realized by the founder of Pennsylvania. The next colonization of North Carolina was voluntary, and, therefore, successful. Settlers came from New England, and exercised the right of self-government by selecting for themselves; and they went at once to the poor soils on which they could raise corn for subsistence, while engaged in the work of clearing richer lands and exchanging the lumber for clothing and other commodities. Other settlers followed; voluntary emigrants from Virginia, driven by persecution for difference of religious opinion: and they also prospered, because they selected for themselves. Prosperity produced union and strength, and when they at a subsequent period found themselves oppressed by the proprietary governor of the state that was to be governed on the system devised by Locke and Shaftesbury, they expelled him and determined to govern themselves. They had become colonists by virtue of the exercise of the right of self-government: and they were ready to work and to fight to maintain that right. They had no great men for leaders, and they would not have landlords claiming rent for the use of lands whose whole rent-producing powers were due to their own exertions. Thus colonized by men who laboured for themselves; thought for themselves; and acted for themselves; North Carolina has always been distinguished among the Southern States for the simplicity of her institutions: for the moderation of her expenditure: and for her attachment to freedom.

Virginia was granted to the noblemen, gentlemen, and

merchants of London, in whom was vested the whole management of the colony; while even the local councillors held their appointment from the king, and at his pleasure. In him was vested supreme legislative authority, the emigrant being denied the exercise of the right of self-government in any single matter: even in that of worshipping the Deity after his own fashion: the Church of England being established as the church, and only church, of the colony. These noblemen and gentlemen were absentee landlords, who wanted rents; and they sent *tenants*, instead of creating land-owners. As a necessary consequence, the character of the emigrants was inferior. They were men who expected to reap from fertile soils the same large profits that have so recently been looked for, and with such entire confidence, by the settlers in Australia; and they were of the same class: poor gentlemen who knew not how to work. Of the first expedition, consisting in all of one hundred and five persons, but twelve were labourers; and the mechanics were very few in number. Their sanguine expectations were disappointed. Food could be obtained only as a reward for labour, and they were of the class not born to work. The next expedition consisted, as before, of "vagabond gentlemen," to whom were now added a few goldsmiths, in search of mines and not of the means of acquiring wealth by honest labour. The landlords now demanded pay from their poor tenants; and threatened that if the ship returned without a full freight, they would leave the colony to perish. In reply to this they were informed by Captain Smith, to whom it was now no secret that men must commence with poor soils, that he wanted "carpenters, husbandmen, gardeners, blacksmiths, masons, and diggers up of trees' roots:" of whom, as he told them, thirty would be more valuable "than a thousand such as we have." Land was abundant, and they could select at pleasure from among the fertile soils; but labour was followed by small returns, because they had to cultivate poor soils. New subscriptions became necessary, and now numbers of the nobility and gentry became proprietors; whereupon grants of new powers were obtained from the government, and the landlords became sole masters. A governor and captain-general, holding his appointment for life, was now sent out; and was accompanied by stately officers with high-sounding titles, and charges with *nominal* duties, but *real* claims to be paid for the services they might be supposed to render. The governor was to possess absolute power: a necessary consequence of which was, that the emigrants who accompanied him were men who, claiming to exercise no rights, respected none: dissolute gallants, impoverished gentlemen, broken tradesmen, rakes, and libertines: men who preferred swords to axes. Idleness and vice, jealousy and hatred, abounded. Poverty, too, abounded, and they could not pay taxes. In default of other modes of contribution, lotteries were instituted, the profits of which went to the support of government; and thus the landlords contributed to maintain in them the gambling spirit which had led them to the New World. As gentlemen could not work, and food could not be obtained without severe labour, the importation of labourers under bonds of servitude had been, from the first, common; and the trade in men became, by degrees, lucrative: those who had cost £8 and £10, being sold as high, sometimes, as £60. Trade was stimulated by such profits; particularly as the importer obtained from the noblemen and gentlemen proprietors a grant of fifty acres of land for each person thus introduced: and thus did the aristocracy of England establish the slave trade of Virginia.* Slaves worked hard, and were hardly treated: the gentlemen owners employed themselves in hunting, fishing, cultivating the breed of horses, and other similar amusements: and the go-

* In the seventeenth century, the gentlemen of England gave the land, and sold the slave. In the nineteenth, the plan is different. They now sell the land, and give the slave. The "systematic colonization" of our time differs in scarcely any thing else from that which distinguished the age of Jeffries and James II.

vernors and officers who represented the noble proprietors plundered the colonists, and cheated their employers.* At the close of fifteen years, after an expenditure of £60,000, we find the former numbering but six hundred. Neither population nor wealth can grow, although fertile land is abundant. Factions arise among the proprietors, discontented with the small returns to their investments. Turbulence among the settlers is followed by massacre by the savages; and the number of plantations is reduced from eighty down to eight.† Next we have "a petition of grace" to the government of England for a monopoly of the right of supplying tobacco: and thus the first application for interference with trade, on this continent, may, we believe, be traced to Virginia. The colonists who do not work themselves, and cultivate their lands by aid of slave labour, cannot compete with other colonists who do work. The petition is granted: but the crown now determines to have the right of monopolizing the tobacco the poor people have to sell, thus converting the grant into a means of taxation. The company of noble proprietors is now dissolved, the result being, as in all similar cases it has been, total loss.‡ The control of the colony passing to the crown, its emancipation is followed by a very brief period of improvement; but governors are now appointed favourable to the claims of those who desire large grants of land, with concessions of jurisdiction: and thus estates grow large, requiring constant increase in the shipments of white slaves from England. Land thus concentrates itself, and man becomes, here as everywhere, poor and disunited. Frequent quarrels with the Indians are followed by massacres of the whites, and population is thus restrained: and without population wealth cannot grow. Slaves cultivate poor soils, and masters amuse

* In this portion of the history, striking resemblances in the two periods may be found.

† New Zealand, in the present century, is the *pendant* to Virginia in the seventeenth.

‡ Here, again, may be found the counterpart of Australia.

themselves with hunting; expending on horses much of the large proportion of the fruits of the soil which falls to their share. The Revolution in England now causes a large addition to the population, in the form of cavaliers: "men of consideration:" bringing with them the dissolute habits engendered by civil war: and churchmen, eager to enforce in the New World the rights, of the exercise of which they had been deprived in the Old. The population is now twenty thousand, of whom the blacks constitute less than one-fiftieth part: although thirty years have now elapsed since the importation of the first African slaves. At the date of the Restoration we find landed proprietors possessing two thousand acres, and spending their lives in indolence. The horse is fully cared for, and the breed is highly improved. The "planter's pace" has become proverbial. Man is, however, less carefully provided for, because of the constant accession of pilgrims to the New World under orders from mayors and justices of the west of England, who divide among themselves the profits of the trade. Land thus continues to grow in power as man declines. The poor soils only are yet cultivated, for wealth grows at "the planter's pace,"—always a slow one in this regard. Roads are mere horse-paths. Bridges are unknown. The only coin known in the payment of debts is tobacco. Exchanges are few, and towns have scarcely an existence. Schools and printing-presses are unknown.

Step by step we trace the progress of an aristocracy, with increasing selfishness and increasing disregard for the rights of those by whom they are surrounded; the natural result of colonization by the class to whom labour is a sacrifice: and here, as everywhere, this is accompanied by increasing incapacity for self-defence, either for the maintenance of their own rights, or those of their fellow-citizens. Royalist emigrants, elated at the Restoration, now become masters. Acts of conformity are passed. Salaries and taxes grow larger, while the land is exempt from contributions. Magistrates assess county taxes at their pleasure, and landholders form courts that judge without appeal. Burgesses pay themselves liberally for their services in voting taxes, while limiting the right of suffrage to freeholders and housekeepers: and submit to the provisions of the navigation act because too poor to own ships by which they may evade it as do the people of New England, now becoming rich from the cultivation of a sterile soil by the hands of freemen. Land grows in power daily, and man, great and small, becomes daily weaker. Voluntary immigration has no existence, because the markets are well supplied with slaves from Bristol and other English ports, and freemen could not exist upon the small proportion retained by the producer out of the very small returns obtained from land constantly cropped: which, too, is cultivated with machinery so indifferent that the top soil alone comes into action. Much of the wealth of the colony goes therefore to "knavish justices," and kidnappers, in England, whereas, under a different system, it would make roads and build ships: and growing wealth would then exercise a gently attractive power over men who could govern themselves, and travel at their own cost. Aristocracy grows daily. The tendency which prevailed in the earlier days of the colony, to a division of property among the members of the family, now ceases to exist, and the law of primogeniture becomes the general rule of action. The land becomes still more powerful, and the people become still more weak. The death of a slave from excess of punishment ceases to be punishable by law, and it is declared lawful to wound, or even to kill them, in making their escape. Among the different portions of society, or among the members of the same portion, there exists no tendency to union or harmony; because, as wealth cannot grow, men are still forced to scatter themselves over the poor soils, and concentration is therefore impossible. Forests still cover the most fertile lands, and swamps capable of yielding vast returns to labour are interspersed between the little settlements. The very few have fine houses: but log-houses, of one story, in which shutters supply the want of glass, are the ordinary residences of men who purchase slaves, read no books or newspapers, and tolerate no lawyers: while children grow up uneducated, because of the total want of schools. What then must be the condition of the slave? What could be his proportion of the product of his labour? Aristocracy is here, as elsewhere in all countries and at all periods, marked by turbulence and discord. Rebellion, civil war, and carnage, coupled with the display of avarice and rapacity in a high degree, fill up several years of the colonial history, during all of which we observe a steady influx of English slaves: sometimes young persons kidnapped and hurried on board of ship; and at others, persons charged with small crimes, who prefer being sold by the magistrates and judges rather than risk confinement in such horrid prisons as those which existed in the days when land was absolute and the people weak.* The arrival of a *noble* governor is distinguished by the doubling of the salary of his office, as necessary to the maintenance of his dignity: and by the relinquishment on the part of the aristocratic assembly of all control over taxation, at a time when from the extreme impoverishment and restless state of the people, economy was more than ever necessary. Failing to respect the rights of those beneath them, they are unable to guard their own, and thus oppression and weakness are seen going hand in hand together. Rebellions and executions follow in the train of tyranny and rapacity. His successor, another of the noble race, *fruges consumere nati*, distinguished, even beyond his successor for rapacity and for meanness, divides perquisites with his clerks. The rebellion of Monmouth now adds largely to the population of

* The whole system has its counterpart in Australia, but the latter presents one feature of barbarism unknown to the seventeenth century, to wit, Norfolk Island, the disgrace of the age.

the colony. The prisoners made on that occasion, and who escape the hangman, are distributed among the queen and courtiers, by whom they are sold at ten or fifteen pounds each: to be resold in Virginia for forty or fifty pounds. Among them are numerous persons of family and education. To this date, the importation of negro slaves has been exceedingly limited, white slaves being found cheaper and better. The tobacco ships have brought them as return cargo, whereas the negro would require a voyage to the coast of Africa, to which no cargo could be carried: and, therefore, so long as the exportation from England can be maintained, the other branch of the slave trade can attain but little development. With the close of the reign of James II. that traffic falls off, even if it be not entirely discontinued; and thereafter the supply comes chiefly from the African coast. Such is the history of the origin of American slavery.

In 1663, Lords Clarendon, Albemarle, and other noblemen, obtained a grant of the country now included in the two Carolinas, with absolute authority, and with the expectation of obtaining large rents from the rich land included within their domain. With the usual rapacity of their class we find them obtaining, two years later, further grants of the land now included in all the States south and west, and extending far into Mexico. The new and great State now to be formed required a constitution that should accord in magnificence with its extent, and to Locke and Shaftesbury are we indebted for that which was then prepared, the only one formed for any portion of the British dominions in America, by the aristocracy exclusively, and therefore the only one in which is avowed the intention of keeping the people in a state of slavery. To the extent of two-fifths the land was to be inalienable, the property of barons, caciques, palatines, &c., with tenants, adscripts of the soil, subject to the jurisdiction of lords from whose decision there was no appeal. The leet men were to be leet men through all generations. A grand council of fifty, of whom fourteen only, holding their seats for life, represented the commons, was mixed up in the scheme with courts of heraldry; of ceremonies and pedigrees; and of fashions and sports: and this absurd scheme it was fully believed would endure for ever. Land was to be all, and man nothing.

The first settlement was formed on rich soils whose fatal atmosphere had destroyed the native inhabitants; and the whites naturally followed them. The second, Charleston, was placed near the junction of two rivers, where the vegetation was luxuriant. The settlers, in keeping with the magnificence of the proprietors, were generally men of noble family impoverished in the civil wars: men who could not work, and who needed others to do the labour. The climate was pestilential and white labourers would not come, even for full wages. Labourers were, therefore, to be purchased; and in a short time the slaves were twice as numerous as the whites. In no part of the Union have the settlers been to the same extent men of high birth and wealthy family connections as in this state; and in none has there existed, at all times, so strong a tendency towards cultivating rich soils in advance of their natural order: and in none, consequently, has there been so great a disparity of condition between the planter and the labourer; the condition of the negro being worse than in any other portion of the Union: the highest aristocracy being here, as everywhere, surrounded by the poorest democracy. The natural consequence is, that population diminishes and land is almost valueless. Aristocracy and disunion, poverty and concentration of land, are ever found in close companionship with each other.

The cause of the existence of slavery in the United States is now, we think, obvious. Impoverished branches or dependents of the English aristocracy sought wealth without labour. Unwilling to work themselves, and unable to offer inducements to the free labourer, who could have land elsewhere for himself, they first enslaved their poorer countrymen; and when that source of supply was stopped, they took the negro. Had no aristocracy existed in England, no negro slavery could have arisen in America. The reader who may chance to be familiar with the books of the recent settlers in Australia, can hardly fail to see in the sketch of Virginian history now furnished very many points of resemblance: all of which are due to the fact that in both the settlers were unused to labour, and therefore unfit for the business of settlement. Everywhere in those books there is a complaint of the high price of labour. The land is good enough, but labour is too dear to work it, and it will not pay. If the labour market could but be over-stocked, so that the land-owners could make their own terms, the latter would be rich. They wanted slaves, although not fully aware of the fact. The man who cannot work and who undertakes the work of settlement, must have slaves, or he must starve: and the reason is, that all rent is consideration paid for the use of those advantages which result from labour expended on land, and not for land itself. *Until labour has been so applied, entitling its owner to a share, it has no value; and he who will work it must have the product, be it what it may, much or little: but it is always little, and with less he could not live. He *must* commence with the poorer lands that he *can* cultivate, while waiting the clearing of the woods and draining of the marshes which cover the rich soils. His wages, therefore, absorb the whole. Virginia and South Carolina were settled by those who consumed without producing, and hence the existence of the curse of negro slavery, which made no way at the north, because the food, and clothing, and lodging, of the slave were more than his labour was worth. He would there have been, as now he would be, an incumbrance on the earth.

---

* "After an enormous expenditure of capital, the returns were far less than might have been derived from a similar amount in England, and property was steadily depreciating in value."—*Henderson's New South Wales.*

THE number of blacks, slave and free, existing in the United States at the first census, was 757,000, of whom 60,000 were free, leaving 697,000 slaves. How many had been imported, it is impossible now to say; but we doubt if the total amount of importation had exceeded 250,000. It was probably short of that number. The slave trade continued to be permitted by law until 1808, a period of eighteen years, during which time the number imported could not have exceeded 100,000, as the whole increase from 1790 to 1810 was only 620,000; and according to the rate of natural increase since that time, it would have been 520,000. We think, therefore, that we are safe in saying that the whole negro race in the Union, amounting now to about 3,250,000, are descended from 350,000 barbarians, whose condition as slaves was far better than it had been when nominally free, and liable at every hour to be robbed or murdered, or both.

At the period of the first census, the country had, in a considerable degree, recovered from the effects of the war of independence. Since that time, it has advanced steadily in population and wealth, but with vastly more rapid pace in the northern than in the southern portions; because in the one every man labours for himself, and every one accumulates something as a contribution to the general stock of wealth. The difference in the relative advance causes the southern portion to appear almost stationary; but such is far from having been the case. Population and wealth have both advanced greatly, and there has been a vast increase in the productive power, accompanied with a corresponding increase in the proportion of the labourer; who is now far better fed, clothed, lodged, and taught, than at any former period. With this increase of wealth the planter has acquired the ability to seek more fertile soils, and we observe him, accompanied by the black race whose services he employs, regularly descending the slope from the mountains of Virginia and Kentucky towards the better lands in the vicinity of the Gulf of Mexico; and with every step in their progress, the value of labour rises. The labourer himself acquires more value in the eyes of his master, who feeds and clothes him better: gives him better shelter; better medical attendance; more privileges in regard to land for his own use and that of his family; and thus enables him more and more to exercise the right of self-government. With every step in this progress he acquires more value in his own estimation, without which he could make no progress in the work of preparing himself for the ultimate perfect exercise of that right. To enable the reader to trace this operation, we give the table on the opposite page, in which the several States occupying the same latitudes are placed together.

The process that is thus exhibited as now going on before our eyes, is frequently stigmatized as an internal slave trade, and legislative action is not unfrequently invoked for its prevention; when it is the precise course that has, in every quarter of the world, led man to freedom. As the people of Italy became more rich, they sought the rich soils at the foot of their hills, and became more free. War drove them back to the hills, and they became slaves. As the people of England now become more rich, they seek the fertile soils, and become more and more free with every stage of the process. So is it with the people of Prussia. So was it with the people of Egypt, of Argos, and of Attica, and so has it been with every nation of the world. To shut up the negro race in Virginia and Kentucky would be their ruin. The Almighty never intended them to mix with the white race, nor is it desirable that they should do so; for as a separate and independent race of free men, they will be happier, better, and more useful, than in any other condition. They are now gradually concentrating on the soils best suited to them, and with results similar to those everywhere else observed. Farms and houses, towns and cities, roads and railroads: steamboats and electric telegraphs, cotton factories, furnaces, and other evidences of increasing power of accumulation,

A TABLE

Showing the Comparative Increase of the White and Coloured Population in several of the Southern States in the same Degrees of Latitude, from the year 1790 *to* 1840.

States.	1790.			1800.			1810.			1820.			1830.			1840.		
	White.	Free Colour-ed.	Slave.	White.	Free Colour-ed.	Slave.	White.	Free Colour-ed.	Slave.	White.	Free Colour-ed.	Slave.	White.	Free Colour-ed.	Slave.	White.	Free Colour-ed.	Slave.
Delaware and Maryland, and Dist. of Colum.	254,000	12,000	112,000	264,000	28,000	114,000	275,000	47,000	116,000	346,000	56,000	117,000	376,000	75,000	111,000	407,000	84,000	97,000
Virginia, Kentucky, and Missouri,	503,000	13,000	305,000	690,000	21,000	387,000	576,000	32,000	473,000	1,115,000	38,000	560,000	1,350,000	53,000	659,000	1,654,000	59,000	689,000
North Carolina, Tennessee, and Arkansas,	288,000	5,000	101,000	430,000	7,000	147,000	588,000	11,000	212,000	787,000	17,000	285,000	1,035,000	24,000	393,000	1,203,000	30,000	449,000
South Carolina,	130,000	2,000	107,000	196,000	3,000	146,000	213,000	4,000	196,000	242,000	7,000	258,000	258,000	8,000	315,000	259,000	8,000	327,000
Georgia, Alabama, Mississippi, Louisiana, and Florida,	53,000		29,000	106,000	2,000	63,000	218,000	9,000	160,000	408,000	20,000	294,000	654,000	23,000	506,000	1,098,000	32,000	923,000

resulting from increased productiveness of labour, are seen to rise with a rapidity totally unknown in the older slave States, where the poor soils are still cultivated: where roads improve but slowly, and railroads are scarcely known. In the new States, the tendency to concentration—to placing the consumer side by side with the producer—exists in a strong degree, whereas, in the older ones it has scarcely an existence. The latter are yet in the transition state. The slave race is going out, and the free race is coming in: and until the change shall be effected, they cannot move with much rapidity. The time is now not far distant when the whole race will be concentrated in the southern tier of States. Including South Carolina, more than one-half were there in 1840. At the next census, the proportion will probably be three-fifths, if not more; and at the end of another decennial period, it will probably exceed four-fifths: and as population and wealth shall increase, as better soils shall be cultivated, and as the consumer shall, more and more, take his place by the side of the producer, their labour will become steadily more productive. With the increase of production they will obtain the control, for their own use, of a largei proportion of the proceeds of their labour: and that proportion will steadily increase until there will be seen to arise a class of free black men, cultivating for their own use their own land, bought from their old masters, who will find in the price of the land a compensation for the price of the labourer. Ultimately, and at no distant period, those States will be owned and inhabited by a race of free citizens, differing in colour but similar in rights, and equal in capacity to their fellow-citizens of the north.

To those who doubt this, and there will be many, we have to say that the laws of nature are the same in the New World as in the old: in the present age and all past ages: for the black man and the white: and that if this result do not arrive, it will be in opposition to all past experience. Man always has become more free as he has passed from the cultivation of poor soils to rich ones, and he always will. He cannot do this unless population and wealth increase. The interest of the planter favours the increase of population, and population cannot increase where morals do not improve. His interest favours increase of wealth, because improved machinery enables him to grow more cotton or corn: improved gins enable him to prepare his cotton better and with less labour: while steamboats and railroads facilitate his connection with the great markets. With another step, he will make his market at home, converting his cotton into cloth by aid of the food grown on his own rich lands, now uncultivated: and with every diminution in the quantity of the machinery of exchange, wealth will still more rapidly increase. The planter desires the growth of wealth and population; and they bear on their wings division of land, and freedom, and happiness, and prosperity, to man. The interests of all are in perfect harmony with each other, and the day is not far distant when all will admit the fact. At present, the majority of planters deny to the minority the right of judging for themselves in the matter of educating slaves, of emancipating them, &c.; but we need desire no better evidence of the tendency to education and emancipation than the fact of the existence of such laws. Without it, they would not be needed. Even as it is, the education law is almost a nullity, and, ere long, the minority will become the majority: and when that shall be the case, the whole class of planters will be restored to the exercise of rights in regard to their property of which they are thus deprived, because, as it is said, the public good requires it. Leagues for the public good always abound where aristocracies exist; but selfishness is their characteristic, wherever found. The war-cry varies, but the object is still the same. Sometimes they fight for the liberties of Europe, while, at others, it is for the plunder of Italy, of India, or of Holland. Such combinations always exist where land is concentrated, and man divided; and they most exist where land is most concentrated, and

31*

man cultivates the poorest soils, as may, at this moment, be seen on both sides of the Atlantic. The history of France shows us several such leagues, the members of which, in every case, had in view the private good alone: and all were willing to be bought at their own prices. We do not allege this of the people of the south. We have no doubt that many, very many, seriously believe that in maintaining such laws they are doing what is best for all, black and white: but they might reflect that their fellow-planter, who educates his slave, has the same right to judge for himself as they: and so he will, and does, and ought: law or no law. Wealth will grow, and freedom will come, let the laws be as they may: provided they remain at peace and diminish the cost of their machinery of exchange. Let them do this, and black senators will ultimately sit in the Congress of the United States: and the Union will then be sounder, and stronger, and richer, and more rapidly advancing in wealth and population, than at any previous period.

It is supposed by many that it is necessary to pass laws to prevent the extension of slavery over new territories: but we are disposed to believe that a very brief examination of the facts of the case will show that such a measure is an unnecessary interference with the rights of those who are equal with themselves. Great natural laws tend now daily to produce the results desired, and evasion of *those* laws is impossible; whereas no law could be made that would exist, or that should exist, did the interests of those subject to it require its repeal.

If we examine attentively the movements of the population of the Southern States, we shall see existing on the part of the planter, a universal tendency downwards towards the richer lands: while, on the part of the free labourer, or the man whose means are limited to the ownership of one or two negroes, there is a tendency, equally universal, towards the higher lands: and thus we see the free population, the farmers, of Virginia, the Carolinas, Georgia and Tennessee, clustering together in the neighbourhood of the mountains, while the country intermediate between them and the ocean is in a great degree occupied by planters: and hence it is that we see an unceasing contest between the eastern and western portions of Virginia for political supremacy. The free man always seeks the heads of the streams: the dry and poor lands: for the commencement of his labours, because his means are small, and he is satisfied if he obtain wages for his time and labour: and his profits are to be found in the value that he gives his land.* The planter is a capitalist, who wants profits of capital, or rent; and as land cannot be made to yield more in return to the labour of the people who work for him than it would do to that of the man who worked for himself, it follows that if the product is to be divided into two parts; one for the labourer, and the other for the labourer's owner; the latter must be a deduction from the former, and the labourer must receive less than the ordinary rate of wages. In

* *Western North Carolina.*

	Slaves.	Total Pop.
Ashe	479	7,467
Cherokee	199	3,427
Haywood	303	4,975
Henderson	466	5,129
Lincoln	2,711	25,660
Burke	3,159	15,799

Western Virginia.

	Slaves.	Total Pop
Brooke	54	7,948
Marshall	46	6,937
Ohio	231	13,367
Lewis	122	3,151
Nicholas	74	2,223
Greenbrier	1,314	8,695

Eastern Tennessee.

	Slaves.	Total Pop
Marion	380	6,070
Monroe	312	12,056
Jefferson	672	12,076
Greene	509	16,076
Blount	383	11,745
Ganger	105	10,552

order that the product may be sufficiently large to bear this division, the planter is forced to seek those soils and those climates in which the powers of his labourers can be employed to the greatest advantage ; and as the negro originated in the torrid region of Africa, it is natural to suppose that it is in a climate corresponding thereto that his powers will be most fully developed : whereas those of the white require a higher and colder one, and he is thus seen to become less active as he passes south. Each is excellent in his place. The negro will do more work than the white man in Florida, but the Yankee will do more than two negroes in Massachusetts. The negro can produce more rice than the white in the low lands of Carolina ; but the white, who lives in the mountainous region of that state, will produce more corn or wheat than his slave. The slave in Maryland and Virginia is competing with the free labourer of Ohio, in the production of wheat and tobacco ; and the latter is beating the former out of market, and thereby producing a necessity for his emigration towards the climate for which nature intended him : and there he will go, and there he will stay, let man make what laws he may.

By law, slavery exists in Missouri, but what is its progress ? In 1830, the slaves were twenty-five thousand, and the free people one hundred and eighteen thousand. In 1840, the former were fifty-eight, and the latter three hundred and twenty-four thousand. The natural increase would give thirty-two thousand. It follows that twenty-six thousand have been taken there : and if we examine where they have gone, we find it is to the counties nearest the Mississippi, where they have been temporarily arrested on their way to the south. If we look to Arkansas, we obtain the following results. The population in 1830 was : slave, five thousand, free twenty-six thousand. In 1840, slave twenty thousand, free seventy-seven thousand. Its numbers increase slowly, because wealth grows slowly, and the free labourer is not attracted there : while the planter finds no attraction sufficient to induce him to ascend the Red River, when he has before him the lower lands of Alabama and Mississippi, where wealth is growing rapidly and attracting forcibly. So strongly is this felt in Arkansas, that lands forfeited for non-payment of taxes are at this moment offered gratuitously to settlers, for freemen will not go where slavery exists, and planters *cannot* ascend rivers to cultivate poor lands. That state must, therefore, soon cease to tolerate slavery within its limits. The planter always *flies* from mountains and hills, and heads of streams, while the free labourer there commences his operations and *works* downwards. The *mass* of the planter is great. He represents fifty, one hundred, or five hundred persons, who are property: and wealth is always strongly attracted by wealth. The railroad now building across the whole of the southern tier of states, constitutes an attractive power that is irresistible, and it is there that the black race tends: *there that it will stay.* Arkansas and Missouri will soon become free states, by virtue of a great general law: the law of self-government. Texas, too, will be a free state. Of the slaves who have been taken there, many have, we understand, already returned: the wild lands of that state, destitute of roads, having proved less attractive than the towns and cities, and steamboats and railroads, of Mississippi and Alabama. The heavily moving planter does not go to the rich lands, but the light and active Yankee, and the hard working German, are going to the poorer ones of the elevated region in which a cool climate and pure air enable them to work, and gradually to prepare the means for subduing the fertile land at their feet. In a short time, the proportion of free to slave population will be, as now in Missouri, so large that the planter will deem it unsafe to venture there, even were it his interest; and *that* it will not be until railroads, and towns, and cities shall become sufficiently numerous to exert a power of attraction greater than Alabama and Mississippi: and that time is very distant. The start those states have taken is so great that they will probably have attracted within their limits the chief part of the negro population before Texas will exercise any attractive influence whatsoever.

If the views thus submitted be true, and they are in strict accordance with the facts which the last ten, twenty and thirty years have presented for examination, there can be no necessity for the passage of laws having for their object interference with the planter's rights of property. He will not go to the high lands of California, for he will not go to those of Arkansas or Texas. He will not go to the low lands of Texas, where no population exists: and still less will he, should Mexico ever unite her fortunes with those of the United States, seek the low lands of that country, where labourers may be *hired* for a less quantity of the necessaries and comforts of life than he is accustomed to give to the slave whom he has *purchased*. Were Mexico this day within the Union no planter would cross the Rio Grande, but tens of thousands of Yankees would be found there, giving life and activity to agriculture, and to commerce: stimulating the labourer, by increased rewards, to increased production; opening new markets for the manufactures, whether of iron or of cotton, of the north, and for the cotton and sugar of the south: for fertile as are the lower lands of Mexico, a long time has yet to elapse before they can be rendered extensively productive. The climate is bad, because vegetation is too luxuriant: and the work of drainage and clearing, essential to improvement of climate, is a very slow one.

Carefully considered, we believe it will be seen that between the two great divisions of the Union there is a perfect harmony of interests, and that all that is needed for the settlement of the great slavery question, is the observance of the most perfect respect for the rights of property: every man of the free states doing to his neighbour of the south as, were their positions changed, he would that his neighbour should do unto him. In so doing, he will do that which will most promote the growth of harmony and peace, union, wealth and population, and without them there can be no improvement in the physical, moral, intellectual or political condition of the objects of his solicitude. "Love one another," is the great law of Christianity, and there is no reason why the planter and the farmer should do otherwise. The former asks only of the latter respect for his rights in property acquired in accordance with law, and he has a right to ask for them perfect respect, but while doing so he should recollect that the whole system of southern legislation is marked by interference by one portion of the planting interest with the rights of another portion, their neighbours. The man who desires to educate, or to emancipate, his slave is as much entitled to the exercise of his judgment in regard to the management of his property as is his neighbour who is resolved to do neither the one nor the other. He should also recollect that the system of separating husbands and wives, parents and children, is not in accordance with the great moral law which teaches that men should do by others as they would that others should do by them, and that persistence in the practice offends the moral sense of those who are most desirous to see enforced most fully the system of non-interference. The more perfectly he respects the rights of his neighbours, and those of the people whom he claims to hold as property, the more fully will he be able to maintain and to defend his own. Such has been the case throughout the world, and the more he shall study its history the better will he be satisfied that obedience to the precepts of Christianity is not more the duty than it is the policy both of men and of nations.

We may now examine the course of events in the British West Indies, the scene of a recent great interference with the rights of property. We have seen the effects of absentee ownership in Virginia, but in the West Indies it was far worse, because much longer continued: and because to the exhaustion thus produced was added that resulting from frequent wars, occasional invasions, and unceasing restrictions on the one hand, and monopolies on the other. The absentees wanted large rents from land on which little capital had been invested. The land would not support the negro, the agent, and the owner, but the wants of the two latter were imperative, and the negro had to suffer to the extent required. To do this, he must begin by working the rich land: the land of fevers and pestilence. He must begin by sugar land, instead of corn or potato land. The forfeit was his life, which was given to make up the rent required. Population could not grow, under such circumstances, and it did not grow. By the census of 1824, there were seven hundred and seventy-five thousand of the negro race in those colonies. In 1834, they were reduced to seven hundred thousand, showing a reduction of ten per cent.

We have seen that in all other countries the fertile lands were abandoned as population decreased, and such must have been the case here. The value of slaves fell, necessarily, from the same cause: and thus to *the tyranny that prevented all increase*, and caused the number emancipated to be far less than the number that had been imported, was due the power of the government to effect emancipation. Had they received the same treatment as the slaves of the United States, there would have been no Maroon wars to waste the population which would have been eight times as great and sixteen times as valuable: and then forced emancipation would have been as impossible as impolitic, and as impolitic as unjust. The majority of the people of England compelled a small minority to do that which if right to be done *at all* should have been done *by all*: but the measure that was to cost perhaps £100,000,000, was held to be fully paid for with £20,000,000. The difference has been since made up in the cost of sugar, which doubled in price, and the labourer of England was thus deprived of a necessary of life. In this way, the landlords of the colonies and the labourers at home have paid the cost of a violent interference with rights acquired under sanction of the law, and guarantied by the law.*

The labourer is now free, and the landlord receives no rent. The former prefers raising yams to sugar. He can raise them on the high lands to which free labour always directs itself, and he can put the whole in his own pocket, as wages. The absentee planter's agent cannot pay the same wages, if he would live and enable his principal to live. The consequence is, an universal cry for labourers, who would be abundant enough at sufficient wages. Cheaper labour is deemed necessary, and a new slave trade is organized. Hill-coolies are imported from India, and distributed to do hard work at low wages, and to be treated little better, if the accounts we have seen be true, than the slaves of old: although still living better than under the Company's government. The whole framework of society in some of the colonies seems to be broken up. In others, owing to peculiar circumstances, it is said to have worked better, but what is the actual state of things in any of them it is exceedingly difficult to say, for all who attempt to describe the workings of the measure are either its determined advocates or its deadly enemies: and the one can see in it no wrong, the other no right. One thing has been proved by it, and that is, that rents cannot come from land upon which labour and capital have not been, and are not continued to be, expended. The mere land can pay nothing but wages, and the labourer must become the owner, unless the owner live on it and improve it and thus entitle himself to receive interest in the form of rent. Were he even to attempt this, it is doubtful if he would succeed; for in all other countries the poor lands have been first cultivated, and the rich lands last: and it would appear that the natural order of things is about to be restored.

* Weakness and tyranny always go hand in hand. The planter of the West Indies destroyed his slave, and had no power to protect himself. The planter of the United States causes his slaves to increase, and therefore it is that he has now the power to protect himself in the enjoyment of his rights of property.

The British islands furnished, of sugar, in	1836 ·········	3,600,000 cwts.
	1839 ·········	2,800,000
	1840–41, average,	2,180,000
	1842–3–4, ·····	2,500,000
	1845 ·········	2,800,000
	1846 ·········	2,100,000

The deficiency in sugar is not made up in coffee, the average amount of which, from the British possessions, was, in 1835–6, above twenty-five millions, whereas the average for 1844–5 and 6, but little exceeded twenty-one millions.

The deficiency in the supply of sugar and coffee cultivated for export, has been attributed to an increasing disposition to raise food for consumption at home, but the *Barbadian* of July last, says, "There is no food in the country, starvation is staring us in the face. What a change has come over Barbadoes! The little island which used to feed more than a hundred and twenty thousand people, and yet export corn, yams and potatoes to the sister colonies, is without supply, and the labouring inhabitants now crowd into Bridgetown to buy American meal, rice, &c., to keep themselves from starving; and so great is the advance on those necessaries of life, that a quarter of a dollar goes very little way indeed. We may judge of the dreadful scarcity of corn and potatoes, by the fact that the town is most abundantly supplied with poultry and butchers' meat, which the cultivators of small tenements are selling off as fast as they can, at a very low price, because they have not the means of feeding their stock."

We have watched this experiment with great interest, but have found it exceedingly difficult to understand the working of it; so far as we have been enabled to form a judgment, it appears to be a total failure. Had it succeeded, it would have been wonderful. By the above statement, it appears that Barbadoes had once a population of a hundred and twenty thousand. In 1834, it was a hundred and three thousand. We should be glad to know what it is now. If population grow, all will come right. But if it diminish as it has heretofore done, the land must relapse into barbarism, and such we have some apprehensions will be the case.

The Spanish colonists commenced with the lower soils—those which in the natural order of things are the last. They wanted gold and silver, which would not pay wages, and therefore the people were enslaved. The results were more disastrous than the working of the sugar lands of the West Indies, for nearly the whole population was destroyed. No land can be made to yield more than wages, except where labour has been expended upon it, or for its advantage: and then its selling price is always less than the cost. The crown of Spain expended no capital but it took a large rent, paid by the sacrifice of millions of lives.

In one case, however, a different system was pursued, and the results contrast so strongly with those afforded by an examination of the British islands, that we cannot omit to notice it. The island of Porto Rico had been for three centuries neglected. It was too rich. In 1802 it had a population of 163,000, scattered over the island, on those parts that would afford food for consumption: and received an annual remittance from Mexico for the support of the government. About thirty years since, Spain invited settlers: offering land, free of expense even for the title papers, and perfect security as regards the control of the property they might bring with them: with freedom to leave when they pleased, and light taxes to pay, if they stayed. The result was that population and wealth increased with great rapidity. The former consisted, in 1830, of 162,000 whites, 127,000 free blacks, and 34,000 slaves, making a total of 323,000, or almost double what it had been before. Immense forests had disappeared before the axe. Marshes had been drained. Roads had been made, and villages and towns had grown up, and cities had increased. The number of proprietors was then

20,000, holding 1,500,000 acres, giving an average of 75 acres to each. The character of the land selected may be seen from the fact that of 85,000 acres under cultivation, there were but 11,000 under sugar cane, and 11,000 under rice, while the remaining 63,000 were employed in growing food for home consumption, except 9000 in coffee trees, which grow on the higher lands. The remaining 1,400,000 acres owned by individuals, were nearly equally divided between meadow and woodlands, waiting until the means of the colonists should enable them to clear and drain them: and affording, in the mean time, food for 200,000 horned cattle, 80,000 horses, and above 170,000 sheep, goats and swine. Here we have a beautiful illustration of the advantage of self-government. Had not the crown offered perfect freedom of entry and departure, and equal freedom as to the selection and mode of occupation of the lands, such results could never have been obtained.

WITH the growth of population and of wealth man acquires increased power to determine for himself what soils he will cultivate; and he takes the near or the distant, the superficial or the profound, as he deems the one or the other best fitted to enable him to improve his condition.] With each step in the progress of the power of man over land, wealth tends to increase with greater rapidity, and with each such step he is enabled to bring into activity better soils with less labour. With each he becomes more and more a being of *power*, and less a victim of *necessity*.

The PAST says to the freeman of the PRESENT: "If you desire that all men should be as free as yourself, respect the rights of your neighbour, and unite with him in exertion for the promotion of the growth of wealth: for freedom always follows wealth."

To the planter, it says: "Labour for the maintenance

of peace, and for the promotion of the growth of wealth. Your property will increase in value, and your lands will become divided. Your slaves will become the free cultivators of those lands, and your rents will then be far greater than they are now."

To all it says: "Avoid war, and preparation for war!"

CHAPTER XII.

IRELAND.

In what we have thus far written, we have purposely omitted all reference to Ireland,—desiring to treat it by itself, and to show, as we think conclusively, that there is no exception to the law that we have submitted for the consideration of our readers.

At the invasion, Ireland was advancing in civilization. It was divided into five little kingdoms, among whom existed those difficulties which in all cases have been seen to exist where men were poor and scattered, because of the necessity for depending on the least productive soils for a supply of food; but, had they been left to themselves, population and wealth would have grown, the better soils would have been brought into cultivation, and Ireland would now occupy the position in the world to which her advantages so eminently entitle her: among the foremost in civilization. To her insular position, England has been indebted for her freedom from invasion, and for the growth of wealth and the habit of peace. Ireland enjoyed the same advantage as regarded the Continent, but she was unhappy in being the near neighbour of the Norman aristocracy, a body whose most distinguishing feature has at all times been unbounded rapacity. Ireland was partially subjugated; and thenceforward the power and wealth of England became an element of perpetual disturbance. The land was filled by English agents, who were anxious for confiscations: and confiscations were to be produced by rebellions. Rebellions were, therefore, to be produced, and the mode of production was oppression. Such is the history of Ireland, the prey of England.

The natural result of this state of things, during the first five centuries, was the entire insecurity of person and property. Population and wealth did not advance, if they did not even retrograde. The people still cultivated the poor soils, and remained in a state of barbarism. The oppressions of the Stuarts gave rise to disturbances, which resulted in the expulsion, under James I., of the whole people of Ulster, who had their choice of 'Hell, or Connaught;' and that province, to the extent of nearly three millions of acres, became the property of the city of London, and other absentee landlords. Ireland afterwards supported the Stuarts, and was repaid for her services by the confiscation of nearly eight millions of acres. Ireland, nevertheless, supported James II., and was punished by his daughter and her husband, by the confiscation of another million. Thus the seventeenth century witnessed the transfer to the aristocracy of England and their friends, of nearly the whole land of Ireland that was fit for cultivation: the whole quantity being twenty millions, of which one-third is still waste.

A conduit was thus provided for all the produce of this unfortunate island, over and above what was absolutely necessary to keep the miserable people from starvation. Some portion of the new owners planted themselves in Ireland: little sovereigns among their hapless dependants: and, as is always the case under such circumstances, there was a perpetual contest among the great men for the division of the spoil; and faction was carried to an extent to be exceeded only in the history of France. The poverty of the people rendered them turbulent, and armies and taxes were rendered more necessary. The people paid the taxes, and their masters filled the offices, and squandered on luxuries in Dublin, what was collected at the point of the bayonet from people who ate potatoes in mud cabins, and went clothed in rags. Every thing tended towards centralizing the wealth of the kingdom in the capital, on its way outward; the necessary consequence of which was that the people still cultivated the poor soils, and concentration was impossible.

More effectually to prevent it, however, every practicable measure was resorted to, for the purpose of preventing the consumer taking his place by the side of the producer. Irish manufactures were prohibited in England; while Ireland was exposed, almost unguarded, to the influence of a system which, by forcing the capital of England from employment on the land, rendered it superabundant and unnaturally cheap, and compelled it to seek manufactures and commerce.* Ireland was then prohibited from all direct intercourse with foreign countries, or even the British colonies; and was thus deprived of the power of exchanging the productions of its fields for sugar or coffee, except through English ports. We see thus, that while the mass of the products of the country was withdrawn never again to return, that portion which was to be exchanged was burdened with the cost of a vast amount of useless and wasteful machinery, tending still further to arrest the progress of wealth and the power of concentration.

That no measure of repression might be omitted, the people who chanced to entertain on the subject of transubstantiation ideas differing from those of the governing few, were deprived of almost all the rights of person and property. They could rise neither in the bar nor in the church: neither in the local corporation nor in the state.† England had pro-

* King William, in one of his speeches to Parliament, declared that he would "do every thing in his power to discourage the woollen manufacture of Ireland."

† The chief disabilities imposed upon the Catholics during the reign of William and Anne, were the following. They could not hold leases for more than thirty-one years; could neither purchase lands, teach publicly in schools, have a horse of more than £5 value, vote for members of Parliament, nor become barristers, or clerks, or attorneys, without taking the oath of allegiance and supremacy; hold any office under the crown, or become magistrates in any town, without taking the sacrament, as prescribed by the English test act, according to the usage of the Church of England; nor take property

vided outlets for the *property* that might otherwise be accumulated in Ireland; and by this measure she provided similar outlets for all the *men of mind*, who desired to rise, and felt that they could rise, if permitted. Such men sought employment in France or Spain, or on the continent of America. The natural consequence of this was, that the control of public affairs fell into the hands of the most rapacious and contemptible band of jobbers, noble and plebeian, that has been exhibited in the annals of the world.

With the Union came perfect freedom of intercourse, and with it came diminished power of concentration. The wealth of Ireland tended now more than ever to England. Dublin lost all its attractions. Power, and place, and pension, were to be sought in London; and there went the landlords of Ireland. The feeble barriers that had been opposed to the perpetual error of English policy now disappeared, and the manufacturers of Ireland were ruined. The copyright law was extended to Ireland, and her printing-offices were closed. From that day to the present, the unfortunate country has been deprived of all power of concentration: of all power to place the consumer by the side of the producer. She is compelled to convert her food into pork, that it may bear transportation to the place where it is to be exchanged for cloth: when, otherwise, she would bring the fashioner of the wool to the place where corn and wool were both produced, and would thus obtain twice the cloth for the same quantity. Could she do this, the gain would be quadruple. She would save the use of a vast amount of bad, and would acquire the use of much of the best, machinery of exchange. The profit derived from this would enable her to bring into

---

from a Protestant by descent, bequest, or devise. Upon death, their inheritances were equally divided among their children; and all regular clergy, friars, jesuits, and Catholic bishops, were enjoined to quit the kingdom. Catholics were in still more general terms deprived of the elective franchise, by an act passed in 1727.

activity her best soils; and the return to labour would be doubled: while the value of the product, in cloth, would also be doubled.

Ireland, thus deprived of all intercourse with the colonies and with the world, might be supposed to be exempt from the cost of supporting the fleets and armies necessary for retaining those colonies, and fighting the battles of the world: but such is not the case. Of what escapes the landlords, the landlord government of England takes four millions, for the maintenance of armies and fleets for keeping Ireland quiet; and for the pay of English viceroys, English chancellors, English secretaries, and English agents of all kinds: whose savings are deposited in English funds, or invested in the stock of English railways. Of what is accumulated in Ireland by people who are there resident, the mass goes to England, because all employment for capital in Ireland is interdicted. From 1821 to 1833, the amount of Irish accumulations transmitted across the Channel for investment in the British funds, exceeded *ten millions of pounds:* and if we could ascertain the investments in corporation stocks, it is possible they might amount to almost as much more. Even the savings of the little capitalist who deposits his shilling in the savings fund, cannot escape absorption. By law, those institutions are compelled to make their investments in the English funds; and thirteen years since, the amount so invested was a million and a half of pounds. Centralization is perfect; and hence the poverty and wretchedness of the whole people.

Having thus shown the numerous conduits provided for the transfer of the wealth of Ireland to England, we may now look to some of the machinery of exchange. That wealth tends to promote the extension of the manufactures of England, the demand for agricultural products, and the demand for labour at certain seasons of the year in agriculture. The labourer of Ireland, deprived of the power of exchanging his products at home with those who will give him cloth, finds that he must confine himself to the cultivation of that commodity of which the land will afford him the greatest quantity, and that will least bear the expense of transportation: the potato. He has, consequently, labour to sell; and as he has rent to pay, he must sell it, or be expelled from his little holding. He travels to Cork or Dublin and makes his way to England, there to employ, in obtaining a pound or two, the labour which might, if employed at home, have given to him and his employer twice as many pounds as he had received shillings. Such is the machinery of exchange provided for Ireland. Under such a system, concentration cannot take place, and without that civilization is impossible.

Such are the causes why the whole population of that beautiful island is dependent upon the single chance of a good crop of potatoes: why they starve if it fail: and why they must continue to starve so long as they continue to constitute a portion of the British empire, subject to laws whose sole end is to draw from the land all that it can be made to give forth, and to return nothing back to the great giver.*

A system better calculated to perpetuate barbarism never was devised; yet English writers gravely ask if the existence of the present state of things is not due to some defect of the Irish character! Had England been made the prey of her continental neighbour, in like manner, such would be now the question of the people of France. In point of physical qualities, the people of Ireland are superior to most of those of the continent, and eminently so to those of France: the reason for which may be found in the perpetual exhaustion of the people of the latter by the

* Mr. Cashlan waited on Sir William Sommerville, the Irish Secretary, with the tidings that in his parish there are sixteen hundred who have neither food nor work. In these quarters, it would seem, nothing will teach the landlords; for he says, Lord Dillon, with a rental of £22,000 per annum, spent in England, has fifteen thousand acres uncultivated there—and not a shilling spent for eighteen months on drainage or reclamation.—*Irish paper*, 1847

drains for purposes of war. Governments are always particular to take the able-bodied, and those exempt from disease. The demands of that portion of the community of France that administered the government: that is, which collected taxes, and made wars for their own gratification or emolument: have at times required *all* that were capable of bearing arms; and even now require, in parts of the kingdom, almost every man that is suited for their purpose. Of the whole mass of conscripts, nearly forty per cent. are rejected for being under the standard, which is four feet ten inches, French, or less than five feet two inches, English measure. In the *Departement du Nord*, out of five thousand four hundred and thirty-three conscripts, that proportion is first dropped for that reason. Then follow those who have constitutional defects, and finally about twenty-eight per cent. are rejected for disease and deformity; and thus the number left is barely sufficient to supply the annual demand. Such has been the case for centuries, and the effect is here the same that would be found on the farm of a man who sold all his best calves to the butcher, and kept the inferior ones for the purpose of propagation. The best men perish in the field, and the blind, the halt, the lame, the stunted, and the miserable, are left at home to labour, and to recruit the population. Poverty prevents marriage, and libertinism is common. Marriages are few, by comparison with those of Ireland. The subjects are bad, and marriages are consequently unprolific. Women cannot marry, because the proportions of the sexes are disturbed, and hence a cause of unchastity. In Ireland the proportions are better maintained, and nearly all marry, as it was intended they should do. Women are therefore chaste, and all have children: but of these many die for want of proper nourishment. Population grows, and therewith wealth advances: and the condition of the people slowly improves.

The growth of population is slow, because the slow growth of wealth perpetually forces the younger and more active portions of the people to seek abroad that subsistence which is denied to them at home. The statements in regard to their numbers during the last century deserve no attention, because of their obvious incorrectness. In 1805, the population was believed to be 5,395,000. In 1841, it was 8,175,000: at which rate, allowing for emigration, it would double itself in about sixty years.

Hundreds of thousands of Irish men and women have transferred themselves to the United States, and we have abundant opportunity of knowing their character. Sometimes turbulent, the natural consequence of the situation in which they have been placed, the men are, in general, hard-working, industrious, and economical, and make excellent citizens: while the women are unquestionably distinguished for chastity. All have been educated in a bad school, but all show what they might have been made, had the school been better.

It is from the frequency of agrarian outrages, that the English writers are disposed to infer the incapacity of the Irish for civilization, yet it is from their occurrence that we should most infer their capacity for it. The system is bad: it destroys the souls and bodies of the men who are subject to it: and the outrages complained of are but the natural result of its existence, while they are evidence that man has not yet been so ground down by slavery as to have lost all consciousness of the existence of a right to resist. The miserable Hindoo when oppressed by his tyrant governor takes his seat before his door, with his wife and children, and threatens to starve himself and them to death if his grievances be not remedied. For centuries the poor peasant of France, *tailleable et corvéeable à merci et à miséricorde*, disappears from the page of history. To raise the Hindoo to civilization, it would be necessary to teach him that he had rights, and to do so would require far greater time than would be required for the Irishman, who, poor and oppressed as he may be, has yet preserved the knowledge that they once existed.

The task of the daughters of Danaüs was that of filling a vessel pierced with holes. Could they have stopped the holes, it would speedily have filled. The task of the people of Ireland is the same, and until they apply that remedy, the effort is hopeless. The mode of remedy is to be found in self-government, and in that alone. Were she alone, she would need neither fleets nor armies, for she has not an enemy in the world. Everywhere regarded as the victim of the policy of England, her sufferings have excited universal commiseration, and all would desire to aid, rather than to interfere with her. Without fleets or armies, she would require scarcely any taxes. She owes no debt, for that of England was contracted by and for England alone. She it was that wanted colonies, and commerce, and glory, in which Ireland was not permitted to participate, and for which Ireland ought not to pay. One leak would thus be closed.

With the diminution of the repulsive power of taxation, the attractive power would increase, and absentee landlords, no longer claimants on the English government, and nc longer driven to France for escape from taxes, would find a residence at home most profitable: while every man, from the highest to the lowest, would find himself animated by the desire to prove that Ireland *was* capable of self-government. Peace and harmony would take the place of riot and outrage, and wealth would grow, in the form of roads and mills: the better soils capable of yielding coal and iron, and larger supplies of food, would come into activity, and concentration would appear: a consequence of the power of the consumer to take his place by the side of the producer. The English manufacturer would find that he could work to more advantage in Connaught, where food was abundant and labour cheap, than in Manchester, where the former was less abundant and the latter dearer: and by degrees factories would make their appearance in every part of Ireland. With every such improvement in the machinery of exchange, the power of production would increase: industry would be stimulated: wages would rise: the million of mud-built cabins would be replaced by neat cottages: the value of land would rise: land would be divided and would pass gradually into the ownership of those who cultivated it: and happiness and prosperity would take the place of the existing scene of misery and wretchedness: and all this would be accomplished without interfering in the slightest degree with one right of property. The man of Ireland wants only to feel that he has a home: that it is his own: to make it one in which he would desire to spend his days, instead of braving all the horrors of the middle passage in search of a place of refuge in the wilds of Canada, to perish on the voyage, or to die of disease on the shores of the St. Lawrence.

The character of the present system is so monstrous that it can be paralleled in India alone. There, as in Ireland, the landholder takes all and gives nothing back to the land. There, as in Ireland, the people perish of famine and pestilence: and both must so continue to perish while their existing relations with England continue to be maintained. India, unhappily, has no newspapers. Ireland has but few, yet we may judge from the few facts that are published, of the vast multitude that are not. The latest journals are filled with accounts of the eviction of tenants, whose houses and cabins are thrown down; their unfortunate inhabitants being compelled to seek refuge in neighbouring glens, or church-yards, there to die of famine or pestilence:* and all

* Sir Edward Waller has ejected eight families, consisting of about forty-seven persons. These most wretched beings have, since the period of their eviction, been squatting in dykes and glens, literally burrowing in the earth for shelter, victims to every inclemency of the weather, death hourly staring them in the face. At Farnee, Maryglen, and Moyrath, in the neighbourhood of Keeper Mountain, Lord Bloomfield, who is in St. Petersburgh, through his agent, has been at the same work of ejectment. About eight families, consisting of

this is the consequence of the pertinacious determination of England that Ireland *shall* send her wool to England, accompanied by food for the man that is to twist and weave it: the whole then to be carried back in the form of cloth, which the poor wretch who raised the food cannot buy, because he has not even potatoes for his family.

The present course of legislation is the most extraordinary that the world has yet seen, and proves the uniform tendency of injustice to produce injustice. The produce of Ireland is transferred to England, there to be employed or consumed, and the impoverished Irishman seeks to follow it. To compel those who are *not yet* paupers to support those who *are*, the Parliament of England passes a poor law, by virtue of which nearly the whole land is confiscated. In one county of the west, the present expenditure under that law exceeds four millions of dollars, while the annual value of all the property subject to the rate is but three millions and a half, and much of this is subject to the claims of mortgagees: but the right of owners, and mortgagees, and all, are extinguished. Over an extent of nearly six millions of acres, the expenditure is at the rate of seventeen millions a year, while the annual value is but twelve millions: and these seventeen millions are to be employed in supporting

---

about forty-five persons, have been also sent abroad, without a roof to protect them from the rigours of the weather. Their condition is immeasurably more lamentable than we can describe.

On the 13th of July, according to the statement, and in the village called "Glen," on the estate of the Earl of Cork, ejectments were executed by the sub-sheriff of Cork, aided by the military and police force, on forty-eight tenants. Their houses or cabins were thrown down, and the forty-eight families, numbering about four hundred human beings, were turned out upon the high road. Of these it is alleged that more than *one hundred were suffering from fever*. They were obliged to take refuge in a neighbouring church-yard. The church-yard of Ballysally contains many flat tombstones and grass-covered graves; and among those graves the ejected families slept for four consecutive nights, huddled together. One poor woman was taken off her bed four days after her confinement, and placed by the side of the ditch with her infant, both in a state of helpless exhaustion. Another woman had a family of seven, all suffering from fever. In a third family there were ten persons in fever at the time of the ejectment.

people who are idle at home because they cannot find employment, *with a view to prevent them from following to England the corn and the pork that they are not permitted to retain at home.* The State is now making loans to promote drainage, and it has lately expended some millions in making roads, also called loans, not a shilling of which can—or ought—ever be repaid. It passes laws to facilitate the sale of encumbered estates, while its system tends to withdraw from the country, to be invested in England, all the means of purchase. It has even been proposed that the State should, under certain circumstances, take possession of lands and administer them in some manner or other. We now forget the process that was to be pursued, but we know that it was most remarkable for its folly and its injustice. Each step is thus worse than the last, and each but renders the case of Ireland more hopeless, and the connection with England more intolerable. Under such circumstances it is not extraordinary that the people of the former should be becoming daily more and more unanimous in favour of a repeal of the Union, and of a recognition of the right to govern herself after her own fashion.

The present forced connection is a curse to both countries, and the sooner it shall be dissolved, the better it will be for both. Free and independent, Ireland will be to England the best of friends, while subjugated Ireland must continue to be, as she always has been, the bitterest of enemies. Allied in feeling, but independent in government, they will be ever ready to combine for self-defence, and wars of offence will pass out of fashion. Peace will promote the growth of wealth in both, and England will find in Ireland a better customer than she has ever yet been, without the cost of governing her. The *blackest chapter in history* is that which contains the recital of Ireland's connection with England, and so long as that country shall continue in her present condition she will stand a living monument of injustice: a great pauper, soliciting alms at home and abroad, and made such by English farmers-general. So long as she shall thus stand, the claims of England to occupy a high place in the history of civilization may well be disputed. She has sown poverty and disunion, and she is now reaping the harvest.

She has compelled the people to cultivate poor soils, while surrounded by millions of acres that require drainage alone to render them as productive as any lands in the world: to content themselves with turf while coal abounded: to buy iron when both ore and fuel existed in unlimited quantity: to buy cloth while wasting more labour than would have manufactured all the cloth consumed in Britain: and all this she has done for the benefit of *her own* landlords, *her own* manufacturers, and *her own* shipping merchants. Her policy towards Ireland has been one of unmixed and unmitigated selfishness, injustice and tyranny: and she has thus established in the sister island, containing eight millions of inhabitants possessing the same rights as their masters her own more favoured people, a realm over the portals of which are inscribed

"Who enters here, leaves Hope behind:'

yet, in defiance of all this, England claims to occupy a high place among civilized nations!*

The PAST says to the Irish landlord of the PRESENT: "If you desire that your land increase in value and that your rents increase in amount: strive for the freedom of Ireland."

To the labourer it says: "If you desire good wages, plenty of food, and a home of your own: and for your

* "It is a strange thing that it should not be admitted in England, *that one nation has no right to govern another nation, and that such government can know no other law than that of force, accompanied by robbery and tyranny;* that the tyranny of a people is of all tyrannies the most intolerable, and that which leaves the least resource to the oppressed, because a despot is arrested by a regard to his own interest, he is restrained by remorse, or by public opinion, but a multitude calculates nothing—it has no remorse—it decrees to itself glory, when it deserves to feel only shame."—*Turgot.*

children, land of their own: strive for the freedom of Ireland."

To all it says: "In union there is strength. Be united and you shall be free. Become free, and you will become prosperous and happy."

NOTE.

As this sheet is going to press, we meet with a statement of the emigration of the present year to the St. Lawrence, by which it appears that out of 99,000, no less than 13,000 died on ship-board, or of disease contracted on the voyage. Of the unhappy remainder, a large portion will probably perish from having been forced abroad to a new and poor country in which exists but small demand for labour, while themselves totally unprovided with the means of purchasing food for themselves and their families. So monstrous a system has never existed in the annals of the world, yet British ships, maintained out of the taxes paid by starving Irishmen, are, at this moment, employed in the suppression of the slave trade!

CHAPTER XIII.

INDIA.

The man who cultivates the poor soils, surrounded by fertile lands covered with fine timber that he cannot clear, is a wanderer, and most frequently a robber. The poor tribe clustered on the side of the great mountain range, looks with longing eyes upon the wealth of more active and industrious men whose labours have subdued to cultivation the richer soils, and have thus enabled millions to obtain abundant food from a surface that but recently gave to a few thousands scarcely the means of supporting life. Envy and jealousy prompt to war and plunder, and hence perpetual interference with the rights of more industrious and richer men.

If we desire to find the seats of early civilization, we must seek them in the lower lands near the foot of the Himalaya range: in India and China: on the shores of the Tigris and the Euphrates: in Asia Minor and in Greece: and, somewhat more distant, on the banks of the Nile. If, now, we trace the history of those countries, we find a constant series of invasions from the higher and poorer lands: one race of barbarians succeeding another until at length civilization disappears from all, and a few scattered people, half savage, are seen obtaining from the cultivation of poor soils a miserable subsistence, where formerly vast nations obtained from the richer soils abundant rewards to labour.

If next we look further westward, we see civilization rising in Italy and Sicily: in Carthage and in Spain: again to disappear under the invasions of poor men, heretofore cultivating poor soils. Again it is found further west, for a time to disappear under the weight of invasion from the east, again to rise, secured by insular position from further interferences from abroad. Standing now in England, and looking upwards towards the Alps, we may see civilization gradually diminishing as our eyes ascend the slope; and with each step upwards, we see the traces of earlier cultivation. Extending our view towards the great range of Asia, we see, on a large scale, the same great fact; and with each step downward in the scale of civilization, we find ourselves approaching nearer the site of early cultivation: nearer to the places occupied by men whose labours were unaided by wealth in the form of spades and axes.

Turning our eyes now towards India, we may see a further illustration of the fact that distance from the seat of early occupation has been essential to permanent civilization. The history of that great country during a long series of centuries, is a record of perpetual invasions from the poor tribes occupying the high and dry lands on the sides of the great mountain range. At each intermission civilization struggles into life, but each is followed by a new incursion, when population is destroyed, the rich lands are again abandoned, and poverty and wretchedness, feebleness and incapacity for self-defence, become again the sole heritage of man. If we now look to the character of man, we may see it change nearly in the ratio that security is increased by distance from these mountain ranges. The Hindoo, aggrieved by his government, sits *dhurnah.* He *will* starve himself, his wife and children, and thus destroy his master's slaves. The Turkish rayah is found one step higher in the scale, which rises gradually until we reach that country of Europe in which security has most existed, and in which wealth and population have most increased—England. On a smaller scale, we may see the same fact illustrated as we descend the Alps, the character of man steadily improving as we pass towards the lands of the richer soils: Guienne and Normandy: the Netherlands and Prussia: the Milanese and Tuscany: and always highest where wealth most exists, for there it is that man is most enabled to apply his labour to the fashioning of the great machine.

At one period in its history, Hindostan appears to have enjoyed a high degree of prosperity. Each village constituted a little republic, having its own officers for the maintenance of the public peace, and for other purposes. The contributions to the state are supposed to have been one-thirteenth of the produce of the land. The best soils were then to a great extent cultivated. Wealth increased, education was generally disseminated, and continued peace and security were alone required for the attainment of the highest civilization. Unhappily, however, for them, they were too near neighbours of poor men who cultivated thin soils, and who saw in labour with the sword returns far larger than could be obtained by labour with the plough. Invasion and destruction of property and life were followed by civil wars and depopulation. The fertile soils were gradually abandoned, and labour yielded less returns. Taxes became less and less productive; and each step downwards in production was followed, necessarily, by a corresponding one upwards in the *proportion* of the great landlord: the collector of rent or tax: until at length the half of the diminished product was held to be his right. Cultivation diminished as with the growth of poverty the inducements to honest labour disappeared, and each diminution in the number of those who lived by their own labour was attended by an increase in the number of those who lived by that of others. The rights of the little land-owner passed away and land gradually concentrated itself in the hands of *the few*, and they did as has been done at all times, and in all ages, by men who exercised power over their fellow men. They plundered those below, and were in turn plundered by those above themselves. The havildar, the head of a village, called his habitation the durbar, and plundered of their meal and roots the wretches within his jurisdiction; the zemindar fleeced him of the small pittance which his penurious tyranny had scraped together; the phoosdar, a military commandant of the province, seized on the zemindar's collections, and bribed the nabob's connivance in his villanies by a share of the spoil; the covetous eye of the nabob ranged over his dominions for prey, and employed the plunder of his subjects in bribing or resisting his superiors.* Great men became very numerous, and, as usual, the poverty of the little men increased with every addition to their number.

Such was the condition of that country forty years since. During a large portion of the previous century it had been the theatre of wars whose object was the determination of the question whether England or France should have the right of taxing its unhappy people; and during the whole period the former was filled with nabobs: men who had accumulated fortunes by a display of rapacity rarely exceeded; who plundered sovereigns, princes, and princesses, with a full knowledge that what was taken from *them* must be furnished by contributions from the poor starving wretches by whom they were surrounded.

Since then, the whole tendency has been that of centralization. Late in the last century Lord Cornwallis had endeavoured to set some bounds to the Company's claim for taxes, but even that effort was accompanied by acts of grievous injustice. The whole class of little village proprietors was first delivered over to the tender mercies of the zemindar, or great landed proprietor, the result of which is that they have been in a great measure, if not altogether, extinguished. Land thus concentrated itself in the hands of the few, but respect for *their* rights had as little existence as respect for those of the unfortunate people below them. Everywhere, zemindary estates were abandoned because of inability to pay the taxes, and in some cases to the extent of a fifth of the whole number. Of the condition of the unfortunate ryot, or labourer, subjected to their control, some idea may be formed from the

* See Orme on the Government of Hindostan.

following passage taken from the fifth report of the select committee of the House of Commons, by which it is seen that the system of indirect taxation united all that is injurious in the French *octroi*, and the Spanish *alcabala*.

"In addition to the assessment on the lands, or the shares of their produce received from the inhabitants, they were subject to the duties levied on the inland trade, which were collected by the renters under the zemindars. These duties, which went by the name of sayer, as they extended to grain, cattle, salt, and all the other necessaries of life, passing through the country, and were collected by corrupt, partial, and extortionate agents, produced the worst effects on the state of society, by not only checking the progress of industry, oppressing the manufacturer, and causing him to debase his manufacture, but also by clogging the beneficial operations of commerce in general, and abridging the comforts of the people at large. This latter description of imposts was originally considered as a branch of revenue too much exposed to abuses to be intrusted to persons not liable to restraint and punishment. It was therefore retained under the immediate management of the government. The first rates were easy, and the custom-houses few; but in the general relaxation of authority, this mode of raising revenue for the support of the government was scandalously abused. In the course of a little time, new duties were introduced, under the pretence of charitable and religious donations, as fees to the chokeydars, or account-keepers' guards, and other officers at the stations, as protection money to a zemindar; or as a present to those who farmed the duties. Not only had the duties been from time to time raised in their amount, and multiplied in their number, at the discretion of the zemindars and the renters under them, but they were at length levied at almost every stage, and on every successive transfer of property; uniformity in the principles of collection was completely wanting; a different mode of taxation prevailing in every district in respect to all the varieties of goods, and other articles subject to impost. This consuming system of oppression had, in some instances, been aggravated by the company's government, which, when possessed of a few factories, with a small extent of territory around them, adopted the measure of placing chokies, or custom stations, in the vicinity of each, for the purpose of ascertaining the state of trade within their own limits, as well as to afford them a source of revenue. Under the head of sayer revenue was also included a variety of taxes, indefinite in their amount, and vexatious in their nature, called moturpha; they consisted of imposts upon houses, on the implements of agriculture, on looms, on merchants, on artificers, and other professions and castes."

The Company, however, could not afford to part with its right to levy taxes to an unlimited extent, under the pretence of taking *rent* for the use of poor lands occupied by men who cultivated the poorest soils: and the further progress of the permanent settlement was therefore stopped after it had been established throughout Bengal, and over a small portion of the Madras presidency. Throughout the remainder of the Madras, and the whole of the Bombay presidencies, the ryotwar system still exists, under which the amount levied on each ryot is left to be determined at the discretion of the European or native revenue officers, it being the practice to compel the ryot to occupy as much land, and consequently pay as much taxes, as is deemed proportioned to his circumstances. He is not allowed, on payment even of the high survey assessment fixed on each field, to cultivate only those fields to which he gives the preference ; his task is assigned to him, and he is constrained to occupy all such fields as are allotted to him by the revenue officers ; and whether he cultivates them or not, he is saddled with the rent of all. If driven by these oppressions to fly, and seek a subsistence elsewhere, he is followed wherever he goes and oppressed at discretion, or deprived of the advantages he might expect from a change of residence.

With every improvement in cultivation; with every improvement in manufactures; with every increase in the quantity of labour; with every indication of increased comfort or wealth; the taxes rise, or would rise: and as a necessary consequence, the poor ryot feels little inducement to exertion. Little as it might be, however, it is lessened when he comes to exchange his productions for the necessaries of life that he cannot produce. At every step in his progress to market he finds a new tax, and when at market, he buys his salt mixed with dirt from the Company's agent, at six times the price at which it should be sold: and thus, of the little that escapes the collector of *rents*, a large portion goes to the collector of *taxes*.* Under such circumstances, it is not extraordinary that the poor ryots should say that "their skins only are left them."

The whole product of that country, over and above what is necessary for the absolute preservation of life in ordinary seasons—for in extraordinary ones the people perish by hundreds of thousands by famine and pestilence—centralizes itself in Calcutta, to go thence forth in the payment of viceroys, and officers without number, charged with managing the affairs of these poor people: that is to say, with the collection of taxes, and with their expenditure for the payment of armies occupied in subduing the people of Burmah, or Scinde, or Affghanistan, or those of the Punjaub; and with the transmission of that large portion which goes to England, to be divided among the owners of East India stock: dividends to men who live in palaces and ride in coaches, out of the proceeds of taxes on salt paid by a poor wretch whose wages are two rupees, or one dollar, per month, out of which he finds himself! Absentee-landlordism *exists* in Ireland, but it *luxuriates* in India. Every thing is taken from the land that can be

* "The government, in purchasing salt, are in the habit of pressing it down with hands and feet in the wooden measure; but when they sell it, of filling it up as light as can be, which makes a difference of twenty per cent.; and other differences of measurement make an additional twenty per cent."—*Letter of Commissioner Gra~nc to the Board of Revenue.*

scratched out, and nothing goes back. Even the zemindar, sometimes enriched by the oppression of the poor ryot, never applies a rupee to the improvement of land subject to the Company's claims for revenue.

Thus far, however, we have seen but a small portion of the holes in this *vast vessel of the Danaïdes.* Forty years since, the people of India supplied the world with cotton manufactured goods. Their machinery was rough, it is true, but it could readily have been improved; and it would have cost far less to carry to Calcutta a few ship-loads of machinery, for the conversion of Hindoo cotton into clothing for Hindoo men and women, by aid of Hindoo labourers eating Hindoo rice; than to carry tens of thousands of ship-loads of cotton and rice to Manchester, to be returned in the form of cloth to Calcutta: thence to be carried into the interior, in a country totally destitute of roads and bridges. Such, however, was not the policy of England. She would *not* cultivate her own fertile soils. She would *not* permit capital to seek employment in fashioning her own great food-producing machine: and she *would* eat the rice of India, even although she might exclude the corn of Canada. She *would not* permit the machinery of manufacture to go to India, or elsewhere; and she *would* insist on supplying India with cotton goods. She *did* take some food in exchange; but, to prevent improvement in that country, she subjected cleaned rice to a heavy duty, from which paddy, or rough rice, was exempted: thus offering a bounty to her people for using an unnecessary quantity of bad machinery of exchange: a measure that could have been exceeded in folly and rapacity only by a similar bounty on the import of cotton in the rough, with a view to secure the profit of ginning it.

England had grown rich. For more than half a century the wealth of India had been transferred to her coffers by aid of Clives, and Hastingses, and numerous other members of the same family: men of the great race: and thus while the one became enriched, the other became poorer from day to day. Towns and villages, by thousands, had been abandoned during endless wars; and extensive districts, embracing the most fertile lands, had relapsed into jungle: and tigers now occupied the ground that before had given food and clothing to hundreds of thousands of poor but industrious people: the consequence of which was, that the poorest soils were cultivated with the worst machinery.

The stock of a ryot consisted of a plough not capable of cutting deep furrows, and only intended to scratch the surface of the soil, with two or three pairs of half-starved oxen. This, a sickle used for a scythe, and a small spade or hoe for weeding, constituted almost his only implements for husbandry. Fagots of loose sticks, bound together, served for a harrow. Carts could be little used in a country where there were no roads, or none but bad ones. Corn, when reaped, was heaped in a careless pile in the open air, to wait his leisure for threshing, which was performed, not by manual labour, but by the simple operation of cattle treading it out of the ear. He had no barns for stacking or storing grain, which was preserved, when required, in jars of unbaked earth, or baskets made of twigs or grass. The cattle were fed in the jungle, or common waste land adjoining his farm; and buffaloes, thus supported, generally supplied him with milk. Horses were altogether unused in husbandry. The fields had no enclosures. Production was small, and the great landlord took one-half of the small amount, thus rendering improvement of machinery impossible. He could not buy looms and spinning-jennies, even if England would have sold them, which she would not. The necessary result was, that the poor manufacturer was first driven out of the market of the world, and then out of his own: and thus the small existing tendency to concentration was diminished. From being a consumer side by side with the producer of cotton, he was driven to seek elsewhere poor soils that he might scratch with his stick, in the almost vain hope of obtaining a sufficiency of food: and thus was the amount of raw cotton to be exported, increased for the supposed benefit of ships and factories owned by British capitalists, who heeded little the sufferings of the poor Hindoo weaver, deprived of all market for his industry. Having thus compelled the use of the inferior machinery of exchange in the form of roads, in place of better machinery previously in use, the export of cotton now went on: but at length the people of the northern United States, driven to the poor soils of new states and territories to raise food instead of concentrating themselves on the rich soils of the old ones for the purpose of consuming it, forced the planter from the production of food to that of cotton with which he filled the world: and now the poor Hindoo could produce for Europe neither the raw material nor the cloth. Next, we find him, in default of other employment, largely engaged in cultivating opium for his neighbours, the Chinese. The trade grows large, and Chinamen use it freely because cheaply supplied. The government takes alarm and destroys the opium, and England takes offence: and now Chinese cities are ruined, their men destroyed, and their women outraged, and the country is laid waste: that English subjects may employ in producing intoxicating drugs the labour that should be employed in converting cotton into cloth, while the labourer ate food produced by the man who was to wear the cloth.

The tendency of the whole system is that of compelling men to waste labour in transportation that might profitably be applied to production. Cotton and rice *must* go to England, that Englishmen may eat the one and fashion the other. Such being the law, it might be supposed that some labour might be applied towards perfecting, in some small degree, that description of the machinery of exchange the use of which was still to be permitted: to wit, roads and bridges: but the reader would greatly err who might suppose that possible. Of the vast revenues of that country, derived from the appropriation of one-half of the gross produce, scarcely a rupee goes back upon the land. We have now before us an account of all the works of improvement in that country, with its population of one hundred millions, during a period of seven years; and it would be exceeded by the state of Rhode Island, with its one hundred thousand inhabitants. It is stated that the government *does* now do something: that it actually expends twelve or fifteen thousand pounds per annum in the repair of roads! and that, too, in a country whose people are forced by erroneous legislation over which they can have no control, to export its great product, because they may not be permitted to obtain machinery for fashioning it at home. The produce of the great cotton-growing districts on the Nerbudda is carried on oxen, each taking one hundred and sixty pounds, at the extreme rate, in fair weather, of seven miles a day. The distance to Mirzapore, on the Ganges, is five hundred miles, and the cost is two and a half pence, or five cents, per pound. Thence it goes to Calcutta, a distance of eight hundred miles, by water, unaided, we believe, by steam. From another portion of the cotton-growing districts, in the Deccan, the transport occupies a continuous journey of two months; and in the rainy season the road is impassable, and the traffic of the country is at a stand. *In the absence of even a defined road*, the carriers, with their pack cattle, are compelled to travel by daylight to prevent the loss of their bullocks in the jungles through which they have to pass, and this under a burning sun of from one hundred to one hundred and forty degrees. If the horde, sometimes amounting to a thousand, is overtaken by rain, the cotton, saturated with moisture, becomes heavy, and the black clayey soil, *through which lies the whole line of road*, sinks under the feet of a man above the ankle, and under that of a laden ox to the knees: and in this predicament the cargo lies sometimes for weeks on the ground, and the merchant is ruined! "Black clayey soils," rich and fertile, are here superabundant; but the poor wretch who raises the cotton must cultivate the high lands that require neither clearing nor drainage, and his masters take half the product of their poor soils, while refusing even to make a road *through* the rich ones: yet forcing him to send his cotton to market to be exchanged for cotton cloth manufactured thousands of miles distant. A system better calculated to compel men to continue cultivating the poorest soils, by aid of sticks, could not be devised.

We have here another of the leaks in this great vessel, but it is by no means the last. Of the revenues of this vast empire no small share is distributed among the infinite number of great men charged with the duties of government, who pay themselves liberally: for a very few years of "exile" are deemed to entitle each to acquire fortune for himself and his children. Salaries are large, and savings are considerable: and these savings are lent to the government to enable it to pay the salaries: for large as are the revenues, the debt grows regularly and rapidly. The lender, having accumulated a fortune and having safely invested it at large interest, now returns home, and thenceforth he is entitled to an annual remittance of the interest: and to pay him and others like him, and to make dividends on East India stock, almost twenty millions of dollars are annually required: a sum sufficient to make yearly a railroad of six hundred miles: and this is to be paid by men who think that they might perhaps continue to grow cotton, if in addition to bullocks *they only had carts!*

Within the last sixty years there has been levied on the poor Hindoos by and for the uses of that government, to aid it in making dividends, paying salaries, and carrying on wars in which, like that of Affghanistan, the poor tax-payers had no interest, more than five thousand millions of dollars! In return for all this, the poor people have received at the hands of their masters neither roads, nor canals, nor public works of any description, except barracks, prisons, and hospitals for their own troops. Deprived of all power to improve their wretched machinery of production, they are compelled to abandon rich lands, and cultivate the poorest: those from which the man who is destitute of a spade and an axe always draws his supplies of food. Such lands can afford no more than is absolutely necessary for the support of existence, yet of the miserable product the company takes one-half and calls it *rent*, and a large portion of the balance and calls it *taxes*. The necessary consequence is, that any thing like accumulation is impossible. Each year must furnish the supplies of the year, and when a failure of crop takes place the miserable people are swept off by hundreds of thousands. In the twenty years, from 1818 to 1838, there were *nine years of famine*. That of 1837–8 was terrific, yet the unfortunate people were surrounded by millions upon millions of acres of the richest lands in the world that they could not cultivate, because the government left them no means. The rivers were choked with dead bodies in the provinces where this very abundance of waste land existed; the air putrefied with the stench of dead and dying human beings, and animals; the jackals and vultures were seen preying on the still animated bodies of our fellow-creatures. Mothers drowned their children by night, unwilling that the morning sun should witness their famishing state; and whole families of respectability poisoned themselves, rather than beg a little rice for their support; and, although a rupee's worth (half-a dollar) of grain would sustain a man for thirty days, hydrophobia was becoming as prevalent as cholera!

In other quarters, the dead were lying in hundreds by the road-side, and it became necessary to form companies to carry them to the river, with a view to the prevention of pestilence. In Agra, the deaths were at the rate of ten thousand per month: and yet at this very period enormous sums, the proceeds of taxes imposed on these wretched beings, were being lavished on the war in Affghanistan!

So exhausted are these unfortunate people, that it becomes necessary frequently to remit the taxes, because of inability to collect them. No better evidence of their wretchedness need be offered than the fact that in lower Bengal, one of the most prosperous portions of the Company's territories: that in which they have been longest and most firmly established; the consumption of salt in three years, from 1834 to 1837, was less by one-fifth than it had been in the three years from 1819 to 1822. Such is the necessary effect of a system that drives men from rich soils to poor ones; and then refuses to supply even a defined road to the unfortunate cultivator, who would consider himself "rich indeed," if that road were made practicable for a cart, to enable him to drag the produce of his miserable soils through the rich black clay that lies between him and the far distant river.

Throughout India, the class of *native* great men: those who live by the labour of others: is large. To them, however, is to be added the whole body of their foreign masters. Till recently one of these latter who might have assaulted a native or ploughed up his land, could drag him to a distant city where the cost of litigation is expensive to a degree five times exceeding those of the courts of England, enormous even as *they* are. Officers of these courts accumulate immense fortunes in a few years, out of the substance of ruined suitors. At Madras the supreme court has, says Mr. Macaulay, fulfilled its mission: it has beggared every rich native within its jurisdiction and is inactive for want of somebody to ruin. Great men are very numerous, and their shares of the produce of the poor soils are always large. The labour of collecting their taxes is great, and they fix themselves their reward. The system is the same wherever men are forced to rely upon those soils for food. The many are weak and disunited, and the few plunder them with impunity.

The Hindoo may well say that nothing is left him but his skin. He knows no freedom but to die: and yet he is the subject of England, whose people are furnishing the world with missionary bishops to teach Christianity; the basis of which is, "Do unto your neighbour as ye would that he should do unto you." He is *the slave* of the same men who look with "holy horror" upon the sugar of Brazil and upon the cotton of Georgia: the latter raised by men who are better fed, better clothed, better lodged, and better taught, than a considerable portion of the people of England itself. He is *their slave;* for they *will not* permit him to combine his exertions with those of his fellow men, to render their joint labour productive. They *will* compel him to send food and cotton to Manchester; that the latter may be twisted and woven, and then sent back to him. They *will not* permit concentration, without which the rich soils cannot be reduced to cultivation: and until they shall be cultivated, famine and pestilence must continue to sweep off the population: and East India proprietors must continue to *waste and destroy*, annually, millions of bushels of salt, that they may be enabled to realize their dividends from selling the balance at a monopoly price to the starving wretch who labours one-half of the year to pay his rent, and one-fourth of the balance to pay for that salt. The *ecorcheurs* of France, who flayed the unhappy people engaged in the preparation of the great food-producing machine, were bad; but those of England in India are worse. It is, throughout, a system of unmatched atrocity. Such is the condition of the men who raise the "free" cotton of India.

Nearly a century has now rolled round, since, by the battle of Plassy, the ascendency of England in that great country was secured; and such is the result. The Hindoo raises cotton, but he consumes only so much as will give him a strip to cover his loins. He raises rice; but he eats little, for he may not even clean it: and all this is done that England may be the workshop of the world, and that great manufacturers may accumulate millions by aid of the labour of over-worked and under-fed operatives. A system more selfish and unsound could not be conceived; nor could one more utterly destructive, both for herself and others, possibly exist. The results, everywhere, are the same: perpetual change of system, and perpetual need of change. Canada stagnates: and governors and forms of government are changed, but Canada still remains motionless. Ireland starves, and Irishmen shoot agents: and curfew laws, and bills prohibiting the carrying of arms, are passed; but Ireland still starves and borrows, and *will not* pay, because she *cannot.* Jamaica tries hill-coolies and free negroes: and coolies and negroes fail: and Jamaica still is poor. India cannot send cotton that will sell, and agents are sent to teach the poor Hindoo: who still cannot send cotton, because the rich soils are so abundant that his half-starved cattle, driven by their half-fed owner, cannot wade through them. Australia raises, on the poorest soils, a small supply of wool for which she must be paid; while paying nothing for six millions of dollars annually charged to her account. English capitalists now propose railroads in India: but railroads never pay when made for people who cultivate the poorest soils, and cannot themselves make roads. India will grow rich, and rapidly grow, when India shall be independent, and shall protect herself against the radical error of the English system; but until she shall do so: until she shall acquire power to place the consumer by the side of the producer: she must remain poor. In few countries of the world would population and wealth grow so rapidly, were she left alone: but so long as she must remit twenty millions to pay interest, and raise so many other millions to pay armies and officers, while compelled to cultivate the poorest soils with the worst machinery, neither can increase. England may change, and change again, abroad: but, before she can effect any improvement, she must learn to look at home, and not abroad: she must abandon the use of temporary machinery and take to that which is permanent: she must *raise her own* food, and permit others to *consume their own.* She must increase her producers, and she must permit others to increase their consumers: and when she shall do that, India and Canada, Jamaica and Australia, will grow rich, while she will grow richer: but she will then cease to want colonies, or armies, or fleets, or great men. In the annals of the world there is recorded no instance of self-deception greater than that which she now exhibits, except, perhaps, in that of France, who seeks dominion by aid of the sword alone, while she goes with sword and yard-stick. To which of the two should be awarded the credit of doing most to prevent the increase of human happiness, it might be difficult to decide; but we are disposed to think that she would carry off the palm. France wasted the Palatinate with fire and sword. The work accomplished, the armies were withdrawn. The poor people who were left breathed again: and, in time, they might restore their houses, and obtain fresh spades and ploughs to enable them to cultivate the rich soils. The yard-stick of England is a much more effective instrument. It produces famines and pestilences, recurring year after year, to sweep off all the population rendered surplus by the denial of the power of concentration. *Her* army is never withdrawn. The houses that it levels *cannot* be rebuilt. The spades and ploughs that it destroys *cannot* be replaced. The people *must* go to the poor soils, and they *must* have famines to keep the population down to the supply of food that England permits them to produce. The Company are disciples of Mr. Malthus. They take rent for the use of the "original and indestructible powers" of a soil that possesses scarcely any power, and thus starve the population down to the level of subsistence.

The PAST says to the people of England of the PRESENT: "I have sinned. I have beggared the people of India. I have taxed them until they have been forced to abandon the rich soils, which are now overgrown. I have applied the proceeds of taxes and contributions to the building of factories that have enabled me to ruin their poor fashioner. I have driven them from making cloth to raising opium. I have destroyed the power of concentration. I have produced famine and pestilence. I have converted people who were free into slaves. I, too, have suffered. My people have starved, because Hindoos were unable to buy cloth, and food was dear. Take warning by my example. Apply your labour to the improvement of the great machine. Raise your own food, and permit the poor Hindoo to make his own cloth. Do unto them as ye would that they should do unto you, and let them govern themselves. They will then increase in numbers and in wealth, and ye will then increase more rapidly."

CHAPTER XIV.

ANNEXATION.

The people who cultivate the poor soils cluster round the hill-sides, and they are separated from their nearest neighbours by large tracts of rich soil covered with forests, and watered by broad rivers. With the growth of wealth and population the rich soils are brought into activity: and with each step the tendency to union is increased, and the numerous tribes ultimately combine to make one great, and rich, and powerful State.

While the people of England cultivated the poor soils of the centre and south, the rich soils of Northumberland and Cumberland, and those of the south of Scotland, were occupied by a race of people, half-savage, to whom plunder offered employment more agreeable than labour: and a state of perpetual war was the natural result. With the growth of population and of wealth, the smaller tribe was annexed to the larger, and the kingdom of Great Britain was formed.

For centuries France has been engaged in the work of annexation: but she has cultivated the poor soils, and failure has been the result. Piedmont has been repeatedly annexed, but annexation would not stand. Italy, and the Netherlands, and Holland, have been annexed: but the strong repulsive power of poverty again produced separation. She is now annexing Algeria: but the union cannot stand, for France is poor and still cultivates poor soils.

Holland and Belgium were annexed, but the first loved ships, colonies, and commerce; and foreign subjects: and looked abroad, while the people of Belgium desired to look to home. The one desired to cultivate the distant poor lands, while the other preferred the near rich ones. The Dutch were expelled, and Belgium adopted the measures necessary for enabling her people to concentrate themselves for the prosecution of the work of improving the great machine. She now advances rapidly in wealth and population, while Holland implores her flying citizens not to desert their country in its hour of distress.

The British colonies are poor, and so they are likely to remain. Unable to protect themselves, they feel in all its force the perpetual vacillation of British policy. Concentration for the cultivation of fertile soils cannot take place. The repulsive power is strong, and their connection with the parent country draws towards its close. From year to year new measures are adopted for their government. Slaves are bought and freed in the west, while slaves are being made in the east: and hill-coolies now cultivate sugar for their masters on the fertile soils of Berbice and Demerara, while the lately emancipated slave raises yams on the higher and more healthy land for himself. At one time slave sugar is prohibited, and arrangements are made for raising free sugar. At another, slave sugar is admitted, and the producer of free sugar is ruined. Thus is the system, internal and external, one of perpetual change, and ruinous to all that are intimately connected with her.

Forced unions are effected, and general associations are now proposed, but at home the measures are the same. The mother country *will* buy food, and will pay for it with the produce of steam-engines and mills, instead of raising her own food and permitting the colonists to have mills and engines of their own. They must be made to continue to use bad machinery of exchange, and they must therefore continue poor. Annexation by the mother country is, therefore, impossible, and separation must come.

In the United States, we witness, at the present moment, the process of annexation on the north and south. On the one hand, the people who cultivate rich soils are rapidly annexing Canada by aid of the peaceful machinery afforded by increasing wealth. On the other, those who cultivate the poor soils of the south and west are striving at the annexation of Mexico by the unprofitable machinery of war. The one is making friends and strength. The other is as busily employed in wasting its powers in making foes. The success of the one is certain. The failure of the other is almost equally so. The one pursues the mode that gave union to the few scattered colonies: that of honest labour. The other that which has in all times given to France disunion and weakness: that of arms. Canada *will* come into the Union, and Mexico most probably *will not*. The north will grow strong by peace, and the south will grow weak by war. The north concentrates its forces and places the consumer by the side of the producer, and hence her attractive power. The south sends the consumer to Mexico while the producer remains at home, and hence her repulsive power. In the north land is valuable, yet greediness of land has no existence. In the south and west land is cheap and abundant, and hence the desire to have more land. If the south and west desire to have power or to retain it, they must study concentration and not dispersion. The more land they have, the weaker they become: while at every step in the growth of northern population, land becomes less abundant and strength increases. The love of land is the characteristic of the barbarian who cultivates poor soils. The love of man is that of the civilized man who cultivates rich soils. The one loves war and remains weak. The other loves peace and grows in strength.

The expenditure of ten millions in placing the consumer of food by the producer of cotton and food, would double the power of the south. The expenditure of a hundred millions in adding Mexico to the Union will diminish that power in the same proportion: yet they will have wars, for throughout the south, in default of concentration, there are always found thousands anxious to manage the affairs of nations, having no business at home to demand their care. Hence it is that claimants for public employment abound at the south of Mason and Dixon's line, while in the land east of the Hudson they are few. The great men of the south seek public life. The greatest men of the north find more advantage in private life. The one furnishes the world with statesmen, generals, and colonels: the class of men who spend much and produce nothing. The other with merchants and manufacturers, who produce much and spend little. The one becomes rich, and with the rich man annexation is easy. The other prevents himself from growing rich, and with him annexation is difficult.

The United States need concentration and not dispersion. Peacefully annexed, Mexico would do no harm, but she would not add materially to the power of the Union, or to the happiness of the people. *She* would gain much. They would gain but little, yet they *would* gain, for all nations prosper by the prosperity of their neighbours. Within the Union, Mexico would speedily double her population, and that population would be as quiet and as industrious as any in the world. *The people* everywhere love peace, and everywhere they will labour, when improvement is felt to follow exertion. Their rulers alone love war. The peaceful annexation of Mexico would be a great work, but the accomplishment of that object requires spades and steam-engines, not swords and cannon. It would be a great boon conferred upon the world. Southern Europe: France, Spain, and Italy: need an outlet for their people, desirous to escape from taxation and misrule, and were Mexico a part of the Union, she would attract much of the best population of those countries; and would do much towards rendering man more valuable in the estimation of men who have land, and of those who exercise power. It would be a great work, and it is deeply to be regretted that the thirst for *land* should have produced a war that tends to prevent a measure so important for the improvement of the condition of *man*.

With the growth of wealth and population men cultivate better soils, and land becomes divided. With the division of land comes the union of man, and with union comes the power of man over himself, his thoughts and actions, his labour and its proceeds. With self-government comes peace. With peace, armies, and navies, and taxes, disappear. With each step in this course the attractive power increases, and the repulsive force diminishes, and the tendency to annexation : or to the union of nations for the maintenance of the perfect freedom of man as a producer, a fashioner, or an exchanger: as a thinker or an actor: grows. With each, wealth and population tend more rapidly to increase, and with each, man becomes more and more a being of *power*, and less a victim of *necessity*.

The PAST says to the people of the PRESENT : I have made war and preparations for war. I have kept on foot large fleets and armies, and have raised heavy taxes. I have prevented the growth of wealth and population. I have compelled men to cultivate the poor soils of the earth. I have prevented the division of land and the union of men and of nations. I have made the few strong and the many weak. Take warning by my example. Cultivate peace. Permit population to grow, and ye will cultivate rich soils. Wealth will then grow rapidly and land will be divided. Men and nations will then become united. Armies, and navies, and taxes, will disappear, and the many will become strong, while the few will become weak. All will then exercise the power of perfect self-government, and all will learn to respect in others those rights they would desire to have respected in themselves.

CHAPTER XVI.

CIVILIZATION.

Civilization has, in all ages and countries, been found where men have accumulated wealth by means of which they have been enabled to subject to cultivation the rich soils of the earth: and it has disappeared as they have been forced to abandon them and fly to the poor soils of the hills for safety. Concentration on the former is essential to the progress of civilization. With each step therein we have diminished machinery of exchange: physical and intellectual. Men exchange more directly with each other the products of their mind and of their hands: and with each step production, material and intellectual, tends to increase. With the increase of material product, the proportion of the labourer increases, while that of land diminishes: and with each step, land tends to become more and more divided. With the increase of intellectual product, the machinery for the communication of ideas improves, and the labourer finds increased facility of obtaining knowledge, while the teacher obtains from a small contribution on the part of each of his readers or hearers a largely increased reward. Each step, therefore, in the progress of civilization is marked by a tendency to equality of physical and intellectual condition, and to the general ownership of wealth, whether in land or other machinery of production: or in the possession of books, pictures, statuary, or other things tending to promote intellectual advancement.

With the division of land and the diffusion of wealth, the power of the few tends to diminish, while the number of persons interested in the maintenance of peace and in the enforcement of perfect security in the enjoyment of the rights of person and property tends to increase; and moral feeling improves, because of the increased facility of obtaining the necessaries, conveniences and comforts of life. Improvement and a tendency towards perfect equality of moral feeling are therefore characteristics of civilization. With each step in this progress, jealousy and avarice disappear, and harmony and good feeling, and liberality of thought and of action, appear: generosity towards the weak takes the place of oppression: woman becomes the companion of man and ceases to be his slave: children cease to be slaves and come to be companions: parents cease to be tyrants, and children respect and love them: and all, men, women and children, acquire the habit of self-government. With each step the *necessity* for the use of the machinery of government, public or private, tends to disappear, and with each the *power* of man to govern himself is seen to increase. With each, the cost of government decreases: and with each, wealth grows with increased rapidity, enabling man to bring into activity better soils, followed by a further increase in the return to labour, and facilitating further accumulation. With each, he acquires more and more the feeling of confidence in himself and in the future, and with each, he becomes more and more animated by Hope. With each, he learns more and more to appreciate the comforts indicated by the good old English word Home, and more and more to find in the great command to "do unto others as he would that others should do unto him," the guide of all his thoughts, his feelings, and his actions.

Civilization is marked by elevation and equality of physical, moral, intellectual, and political condition, and by the tendency towards union and harmony among men and nations. The highest civilization is marked by the most perfect individuality and the greatest tendency to union, whether of men or of nations.

In the early history of Attica, the tendency towards civilization was very great, but the destruction of wealth and consequent deterioration of physical condition attendant upon the

Persian wars, was followed by a deterioration of moral and political condition. The people learned to live on the labours of others, while themselves the slaves of demagogues who distributed among their followers small wages, the proceeds of taxation and oppression; and who employed their share of the plunder in creating gardens, and building temples, to hand down to admiring posterity their illustrious names. Individuals now give names to the times in which they live, always a sign of declining civilization. The period most distinguished by lust for power and "glory," and known as the age of Pericles, which owes its celebrity to men whose existence was one of the results of the previous age of peace and growing wealth, bequeathed to posterity Aristophanes, to whom we are indebted as the vivid painter of the vices of the "lazy, cowardly, talkative, and money-loving" tribe by whom he was surrounded. With each step downward the few become greater and more profligate. Generals plunder cities and betray their fellow-citizens. Great orators make speeches on one side and take bribes on the other, while the people become more and more impoverished and enslaved. Depravity and corruption, the necessary consequences of unceasing war and growing inequality, become universal, and with the decay of morals we mark a steady increase of superstition and fanaticism, and all other of the characteristics of increasing barbarism.

In early Rome we find a compliance with all the conditions of advancing civilization, but with each step in the progress of war and waste, we mark its decline. Great men have palaces filled with their poor and enslaved debtors. Scipio, Metellus, and others, form courts around themselves, wherein the arts are exercised and the sciences taught by slaves, while the streets of Rome witness exhibitions of captured princes and princesses, followed by thousands of captives and the plunder of conquered nations; and terminating in the execution, in cold blood, at the capitol, of all who might be supposed to possess power to affect the future distribution of the spoils of the world.* With each step in the downward progress, festivals and games become more magnificent and more brutal, and the people become more and more pauperized: the great men become greater, and the little men become less: until at length the exhausted empire becomes the property of barbarians, and civilization disappears from the earth.

In the history of France, we see little tendency towards civilization. Wealth could not grow, and man could not concentrate himself for the cultivation of the fertile soils: and therefore has he remained always poor and disunited. For want of roads, he has been unable to meet his fellow man for the exchange of physical or intellectual products: and, for want of a common language, he and his fellow man have been unable to correspond, or to understand each other if they met.† None of the conditions of civilization are here complied with. Everywhere we see inferiority and inequality of physical, moral, intellectual, and political condition.‡

M. Guizot regards France as "the centre: the focus: of the civilization of Europe." That country is and has been, in his estimation, the great leader in European civilization, at the

---

* In relation to this period, M. Guizot says: "Take Rome, for example, in the splendid days of the republic, at the close of the second Punic war; the moment of her greatest virtues, when she was rapidly advancing to the empire of the world—*when her social condition was evidently improving.*"

† German is even now the language of an important portion of the people, and the *patois* of one part of the kingdom is scarcely understood in another.

‡ "The official returns of particular classes of the population, such as the conscripts and the convicts, recognise three degrees of ignorance and three of instruction. Taking these returns as the basis of our calculations, we find the following results for the whole of the population:—

1. Unable to read and to write	16,855,000
2. Able to read, but not to write	7,097,000
3. Reading and writing, but incorrectly	6,968,000
4. Reading and writing correctly	2,430,000
5. Having the elements of classical education	735,000
6. Having completed their classical studies	315,000
	34,400,000"

France. London, 844.

nead of which, from its peculiar qualities, "it has been eminently qualified to march."

To us, she appears in the light of the constant and unwearied foe of civilization. To her was due the destruction of the Lombard kingdom of Italy, in which civilization was rapidly advancing. By her was Italy afterwards exhausted and delivered over to the ferocious Spaniard. By her have since been commenced all the wars that, from the days of Ferdinand and Charles V., have prevented any advance towards the improvement of the condition of its inhabitants: ever unfortunate in their proximity to poor neighbours, who saw in their wealthy cities, and in their treasures of art, plunder that they desired to appropriate.

By her were the Netherlands and Holland ruined. To her are due the expulsion of the best citizens of both: the exhaustion of their wealth: the abandonment of rich soils, and the cultivation of poor ones: and to her is due the present enormous debt under which the industry of Holland is paralyzed.

If we turn our eyes southward, the same picture meets our eye. Catalonia was advancing in civilization, and therefore was it coveted. Therefore was it made the scene of ceaseless wars in which was destroyed enormous wealth, while the poor inhabitants were driven to seek from the poor soils of the hills the return to labour which the fertile soils were no longer permitted to yield. Had France not existed, civilization would have spread throughout Spain: for had France not existed, the people who cultivated the poor soils of Spain could not have drawn from Italy the means of destroying the civilization of those who cultivated the rich ones.

If now we look towards Germany, we see France the perpetual enemy of the free cities: the perpetual ravager of the rich lands, and unceasingly engaged in their depopulation. To her intrigues was due the desolation of the Thirty Years' war. To her was due the control by the house of Austria of the passage of the Valteline, by means of which Spanish troops from Italy were enabled to co-operate with those of the execrable Ferdinand in the destruction of the wealth of Germany: and in the establishment of unlimited control over the modes of thinking and acting of the people of Bohemia, till then ranking among the most civilized people of Europe. To her unceasing jealousy of Austria were due the perpetual invasions of her Turkish allies, by which all eastern Europe was impoverished.

If we turn our eyes towards Genoa, or Venice, or Sicily, or Corsica, the result is the same. Wherever civilization endeavoured to raise its head, there were found French armies engaged in the work of its destruction. It could not be otherwise. France kept herself poor, and her people were driven to the cultivation of the least fertile soils: and hence they were always preying upon each other. Hence the barbarism of the Feudal System, which she inflicted upon Europe: hence the horrors of the Jacquerie: hence the universal proscription of the industrious Huguenots: the atrocities of St. Bartholomew's night, and of the *dragonnades:* and hence the enormous mass of crime and misery that attended the Revolution. The tendency of every thing in France has been to produce poverty and inequality: and thus it is that we see such vast wealth side by side with extreme wretchedness. The few have been, and are, the controllers of the destinies of the people, who have had no voice in the regulation of their own actions: or in the disposal of the proceeds of their labour: or in the determination of their modes of thought.

M. Guizot informs us that, "as a general thing, in France, ideas have preceded and impelled the progress of the social order; they have been prepared in doctrine before being accomplished in things, and in the march of civilization mind has taken the lead." Theories *have* certainly always preceded the accomplishment of "things," and to the fact that it has been so it is due that the latter have made so little progress. Knowledge is acquired from the study of the laws of nature, and where those laws are habitually set aside they cannot be studied. They have been set aside, uniformly and steadily, in France; and hence it is that "mind" has taken the lead, and that laws have been manufactured by great men, who have "impelled the progress of the social order" in the direction that suited their purpose. The theory of the barons of the middle ages was, that they held their power from God himself, and that they had a right to make war on their own account: to exercise the *droit de jambage et de cuissage:* and to follow the serf and seize his person and his goods: most of which may be found reasserted almost in our own day, by *Montlosier.* They held that "the liberties of the Gallican church" were perfectly secured when the right of nomination to all places in that church was in their hands, and when they could accumulate bishoprics with immense revenues in the hands of their bastards and dependents. They held, too, that "glory" was the great pursuit of gentlemen, while labour was worthy only of slaves. France has always been the land of very great and very little men: of those who respected no rights in others, and could command from others no respect for their own. The great had no leisure to study the laws of nature, and the small were too poor and too miserable to have time or mind so to do. The starving man has no leisure to study any thing but how to obtain food. Wherever civilization has existed, it has gone from below upwards: from the people who minded their own business, to those who lived by managing the affairs of others. The great have always been the foes of civilization: while the small have been its friends. From the ranks of *the people* sprang Bacon and Locke, Shakspeare and Milton, Watt and Arkwright; men to whom mankind are more indebted than to all the kings and princes the earth has seen. These men were observers of nature, and recorders of her modes of operation. They lived among a people accustomed more than any other in Europe to permit the laws of nature to act: and there, and there alone, could her laws be studied. The essential difference between English and French mind is that one is based upon observation and the other is not, and therefore it is that in France "ideas" have been so numerous; but there, as everywhere else, theory has been in the inverse ratio of knowledge. Theories in relation to Christianity most abounded when its practice least existed. The immaculate conception was most ardently debated at the time when the Church sold absolution for the worst crimes at the cheapest rate. The theory of France, at all times, has been that her own grandeur was in ratio of the littleness of her neighbours: yet littleness has been her characteristic, in the field and in the cabinet. To that theory it is due that she has at all times made herself "the focus: the centre:" not of civilization, but of corruption and intrigue, and hence it is that she is dreaded by all the friends of freedom. She abounds now in theories. St. Simonianism and other systems of forced union have their origin where the tendency to voluntary union least exists. The advocates of each successive theory hold that they alone have the truth: and thus St. Simonianism is now persecuted, as Jansenism, and Molinism, and Jesuitism, have been in past times. Intolerance towards freedom of thought marks her whole history. Theories of liberty have always abounded, because practical liberty has been unknown. Politico-economical theories abound, yet in no part of the world is the true political economy: that which teaches man to respect in others those rights of which he desires the enjoyment for himself: so little known. Theories of government, and constitutions, have been innumerable: yet government has always, and under every constitution, been administered for the sole benefit of those charged with the performance of its duties. The present theory of France is that Algeria will make her rich: yet she becomes poorer. Her great theory is, that power and influence are to be sought abroad, and she maintains great fleets and armies out of the taxes of a starving people: and then distributes bread-tickets to half the population of Paris. Throughout her whole system, past and present, every thing *has been* "prepared in doctrine before being accomplished in things:" that is, the few have undertaken to teach the many, and they have made laws to suit themselves, instead of studying the laws that nature made. The consequence has been, that nothing has been accomplished; that French theories have been barren, as must be all that are not based upon observation, which cannot take place where practice does not exist. We are not aware, at this moment, of a single idea in moral or political science that is throughout the world received as true, for which we are indebted to that country. Whenever she shall come to be a little practical; whenever she shall have acquired a little knowledge of the science of self-government; her theories of governing others will cease to exist: and whenever she shall arrive at that point in the progress of wealth when she shall cease to limit her cultivation to the poorest soils, voluntary unions may arise, and then the system of forced unions, whether for the building of forts, or the cultivation of farms, will pass away. The healthy man never studies the theory of disease or health. The sick man does, and the very sick man gives to it his whole time and mind. In no part of Europe is practice so unsound as in France. In none do theories so much abound: and in none, consequently, should we have a right to expect to find the body-politic more sick. In none should we find it so. In none is the tendency towards civilization at home so small: in none is the tendency to the obstruction of civilization abroad so great. For centuries nearly all the wars of Europe have had their origin in France, and at this moment her intrigues are the cause of nearly all the existing disturbances.

The insular position of England has given her peace, and the laws of nature have there been far less habitually set aside than in France. Hence it is that she has given to the world the great men to whom we have already referred: men who owed their knowledge to a careful study of nature and her laws, and to that labour which is required of every man who desires to cultivate the richest soils, whether physical or intellectual.

In no part of Europe has the tendency to civilization been so great as in England: yet, if we now examine her condition, the conditions of civilization are complied with in but a very limited degree. She uses much of the worst machinery of exchange, that she may cultivate poor and distant soils while neglecting the rich ones at her feet: and therefore it is that land remains undivided in the hands of great land-owners whose debts are counted by millions of pounds, while surrounded by labourers living in mud hovels, and earning 9*s*. a week.* Here we have the civilization of Rome in the days of Pompey and Cæsar: or that of Pomerania, before the changes of the early years of the present century. Where such things are, true civilization has made little progress.

Neither can we see much of it in a system that enables great manufacturers to accumulate fortunes of millions of pounds out of the labours of the people who occupy the wretched cellars of Manchester: great ship-owners to do the same, while surrounded by the poverty and starvation that may be found in Liverpool: or great coal-proprietors, to fix monopoly prices upon coal mined by naked women and children, to enable them to accumulate fortunes at the expense of poor consumers in London. There is no civilization in the lanes and alleys of Glasgow; nor in its numerous brothels, filled with the daughters of peasants who have been hunted out of their hills, until in the northern Highlands the poor remainder have degenerated into a meagre and stunted race. There is none in a system which exhibits throughout the western Highlands and the Isles, a population of from sixty to eighty thousand always in a state of destitution and habitually dependent upon charity; and compelled, in case of

* The debts of one noble duke are stated to exceed two millions of pounds sterling: and those of another have been stated to require sixty thousand pounds for the payment of interest alone.

any deficiency of crops, to seek foreign aid to save them from the horrors of starvation. These poor people pay, for the use of very poor soils, high rents to men who live in palaces: great men: always the bane of little men. There is no civilization in starving Ireland; none in India depopulated by starvation produced by enormous taxation for the support of great armies maintained for securing the sale of English cloths, or for the payment of interest on loans made to their masters by English subjects, and dividends on stock held by absentee landlords.

So long as England shall continue to constitute herself head of a great empire, that empire must be considered as one in its whole length and breadth; and her claims to rank in civilization must be weighed after an examination of the condition of her whole people: the powerful duke and the occupant of the mud hovel: the great chief of the clan and his miserable tenant: the wealthy manufacturer and the poor operative: the Irish landholder and his starving tenant: the rich West India proprietor and his late slave: the East India proprietor and his present slaves, decimated, at brief intervals, by famine and pestilence. So considered, the claims of England to civilization do not stand high: nor can they do so while she shall continue to present to view such enormous contrasts.

Half a century since, and perhaps even more recently, might be seen in the streets of Lisbon, men with good coats on their backs, cocked hats upon their heads, and swords by their sides, but with bare feet and legs. These men thought themselves civilized, and so does England: and the civilization of the two is nearly alike. England has a very good coat, by which her body is well covered: but it has very short sleeves. The arms, to a great extent, are naked: and those arms represent a large portion of the people of England, badly fed, badly clothed, and very badly educated; while surrounded by rich lands, great mills, well-endowed colleges, and vastly rich bishops and archbishops. Her body is well covered, but her feet and legs, Ireland and India, are bare: and she keeps them bare, that she may have more to put upon her body: and she retains the sword by her side, that she may compel them to remain bare: that she may compel them to continue cultivating poor soils in sight of rich ones undrained because of poverty, and uncultivated because undrained. In all this there is no civilization.

In the United States, the conditions of civilization are complied with to an extent far beyond what elsewhere exists, and if they are not fully and completely so the cause is to be found in the fact that they cannot control their own actions.* So soon as they shall resolve that they *will* do so, they can place themselves at once at the head of all civilization. Massachusetts does now occupy that place, because she cultivates her richest soils; but the whole nation may cultivate rich soils, when it wills that it *shall* be done. Then men will concentrate themselves, and the infinity of little schools will become larger and better schools, when children will be better taught at less cost. Then the vast skeleton of railroads and canals will be filled up with branches leading to every little town: and the little towns will become great towns, because land will increase in value from the great increase of the product and the diminished *necessity* for use of the machinery of exchange. Then land will become more and more divided: men will have large libraries

* Perfect individuality and the strongest tendency to combination of action mark the highest civilization, and where they exist their effects will be seen in the events of war, as well as those of peace. However little we may be disposed to approve of the existing war, it is impossible to read the accounts of the recent proceedings in the valley of Mexico without being struck with the extent to which individuality and union have there been manifested. Generals, colonels, captains, and lieutenants, seem to be acting for, and by, themselves, yet never was union more complete, and never was the wonderful power of union more fully exhibited. We seem to know each regiment, each officer, and almost each man. The perfection of individuality is seen in the election of a colonel on the battle-field, by the men whom he was to command: and in the return of the name of every man killed or wounded, from the highest officer to the lowest private. The perfection of the power of union which accompanies this individuality is seen in the results.

instead of small ones, and the farmer will have his daily newspaper instead of his weekly one: and he will meet and exchange ideas with the consumers of his products: and his mind will become better informed: and he will learn daily more and more how to manage his farm and to govern himself.

Then will his wife become more and more exempt from the hardships of labour, and his children will marry and remain near him: and then he will learn daily more and more to appreciate the comforts of home: and he will more and more desire to render that home agreeable by the cultivation of flowers and trees, and by the collection of books and of instruments calculated to aid him in the development of his intellect, and that of those by whom he is surrounded. Then will the consciousness of power diminish, and the sense of his duty towards his fellow man increase: and then will he be seen daily more and more exerting himself to aid the afflicted and to help the weak: doing to all, and daily more and more, as he would that others should do unto him.*

The PAST says to the people of the PRESENT: "Civilization comes with wealth and the cultivation of the rich soils. With them come concentration, large wages, increased productiveness of land, and increased rents for the use of that land. Wealth comes with peace. Labour then for the maintenance of peace."

* Efforts have been made to show that crime is more abundant in the United States than in Europe. In the former, newspapers abound and every thing is published. In the latter, newspapers are few, and little is published. Archbishop Whateley says, and most correctly, that he has "no doubt that a single murder in Great Britain has often furnished matter for discourse to more than twenty times as many persons as any twenty such murders would in Turkey." He adds that "we should remember, that there are not more particles of dust in the sunbeam than in any other part of the room, though we see them more where the light is stronger."

THE FUTURE.

The population of the United States is at the present moment about twenty-one millions; and the surface comprised within the existing states and territories exceeds a million of square miles, or six hundred and forty millions of acres, each of which is capable, at a moderate estimate, of feeding a full-grown man: and were it properly cultivated, it would clothe him too. The surface, then, that is already organized, is capable of maintaining six hundred and forty millions of people, or two-thirds of the whole population of the globe: and yet men are seen, by thousands and almost tens of thousands, removing to Oregon and California to appropriate more land, of which they must cultivate the poor soils: while behind them are left fertile lands covered with the finest timber, almost utterly valueless; as we have already shown.

For the benefit of the rich lands from which man thus flies, his predecessors have laboured during more than a century. For their benefit, they have made roads, railroads, and canals: have built houses, and towns, and cities: and he can purchase them, with all their advantages of timber and soil, at the price sometimes of sixty cents an acre—or one-twentieth of the interest they have acquired in these improvements: yet he flies from them to commence the work of cultivation upon poor land that has no value, and that can never acquire any but from the labour that he bestows upon it. He flies from rich lands that he may have at far less than cost, to obtain poor ones at full cost: and a heavy cost it is. He flies from lands that are covered with manure that has accumulated for ages, and that he may have for little more than the labour of clearing them, while men near towns pay thousands of dollars a year for the manure yielded by the produce of poor lands cultivated by him and others like himself.

The natural tendency of man is to combine his labours with those of his fellow man. He knows that two can roll, and four can lift, a log, that one alone could neither roll nor lift. Here, however, men are seen flying from their fellow men, each one seeking to roll his own log, for lift it he cannot. The labour of each is thus wasted on the road. The manure of his horses is wasted on the road: and his labour is unprofitably employed at the end of his journey.

The natural tendency of man is to combine his axe with his neighbour's spade: lending one and borrowing the other. Here, however, the man with the axe flies from the man who has a spade.

The natural tendency of man is to begin on the thin soil at the side of the hill, and to work down towards the rich soil at its foot, gathering manure on the one with which to enrich the other: but here man flies from the rich soils near him, to seek the poor ones distant from him.

The natural tendency of man is to combine with his neighbours for improving old roads: but here man flies to a distance that he may employ his labour on new ones, while the old ones remain unimproved: and henceforth two are to be maintained instead of one.

The natural tendency of man is to combine with his neighbours for improving the character of education in old schools: but here he flies from his neighbours to places where there are no schools, and where none can be until he shall build it himself.

The natural tendency of man is to hold in regard old places and old churches, mellowed by time and sanctified by the recollection of those who had before inhabited them: but here he flies from them, to cut out new places in the woods, whose harshness and hardness are quintupled by the recollection of the places he has left, occupied by the friends of his early years.

Why is this so? Why is it that men should fly from western New York, where railroads run through rich lands, covered with dense forests: through swamps that need drainage alone to give to cultivation the richest soils in the world: to seek the West, where they must cultivate poor soils distant from market, and yielding but ten bushels of wheat to the acre, and that small yield, too, annually decreasing* because of the necessity for starving the great machine, by wasting on the road the manure yielded by the horses or oxen employed in the work of transportation: while the wheat itself is consumed abroad, leaving nothing whatever to return to the land? Why is it that throughout that rich country, with its canals and railroads, its towns and its telegraphs, population diminishes, and land concentrates itself in fewer hands: always the signs of diminishing wealth?

Why is it that men fly the fertile valleys and rich slopes of northern New York, near neighbours to both the St. Lawrence and Lake Champlain, where steamboats abound: to seek the shores of Lake Superior, there to obtain from the poorer soils that *always must be* first cultivated, a reward of little more than five times the seed? Why is it that rich meadow-lands on the Schuylkill remain unimproved, while men seek Oregon and California? Why is it that vast forests still cover fine meadow-lands on the Susquehanna, capable of yielding crops whose *tons* would number more than the *bushels* obtained from the wheat lands of Ohio: furnishing manure in tons for fertilizing the poor soils of the hills, on which now stand farm-houses in the midst of farms that have been in cultivation for half a century? Why do men seek Iowa, to raise from an acre thirty bushels of Indian corn, that before it can reach market must be con

* See Report of Commissioner of Patents, January, 1845, p. 25.

verted into pork, while the lower lands of Virginia and Maryland are abandoned: lands that are nearer to the great market of Europe, and from which, by careful cultivation, a hundred bushels might be obtained? Why is it that men fly from the meadow lands of South Carolina, leaving the remaining inhabitants a prey to fevers and malaria consequent upon diminished population, to seek the thin lands of Texas, at the heads of the streams; there to raise small crops to be wagoned over half-made roads down to new towns, possessing no one of the conveniences that tend so greatly to diminish the friction between the consumer and the producer? Why is it that men are everywhere seen flying from their fellow men: from those destined by the Deity to be their helpmates: from parents and relations: from old houses, and old churches, and old school-houses; old comforts, and old feelings: and from all the conveniences and advantages that tend so largely to promote their happiness and their respectability, and to increase their powers of exertion: to seek in Texas and Iowa, Oregon and California, new homes and new relations, amidst woods that they cannot fell, and swamps that they cannot drain, and upon the poor soils that yield, invariably, the smallest return to labour?

These things would seem almost impossible: yet if we turn to India, we may see the poor Hindoo cultivating the poorest soils, and then labouring, almost in vain, to drive through the rich black clay that lies between him and his market, the half-starved cattle that bear his miserable crop. Here we have the same state of things; and both here and there it may be traced to the same cause: *necessity.* In neither can men exercise *power* over the rich soils, because *in neither have men power over themselves;* and until they shall have it, they must continue to fly from rich soils capable of yielding tons, by aid of whose manure poor soils might be enriched, to poor soils becoming daily poorer, because to them even the manure yielded by their own little product cannot be returned. They borrow from the earth, and they do not repay: and therefore it is that they find an empty exchequer: performing thus the process that farmers are enabled to avoid, when, as in England and New England, the consumer takes his place by the side of the producer.* Therefore it is that the average produce of New York is but fourteen bushels of wheat to the acre, while that of Ohio is even less, although acres may readily be made to yield forty or fifty bushels: and therefore it is that the average produce of Indian corn is but twenty-five, when it should be a hundred bushels, and that of potatoes but ninety when it might be four hundred bushels.

If we desire to understand the cause of these extraordinary facts, we may perhaps obtain what we want by taking a bird's-eye view of a farm-house of western Pennsylvania, near neighbour to the rich meadow-land above described. The farmer is reading the newspaper, anxious to know what are the crops of England, and whether or not the rot has destroyed the potato crop in Ireland. Last year many of the people of Europe starved: but he sold his crop at a good price, and paid off his debts. This year he wishes to purchase a new wagon, and to add to his stock of horses: but, unhappily for him, the farmers of England have had a favourable season, and the rot has not appeared in Ireland. Starvation will not sweep off its thousands, and he will get neither horses nor wagon.

His eldest son is preparing to remove to the west, to raise wheat on dry lands in Wisconsin or Iowa, and to send to the already overstocked markets increased supplies of food. His daughter is grieving for the approaching loss of her brother; and of her sweetheart, the son of the neighbouring wool-grower, who is about to leave for Michigan to raise wool, that he may compete with his father who is studying carefully the newspapers hoping to see that the sheep of Aus-

* For the remarkable results produced by the proper application of manures, we would refer the reader to the account of a meeting at Drayton Manor, the residence of Sir Robert Peel, in Skinner's Farmer's Library.

tralia have rotted off and thus diminished the supply of wool. He wants to pay off his debts: but this he cannot do, unless the price of wool should rise, and thus increase the difficulty of obtaining clothing. Why do these sons move off? It is because there is no demand for labour. All the land is held in large farms because the poor soils alone are cultivated; and farmers that would live at all must farm and fence in a great deal of land, where a dozen bushels to the acre are considered a good crop. Why does he not clear some of the meadow-land? It is because there is no demand for milk, or for fresh meat: for hay, or turnips, or potatoes: or for any of those things of which the earth yields largely, and which from their bulk will not bear carriage. He knows that when the great machine yields by tons the product is worth little unless there be mouths on the spot to eat, but that when he restricts it to bushels the product may be transported to the mouths. There is no demand for timber; for all the young men fly to the west, and new houses are not needed. The timber is valueless; and the land is not worth clearing to raise wheat, almost the only product of the earth that *will* bear carriage. To clear an acre would cost as much as would buy a dozen in Iowa; and the product of four acres, at ten bushels each, would be equal to one of forty. He therefore goes to the west to raise more wheat; and his friend goes to raise more wool; and his sister remains at home unmarried. Why does she not marry, and accompany her lover? It is because she has found no demand for her labour, and has earned no wages to enable her to contribute to the expense of furnishing the house.

Here, then, we have labour, male and female, superabundant for want of wages with which to buy food, and clothing, and houses: food superabundant, for want of mouths to eat it: clothing material superabundant, for want of people to wear it: timber superabundant, for want of people desiring to build houses: fertile land superabundant, for want of people to drink milk and eat butter and veal: and poor land superabundant, for want of the manure that has for ages accumulated in the river bottom; while the men who might eat the veal and drink the milk produced on rich lands, are flying to the west to waste their labour on poor ones: *those who should be consumers of food becoming producers of food.*

Why is this? It is because they want a market at which the labour, male and female: the food and the wool: can be exchanged for each other. They want a woollens mill, and had they this, the sons would stay at home and eat food, instead of going abroad to produce more. The daughters would marry, and would want houses. The timber would be cleared, and the fertile lands would be cultivated. The manure would be made, and the poor lands would be made rich. The milk would be drunk, and the veal would be eaten, and the swamps would be drained to make meadows. The saw-mill would come, and the sawyer would eat corn. The blacksmith, the tailor, the hatter, and the printer would come, and all would eat corn. The town would grow up, and acres would become lots. The farms would be divided, and the fencing of each diminished. The railroad would be made, and the coal and iron would come: and with each step in this progress, the farmer would obtain a better price for his corn and his wool, enabling him from year to year to appropriate more and more labour to the development of the vast treasures of the earth; to building up the great machine, whose value would increase in the precise ratio of the increase in the return to his labour. The more he could take out of it, the more it would be worth.

The good people of this neighbourhood now use bad machinery of exchange. They send to market annually five thousand tons of food and wool: a fourth of which is absorbed by the horses, and men, and machines, required for its transportation and exchange; and thus they pay annually as much as would be required for the erection of a place of home exchange. The amount thus spent is lost for ever. The following year the same expenditure is needed: and the next, and every succeeding one. The same labour once applied at home, would stand; and in the following year the wagons, and horses, and men would be at work upon the farms, clearing richer lands, and carrying manure to the old ones; and with every year new combinations would arise: new and better lands would be cleared: new houses would be needed: new demands for timber would arise: new marriages would take place: new children would be born: and with each step in the progress of population and wealth, men would become richer and happier: and land would be more divided: and farms would be better cultivated: and schoolmasters and preachers would be better: and man would acquire more power over land and over himself.

Let us now take a similar view of one of our planting friends in the south. His cotton is half picked, but early frost has come and killed the rest. Why is this? He had not hands to pick it. Why had he not? Because throughout the year there is no demand for labour. His best lands are uncleared, because there is no demand for lumber. His meadow lands are undrained, because there is no demand for milk or veal. He raises bushels of corn, when he might have tons of turnips or potatoes. He, too, wants a market-house. His neighbour is going west to the light soils of Texas, leaving the rich soils untouched. He is going to raise more cotton. If he stayed, he might be a consumer of corn, and cotton, and milk, and veal, and beef.

If we now ask the worthy planter why he does not clear the rich land close to the poorer soil that he now cultivates, his answer will be, that he has offered twenty dollars an acre for clearing it, and destroying the timber, but in vain: nobody will undertake it. Nobody wants timber. There are no houses wanted, for his neighbours are flying to poorer and more distant soils. There are no railroad sills needed, for the production of the neighbourhood diminishes, and men will not make roads when such is the case. If we look in upon him at his hours of leisure, we shall find him intent upon the last news from England: desiring to know how many mills are closed: how many are working half time: how many operatives have been discharged to starve: and wondering within himself if a time will ever arrive when it will be possible to calculate upon a continuance of the same state of things in that country during any single half year. If we look in upon him when meeting with his neighbour planters, we shall find them discussing the expediency of restricting the culture of cotton; or of holding conventions for the purpose of determining how much shall be grown, with a view to acquire some *power* over their own actions, and thus to diminish their *necessities*—but all in vain. Each successive arrival brings with it the news of a further reduction in prices, yet no means can be devised to bring the supply down to the demand: and yet his neighbour goes to Texas *to raise more cotton.*

He and his neighbours send annually to market four thousand bales, of which a fourth is swallowed up by the men and horses and machines employed in the business of transportation and exchange. A thousand bales would build a market-house for labour, and corn, and cotton: and the new machinery of exchange would stand. Thenceforward, the produce of hundreds of these bales would go upon the land, and newer and better soils would be cleared: and labour would become more valuable: and wages would rise: and men would marry, and houses would be needed, and children would be born: and land would become divided: and the planter would in time become the landlord of happy tenants, cultivating their own little farms for their own advantage: and slaves would become free, while their masters would become rich.

If we desire to see this process in full operation, we must turn our eyes towards New England. The best soils are there cultivated, because there is a market on the spot for those productions which our great mother earth supplies in such profusion that they will not bear carriage. The Yankee can take tons from the land, and he can return tons of manure back to it, because he uses the best machinery of exchange. He concentrates his population by tens of thousands upon the poor soils of Massachusetts and Rhode Island, and there he consumes the corn raised by the people of the west, and places on his own thin soil the manure that they lose. His soils double in productive power, while theirs fall off. He becomes rich and richer every day, by concentration. They remain poor, and then they scatter themselves over new thin soils, to repeat in Iowa and Oregon the process of exhaustion already so well commenced in New York, Virginia, and Ohio.

If we desire to see it elsewhere, we must turn to Eastern Pennsylvania. Population is there concentrating itself in the coal and iron regions: and what is the result? She has ceased to be a corn-exporting State. Her miners now eat the wheat of Michigan and Iowa. Her farmers are now clearing richer land. Houses are needed, and mine-props are needed: and railroad sills are needed: and boat timber is needed: and in every spot, for fifty miles around the coal region, the farmers are felling their trees, which yield them the means of draining their meadows, while the demand for milk, and beef, and veal, and potatoes, and turnips, and all those vegetable products that the earth yields in greatest abundance, enables them to grow rich themselves and to make their poor soils rich. She has ceased to be a rival to Ohio or Wisconsin in the market of the world, and therefore their products are more valuable; and with the increased value of their productions the planter of Mississippi and Alabama is enabled advantageously to devote more of his land to raising food, and less to raising cotton, the effect of which is found in the increased price of the latter. Were the mines to be discontinued: were the furnaces to be abandoned: her people would scatter over the west, to become producers of food instead of consumers, and then more planters would raise cotton, and fewer would raise food: the result of which would be seen in the fall in the price of cotton.

Such is the effect of a trade of six millions of dollars, the establishment of which has required fifty millions of dollars. A million and a half more would put up fifty furnaces, capable of producing two hundred and fifty thousand tons of iron, the producers of which would eat as much food, occupy as many houses, and wear as much cloth, as those who have been set in motion by the fifty millions already expended. In the fashioning of the great machine, it is the first step that costs, and each is but preparatory to a new and greater one.

Three millions more would erect rolling-mills to convert all this iron into bars, and thus to produce a demand upon the farmer and the planter as great as is now produced by the fifty millions.

Ten millions would build a hundred great cotton factories, furnishing a market for two hundred thousand bales of cotton, and five millions of dollars' worth of corn and clothing.

The people who made the machinery and built the houses, would be consumers of corn and cotton, and not producers of either. They would want houses at home, instead of houses in Texas or Iowa. The demand for houses would make a market for timber. The demand for timber would clear the rich soils with profit to their owner, who would sell his trees instead of paying men for killing them. He would produce more food, and more people would come to eat it, and they would want more clothes, and more mills would be needed, and more stone, and timber, and lime, and clay, would be required: and with each step he would be improving the great machine, while concentration would afford him means of improving his mind and his tastes, and of educating his children.

Six millions would build two hundred woollen factories, that would use thirty millions of pounds of wool in a year;

and distribute among farmers, workmen, and workwomen, twenty millions of dollars in a year, to be applied to the purchase of food, by which the farmer would be enabled to improve his better lands: of wool, by means of which he would be enabled to improve his breed, and increase his product: of timber, by aid of which he would be enabled to clear his land: and of stone, by aid of which he would be enabled to bring his quarries into use: while the constantly increasing circulation of man and of machinery, and of their products, would offer large inducements to improve the roads by which he could transport to market the surplus, for which he would obtain better prices; because population would increase far more rapidly than at present, and all would stay at home instead of seeking the wilds of the west: and the increased demand for labour throughout the country would enable all to consume more: and thus his *powers* when at market would increase as his *necessity* for seeking that market decreased.

But is this all? It is not. The future annual saving of the machinery of exchange would go again upon the land, and more would be raised, and wages would be greater, and the demand for houses and machinery would make a market for the labour of thousands, all of whom would themselves want houses, and all would consume more food and clothing than now:—and the quantity to be sent into the great market of the world would be diminished, and prices would rise. The farmer and planter would double their crops, while the machinery of transportation would itself improve, and the loss in exchanging would diminish: and all would grow rich, and all would acquire more power over land, and over themselves: while their land would improve hourly in value. Their *necessities* would diminish, and their *power* would increase, and as they made their own iron and cloth, and ate their own food, they would want more silks, and books, and newspapers, and pictures, and statues: and intellectual power would grow with physical and moral power, and thus would improvement keep pace with freedom.

Why is not all this done? Let us ask the farmer. He will tell us that cloth is sometimes high and sometimes low: that the woollen manufacturers have invariably been ruined by the perpetual fluctuations of England. Again, he will say that if he and his neighbour farmers desired to associate for the purpose of building a mill, they would have to be bound, each for all: and that they cannot get a charter, as there is no general law for that purpose, and the power freely to associate has no existence.

Ask the planter. He will tell us that the cotton manufacturers have been ruined over and over again: that cotton goods are sometimes high and sometimes low: that last year they were high, and that now England is forcing them into every market of the world:* that he has no charter, and that without this he and his fellow planters cannot associate; whereas if they had a general law for the purpose, every man in the neighbourhood would subscribe a little, and that they might make an effort at concentration.

---

* Of 175 mills in Manchester, there were working full time, September 28, 1847, only	130
At the close of the following week, the number had diminished to	125
In the first week the number altogether stopped was	22
In the second, it was	24
In the first, the number working short time, was	23
In the second, it was	26
The average number of hours was in the first but	$7\frac{3}{4}$
In the second it was reduced to	$7\frac{1}{2}$
In both, the number of persons working short time was about	8000
In the first, the number altogether unemployed, was	7654
In the second, it had increased to	8736

October 19, the number working short time had risen to 12,198, and those altogether unemployed to 10,341. The number unemployed in Lancashire is said to exceed 50,000.

But a little while since, all were employed, and the labourers demanded a limitation of the hours of labour. Now, the employers reduce the hours, and the labourers suffer for want of employment. These changes occur in a time of perfect peace, and are produced by changes of policy over which foreign nations have no control. They are destructive of the happiness, and comfort, and respectability, of the people of England, as they are of those of all her unfortunate subjects.

Ask the farmer of Pennsylvania why he does not associate with his neighbours to erect a furnace, and his answer will be that three years since all the iron-masters were nearly ruined: that iron is now £10 per ton, but that before a furnace could be built it would be down to £5, and their capital would be sunk. He, too, would say that charters were needed, and that charters could not be obtained.

Here lies the secret of dispersion. Here is to be found the cause of the impossibility of concentration. The people of the United States have no power over their own actions. They waste annually more labour in hauling *their products to market*, and *their consumers from market*, to the west, there to be employed in raising more food and cotton, than would build markets for themselves. They waste on the roads the manure yielded by the products of poor soils, and they leave on the rich ones the manure that has accumulated for ages, and that would render their poor ones rich; and while they shall continue so to do, they must scatter themselves over the far west: they must leave home, and friends, and school-houses, behind: they must continue to be hewers of wood and drawers of water on the poor soils, instead of becoming rich on the fertile ones: they must continue to obtain bushels where they might have tons: they must continue to do as do the people of India:—cultivate poor soils and find themselves bogged in the rich ones, through which they have to drag their products to market.

The annual loss to the people of the Union from the want of the power to concentrate themselves on the rich soils, is far more than the value of the whole exports of England *to all parts of the world*, and, were she to give them the whole, the gift would be injurious. It would tend only to scatter the people more widely, for concentration would then be impossible, and *without that the earth cannot be made to yield*: and unless it be made to do so, the poor soils cannot be made rich. *Population makes the food come from the rich soils*, while depopulation forces men back to the poor ones.

The number of States employed in producing cotton is ten. The whole product is about two millions of bales, and the average is therefore about two hundred thousand bales per State. To prepare a State for producing that quantity, and the food that is to be consumed by the men who raise it, has cost hundreds of millions of dollars. To place in that State machinery requisite for its conversion into cloth would cost ten millions of dollars, *or less than the amount annually wasted:* of labour for want of employment at home: of labour and manure in transporting the product to market: of labour and manure in transporting men to new lands: of crop from the want of hands to pick it: of freights, because of the increased demand for ships and wagons: and of prices, because of the surplus in the markets of the world: and *less than half the amount annually wasted*, because of the necessity for cultivating poor soils while rich ones lie idle.

The cost of transporting the hides and the food to the shoemaker, his awl and his lapstone, is great, and all the manure is lost, and lost for ever. The cost of bringing the awl and the lapstone to the hides and the food is small, and all the manure is saved: and the great machine is improved, because the manure is saved and the shoemaker wants a house; and the house wants timber and stone, by the furnishing of which the land is cleared. A large portion of the people of the United States are busily employed in carrying the hides and the food to the awl and the lapstone, and in driving people who might use the awl to other places where they must raise more hides and food.

What is the remedy for this state of things? The answer is easy: England must be made to raise her own food, and she must be made to let other nations consume theirs. The resistance of the United States put an end to the navigation laws. Their resistance killed the right of search. Their resistance killed the corn laws. Their resistance will kill the colonial system, and give freedom to India and Ireland, to *the people* of England, and to themselves.

To their resistance is due the fact that England has already turned her attention, in some degree, homeward; but the work is not half done. To make a short war, it must be a strong one. No set of men can now feel any confidence in erecting iron-works, cotton-mills, or woollen-mills; and until all shall feel full confidence, the little capitalists cannot get to work, and the business must remain in the hands of great ones, who can run great risks: and while that shall be the case, but little will be done. Almost all that exists in the Union is the work of the millions of little men engaged in improving the great machine, and when they, the little farmers, and little mechanics, and little shopkeepers, shall get to work, the production of iron, and of cotton and woollen cloth, will go ahead as rapidly as farming has done, and then concentration will take place, and the rich soils will come into cultivation, and every county in the Union will have its iron, or its cotton, or its woollens exchange, and then land will double in product and in value. There is not one county that could not supply the stone, the timber, and the labour necessary for building a furnace or a mill, and the money necessary for the purchase of machinery: thus making a place of home exchange. Once built, further capital is not needed. The grower of corn, and hay, and oats, and wool, and the young men and young women who have labour to sell, perform their exchanges at the factory, which becomes a little bank in which each man buys a share while accumulating means to build a house or buy a farm, selling it again when the house is built or the farm is bought. Throughout the Union, south of the Hudson, there is scarcely a single county in which there is not more capital unemployed than would build such a place of exchange: and scarcely one in which, for want of such a place, there are not more people idle than would suffice to carry it on. Were each county to help itself, all would be helped.

Wealth is power. The people of the United States have the wealth. That wealth has given them power, dispersed as they were, to do much. Concentration will give them greater wealth, and greater power. Their twenty-one millions produce at this moment a greater quantity of commodities than the people of England, while they build twice as many houses; make twice as many roads; apply thrice the labour to the improvement of land; build four times as many school-houses and churches; and print ten times as many newspapers. The machinery of production is greater than that of England, and all they now want is better machinery of exchange. Let the farmers and planters have this and population will increase with greater rapidity than ever, for young men will stay at home and marry instead of going to the west; and tens of thousands of mechanics, and of coal and iron miners, will seek the United States; while labourers will come by hundreds of thousands, and every man will furnish a mouth to be fed, instead of, as now, furnishing hands to produce food. They will then be consumers of corn, and wool, and cotton, instead of producers: customers instead of rivals. Corn and cotton will be produced at less cost of labour, and wages in corn and cotton will be higher: while cloth and iron will be cheaper, and the farmer will cease to have to pray for bad crops in Europe: while the planter will find in the increased demand for his product consequent upon the higher wages of England, and of Europe, a certainty of a good market for all he has to spare. Coffee, and tea, and sugar, will then be paid for in cotton cloths, and the men who make the cloth will be customers to himself and to his brother agriculturists of the north, who will use more cotton than at present; while Brazil and Cuba will want more cloths, because they will have a better market for their sugar. Every diminution in the machinery of exchange tends to give more time for improving the great machine of production, whether for cotton or sugar, wheat, rye, oats or hemp: to increase the quantity produced: to increase the wages of the labourer and the profits of the capitalist, landed or moneyed: and to increase the comfort and happiness of all.

Let but the people of the United States set the example of a determined resistance to the system, and it will be followed by all Europe. French artisans will then seek America and Germany, and France too will have to raise her own food. Her swords will be changed for ploughshares, and her forests will disappear, while her coal mines will be opened. She, too, will learn the art of concentration, and with each step of her progress, the few will become less and the many greater.

The people of the United States owe this to themselves, and to the world. They enjoy a higher degree of happiness than has fallen to the lot of any other nation, and they should desire to aid their fellow men in England, in Ireland, in Germany and in India, and by helping themselves they will help them. As colonies, India and Ireland will remain poor. As independent nations, they will become rich, for they too will insist on the right of placing the consumer by the side of the producer.

Westward, the star of empire wends its way. From the west to the east civilization has gone, and so it has yet to go: from the base of the Alleghenies to the foot of the Himalaya. The measure is one of peaceful and quiet, but determined, and it should be of united, action. It is one that interests

Every man that wishes to cultivate rich lands instead of poor ones:

Every man that would raise tons instead of bushels:

Every father that would wish to see his sons, and his sons' sons settle round him:

Every mother that wishes to see her daughters married:

Every son that would have a wife and a home of his own:

Every daughter that would have a husband:

Every journeyman that would be an employer:

Every labourer that would have a farm and house, or shop, of his own:

Every property-holder that desires higher rents:

Every man that hates crime and loves virtue:

Every man that loves literature and art:

Every man that loves freedom:

Every man that loves *the people* of England: or of France:

Every man that loves Ireland:

Every man that feels for India:

Every man that loves his old fatherland, Germany:

Every man that loves free trade:

Every man that loves peace:

Every man that loves his fellow man:

Every man that loves his Creator:

Every man that desires that the great law of Christ, "Do unto others as ye would that others should do unto you," should become universally operative.

It is the great work reserved for the people of these United States, and they have the power to accomplish it. It should be entered upon with the same feeling that animated the Puritans of old: the same that gave confidence to the men who, seventy years since, signed the Declaration of Independence. It should be preceded by a return to peace with an unfortunate neighbour, towards whom they now occupy the position of a strong man pummeling a weak one already on his back, to make him cry enough. That war has already cost more than would have given to every county in the Union a place for exchanging labour, corn, and cotton, or wool, or iron ore, for cotton or woollen cloth, or iron: and if it continue another year, it will cost at least as much more. They have too much land already. They want but concentration to enable them to become both rich and strong.

For two centuries past, the world has been perpetually disturbed by the wars of England and France, for ships, colonies, and commerce. Had France had no colonies, there would, probably, have been no wars of the French Revolution after the failure of the invasion of 1792. But for them, France would have been permitted quietly to settle down, in which case Italy and Spain, Holland, Germany, and Russia would have escaped the war of twenty years, and France might now be rich, powerful, and free. The system of both nations is one of perpetual interference. At one time, Poland is to be excited: at another, she is to be abandoned. At one time, Greece is to be aided: at another, Syria is to be delivered over to the tender mercies of the Egyptian pasha: at a third, China is to be made to buy opium, and to open her ports to the cloths of the men who have ruined the poor fashioners of India. At one moment, the affairs of Spain require the interposition of England: at the next, we see her fleets in Portugal, dictating terms to people driven by oppression to revolt. At another, France governs Spain, and the country is made a scene of murderous war, while the court is one of endless intrigue, having for its object the promotion of the interests—not of France, but—of the family of Louis Philippe: all anxious, as French princes have at all times been, for *appanages* at home, and thrones abroad. For centuries has the European world been agitated by the princes of the houses of Valois and Bourbon, and those of the house of Orleans are well disposed to follow their example. For two years past has all commerce with the La Plata been interdicted, because England and France chose to interfere in affairs that were not their own. They have failed, and the country is worse by two years of war and poverty. Three years since, the affairs of Texas claimed their attention. Now Switzerland is menaced, while Italy, fearing France, looks to England. But a short time since, the people of the United States were to be *compelled* to join in a crusade against the slave trade; which would soon cease to exist, were England and France to permit the world to remain at peace. At every difference of opinion as to rights, they are menaced with the destruction of their towns and cities, and the seizure of their ships. At every quarrel, whether to maintain the trade in opium, or to put down that in slaves, their trade is interrupted. The two nations are everywhere seen meddling with everybody's business, and neglecting their own.

They are the great bullies of the world. Italy would now be strong to help herself, but for the wars of France and

England. So would Spain and Germany. Wars made for private ends are afterwards carried on for "the public good," and in defence of "the liberties of Europe," which will take care of themselves whenever the armies and fleets of England and France shall disappear, and not until then. Both countries should be placed under bonds to keep the peace; and the peace-loving portions of the earth can take those bonds when they will. Both should be made to turn their attention homeward: to raise their own food: to feed their starving artisans: to improve their own morals: to free their own people from the thousand restrictions under which they labour: and thus would they set to the world an example far more worthy to be followed than when they are seen preaching liberty and practising oppression: paying for slaves in the West Indies, and making slaves in the East by means of taxes on salt for the payment of dividends on India stock. Nations that pursue the natural system of concentration will find that the first of all rules is the simple one, "Let every man mind his own business." The people of the United States possess the power of compelling both nations to follow this rule, for if they determine on the course that is essential to their prosperity, it will be followed throughout Europe: and then fleets and armies must be abandoned, and colonies must be left to exercise the right of self-government.

The "true grandeur of nations" consists in the perfection of the self-defensive power: and that is now possessed by the United States in a degree greater than any other nation of the world. They have laid the foundation of a pyramid whose base is a million of square miles, occupied by twenty-one millions of people, and filled with little communities, each with its little school-house, its church, and its newspaper. Each of these little communities occupies space sufficient for a large one, with its academy, or its college, its numerous churches, its newspapers, its bookstores, and its libraries, all aiding to give to the structure a height proportioned to its base: and that height may be obtained whenever the planters and farmers of the Union shall determine to exercise the right peaceably to defend themselves. Until they shall do so, concentration cannot take place. Until they shall do so, their people must continue to waste their labour upon poor soils, yielding bushels, while neglecting rich ones that would yield tons. Whenever they shall do so, they will at once take the place to which they are entitled by two centuries of peaceful action, in which it is difficult to discover a single important error until the occasion of the present war: and we cannot but hope that they will speedily exhibit to the world a specimen of real greatness, in abandoning a contest for land that they do not want, with an enemy incapable of self-defence. They are strong, and they can afford to be generous. With England and with France lies the great contest, and it is for the exercise of power over their own actions: for the exercise of the right to stay at home and become rich by the cultivation of rich soils, in preference to flying from home to remain poor while cultivating poor ones: and every dollar spent in the present contest tends to lessen the power vigorously to maintain that one which is to result in the emancipation of the world from the tyranny of fleets and armies, and the establishment of perfect peace. The truest grandeur consists in the most perfect power over ourselves, our thoughts and actions, and in conceding to all men the exercise of the same powers that we desire for ourselves. The people of the United States do not exercise that power: but they may do so, and we trust they will. Their position is one of surpassing strength. They are twenty-one millions, among whom there is universal activity and intelligence. Of these seven hundred and fifty thousand are the product of the present year, and soon the addition of a year will reach a million. They have more school-houses and more scholars in them, more churches and more hearers in them, more public libraries and more books in them, than any other nation of the world. They have more and better printing presses, and they consume more paper; and their authors are better paid.* They have a mercantile marine that can perform more service in a given time than any other. Their machinery of manufacture now takes precedence of that of England. They have railroads, canals, and magnetic telegraphs, over a surface of five hundred millions of acres. They have twenty millions of sheep, five millions of horses and mules, fifteen millions of cattle, and thirty millions of hogs.† They raise a thousand millions of bushels of food for man, and almost a thousand millions of pounds of cotton; and this vast product can be doubled by the application of the same quantity of labour, whenever they shall determine that *they will* make their own cloth, and their own iron, and by thus placing the consumer by the side of the producer enable the latter to cultivate rich soils instead of poor ones. So soon as they shall have thus determined, thousands of tons of the surplus machinery of England, and tens of thousands of her artisans, will be seen leaving her shores to place themselves where food and cotton together grow, and where liberal and constant wages will be the reward of moderate but steady labour.

England presents to view a pyramid, but an inverted one, the apex of which rests upon a vast population, a portion of which is uninstructed to a degree almost incredible, while another large portion is instructed in a very small degree; and the whole are wanting in the activity which in the United States results from perfect self-government. Piled on these is a vast poor-house establishment with its host of officers. On this again stands Manchester: and on this rests a large mass of great merchants and bankers, trading largely on credit

* We except from this the authors of such trash as "*Le Juif Errant*," and of histories whose object is to teach that "glory" is the great object of life, and that it is to be sought at any sacrifice of honour or honesty. Such writers are better paid in France.

† Great Britain and Ireland, with a population of twenty-eight millions, have forty millions of sheep, two millions of horses, and five millions of cattle. France, with a population of thirty-five millions, has thirty millions of sheep, three millions of horses, seven millions of cattle, and five millions of hogs.

and but little on capital. On the top of this rest numerous great corporations making large dividends out of *Irish rents*, and taxes on the coal consumed by the artisans of London, or the salt eaten by the unfortunate people of India: or the proceeds of high interest charged to unhappy traders and railroad speculators seduced, by liberal offers of loans at low interest, to risk their fortunes and their happiness upon the chance of an approach towards steadiness in the action of a great bank, that is governed by no principle but that of momentary expediency.* On top of this, we see a great Church collecting millions to be divided among archbishops, bishops, prebends, and rectors, while curates do the work and starve on servant's wages. Next, we see a great aristocracy, with vast possessions cultivated by men who live in mud hovels and earn nine shillings a week; and mortgages so heavy that record offices are held in small esteem and deemed to be undesirable. Piled on this, Pelion upon Ossa, we have a fleet and army, and colonies, requiring a hundred millions of dollars annually for their support. Over all, stand the ministers

* Five weeks ago, when money was selling in the market at 6 per cent., the managers of the Bank of England, having a great mass of that commodity accumulating on their hands belonging to the public, notwithstanding that their published weekly returns proclaimed that the value of money was steadily increasing, commenced underselling their rivals in the market, and offered their commodity at five per cent. The immediate effect of this extra issue was what is called "relief;" money was easier, traders obtained discounts rather more freely, and at a lower rate than before, property moved, and persons were tempted to accept contracts which they would otherwise have rejected. In the meanwhile, the weekly bank returns went on announcing that the stock of gold was diminishing, and that the natural value of money was enhancing, and such bystanders as ourselves awaited in breathless expectation the inevitable result of this terrific proceeding on the part of the managers of the bank. It came—those managers met one morning last week, and found that they had got no more money than they should want for paying the public dividends. They turned round in an instant upon the unfortunates whom they had been pampering with treacherous nourishment, (as they had often done before,) and whom they had led and lulled into a fatal security, and, by a contraction and denial of loans more sudden, more perfidious, and more remorseless than we ever before heard of, (but indispensably necessary to save themselves from the consequences of the criminal act of which they had been previously guilty,) plunged thousands into distress and hundreds into ruin.—*Examiner*, October, 1847.

and great officers of state, surrounded by hosts of chancellors and ex-chancellors, pensioners, sinecurists, and recipients of the public moneys, of all grades and conditions of life, from the great Duke himself down to the tide-waiter and letter-sorter.

The machine is top-heavy. It rests on the shoulders of the very poor: upon those of the little children and poor women of Manchester: and at the slightest disturbance there, it will topple over.* Such will be the case when the people of the United States shall determine that *they will* place the consumer of food by the side of the producer of food and cotton. That done, of all this vast mass little will remain but the land and the mortgages: and then machinery will become, as it has already somewhat done, superabundant, and much of it will find its way to America and Ireland, India and Germany. Mechanics and coal miners will become superabundant, and many will find their way to the United States. Capital, no longer needed in manufactures, will go upon the land, and food will become more abundant: and labour in agriculture will be more and more needed, and better paid; because land-owners will find that they must offer bounties to men to stay, instead of granting premiums to those who will carry them into slavery in Van Diemen's land and Norfolk Island. Systematic colonization will be forgotten. Landlords will dispense with great farmers, and manage their affairs themselves: and the return to capital will rise, because its employment will be directed by mind. Great farms will be broken into little farms, and little farms

* The extreme unsoundness of the system is proved by the apprehensions felt by the government on every occasion of stoppage of work. The *Britannia*, of October 23, says, "The state of the manufacturing districts is so alarming that government, though it refuses all measures of relief, is providing a strong military force to keep the peace. At Carlisle the local authorities have received warrants from Sir George Grey, the Home Secretary, authorizing them to call and enroll the pensioners of the district; and a strong force of cavalry is now stationed at Newridge. No one supposes that the winter can be got through, should the distress not be mitigated, without some desperate rioting."

will require cottages; and land will be better cultivated, and pay more rent. Land will pay more taxes, and labour less: and landlords will cease to want fleets, or armies, or colonies, because they will dislike taxes. Landlord's sons will have to work, and landlord's properties will have to be divided. Titles will disappear. The price of perpetual annuities will fall, and the government will be unable to make loans.* Great bankers will break and little ones will take their place. The great will become less, and the little will become greater and stronger; and all will become happier. Wealth will grow more rapidly, and wages will advance. Great corporations will die, and little unions will start into existence. Ireland and India and Germany will be permitted to eat their own food, and make their own cloth; and England will sell them steam-engines and power-looms, while for a time she will send the people of the United States the finer articles that they will want in vast abundance when they shall have acquired power to make the commoner ones for themselves.

The people of England are the friends of the people of the United States. They are part and parcel of themselves. To the aristocracy, landed, or moneyed, the latter owe nothing. *They* sent slaves, and because the people of the United States fed and clothed them well, and caused their numbers to increase, they branded them as "slave breeders." They seized the vessels of the United States by thousands, ruining their owners, and then reproached them as "bankrupts." They forced the people to scatter to the west, and then forced loans upon them to make roads: then ruined them, and reproached them with "repudiation." Time after time they have filled the western world with ruin, and ruin has invariably been followed by invective. *To them*, there

* This operation is now going on in Germany as well as in England. The Austrian government has just prohibited the sale of railroad shares, in hopes of compelling capitalists to make investments in the worthless stock of a government by which repudiation has been repeatedly resorted to, to the ruin of all who have trusted it. The day of Austrian loans and power is over.

is no friendship due. Their system is unsound, unsteady, and ruinous to the world, and to themselves; and so will it continue until the many shall have acquired more power, and the few shall exercise less. Their power hangs on fleets, and armies, and colonies, and when these shall have passed away order will succeed disorder and the world may hope for peace.

With each step in this progress, England will acquire the power of self-protection, which now has no existence. Her policy is dependent upon that of foreign nations, and hence the endless waste upon diplomacy. Foreign tariffs affright her merchants, and compel the repeal of her corn laws. The fear of losing her supplies of cotton compels the abandonment of the right of search, and the settlement of boundary questions. She has no fixed system, and she can have none: she can exercise in no degree the power of self-government while she relies on poor soils abroad in preference to rich ones at home. At this moment her whole policy is dependent on the action of the United States. If they determine that they will eat their own food, and work up their own cotton, and smelt their own iron ore, the downfall of the system of ships, commerce, and colonies is as certain to take place as it is now certain that the navigation and corn laws have been repealed. In confirmation of this view we take the following passage from an English journal:

"It is a great mistake to date trading on reciprocity principles at the treaties of 1824; a still greater to suppose that the accession to these treaties by Great Britain was voluntary, and that she had it in her power to resist them. The most indisputable fact is, that these treaties have each in their turn been as much forced upon us—that we were as much driven into them—as if they had been dictated at the triumphant cannon's mouth. In 1815, after the long, exhausting, desolating war with Bonaparte, Europe was only too eager to obtain any peace; nations and governments forbade longer destruction, bloodshed, and misery; and then in the peace concluded between Great Britain and America the United States, by the articles which placed British and American shipping on terms of equality with each other, exacted such a recognition and establishment of the principles of reciprocity, that, whether they demanded it sooner or later, the concession of them could no longer be refused to other nations. In fact, the United States, by thus setting the example in this instance, as much abrogated our general navigation laws, as, by resisting the search on the high seas, they have dealt the death-blow to that vexatious and presumptuous claim. For it was, and still is becoming every day more and more apparent, that Great Britain, as a commercial nation, cannot wage a war of custom-houses. To her, international retaliation of duties would be more fatal than defeat at Trafalgar and Waterloo. Wherefore, the threat of custom-house hostility repealed our navigation laws—though our legislature went through the form of doing so, and though Mr. Huskisson affected to originate it in 1824 in the House of Commons, as a necessary and prudential measure, when he announced the orders in council and the tariff on which the government had decided."*

France presents to view another great inverted pyramid, resting on the shoulders of the miserable people of Paris, one-half of whom receive alms, in the form of bread tickets, when crops are short: and the equally miserable owners of millions of acres and half acres, cultivated by men who scarcely obtain the means of subsistence: and the more miserable operatives of Lyons and Sedan. The part which stands high in air, and which should be the bottom, is broad, and there we see the King busily employed in raising materials from below for the purpose of widening the top; creating *appanages* and vice-royalties for his children, while all around are watching for the time when the whole machine shall topple over, burying in its ruins, king, princes, princesses, *appanages*, vice-

* New Quarterly Review, p. 136, vol. 6, 1845.

royalties, and all other of the bad machinery now so extensively in use. Let but the people of the United States determine that *they will* place the consumer by the side of the producer, and thousands of the most useful men in that country: great and little capitalists, and the best operatives of all descriptions: will transfer themselves to the place where labour is in demand, wages are high, and food is abundant.* Then will it become necessary to offer them inducements to stay at home: then will the people acquire power: and then may the world see an approach to peace, for the people everywhere love peace. Their rulers alone love war, and war abounds where man is cheap and food is dear.

France and England are both hollow. With both power is apparent, not real, and both must lay down their arms when other nations shall determine that *they will consume* their own food, and that France and England *shall raise their own*. Wealth alone gives power. France is poor. England is apparently very rich, but far less so than she appears to be; and no better evidence of the fact need be desired than is to be found in the general ruin caused by the appropriation of a few millions' worth of land, and corn, and coal, and iron ore, to the purpose of making roads. She dams up capital, and when it accumulates to the amount of eight or ten millions she fancies herself very rich, and commences the investment of twenty or thirty millions: and when the work is half done, half the merchants and traders are ruined, and half the operatives thrown out of work and obliged to expend their little savings in the effort to obtain food.† Such has been the course of events in every cycle of seven years

* "Workmen! we who are now tied, abused, chained—who have no rights, are not cared for; no work, no bread, no future, as at present—let us go and seek elsewhere, for the Providence or nature which offers us all the treasures of their love and beneficence. Let us go and make the foundations of Icaria on the American land."—*Le Populaire.*

† The *Times* says, that "England is poor." England is very much less rich than the world is accustomed to believe. She wastes too much to be very rich.

for the last half century, and such will it continue to be until she shall be compelled to raise her own food. Should the United States take the lead in the measures necessary to this end by adopting vigorous measures for the specific end of enabling themselves to dispense with the present cumbrous and wasteful machinery of exchange, adopting for it the cheap substitute that would be afforded by placing the consumer side by side with the producer, the close of *another cycle of seven years* would almost see the termination of the system. With its termination trade may become free: absolutely free: for in a natural state of things, those who possess abundant supplies of food, the great raw material of manufacture, can need no protection.

With each step in the progress towards that point, the people of Germany and Russia, and Spain, and Italy, and Ireland, will acquire power to consume more and more the food yielded by their own soil, on the ground on which it is produced; and with each they will acquire power to consume more clothing, for which they will require more cotton, to be paid for in those commodities for which their soils and climates are best fitted. With each, exchanges will be made more and more directly between the consumer and the producer, and the existing barbarous system of sending cotton to Manchester to be there spun for Germany and Russia; and food from Germany and Russia to be eaten by those who spin it; will tend to pass away. With each, the planter will produce his cotton at less cost of labour, and the cost of exchanging for the products of other portions of the world will diminish. With each, the power of the peace-loving portions of the world will grow, while that of the war-making portions will decline; and with each, the power of man everywhere over land and over himself, his thoughts, his feelings, and his actions, will advance, with a steady tendency towards the establishment of perfect self-government. To the cotton planter this change is almost indispensable. So long as England shall continue to be the chief distributor of his great product, he can know nothing of self-government, for he must continue to be subject to the periodical revulsions with which that country is afflicted. At the present moment numerous mills are closed, not for want of orders but for want of means to execute them, and his cotton falls heavily in price because of his dependence upon English cotton manufacturers who are themselves dependent on the movements of English banks and English politicians. The intervention of England between the producer in America and the consumers of the continent constitutes a cumbrous, costly, and wasteful portion of the machinery of exchange, and the substitution of direct intercourse with the consumer would be attended with advantage similar to that which results from replacing the cart or wagon by the railroad car. The more perfect the machinery the less is the friction, and the greater the power.

Thus far, resistance to the great error of English policy has been in the form of tariffs having for their object the raising of revenue, and thereby affording incidental protection to the consumer of food, and cotton, and wool, who desires to place himself by the side of the producer. The system is vicious and unsound. It is part and parcel of that which it proposes to correct: of that which produces the depopulation of India, and compels the people of the United States to fly from rich soils to poor ones.

When the government of England prohibited the export of machinery and the emigration of mechanics, the object in view was precisely the same that was sought in discouraging the manufacture of woollens in Ireland, and that of nails in America: in depriving the people of the southern provinces of this country of the right of exchanging with those of the north, and the people of Ireland from exchanging with those of the West Indies, except through the medium of English ports and English merchants: that of establishing a system of indirect taxation.

How perfectly that object has been accomplished, we propose now to show. The man who raises cotton in India, receives less than one penny per pound for it. When it returns to him from Manchester in the form of cloth, after having been dragged through the "rich black clay" that lies between him and the Ganges, it costs him certainly not less than four pence a yard. He gives, therefore, four pounds of cotton for one yard of cloth. A pound of cotton will make three yards of coarse cloth. With proper machinery, such as would be now in India but for the determination of England to tax the world for the maintenance of her system, a pound of cotton could be converted into cloth with less labour than is required for the production of the wool itself. Such being the case, a fair division would give the producer of the cotton at least one-half of the cloth, and he would receive a yard and a half for a pound, whereas he now gives for one yard four pounds. If we now add to this that because of the impoverishment that is thus produced he is compelled to fly from the richest soils of the world, and apply himself to the cultivation of poor ones that yield for wages but two rupees, or one dollar, per month, and for profits of capital but sixpence, or twelve cents, per acre,* we may be enabled to form some small conception of

* "General Briggs states, that the greater portion of the soil in the districts ceded by the Nizam to the British government in 1800, was the rich black land termed cotton ground. On the occasion of the survey, made between 1803 and 1807, there were entered in one district only (Bellary) 1,460,993 acres fit for producing cotton, of which 911,803 were in actual cultivation, and which, according to Dr. Wight's table of produce, in that part of India should have yielded 98,474,724 pounds: but in 1814-15, we find 740,845 acres had been abandoned, and that the produce of the whole district did not exceed 5,278,000 pounds, instead of 98,474,724 pounds a few years before; and strange to say, that the same public report shows that more cotton passed into and through the district in the same year from the remote districts of the Nizam, than was produced in the district alluded to. The cause of the falling off of the cotton culture under our government is but too apparent, for we find on the same authority, namely, the public reports of the revenue collector

the extent of indirect taxation levied by England on that unfortunate people, and we shall be safe in placing it at more than twenty times the value of all the cloth and yarn produced in England from all the cotton wool grown in India, Egypt, and America.

The poor Irishman is, by the system, denied the use of machinery, and he obtains one yard of cloth for the same quantity of grain or pork that would give him two, three, or four, if he could place the consumer by the producer. He too cultivates poor lands, and then he travels to England and spends half a dozen weeks in obtaining a fortnight's wages. What is the extent of the indirect taxation here it would be difficult to calculate, but it is quite sufficient to account for all the misery of Ireland.

The planter in Tennessee sells his cotton for five cents per pound. By the time it reaches Manchester, it costs eight. He buys it back again, obtaining one yard of cloth for two pounds of cotton, whereas, if he had the consumer of food in his neighbourhood, he would obtain half the cloth yielded by his cotton, and would have three yards in place of one. He would then clear and cultivate rich soils, and would obtain a bale to the acre instead of half a bale, and would sell his timber instead of wasting it as now he does.

The farmer of Ohio sells his wheat, grown on land that yields ten bushels to the acre, at seventy cents. By the time it reaches Manchester it is worth a dollar and a half, at which price, with the addition of numerous charges, the farmer buys it back: the result of which is, that he obtains for the produce of an acre of wheat ninety yards of cloth, the produce of about thirty pounds of cotton, for which the producer in Tennessee has received a dollar and fifty cents, and which could be converted into cloth for as much more.

in 1814–15, that the profit on cotton, according to his own estimate, did not exceed six and a half-pence per acre, while, according to the native collector, whose account is more likely to be correct, there was a dead loss in ordinary seasons of five pence per acre."—*Economist.*

He cultivates poor soils, whereas, if he had the consumer by his side, he might clear and cultivate rich ones that would yield forty bushels to the acre, and he too could sell his timber.

What is the extent of indirect taxation upon the people of the United States by means of the system may perhaps be estimated if we take into consideration the following facts:—

I. The labour annually expended in the construction of carts, and wagons, and ships, that would be unnecessary if the consumer and producer could be permitted to take their place by the side of each other, would produce as many mills and furnaces as would convert into cloth half the cotton and wool produced, and smelt the ore for making all the iron used in the Union. To the carts, and wagons, and ships, may be added the labour of horses and mules employed in the same wasteful work.

II. The time lost by the persons employed in the work of unnecessary transportation and exchange; by those who are idle in whole or in part for want of a regular demand for labour; and by those who are on the road seeking for new places of residence; is more than would be required for the work of converting all the wool into cloth, and all the ore into iron.

III. The labour that is now given to the work of cultivating poor soils yielding ten bushels to the acre, instead of rich ones that are capable of affording tons of food by aid of which poor soils might be enriched, would yield double the return could the consumer take his place by the side of the producer and thus save the manure that is now wasted.

IV. The labour that is now wasted in making and repairing roads through new states and territories, and among scattered settlements in both old and new states, if applied to the improvement of old roads would diminish annually, and largely, the cost of transportation of those portions of the products of the earth requiring to be exchanged.

It may safely be asserted that the labour of man as now applied is, on an average, but half as productive as it would be were it possible for the consumer and the producer to be near neighbours to each other, and if so, it follows that the indirect taxation by aid of the colonial system is equal to the whole of the present product of the Union, which we have estimated at two thousand millions of dollars. If we wish evidence of the extent to which taxation is pushed by aid of this system, we need only to look to all the colonies of England throughout the world, Ireland, India, the West Indies, Canada, Nova Scotia, and South Africa, and we shall find exhaustion and depopulation universal, as it must continue to be wherever the power of self-protection has no existence.*

* "Both from observation and reflection, I am convinced that a state entirely destitute of manufactures, whatever may be the extent and nature of its staple productions, will always be inferior to one that combines manufactural industry with agricultural wealth. In the first place, materials to a very large amount, which might be worked up to advantage, but which will not bear the cost of distant transportation, are wasted for want of neighbouring manufactures. In the next, it is destitute of those towns and villages that grow up around such establishments, affording home markets for the produce of the farmer, more advantageous than those at a distance, and supplying him with necessary articles at a cheaper rate, the price being diminished to the amount of the cost of transportation. Again, manufactures greatly increase the productive resources of a country; the use of steam and water power, and the vast number of mechanical contrivances and labour-saving machines set in motion by them, augment to an almost indefinite extent the productive industry of the country; while every discovery in science applicable to the useful arts which manufactures give rise to, adds still further to its wealth. It is true that the application of science to agriculture has increased its products, and that we have some few labour-saving machines, but how few and insignificant are they when compared with those that multiply a thousand-fold the industrial capital of a manufacturing district! Where manufactures exist, the individuals interested in their success and prosperity, from their proximity to each other, easily unite their efforts for all purposes of common interest, and good roads and canals result naturally from such combinations, and convenient lines of communication are everywhere established, so as to give to each one his fair share of the advantages of trade. We, on the contrary, live far apart, and meet but rarely to take into consideration our common interests; and when we do meet, we remain together too short a time to originate or perfect any great measure of general improvement. In purely agricultural districts, therefore, the products of industry find their way to market by miserable roads and circuitous lines of communication, to the great loss and inconvenience of the farmer."—*Poinsett's Address to the South Carolina State Agricultural Society.*

The benefit to the man who plunders towns is small compared with the injury inflicted upon those who are plundered. So is it with taxation, direct or indirect. The amount produced is small when compared with the loss that is caused by compelling men to cultivate poor soils, when they might have rich ones were they enabled to improve their machinery of cultivation. England gains nothing by this course of action. While thus taxing all the world to an amount almost inconceivable, she pays heavily herself. She drives capital from employment that would be profitable to that which is unprofitable—from the cultivation of her own soil to the fashioning of the products of other soils—and the consequence is that the profits derived from its use are less by more than one-half than they would otherwise be. She drives labour from the profitable to the unprofitable, and wages are also less by one-half. Capital is cheap and governments borrow readily for the purposes of war; and man is cheap while food is dear, and therefore men are readily hired for the purpose of keeping in subjection the people of England, Ireland, and India, while undergoing the operation of having extracted from them a large portion of the small wages they are permitted to earn. The system is unnatural and unsteady, and therefore it is that her workmen are often unemployed by tens of thousands, while at other times they are overworked: and therefore too it is that her neighbours are perpetually ruined by its unceasing instability.

To the unsoundness of the system it is due that throughout the world protective tariffs exist, having for their object the exclusion of British manufactures. Nothing less could have introduced the system of protection into these United States. Everywhere, however, it has been attempted to correct error resulting from the effort by England at indirect taxation, by other error in desiring to use tariffs as a means of similar taxation at home. It has been the substitution of plunder by a pickpocket for that of a highwayman. The whole system of indirect taxation is mere petty larceny. It is an attempt to filch that which cannot be openly demanded. It is one of those "inventions" of man by which the few are enabled to grow rich at the expense of the many, and is therefore greatly favoured by that class of men who prefer living by the labour of others to living by their own. The man who plunders a city is of the same species with the highway robber. The one who imposes indirect taxes is of the same species with the *chevalier d'industrie.* All belong to the *genus* of great men. All are equally destitute of manly or generous feeling. The plunderer of cities selects those which are weak and defenceless, and the collector of indirect taxes selects the commodities used by poor men who cannot defend themselves, and where the system most prevails men are most weak and cheap, and food most dear.

In India it is found in perfection. The Company taxes princes and sovereigns by millions, and through them their subjects. It then seizes on salt, and retails it at a profit of from eight hundred to fifteen hundred per cent. Next, it taxes commodities on their way to and from market, wherever they can be found, and then hands over its poor subjects to the tender mercies of judges, generals, captains and lieutenants, zemindars, mundils, potails, and all others of the *genus* whose *forte* lies in picking pockets with dexterity.

France has always been governed by financiers, stock-jobbers, and other members of the same great family, and there the system is carried to greater perfection than elsewhere in Europe. The government takes all that can be obtained by direct taxes, then seizes on salt, tobacco, and all other of the commodities used by little men, and then leaves them in charge of innumerable subordinates engaged in abstracting from their pockets by taxes at the gates of towns, monopolies, interest upon innumerable mortgages, and endless fees to lawyers, most of the little that is left.

England exhibits the same system on a grand scale. The nation taxes the world, and each portion of it that exercises power is engaged in the same great work at home. That portion which calls itself "The State" seizes on sugar, and coffee, and tea, and all other of the commodities used by little men, and thus levies contributions that could not otherwise be obtained. The land-holder picks pockets by aid of corn laws. Railroad kings plunder the unhappy traveller by high fares, and hereditary legislators pick his pocket by doubling the cost of making the road. Lawyers oppose local courts lest they should diminish fees. The Bank makes loans at two per cent., and renews them to the almost ruined debtor at nine. The city of London taxes transportation by seizing on the poor carter and taxing his cart, that he may contribute to the Lord Mayor's dinner. The number engaged in the work of indirect taxation—in that of picking pockets by aid of monopolies and restrictions—is great, and the business appears to be profitable; but it is one that, like all other of the modes of plunder, yields small return to the capital and labour that are employed.

Where highwaymen are numerous, pickpockets will always abound. Where wars are frequent, indirect taxes will be numerous, and the people will be poor. The people of the United States, happily, have preserved peace more steadily than other nations; the consequence of which is found in the fact that indirect taxes are fewer, and the class that lives by the labour of others is smaller than in other parts of the world. In the south and west, where poor soils are cultivated and land is held in large quantities, many modes of indirect taxation may be found. Some States own banks, and others make canals and railroads, by aid of all of which taxes are collected from the many to be expended by the few. Pennsylvania presents to view a considerable class that lives by the labour of others, and various modes of picking pockets by aid of indirect taxation have been there in use. With the gradual substitution of direct taxation, the class is becoming less numerous, and soon we may hope to see it disappear. In New Jersey, we find an ingenious compound of highway robbery and petty larceny. The

State sells to a Company distinguished for its rapacity, the exclusive privilege of transporting passengers and merchandise by railroad between the two principal cities of the Union; the consequence of which is that they are worse accommodated, at higher cost, than in any other part of the country where the same amount of business is done. The Company puts the pistol to the head of the traveller, and the State picks his pocket of its fee. The nation is thus taxed to the amount of millions by means of the money that is thus extorted, and by vast interferences with trade and travel. The State itself loses, because high freights prevent the clearing of its land which remains in many places a wilderness where it should be a garden: and thus at the cost of millions it acquires a revenue equal to little more than one cent per acre of its surface.

New York makes canals, and then, to avoid laying direct taxes, imposes a tax on all merchandise carried on railroads, with a view, apparently, to prevent the clearing and drainage of its best lands, which yet remain in a state of nature. Here we find the practice of petty larceny on an extensive scale. That the State may borrow money cheaply by reason of its obligations commanding a high price in the market, its creditors are invested with a monopoly of furnishing that species of currency that men most desire to use, to wit, bank notes; and by aid of this grant they are enabled to impose heavy taxes upon those who use them, by paying them out at par and buying them in at a discount: whereas, were the trade in money free, notes would be supplied that would be always, and everywhere through the State, at par. That trade has in all ages been found by legislators, whether hereditary or elective, to afford a convenient mode of picking pockets, and therefore it has been kept always under their especial care, and where most cared for the robbery has invariably been greatest. Here, however, the system is likely soon to see its close, for here the people have acquired an increase of power.

New England is, more than any other part of the world, free from this system of plunder. Massachusetts expends two millions, all of which, with the exception of a very injurious tax on bank stock, and another on sales by auction, is honestly taken in the form of taxes demanded directly from the owner of the property himself. The people there cultivate all their soils. They know what they pay for, and they receive value for their money. The pickpocket collector of indirect taxes has little existence there.

In the government of the Union, on the contrary, the system of indirect taxation is universal. The forms it assumes are different at different times. Sometimes duties are specific, and the honest man then pays no more than his dishonest neighbour. At other times they are *ad valorem*, and then the pickpocket, by aid of a false invoice, collects his share of the indirect taxation by paying less duty than his honest neighbour. The few who employ themselves in managing the affairs of the many: those who trade in politics: have availed themselves of the necessity for protection against the perpetual and enormous error of the English system to establish revenue tariffs with incidental protection, and thus to swell the amount of taxes to thirty millions of dollars, by aid of which armies of officers, civil, military, and naval, are supported, and wars are made, and loans are effected: whereas, were the system of direct taxation once adopted wars would become impossible, for no chief magistrate would dare to recommend one for which the people were to be required to pay down in taxes upon their lands, their houses, and their merchandise.

As we pass from the north and east, the land where population is most numerous and land least abundant, to the south and west, where land most abounds and men cultivate the poorer soils, the love of war increases, and wars flow from indirect taxation. If we desire to diminish the love of war we must diminish the power of the few to impose such taxes. That power is greatest where men are most scattered, and every increase in the tendency to depopulation tends to increase that power, while every increase in the tendency to concentration tends to its diminution. If we wish, then, that the whole people shall become as rich, and strong, and free and peaceful, as the people of Massachusetts, we must place the consumer by the side of the producer in Pennsylvania, Virginia, South Carolina, and other States, and thus enable the latter to cultivate rich soils, instead of compelling the former to fly to Oregon or Texas, there to become himself a producer, cultivating poor ones.

Concentration, even to its present extent, cannot be maintained without protection. To repeal even the existing tariff would be to drive to the west, there to raise food from poor soils, the men who now cultivate rich ones, and with each step the power of the few to obtain large revenues by indirect taxation, and the power to make wars, would increase. If we desire to preserve peace, we must arrest the progress of depopulation and promote concentration upon rich soils, and that can be done only by increased protection, by aid of *a tariff that is not for revenue*—a tariff whose direct object shall be that of establishing the right of every man to determine for himself where he will live, and how he will employ his labour, or his capital, or both. What is needed is a distinct declaration of a *determination* on the part of the whole nation, farmers and planters, to pursue the course necessary for bringing the consumer of cotton, and wool, and food, to the side of the producers of those commodities: for bringing the lapstone to the hides and the food, instead of carrying the hides and the food to the lapstone: and thus to terminate the system of indirect taxation by both England and France, and to annihilate, by means of measures of peaceful but vigorous resistance, the power of those countries to disturb the world by means of fleets and armies. Were such a measure once deliberately adopted as the policy of the whole nation, evasion of its provisions would be impossible, for all, males and females, old and young, rich and poor, land-owner and labourer, would feel that their own interests were directly concerned in their enforcement. All would feel that the object in view was the establishment of their own right to cultivate rich soils instead of poor ones, and to receive large wages and large rents instead of small ones. The example once set and its object distinctly avowed by the United States, it would be followed by every nation in Europe, and then capital, in the form of machinery, would be seen travelling to place itself by the side of the food, the cotton, the wool, and the iron ore, and mechanics and labourers would seek the lands where food was cheap and man was dear. A brief period of determined action would suffice to restore the equilibrium, now disturbed, between the demand for, and the supply of, both labour and capital in England and France. Both would cease to be superabundant, and landlords would be found paying high interest for the one, and high wages to secure the services of the other. The effort then would be to retain both at home, and contrivances for expelling them would pass out of use. Food would become cheap, while man would become dear, and the power to maintain large armies would soon cease to exist. Labourers would then vote, and then taxes would be laid on land: and then fleets, and armies, and colonies would pass out of existence, while custom-houses would be turned into factories.

In a natural state of things, the people of the United States can manufacture more cheaply than any nation of the world. The mechanic wants food, and lodging, and clothing. The first they have in vast abundance, and the materials for the others equally abound. All that is wanted is that the shoemaker with his lapstone shall be *permitted* to take his place by the side of the hides and the food, as he would long since have done but for the existence of a disturbing force of prodigious power, that needs now a decided, and vigorous, and united, exertion for its correction. So long as it shall be permitted to exist, depopulation and the system of large revenues raised by means of indirect taxation, to be squandered by those who live by managing the affairs of others, must continue. So long as it exists, the planter and farmer must continue to cultivate poor soils instead of rich ones, and to give a large portion of their small product in exchange for a small quantity of clothing. So long as it exists, every attempt at the establishment of freedom of trade must be a failure. With its correction, every obstacle to the establishment of perfect freedom will disappear, and the tariff will pass out of existence. Its enactment would be a declaration of war for the establishment of peace and free trade, and when the object of the war should be attained a continuance of hostilities would be found unnecessary.

The interest of every farmer and planter, and of every labourer and mechanic, is directly concerned in the adoption of a measure of this kind, and one that shall be calculated promptly to produce the effect desired; but it is not more his interest than it is his duty. So long as the present system shall endure, trade of every kind must continue subject to the violent fluctuations which enable the few to enrich themselves at the expense of the many, and enable gambling speculators to live in palaces and ride in coaches by aid of the indirect taxation levied upon the hard-working mechanic and honest trader ruined by changes in the value of their property. So long as it shall continue to endure, usury laws must continue to exist, whereas, when trade shall once be permitted to take its natural course, it will be found that of all commodities money is the one that tends most to permanence of value. So long as it shall endure, England will continue to maintain expensive establishments on barren rocks that she may be enabled, by aid of the smuggler, to set at defiance every effort at concentration on the part of the people of Spain, Italy, and Germany, and so long must false invoices and perjury characterize the whole of her foreign trade. So long as it shall endure, the people of the United States must continue to barbarize themselves by flying from friends, relatives, schoolhouses, and churches: those of Ireland must continue to shoot landlords and landlord's agents: and those of India to play the part of assassins, under the name of *thugs* and *phansigars*. It is therefore the bounden duty of every man desirous to promote the great cause of morality, of justice, and of truth, to unite his efforts with those of his neighbour for the early accomplishment of the great object.

But, it may be asked, what will become of the revenue? Tariffs for revenue should have no existence. Interferences with trade are to be tolerated only as measures of self-protection. Every man who enjoys security should contribute directly for its maintenance, and then he would have cheap government, and good government. With every step in the progress towards placing the consumer by the side of the producer there would be diminished necessity for the maintenance of costly missions and expensive negotiations, and the trader in politics would have diminished chances of profit or distinction. Great men would become less, while the little men: those who minded their own business: would become greater. With the abolition of British and French fleets and armies the necessity for maintaining American fleets and armies would diminish and finally pass away, while the power of self-defence would increase, by the concentration of population and increase of means of intercourse. Men would cease to disperse themselves so widely over the west. Colonization would proceed naturally, and colonists would cease to require forts or troops to defend them, because they would be strong in union with each other, and because they would cease to press so heavily upon the poor natives of the forest. Trade with the consumers of cotton, and of other of the commodities produced in the Union, would increase as those consumers were more and more enabled to consume their own food, and the *power* to maintain ships would increase as the *necessity* for dependence upon them diminished. The ocean would be covered with steam-ships capable of defending themselves, and also capable of being converted into ships of war should war occur in self-defence, but wars would cease. The people everywhere love peace, as will be fully shown when the system of indirect taxation at home, and that of ships, colonies, and commerce abroad: the systems which great men patronize: shall have seen their end, a consummation devoutly to be wished. By degrees exportations of food would cease, except in the form of cloth, or yarn, or iron, or other manufactured commodities: and importations would become limited to those commodities for which the climate was unsuited, or those finer articles on which small duties could alone, under any circumstances, be levied, of which the consumption would be vastly increased, to the improvement of both knowledge and taste. Revenue and expenditure would fall together, and ultimately it might, and we think would, prove that five millions of dollars would more than suffice for all the necessary expenses of a people of thirty millions, while the product of those thirty millions would be more than double that of the present twenty-one millions. That sum would be equal to one-sixth of a dollar per head, and it might be raised without the necessity for a single revenue officer of the general government. With each step in the progress of diminution in the quantity of the machinery of exchange, its quality would improve, and men would travel by thousands where now go hundreds; their *power* of locomotion, and their disposition to see the world increasing as the *necessity* therefor diminished: and ultimately it would be seen that in a natural state of things man and machinery move, and food tends to stay at home: whereas, in Europe, *where he is kept poor*, it is held that man is the most difficult of all commodities to be moved. Man and machinery can afford to pay high freights, while fuel and food must be carried cheaply, or not at all. The increased transport of the former, and more valuable, commodities, would tend to give perfect roads and perfect ships, and both man and machinery would travel at far less cost than now.

The first and great desire of man is that of maintaining and improving his condition. With each step in the progress of concentration, his physical condition would improve, because he would cultivate more fertile lands, and obtain increased power over the treasures of the earth. His moral condition would improve, because he would have greater inducements to steady and regular labour; and the reward of good conduct would steadily increase. His intellectual condition would improve, because he would have more leisure for study, and more power to mix with his fellow men at home or abroad; to learn what they knew, and to see what they possessed; while the reward of talent would steadily increase, and that of mere brute wealth would steadily decline. His political condition would improve, because he would acquire an increased power over the application of his labour and of its proceeds. He would be less governed, better governed, and more cheaply governed: and all because more perfectly self-governed.

NOTE.—We take the following from the last (October) number of the Edinburgh Review:—"If we are unjust enough, and insane enough, to allow a combination for retaliatory measures of this description to be once formed, there is no knowing to what purposes it may not be afterwards applied. One of our greatest perils is the universal jealousy of our commercial power. We would piously hope that our legislators may be just, and fear not. But we must be just. Retaliation, once entered upon, will not be confined to Europe. The United States of America are never backward in pressing their supposed interests, and in extorting privileges from others. We now export to those states large quantities of the produce of every region. Our trade with America involves a hundred interests, of which, if our cotton manufactures are the greatest, they are but one. Let the legislature of Washington pass a Navigation Law, in all respects the counterpart of our own! We need say no more. But we are shocked to think into what a condition the following out of our example would bring the world."

The time has come for the people of the United States to insist upon the enjoyment by their ships of every right conceded to those of England, and the people of the continent of Europe are fully prepared to second them. The time has come for the abolition of the system of indirect taxation by which the nations of the world are compelled to contribute towards the maintenance of fleets and armies employed in disturbing the repose of the world, and the more vigorous the measures the sooner shall we see arrive the æra of universal peace and universal freedom of trade.

THE END.

CATALOGUE

OF

PRACTICAL AND SCIENTIFIC BOOKS,

PUBLISHED BY

HENRY CAREY BAIRD,

INDUSTRIAL PUBLISHER,

No. 406 WALNUT STREET,

PHILADELPHIA.

☞ Any of the Books comprised in this Catalogue will be sent by mail, free of postage, at the publication price.

☞ MY NEW AND ENLARGED CATALOGUE, 95 pages 8vo., with full descriptions of Books, will be sent, free of postage, to any one who will favor me with his address.

ARMENGAUD, AMOUROUX, AND JOHNSON.—THE PRACTICAL DRAUGHTSMAN'S BOOK OF INDUSTRIAL DESIGN, AND MACHINIST'S AND ENGINEER'S DRAWING COMPANION: Forming a complete course of Mechanical Engineering and Architectural Drawing. From the French of M. Armengaud the elder, Prof. of Design in the Conservatoire of Arts and Industry, Paris, and MM. Armengaud the younger and Amouroux, Civil Engineers. Rewritten and arranged, with additional matter and plates, selections from and examples of the most useful and generally employed mechanism of the day. By WILLIAM JOHNSON, Assoc. Inst. C. E., Editor of "The Practical Mechanic's Journal." Illustrated by 50 folio steel plates and 50 wood-cuts. A new edition, 4to. . $10 00

ARLOT.—A COMPLETE GUIDE FOR COACH PAINTERS. Translated from the French of M. ARLOT, Coach Painter; late Master Painter for eleven years with M. Ehrler, Coach Manufacturer, Paris. With important American additions . . $1 25

ARROWSMITH.—PAPER-HANGER'S COMPANION: A Treatise in which the Practical Operations of the Trade are Systematically laid down: with Copious Directions Preparatory to Papering; Preventives against the Effect of Damp on Walls; the Various Cements and Pastes adapted to the Several Purposes of the Trade; Observations and Directions for the Panelling and Ornamenting of Rooms, &c. By JAMES ARROWSMITH. 12mo., cloth $1 25

BAIRD.—THE AMERICAN COTTON SPINNER, AND MANAGER'S AND CARDER'S GUIDE:

A Practical Treatise on Cotton Spinning; giving the Dimensions and Speed of Machinery, Draught and Twist Calculations, etc.; with notices of recent Improvements: together with Rules and Examples for making changes in the sizes and numbers of Roving and Yarn. Compiled from the papers of the late ROBERT H. BAIRD. 12mo. . . . $1 50

BAKER.—LONG-SPAN RAILWAY BRIDGES:

Comprising Investigations of the Comparative Theoretical and Practical Advantages of the various Adopted or Proposed Type Systems of Construction; with numerous Formulæ and Tables. By B. Baker. 12mo. $2 00

BAKEWELL.—A MANUAL OF ELECTRICITY—PRACTICAL AND THEORETICAL:

By F. C. BAKEWELL, Inventor of the Copying Telegraph. Second Edition. Revised and enlarged. Illustrated by numerous engravings. 12mo. Cloth . . . . .

BEANS.—A TREATISE ON RAILROAD CURVES AND THE LOCATION OF RAILROADS:

By E. W. BEANS, C. E. 12mo. . . . $2 00

BLENKARN.—PRACTICAL SPECIFICATIONS OF WORKS EXECUTED IN ARCHITECTURE, CIVIL AND MECHANICAL ENGINEERING, AND IN ROAD MAKING AND SEWERING:

To which are added a series of practically useful Agreements and Reports. By JOHN BLENKARN. Illustrated by fifteen large folding plates. 8vo. $9 00

BLINN.—A PRACTICAL WORKSHOP COMPANION FOR TIN, SHEET-IRON, AND COPPER-PLATE WORKERS:

Containing Rules for Describing various kinds of Patterns used by Tin, Sheet-iron, and Copper-plate Workers; Practical Geometry; Mensuration of Surfaces and Solids; Tables of the Weight of Metals, Lead Pipe, etc.; Tables of Areas and Circumferences of Circles; Japans, Varnishes, Lackers, Cements, Compositions, etc. etc. By LEROY J. BLINN, Master Mechanic. With over One Hundred Illustrations. 12mo. $2 50

BOOTH.—MARBLE WORKER'S MANUAL:
Containing Practical Information respecting Marbles in general, their Cutting, Working, and Polishing; Veneering of Marble; Mosaics; Composition and Use of Artificial Marble, Stuccos, Cements, Receipts, Secrets, etc. etc. Translated from the French by M. L. BOOTH. With an Appendix concerning American Marbles. 12mo., cloth . . $1 50

BOOTH AND MORFIT.—THE ENCYCLOPEDIA OF CHEMISTRY, PRACTICAL AND THEORETICAL:
Embracing its application to the Arts, Metallurgy, Mineralogy, Geology, Medicine, and Pharmacy. By JAMES C. BOOTH, Melter and Refiner in the United States Mint, Professor of Applied Chemistry in the Franklin Institute, etc., assisted by CAMPBELL MORFIT, author of "Chemical Manipulations," etc. Seventh edition. Complete in one volume, royal 8vo., 978 pages, with numerous wood-cuts and other illustrations. $5 00

BOWDITCH.—ANALYSIS, TECHNICAL VALUATION, PURIFICATION, AND USE OF COAL GAS:
By Rev. W. R. BOWDITCH. Illustrated with wood engravings. 8vo. $6 50

BOX.—PRACTICAL HYDRAULICS:
A Series of Rules and Tables for the use of Engineers, etc. By THOMAS BOX. 12mo. $2 50

BUCKMASTER.—THE ELEMENTS OF MECHANICAL PHYSICS:
By J. C. BUCKMASTER, late Student in the Government School of Mines; Certified Teacher of Science by the Department of Science and Art; Examiner in Chemistry and Physics in the Royal College of Preceptors; and late Lecturer in Chemistry and Physics of the Royal Polytechnic Institute. Illustrated with numerous engravings. In one vol. 12mo. . $1 50

BULLOCK.—THE AMERICAN COTTAGE BUILDER:
A Series of Designs, Plans, and Specifications, from $200 to to $20,000 for Homes for the People; together with Warming, Ventilation, Drainage, Painting, and Landscape Gardening. By JOHN BULLOCK, Architect, Civil Engineer, Mechanician, and Editor of "The Rudiments of Architecture and Building," etc. Illustrated by 75 engravings. In one vol. 8vo. $3 50

BULLOCK.—THE RUDIMENTS OF ARCHITECTURE AND BUILDING:

For the use of Architects, Builders, Draughtsmen, Machinists, Engineers, and Mechanics. Edited by JOHN BULLOCK, author of "The American Cottage Builder." Illustrated by 250 engravings. In one volume 8vo. $3 50

BURGH.—PRACTICAL ILLUSTRATIONS OF LAND AND MARINE ENGINES:

Showing in detail the Modern Improvements of High and Low Pressure, Surface Condensation, and Super-heating, together with Land and Marine Boilers. By N. P. BURGH, Engineer. Illustrated by twenty plates, double elephant folio, with text. $21 00

BURGH.—PRACTICAL RULES FOR THE PROPORTIONS OF MODERN ENGINES AND BOILERS FOR LAND AND MARINE PURPOSES.

By N. P. BURGH, Engineer. 12mo. . . . $2 00

BURGH.—THE SLIDE-VALVE PRACTICALLY CONSIDERED:

By N. P. BURGH, author of "A Treatise on Sugar Machinery," "Practical Illustrations of Land and Marine Engines," "A Pocket-Book of Practical Rules for Designing Land and Marine Engines, Boilers," etc. etc. etc. Completely illustrated. 12mo. $2 00

BYRN.—THE COMPLETE PRACTICAL BREWER:

Or, Plain, Accurate, and Thorough Instructions in the Art of Brewing Beer, Ale, Porter, including the Process of making Bavarian Beer, all the Small Beers, such as Root-beer, Ginger-pop, Sarsaparilla-beer, Mead, Spruce beer, etc. etc. Adapted to the use of Public Brewers and Private Families. By M. LA FAYETTE BYRN, M. D. With illustrations. 12mo. $1 25

BYRN.—THE COMPLETE PRACTICAL DISTILLER:

Comprising the most perfect and exact Theoretical and Practical Description of the Art of Distillation and Rectification; including all of the most recent improvements in distilling apparatus; instructions for preparing spirits from the numerous vegetables, fruits, etc.; directions for the distillation and preparation of all kinds of brandies and other spirits, spirituous and other compounds, etc. etc.; all of which is so simplified that it is adapted not only to the use of extensive distillers, but for every farmer, or others who may wish to engage in the art of distilling. By M. LA FAYETTE BYRN, M. D. With numerous engravings. In one volume, 12mo. $1 50

BYRNE.—POCKET BOOK FOR RAILROAD AND CIVIL ENGINEERS:

Containing New, Exact, and Concise Methods for Laying out Railroad Curves, Switches, Frog Angles and Crossings; the Staking out of work; Levelling; the Calculation of Cuttings; Embankments; Earth-work, etc. By OLIVER BYRNE. Illustrated, 18mo., full bound $1 75

BYRNE.—THE HANDBOOK FOR THE ARTISAN, MECHANIC, AND ENGINEER:

By OLIVER BYRNE. Illustrated by 185 Wood Engravings. 8vo. $5 00

BYRNE.—THE ESSENTIAL ELEMENTS OF PRACTICAL MECHANICS:

For Engineering Students, based on the Principle of Work. By OLIVER BYRNE. Illustrated by Numerous Wood Engravings, 12mo. $3 63

BYRNE.—THE PRACTICAL METAL-WORKER'S ASSISTANT:

Comprising Metallurgic Chemistry; the Arts of Working all Metals and Alloys; Forging of Iron and Steel; Hardening and Tempering; Melting and Mixing; Casting and Founding; Works in Sheet Metal; the Processes Dependent on the Ductility of the Metals; Soldering; and the most Improved Processes and Tools employed by Metal-Workers. With the Application of the Art of Electro-Metallurgy to Manufacturing Processes; collected from Original Sources, and from the Works of Holtzapffel, Bergeron, Leupold, Plumier, Napier, and others. By OLIVER BYRNE. A New, Revised, and improved Edition, with Additions by John Scoffern, M. B , William Clay, Wm. Fairbairn, F. R. S., and James Napier. With Five Hundred and Ninety-two Engravings; Illustrating every Branch of the Subject. In one volume, 8vo. 652 pages . $7 00

BYRNE.—THE PRACTICAL MODEL CALCULATOR:

For the Engineer, Mechanic, Manufacturer of Engine Work, Naval Architect, Miner, and Millwright. By OLIVER BYRNE. 1 volume, 8vo., nearly 600 pages $4 50

BEMROSE.—MANUAL OF WOOD CARVING: With Practical Illustrations for Learners of the Art, and Original and Selected designs. By WILLIAM BEMROSE, Jr. With an Introduction by LLEWELLYN JEWITT, F. S. A., etc. With 128 Illustrations. 4to., cloth $3 00

BAIRD.—PROTECTION OF HOME LABOR AND HOME PRODUCTIONS NECESSARY TO THE PROSPERITY OF THE AMERICAN FARMER:
By HENRY CAREY BAIRD. 8vo., paper 10

BAIRD.—THE RIGHTS OF AMERICAN PRODUCERS, AND THE WRONGS OF BRITISH FREE TRADE REVENUE REFORM.
By HENRY CAREY BAIRD. (1870) 5

BAIRD.—SOME OF THE FALLACIES OF BRITISH-FREE-TRADE REVENUE-REFORM.
Two Letters to Prof. A. L. Perry, of Williams College, Mass. By HENRY CAREY BAIRD. (1871.) Paper 5

BAIRD.—STANDARD WAGES COMPUTING TABLES:
An Improvement in all former Methods of Computation, so arranged that wages for days, hours, or fractions of hours, at a specified rate per day or hour, may be ascertained at a glance. By T. SPANGLER BAIRD. Oblong folio $5 00

BAUERMAN.—TREATISE ON THE METALLURGY OF IRON.
Illustrated. 12mo. $2 50

BICKNELL'S VILLAGE BUILDER.
55 large plates. 4to. $10 00

BISHOP.—A HISTORY OF AMERICAN MANUFACTURES:
From 1608 to 1866; exhibiting the Origin and Growth of the Principal Mechanic Arts and Manufactures, from the Earliest Colonial Period to the Present Time; By J. LEANDER BISHOP, M. D., EDWARD YOUNG, and EDWIN T. FREEDLEY. Three vols. 8vo., $10 00

BOX.—A PRACTICAL TREATISE ON HEAT AS APPLIED TO THE USEFUL ARTS:
For the use of Engineers, Architects, etc. By THOMAS BOX, author of "Practical Hydraulics." Illustrated by 14 plates, containing 114 figures. 12mo. $4 25

CABINET MAKER'S ALBUM OF FURNITURE:
Comprising a Collection of Designs for the Newest and Most Elegant Styles of Furniture. Illustrated by Forty-eight Large and Beautifully Engraved Plates. In one volume, oblong $5 00

CHAPMAN.—A TREATISE ON ROPE-MAKING:
As practised in private and public Rope-yards, with a Description of the Manufacture, Rules, Tables of Weights, etc., adapted to the Trade; Shipping, Mining, Railways, Builders, etc. By ROBERT CHAPMAN. 24mo. $1 50

CRAIK.—THE PRACTICAL AMERICAN MILLWRIGHT AND MILLER.

Comprising the Elementary Principles of Mechanics, Mechanism, and Motive Power, Hydraulics and Hydraulic Motors, Mill-dams, Saw Mills, Grist Mills, the Oat Meal Mill, the Barley Mill, Wool Carding, and Cloth Fulling and Dressing, Wind Mills, Steam Power, &c. By DAVID CRAIK, Millwright. Illustrated by numerous wood engravings, and five folding plates. 1 vol. 8vo. $5 00

CAMPIN.—A PRACTICAL TREATISE ON MECHANICAL ENGINEERING:

Comprising Metallurgy, Moulding, Casting, Forging, Tools, Workshop Machinery, Mechanical Manipulation, Manufacture of Steam-engines, etc. etc. With an Appendix on the Analysis of Iron and Iron Ores. By FRANCIS CAMPIN, C. E. To which are added, Observations on the Construction of Steam Boilers, and Remarks upon Furnaces used for Smoke Prevention; with a Chapter on Explosions. By R. Armstrong, C. E., and John Bourne. Rules for Calculating the Change Wheels for Screws on a Turning Lathe, and for a Wheel-cutting Machine. By J. LA NICCA. Management of Steel, including Forging, Hardening, Tempering, Annealing, Shrinking, and Expansion. And the Case-hardening of Iron. By G. EDE. 8vo. Illustrated with 29 plates and 100 wood engravings. $6 00

CAMPIN.—THE PRACTICE OF HAND-TURNING IN WOOD, IVORY, SHELL, ETC.:

With Instructions for Turning such works in Metal as may be required in the Practice of Turning Wood, Ivory, etc. Also an Appendix on Ornamental Turning. By FRANCIS CAMPIN, with Numerous Illustrations, 12mo., cloth . . $3 00

CAPRON DE DOLE.—DUSSAUCE.—BLUES AND CARMINES OF INDIGO.

A Practical Treatise on the Fabrication of every Commercial Product derived from Indigo. By FELICIEN CAPRON DE DOLE Translated, with important additions, by Professor H. DUSSAUCE. 12mo.

CAREY.—THE WORKS OF HENRY C. CAREY:

CONTRACTION OR EXPANSION? REPUDIATION OR RESUMPTION? Letters to Hon. Hugh McCulloch. 8vo. 38

FINANCIAL CRISES, their Causes and Effects. 8vo. paper 25

HARMONY OF INTERESTS; Agricultural, Manufacturing, and Commercial. 8vo., paper $1 00
Do. do. cloth $1 50

LETTERS TO THE PRESIDENT OF THE UNITED STATES. Paper $1 00

MANUAL OF SOCIAL SCIENCE. Condensed from Carey's "Principles of Social Science." By KATE MCKEAN. 1 vol. 12mo. $2 25

MISCELLANEOUS WORKS: comprising "Harmony of Interests," "Money," "Letters to the President," "French and American Tariffs," "Financial Crises," "The Way to Outdo England without Fighting Her," "Resources of the Union," "The Public Debt," "Contraction or Expansion," "Review of the Decade 1857—'67," "Reconstruction," etc. etc. 1 vol. 8vo., cloth $4 50

MONEY: A LECTURE before the N. Y. Geographical and Statistical Society. 8vo., paper 25

PAST, PRESENT, AND FUTURE. 8vo. $2 50

PRINCIPLES OF SOCIAL SCIENCE. 3 volumes 8vo., cloth $10 00

REVIEW OF THE DECADE 1857—'67. 8vo., paper 50

RECONSTRUCTION: INDUSTRIAL, FINANCIAL, AND POLITICAL. Letters to the Hon. Henry Wilson, U. S. S. 8vo, paper 50

THE PUBLIC DEBT, LOCAL AND NATIONAL. How to provide for its discharge while lessening the burden of Taxation. Letter to David A. Wells, Esq., U. S. Revenue Commission. 8vo., paper 25

THE RESOURCES OF THE UNION. A Lecture read, Dec. 1865, before the American Geographical and Statistical Society, N. Y., and before the American Association for the Advancement of Social Science, Boston . . . 50

THE SLAVE TRADE, DOMESTIC AND FOREIGN; Why it Exists, and How it may be Extinguished. 12mo., cloth $1 50

LETTERS ON INTERNATIONAL COPYRIGHT. (1867.) Paper 50

REVIEW OF THE FARMERS' QUESTION. (1870.) Paper 25

RESUMPTION! HOW IT MAY PROFITABLY BE BROUGHT AROUT. (1869.) 8vo., paper 50

REVIEW OF THE REPORT OF HON. D. A. WELLS, Special Commissioner of the Revenue. (1869.) 8vo., paper 50

SHALL WE HAVE PEACE? Peace Financial and Peace Political. Letters to the President Elect. (1868.) 8vo., paper 50

THE FINANCE MINISTER AND THE CURRENCY, AND THE PUBLIC DEBT. (1868.) 8vo., paper . . 50

THE WAY TO OUTDO ENGLAND WITHOUT FIGHTING HER. Letters to Hon. Schuyler Colfax. (1865.) 8vo., paper $1 00

WEALTH! OF WHAT DOES IT CONSIST? (1870.) Paper 25

CAMUS.—A TREATISE ON THE TEETH OF WHEELS:

Demonstrating the best forms which can be given to them for the purposes of Machinery, such as Mill-work and Clock-work. Translated from the French of M. CAMUS. By JOHN I. HAWKINS. Illustrated by 40 plates. 8vo. $3 00

COXE.—MINING LEGISLATION.

A paper read before the Am. Social Science Association. By ECKLEY B. COXE. Paper 20

COLBURN.—THE GAS-WORKS OF LONDON:

Comprising a sketch of the Gas-works of the city, Process of Manufacture, Quantity Produced, Cost, Profit, etc. By ZERAH COLBURN. 8vo., cloth 75

COLBURN.—THE LOCOMOTIVE ENGINE:

Including a Description of its Structure, Rules for Estimating its Capabilities, and Practical Observations on its Construction and Management. By ZERAH COLBURN. Illustrated. A new edition. 12mo. $1 25

COLBURN AND MAW.—THE WATER-WORKS OF LONDON:

Together with a Series of Articles on various other Waterworks. By ZERAH COLBURN and W. MAW. Reprinted from "Engineering." In one volume, 8vo. . . $4 00

DAGUERREOTYPIST AND PHOTOGRAPHER'S COMPANION:

12mo., cloth $1 25

DIRCKS.—PERPETUAL MOTION:

Or Search for Self-Motive Power during the 17th, 18th, and 19th centuries. Illustrated from various authentic sources in Papers, Essays, Letters, Paragraphs, and numerous Patent Specifications, with an Introductory Essay by HENRY DIRCKS, C. E. Illustrated by numerous engravings of machines. 12mo., cloth $3 50

DIXON.—THE PRACTICAL MILLWRIGHT'S AND ENGINEER'S GUIDE:

Or Tables for Finding the Diameter and Power of Cogwheels; Diameter, Weight, and Power of Shafts; Diameter and Strength of Bolts, etc. etc. By THOMAS DIXON. 12mo., cloth. $1 50

DUNCAN.—PRACTICAL SURVEYOR'S GUIDE:

Containing the necessary information to make any person, of common capacity, a finished land surveyor without the aid of a teacher. By ANDREW DUNCAN. Illustrated. 12mo., cloth. $1 25

DUSSAUCE.—A NEW AND COMPLETE TREATISE ON THE ARTS OF TANNING, CURRYING, AND LEATHER DRESSING:

Comprising all the Discoveries and Improvements made in France, Great Britain, and the United States. Edited from Notes and Documents of Messrs. Sallerou, Grouvelle, Duval, Dessables, Labarraque, Payen, René, De Fontenelle, Malapeyre, etc. etc. By Prof. H. DUSSAUCE, Chemist. Illustrated by 212 wood engravings. 8vo. $10 00

DUSSAUCE.—A GENERAL TREATISE ON THE MANUFACTURE OF SOAP, THEORETICAL AND PRACTICAL:

Comprising the Chemistry of the Art, a Description of all the Raw Materials and their Uses. Directions for the Establishment of a Soap Factory, with the necessary Apparatus, Instructions in the Manufacture of every variety of Soap, the Assay and Determination of the Value of Alkalies, Fatty Substances, Soaps, etc. etc. By PROFESSOR H. DUSSAUCE. With an Appendix, containing Extracts from the Reports of the International Jury on Soaps, as exhibited in the Paris Universal Exposition, 1867, numerous Tables, etc. etc. Illustrated by engravings. In one volume 8vo. of over 800 pages $10 00

DUSSAUCE.—PRACTICAL TREATISE ON THE FABRICATION OF MATCHES, GUN COTTON, AND FULMINATING POWDERS.

By Professor H. DUSSAUCE. 12mo. $3 00

DUSSAUCE.—A PRACTICAL GUIDE FOR THE PERFUMER: Being a New Treatise on Perfumery the most favorable to the Beauty without being injurious to the Health, comprising a Description of the substances used in Perfumery, the Formulæ of more than one thousand Preparations, such as Cosmetics, Perfumed Oils, Tooth Powders, Waters, Extracts, Tinctures, Infusions, Vinaigres, Essential Oils, Pastels, Creams, Soaps, and many new Hygienic Products not hitherto described. Edited from Notes and Documents of Messrs. Debay, Lunel, etc. With additions by Professor H. DUSSAUCE, Chemist. 12mo. $3 00

DUSSAUCE.—A GENERAL TREATISE ON THE MANUFACTURE OF VINEGAR, THEORETICAL AND PRACTICAL. Comprising the various methods, by the slow and the quick processes, with Alcohol, Wine, Grain, Cider, and Molasses, as well as the Fabrication of Wood Vinegar, etc. By Prof. H. DUSSAUCE. 12mo. $5 00

DUPLAIS.—A COMPLETE TREATISE ON THE DISTILLATION AND MANUFACTURE OF ALCOHOLIC LIQUORS: From the French of M. DUPLAIS. Translated and Edited by M. McKENNIE, M D. Illustrated by numerous large plates and wood engravings of the best apparatus calculated for producing the finest products. In one vol. royal 8vo. $10 00

☞ This is a treatise of the highest scientific merit and of the greatest practical value, surpassing in these respects, as well as in the variety of its contents, any similar volume in the English language.

DE GRAFF.—THE GEOMETRICAL STAIR-BUILDERS' GUIDE: Being a Plain Practical System of Hand-Railing, embracing all its necessary Details, and Geometrically Illustrated by 22 Steel Engravings; together with the use of the most approved principles of Practical Geometry. By SIMON DE GRAFF, Architect. 4to. $5 00

DYER AND COLOR-MAKER'S COMPANION: Containing upwards of two hundred Receipts for making Colors, on the most approved principles, for all the various styles and fabrics now in existence; with the Scouring Process, and plain Directions for Preparing, Washing-off, and Finishing the Goods. In one vol. 12mo. $1 25

EASTON.—A PRACTICAL TREATISE ON STREET OR HORSE-POWER RAILWAYS:

Their Location, Construction, and Management; with General Plans and Rules for their Organization and Operation; together with Examinations as to their Comparative Advantages over the Omnibus System, and Inquiries as to their Value for Investment; including Copies of Municipal Ordinances relating thereto. By ALEXANDER EASTON, C. E. Illustrated by 23 plates, 8vo., cloth $2 00

FORSYTH.—BOOK OF DESIGNS FOR HEAD-STONES, MURAL, AND OTHER MONUMENTS:

Containing 78 Elaborate and Exquisite Designs. By FORSYTH. 4to., cloth $5 00

*** This volume, for the beauty and variety of its designs, has never been surpassed by any publication of the kind, and should be in the hands of every marble-worker who does fine monumental work.

FAIRBAIRN.—THE PRINCIPLES OF MECHANISM AND MACHINERY OF TRANSMISSION:

Comprising the Principles of Mechanism, Wheels, and Pulleys, Strength and Proportions of Shafts, Couplings of Shafts, and Engaging and Disengaging Gear. By WILLIAM FAIRBAIRN, Esq., C. E., LL. D., F. R. S., F. G. S., Corresponding Member of the National Institute of France, and of the Royal Academy of Turin; Chevalier of the Legion of Honor, etc. etc. Beautifully illustrated by over 150 wood-cuts. In one volume 12mo. $2 50

FAIRBAIRN.—PRIME-MOVERS:

Comprising the Accumulation of Water-power; the Construction of Water-wheels and Turbines; the Properties of Steam; the Varieties of Steam-engines and Boilers and Wind-mills. By WILLIAM FAIRBAIRN, C. E., LL. D., F. R. S., F. G. S. Author of "Principles of Mechanism and the Machinery of Transmission." With Numerous Illustrations. In one volume. (In press.)

GILBART.—A PRACTICAL TREATISE ON BANKING:

By JAMES WILLIAM GILBART. To which is added: THE NATIONAL BANK ACT AS NOW IN FORCE. 8vo. . . . $4 50

GESNER.—A PRACTICAL TREATISE ON COAL, PETROLEUM, AND OTHER DISTILLED OILS.

By ABRAHAM GESNER, M. D., F. G. S. Second edition, revised and enlarged. By GEORGE WELTDEN GESNER, Consulting Chemist and Engineer. Illustrated. 8vo. . . . $3 50

GOTHIC ALBUM FOR CABINET MAKERS:

Comprising a Collection of Designs for Gothic Furniture. Illustrated by twenty-three large and beautifully engraved plates. Oblong $3 00

GRANT.—BEET-ROOT SUGAR AND CULTIVATION OF THE BEET:

By E. B. GRANT. 12mo. $1 25

GREGORY.—MATHEMATICS FOR PRACTICAL MEN:

Adapted to the Pursuits of Surveyors, Architects, Mechanics, and Civil Engineers. By OLINTHUS GREGORY. 8vo., plates, cloth $3 00

GRISWOLD.—RAILROAD ENGINEER'S POCKET COMPANION.

Comprising Rules for Calculating Deflection Distances and Angles, Tangential Distances and Angles, and all Necessary Tables for Engineers; also the art of Levelling from Preliminary Survey to the Construction of Railroads, intended Expressly for the Young Engineer, together with Numerous Valuable Rules and Examples. By W. GRISWOLD. 12mo., tucks. $1 75

GUETTIER.—METALLIC ALLOYS:

Being a Practical Guide to their Chemical and Physical Properties, their Preparation, Composition, and Uses. Translated from the French of A. GUETTIER, Engineer and Director of Founderies, author of "La Fouderie en France," etc. etc. By A. A. FESQUET, Chemist and Engineer. In one volume, 12mo. $3 00

HATS AND FELTING:

A Practical Treatise on their Manufacture. By a Practical Hatter. Illustrated by Drawings of Machinery, &c., 8vo. $1 25

HAY.—THE INTERIOR DECORATOR:

The Laws of Harmonious Coloring adapted to Interior Decorations: with a Practical Treatise on House-Painting. By D. R. HAY, House-Painter and Decorator. Illustrated by a Diagram of the Primary, Secondary, and Tertiary Colors. 12mo. $2 25

HUGHES.—AMERICAN MILLER AND MILLWRIGHT'S ASSISTANT:

By WM. CARTER HUGHES. A new edition. In one volume, 12mo. $1 50

HUNT.—THE PRACTICE OF PHOTOGRAPHY.

By Robert Hunt, Vice-President of the Photographic Society, London. With numerous illustrations. 12mo., cloth . 75

HURST.—A HAND-BOOK FOR ARCHITECTURAL SURVEYORS:

Comprising Formulæ useful in Designing Builders' work, Table of Weights, of the materials used in Building, Memoranda connected with Builders' work, Mensuration, the Practice of Builders' Measurement, Contracts of Labor, Valuation of Property, Summary of the Practice in Dilapidation, etc. etc. By J. F. Hurst, C. E. 2d edition, pocket-book form, full bound $2 50

JERVIS.—RAILWAY PROPERTY:

A Treatise on the Construction and Management of Railways; designed to afford useful knowledge, in the popular style, to the holders of this class of property; as well as Railway Managers, Officers, and Agents. By John B. Jervis, late Chief Engineer of the Hudson River Railroad, Croton Aqueduct, &c. One vol. 12mo., cloth $2 00

JOHNSON.—A REPORT TO THE NAVY DEPARTMENT OF THE UNITED STATES ON AMERICAN COALS:

Applicable to Steam Navigation and to other purposes. By Walter R. Johnson. With numerous illustrations. 607 pp. 8vo., ... $10 00

JOHNSTON.—INSTRUCTIONS FOR THE ANALYSIS OF SOILS, LIMESTONES, AND MANURES.

By J. W. F. Johnston. 12mo. 35

KEENE.—A HAND-BOOK OF PRACTICAL GAUGING,

For the Use of Beginners, to which is added a Chapter on Distillation, describing the process in operation at the Custom House for ascertaining the strength of wines. By James B. Keene, of H. M. Customs. 8vo. . . . $1 25

KENTISH.—A TREATISE ON A BOX OF INSTRUMENTS,

And the Slide Rule; with the Theory of Trigonometry and Logarithms, including Practical Geometry, Surveying, Measuring of Timber, Cask and Malt Gauging, Heights, and Distances. By THOMAS KENTISH. In one volume. 12mo. . . $1 25

KOBELL.—ERNI.—MINERALOGY SIMPLIFIED:

A short method of Determining and Classifying Minerals, by means of simple Chemical Experiments in the Wet Way. Translated from the last German Edition of F. VON KOBELL, with an Introduction to Blowpipe Analysis and other additions. By HENRI ERNI, M. D., Chief Chemist, Department of Agriculture, author of "Coal Oil and Petroleum." In one volume. 12mo. $2 50

LANDRIN.—A TREATISE ON STEEL:

Comprising its Theory, Metallurgy, Properties, Practical Working, and Use. By M. H. C. LANDRIN, Jr., Civil Engineer. Translated from the French, with Notes, by A. A. FESQUET, Chemist and Engineer. With an Appendix on the Bessemer and the Martin Processes for Manufacturing Steel, from the Report of ABRAM S. HEWITT, United States Commissioner to the Universal Exposition, Paris, 1867. 12mo. . . $3 00

LARKIN.—THE PRACTICAL BRASS AND IRON FOUNDER'S GUIDE.

A Concise Treatise on Brass Founding, Moulding, the Metals and their Alloys, etc.; to which are added Recent Improvements in the Manufacture of Iron, Steel by the Bessemer Process, etc. etc. By JAMES LARKIN, late Conductor of the Brass Foundry Department in Reany, Neafie & Co.'s Penn Works, Philadelphia. Fifth edition, revised, with extensive Additions. In one volume. 12mo. $2 25

LEAVITT.—FACTS ABOUT PEAT AS AN ARTICLE OF FUEL:
With Remarks upon its Origin and Composition, the Localities in which it is found, the Methods of Preparation and Manufacture, and the various Uses to which it is applicable; together with many other matters of Practical and Scientific Interest. To which is added a chapter on the Utilization of Coal Dust with Peat for the Production of an Excellent Fuel at Moderate Cost, especially adapted for Steam Service. By H. T. LEAVITT. Third edition. 12mo. $1 75

LEROUX.—A PRACTICAL TREATISE ON THE MANUFACTURE OF WORSTEDS AND CARDED YARNS:
Translated from the French of CHARLES LEROUX, Mechanical Engineer, and Superintendent of a Spinning Mill. By Dr. H. PAINE, and A. A. FESQUET. Illustrated by 12 large plates. In one volume 8vo. $5 00

LESLIE (MISS).—COMPLETE COOKERY:
Directions for Cookery in its Various Branches. By MISS LESLIE. 60th edition. Thoroughly revised, with the addition of New Receipts. In 1 vol. 12mo., cloth . . $1 50

LESLIE (MISS). LADIES' HOUSE BOOK:
a Manual of Domestic Economy. 20th revised edition. 12mo., cloth $1 25

LESLIE (MISS).—TWO HUNDRED RECEIPTS IN FRENCH COOKERY.
12mo. 50

LIEBER.—ASSAYER'S GUIDE:
Or, Practical Directions to Assayers, Miners, and Smelters, for the Tests and Assays, by Heat and by Wet Processes, for the Ores of all the principal Metals, of Gold and Silver Coins and Alloys, and of Coal, etc. By OSCAR M. LIEBER. 12mo., cloth $1 25

LOVE.—THE ART OF DYEING, CLEANING, SCOURING, AND FINISHING:
On the most approved English and French methods; being Practical Instructions in Dyeing Silks, Woollens, and Cottons, Feathers, Chips, Straw, etc.; Scouring and Cleaning Bed and Window Curtains, Carpets, Rugs, etc.; French and English Cleaning, etc. By THOMAS LOVE. Second American Edition, to which are added General Instructions for the Use of Aniline Colors. 8vo. 5 00

MAIN AND BROWN.—QUESTIONS ON SUBJECTS CONNECTED WITH THE MARINE STEAM-ENGINE:

And Examination Papers; with Hints for their Solution. By THOMAS J. MAIN, Professor of Mathematics, Royal Naval College, and THOMAS BROWN, Chief Engineer, R. N. 12mo., cloth $1 50

MAIN AND BROWN.—THE INDICATOR AND DYNAMOMETER:

With their Practical Applications to the Steam-Engine. By THOMAS J. MAIN, M. A. F. R., Ass't Prof. Royal Naval College, Portsmouth, and THOMAS BROWN, Assoc. Inst. C. E., Chief Engineer, R. N., attached to the R. N. College. Illustrated. From the Fourth London Edition. 8vo. $1 50

MAIN AND BROWN.—THE MARINE STEAM-ENGINE.

By THOMAS J. MAIN, F. R. Ass't S. Mathematical Professor at Royal Naval College, and THOMAS BROWN, Assoc. Inst. C. E. Chief Engineer, R. N. Attached to the Royal Naval College. Authors of "Questions Connected with the Marine Steam-Engine," and the "Indicator and Dynamometer." With numerous Illustrations. In one volume 8vo. $5 00

MARTIN.—SCREW-CUTTING TABLES, FOR THE USE OF MECHANICAL ENGINEERS:

Showing the Proper Arrangement of Wheels for Cutting the Threads of Screws of any required Pitch; with a Table for Making the Universal Gas-Pipe Thread and Taps. By W. A. MARTIN, Engineer. 8vo. 50

MILES—A PLAIN TREATISE ON HORSE-SHOEING.

With Illustrations. By WILLIAM MILES, author of "The Horse's Foot"

MOLESWORTH.—POCKET-BOOK OF USEFUL FORMULÆ AND MEMORANDA FOR CIVIL AND MECHANICAL ENGINEERS.

By GUILFORD L. MOLESWORTH, Member of the Institution of Civil Engineers, Chief Resident Engineer of the Ceylon Railway. Second American from the Tenth London Edition. In one volume, full bound in pocket-book form $2 00

MOORE.—THE INVENTOR'S GUIDE:

Patent Office and Patent Laws: or, a Guide to Inventors, and a Book of Reference for Judges, Lawyers, Magistrates, and others. By J. G. MOORE. 12mo., cloth $1 25

NAPIER.—A MANUAL OF ELECTRO-METALLURGY:

Including the Application of the Art to Manufacturing Processes. By JAMES NAPIER. Fourth American, from the Fourth London edition, revised and enlarged. Illustrated by engravings. In one volume, 8vo. $2 00

NAPIER.—A SYSTEM OF CHEMISTRY APPLIED TO DYEING:

By James Napier, F. C. S. A New and Thoroughly Revised Edition, completely brought up to the present state of the Science, including the Chemistry of Coal Tar Colors. By A. A. Fesquet, Chemist and Engineer. With an Appendix on Dyeing and Calico Printing, as shown at the Paris Universal Exposition of 1867, from the Reports of the International Jury, etc. Illustrated. In one volume 8vo., 400 pages $5 00

NEWBERY.—GLEANINGS FROM ORNAMENTAL ART OF EVERY STYLE;

Drawn from Examples in the British, South Kensington, Indian, Crystal Palace, and other Museums, the Exhibitions of 1851 and 1862, and the best English and Foreign works. In a series of one hundred exquisitely drawn Plates, containing many hundred examples. By Robert Newbery. 4to. $15 00

NICHOLSON.—A MANUAL OF THE ART OF BOOK-BINDING:

Containing full instructions in the different Branches of Forwarding, Gilding, and Finishing. Also, the Art of Marbling Book-edges and Paper. By James B. Nicholson. Illustrated. 12mo. cloth $2 25

NORRIS.—A HAND-BOOK FOR LOCOMOTIVE ENGINEERS AND MACHINISTS:

Comprising the Proportions and Calculations for Constructing Locomotives; Manner of Setting Valves; Tables of Squares, Cubes, Areas, etc. etc. By Septimus Norris, Civil and Mechanical Engineer. New edition. Illustrated, 12mo., cloth
$2 00

NYSTROM.—ON TECHNOLOGICAL EDUCATION AND THE CONSTRUCTION OF SHIPS AND SCREW PROPELLERS:

For Naval and Marine Engineers. By John W. Nystrom, late Acting Chief Engineer U. S. N. Second edition, revised with additional matter. Illustrated by seven engravings. 12mo.
$2 50

O'NEILL.—A DICTIONARY OF DYEING AND CALICO PRINTING:

Containing a brief account of all the Substances and Processes in use in the Art of Dyeing and Printing Textile Fabrics: with Practical Receipts and Scientific Information. By Charles O'Neill, Analytical Chemist; Fellow of the Chemical Society of London; Member of the Literary and Philosophical Society of Manchester; Author of "Chemistry of Calico Printing and Dyeing." To which is added An Essay on Coal Tar Colors and their Application to

Dyeing and Calico Printing. By A. A. FESQUET, Chemist and Engineer. With an Appendix on Dyeing and Calico Printing, as shown at the Exposition of 1867, from the Reports of the International Jury, etc. In one volume 8vo., 491 pages . . $6 00

OSBORN.—THE METALLURGY OF IRON AND STEEL:

Theoretical and Practical: In all its Branches; With Special Reference to American Materials and Processes. By H. S. OSBORN, LL. D., Professor of Mining and Metallurgy in Lafayette College, Easton, Pa. Illustrated by 230 Engravings on Wood, and 6 Folding Plates. 8vo., 972 pages $10 00

OSBORN.—AMERICAN MINES AND MINING:

Theoretically and Practically Considered. By Prof. H. S. OSBORN, Illustrated by numerous engravings. 8vo. (*In preparation.*)

PAINTER, GILDER, AND VARNISHER'S COMPANION:

Containing Rules and Regulations in everything relating to the Arts of Painting, Gilding, Varnishing, and Glass Staining, with numerous useful and valuable Receipts; Tests for the Detection of Adulterations in Oils and Colors, and a statement of the Diseases and Accidents to which Painters, Gilders, and Varnishers are particularly liable, with the simplest methods of Prevention and Remedy. With Directions for Graining, Marbling, Sign Writing, and Gilding on Glass. To which are added COMPLETE INSTRUCTIONS FOR COACH PAINTING AND VARNISHING. 12mo., cloth, $1 50

PALLETT.—THE MILLER'S, MILLWRIGHT'S, AND ENGINEER'S GUIDE.

By HENRY PALLETT. Illustrated. In one vol. 12mo. . $3 00

PERKINS.—GAS AND VENTILATION.

Practical Treatise on Gas and Ventilation. With Special Relation to Illuminating, Heating, and Cooking by Gas. Including Scientific Helps to Engineer-students and others. With illustrated Diagrams. By E. E. PERKINS. 12mo., cloth . . . $1 25

PERKINS AND STOWE.—A NEW GUIDE TO THE SHEET-IRON AND BOILER PLATE ROLLER:

Containing a Series of Tables showing the Weight of Slabs and Piles to Produce Boiler Plates, and of the Weight of Piles and the Sizes of Bars to Produce Sheet-iron; the Thickness of the Bar Gauge in Decimals; the Weight per foot, and the Thickness on the Bar or Wire Gauge of the fractional parts of an inch; the Weight per sheet, and the Thickness on the Wire Gauge of Sheet-iron of various dimensions to weigh 112 lbs. per bundle; and the conversion of Short Weight into Long Weight, and Long Weight into Short. Estimated and collected by G. H. PERKINS and J. G. STOWE $2 50

PHILLIPS AND DARLINGTON.—RECORDS OF MINING AND METALLURGY:

Or, Facts and Memoranda for the use of the Mine Agent and Smelter. By J. ARTHUR PHILLIPS, Mining Engineer, Graduate of the Imperial School of Mines, France, etc., and JOHN DARLINGTON. Illustrated by numerous engravings. In one vol. 12mo. . $2 00

PRADAL, MALEPEYRE, AND DUSSAUCE.—A COMPLETE TREATISE ON PERFUMERY:

Containing notices of the Raw Material used in the Art, and the Best Formulæ. According to the most approved Methods followed in France, England, and the United States. By M. P. PRADAL, Perfumer-Chemist, and M. F. MALEPEYRE. Translated from the French, with extensive additions, by Prof. H. DUSSAUCE. 8vo. $10

PROTEAUX.—PRACTICAL GUIDE FOR THE MANUFACTURE OF PAPER AND BOARDS.

By A. PROTEAUX, Civil Engineer, and Graduate of the School of Arts and Manufactures, Director of Thiers's Paper Mill, 'Puy-de-Dômé. With additions, by L. S. LE NORMAND. Translated from the French, with Notes, by HORATIO PAINE, A. B., M. D. To which is added a Chapter on the Manufacture of Paper from Wood in the United States, by HENRY T. BROWN, of the "American Artisan." Illustrated by six plates, containing Drawings of Raw Materials, Machinery, Plans of Paper-Mills, etc. etc. 8vo. $5 00

REGNAULT.—ELEMENTS OF CHEMISTRY.

By M. V. REGNAULT. Translated from the French by T. FORREST BENTON, M. D., and edited, with notes, by JAMES C. BOOTH, Melter and Refiner U. S. Mint, and WM. L. FABER, Metallurgist and Mining Engineer. Illustrated by nearly 700 wood engravings. Comprising nearly 1500 pages. In two vols. 8vo., cloth $10 00

REID.—A PRACTICAL TREATISE ON THE MANUFACTURE OF PORTLAND CEMENT:

By HENRY REID, C. E. To which is added a Translation of M. A. Lipowitz's Work, describing a new method adopted in Germany of Manufacturing that Cement. By W. F. REID. Illustrated by plates and wood engravings. 8vo. $7 00

RIFFAULT, VERGNAUD, AND TOUSSAINT.—A PRACTICAL TREATISE ON THE MANUFACTURE OF COLORS FOR PAINTING:

Containing the best Formulæ and the Processes the Newest and in most General Use. By MM. RIFFAULT, VERGNAUD, and TOUSSAINT. Revised and Edited by M. F. MALEPEYRE and Dr. EMIL WINCKLER. Illustrated by Engravings. In one vol. 8vo. (*In preparation.*)

RIFFAULT, VERGNAUD, AND TOUSSAINT.—A PRACTICAL TREATISE ON THE MANUFACTURE OF VARNISHES:
By MM. RIFFAULT, VERGNAUD, and TOUSSAINT. Revised and Edited by M. F. MALEPEYRE and Dr. EMIL WINCKLER. Illustrated. In one vol. 8vo. (*In preparation.*)

SHUNK.—A PRACTICAL TREATISE ON RAILWAY CURVES AND LOCATION, FOR YOUNG ENGINEERS.
By WM. F. SHUNK, Civil Engineer. 12mo., tucks . . $2 00

SMEATON.—BUILDER'S POCKET COMPANION:
Containing the Elements of Building, Surveying, and Architecture; with Practical Rules and Instructions connected with the subject. By A. C. SMEATON, Civil Engineer, etc. In one volume, 12mo. $1 50

SMITH.—THE DYER'S INSTRUCTOR:
Comprising Practical Instructions in the Art of Dyeing Silk, Cotton, Wool, and Worsted, and Woollen Goods: containing nearly 800 Receipts. To which is added a Treatise on the Art of Padding; and the Printing of Silk Warps, Skeins, and Handkerchiefs, and the various Mordants and Colors for the different styles of such work. By DAVID SMITH, Pattern Dyer, 12mo., cloth $3 00

SMITH.—THE PRACTICAL DYER'S GUIDE:
Comprising Practical Instructions in the Dyeing of Shot Cobourgs, Silk Striped Orleans, Colored Orleans from Black Warps, ditto from White Warps, Colored Cobourgs from White Warps, Merinos, Yarns, Woollen Cloths, etc. Containing nearly 300 Receipts, to most of which a Dyed Pattern is annexed. Also, a Treatise on the Art of Padding. By DAVID SMITH. In one vol. 8vo. $25 00

SHAW.—CIVIL ARCHITECTURE:
Being a Complete Theoretical and Practical System of Building, containing the Fundamental Principles of the Art. By EDWARD SHAW, Architect. To which is added a Treatise on Gothic Architecture, &c. By THOMAS W. SILLOWAY and GEORGE M. HARDING, Architects. The whole illustrated by 102 quarto plates finely engraved on copper. Eleventh Edition. 4to. Cloth. $10 00

SLOAN.—AMERICAN HOUSES:
A variety of Original Designs for Rural Buildings. Illustrated by 26 colored Engravings, with Descriptive References. By SAMUEL SLOAN, Architect, author of the "Model Architect," etc. etc. 8vo. $2 50

SCHINZ.—RESEARCHES ON THE ACTION OF THE BLAST-FURNACE.
By CHAS. SCHINZ. Seven plates. 12mo. . . . $4 25

SMITH.—PARKS AND PLEASURE GROUNDS:
Or, Practical Notes on Country Residences, Villas, Public Parks, and Gardens. By CHARLES H. J. SMITH, Landscape Gardener and Garden Architect, etc. etc. 12mo. $2 25

STOKES.—CABINET-MAKER'S AND UPHOLSTERER'S COMPANION:
Comprising the Rudiments and Principles of Cabinet-making and Upholstery, with Familiar Instructions, Illustrated by Examples for attaining a Proficiency in the Art of Drawing, as applicable to Cabinet-work; The Processes of Veneering, Inlaying, and Buhl-work; the Art of Dyeing and Staining Wood, Bone, Tortoise Shell, etc. Directions for Lackering, Japanning, and Varnishing; to make French Polish; to prepare the Best Glues, Cements, and Compositions, and a number of Receipts, particularly for workmen generally. By J. STOKES. In one vol. 12mo. With illustrations $1 25

STRENGTH AND OTHER PROPERTIES OF METALS.
Reports of Experiments on the Strength and other Properties of Metals for Cannon. With a Description of the Machines for Testing Metals, and of the Classification of Cannon in service. By Officers of the Ordnance Department U. S. Army. By authority of the Secretary of War. Illustrated by 25 large steel plates. In 1 vol. quarto $10 00

SULLIVAN.—PROTECTION TO NATIVE INDUSTRY.
By Sir EDWARD SULLIVAN, Baronet. (1870.) 8vo. . $1 50

TABLES SHOWING THE WEIGHT OF ROUND, SQUARE, AND FLAT BAR IRON, STEEL, ETC.
By Measurement. Cloth 63

TAYLOR.—STATISTICS OF COAL:
Including Mineral Bituminous Substances employed in Arts and Manufactures; with their Geographical, Geological, and Commercial Distribution and amount of Production and Consumption on the American Continent. With Incidental Statistics of the Iron Manufacture. By R. C. TAYLOR. Second edition, revised by S. S. HALDEMAN. Illustrated by five Maps and many wood engravings. 8vo., cloth $6 00

TEMPLETON.—THE PRACTICAL EXAMINATOR ON STEAM AND THE STEAM-ENGINE:
With Instructive References relative thereto, for the Use of Engineers, Students, and others. By WM. TEMPLETON, Engineer 12mo. $1 25

THOMAS.—THE MODERN PRACTICE OF PHOTOGRAPHY.
By R. W. THOMAS, F. C. S. 8vo., cloth 75

THOMSON.—FREIGHT CHARGES CALCULATOR.
By ANDREW THOMSON, Freight Agent $1 25

TURNING: SPECIMENS OF FANCY TURNING EXECUTED ON THE HAND OR FOOT LATHE:
With Geometric, Oval, and Eccentric Chucks, and Elliptical Cutting Frame. By an Amateur. Illustrated by 30 exquisite Photographs. 4to. $3 00

TURNER'S (THE) COMPANION:
Containing Instructions in Concentric, Elliptic, and Eccentric Turning; also various Plates of Chucks, Tools, and Instruments; and Directions for using the Eccentric Cutter, Drill, Vertical Cutter, and Circular Rest; with Patterns and Instructions for working them. A new edition in 1 vol. 12mo. $1 50

URBIN—BRULL.—A PRACTICAL GUIDE FOR PUDDLING IRON AND STEEL.
By ED. URBIN, Engineer of Arts and Manufactures. A Prize Essay read before the Association of Engineers, Graduate of the School of Mines, of Liege, Belgium, at the Meeting of 1865–6. To which is added a COMPARISON OF THE RESISTING PROPERTIES OF IRON AND STEEL. By A. BRULL. Translated from the French by A. A. FESQUET, Chemist and Engineer. In one volume, 8vo. $1 00

VOGDES.—THE ARCHITECT'S AND BUILDER'S POCKET COMPANION AND PRICE BOOK.
By F. W. VOGDES, Architect. Illustrated. Full bound in pocket-book form. $2 00
In book form, 18mo., muslin 1 50

WARN.—THE SHEET METAL WORKER'S INSTRUCTOR, FOR ZINC, SHEET-IRON, COPPER AND TIN PLATE WORKERS, &c.
By REUBEN HENRY WARN, Practical Tin Plate Worker. Illustrated by 32 plates and 37 wood engravings. 8vo. . . $3 00

WATSON.—A MANUAL OF THE HAND-LATHE.
By EGBERT P. WATSON, Late of the "Scientific American," Author of "Modern Practice of American Machinists and Engineers," In one volume, 12mo. $1 50

WATSON.—THE MODERN PRACTICE OF AMERICAN MACHINISTS AND ENGINEERS:

Including the Construction, Application, and Use of Drills, Lathe Tools, Cutters for Boring Cylinders, and Hollow Work Generally, with the most Economical Speed of the same, the Results verified by Actual Practice at the Lathe, the Vice, and on the Floor. Together with Workshop management, Economy of Manufacture, the Steam-Engine, Boilers, Gears, Belting, etc. etc. By EGBERT P. WATSON, late of the "Scientific American." Illustrated by eighty-six engravings. 12mo. $2 50

WATSON.—THE THEORY AND PRACTICE OF THE ART OF WEAVING BY HAND AND POWER:

With Calculations and Tables for the use of those connected with the Trade. By JOHN WATSON, Manufacturer and Practical Machine Maker. Illustrated by large drawings of the best Power-Looms. 8vo. $10 00

WEATHERLY.—TREATISE ON THE ART OF BOILING SUGAR, CRYSTALLIZING, LOZENGE-MAKING, COMFITS, GUM GOODS,

And other processes for Confectionery, &c. In which are explained, in an easy and familiar manner, the various Methods of Manufacturing every description of Raw and Refined Sugar Goods, as sold by Confectioners and others $2 00

WILL.—TABLES FOR QUALITATIVE CHEMICAL ANALYSIS.

By Prof. HEINRICH WILL, of Giessen, Germany. Seventh edition. Translated by CHARLES F. HIMES, Ph. D., Professor of Natural Science, Dickinson College, Carlisle, Pa. . . $1 25

WILLIAMS.—ON HEAT AND STEAM:

Embracing New Views of Vaporization, Condensation, and Expansion. By CHARLES WYE WILLIAMS, A. I. C. E. Illustrated. 8vo. $3 50

WORSSAM.—ON MECHANICAL SAWS:

From the Transactions of the Society of Engineers, 1867. By S. W. WORSSAM, Jr. Illustrated by 18 large folding plates. 8vo. $5 00

WÖHLER.—A HAND-BOOK OF MINERAL ANALYSIS.

By F. WÖHLER. Edited by H. B. NASON, Professor of Chemistry, Rensselaer Institute, Troy, N. Y. With numerous Illustrations. 12mo. $3 00

www.ingramcontent.com/pod-product-compliance
Lightning Source LLC
LaVergne TN
LVHW020914110826
845150LV00004B/668